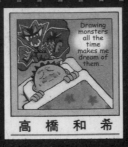

Drawing monsters all the time makes me dream of them..

高 橋 和 希

"THE OTHER PERSONALITY THAT LIVES IN YOUR HEART"...THIS IS THE CENTRAL THEME OF YU-GI-OH!. PERHAPS THE CHARACTERS I DRAW ARE ALSO PERSONALITIES THAT EXIST INSIDE ME. YUGI IS IN MY HEART. BUT ALSO JONOUCHI AND KAIBA...PEGASUS AND MAI...USHIO THE BULLY, INSECTOR HAGA, ESPER ROBA...AND THE COUNTLESS MONSTERS! JUST WHAT KIND OF PERSON AM I?
-KAZUKI TAKAHASHI, 2000

Artist/author Kazuki Takahashi first tried to break into the manga business in 1982, but success eluded him until **Yu-Gi-Oh!** debuted in the Japanese **Weekly Shonen Jump** magazine in 1996. **Yu-Gi-Oh!**'s themes of friendship and fighting, together with Takahashi's weird and wonderful art, soon became enormously successful, spawning a real-world card game, video games, and two anime series. A lifelong gamer, Takahashi enjoys Shogi (Japanese chess), Mahjong, card games, and tabletop RPGs, among other games.

YU-GI-OH!: DUELIST VOL. 11
The SHONEN JUMP Graphic Novel Edition

STORY AND ART BY
KAZUKI TAKAHASHI

Translation & English Adaptation/Joe Yamazaki
Touch-up Art & Lettering/Eric Erbes
Design/Andrea Rice
Editor/Jason Thompson

Managing Editor/Elizabeth Kawasaki
Director of Production/Noboru Watanabe
Vice President of Publishing/Alvin Lu
Vice President & Editor in Chief/Yumi Hoashi
Sr. Director of Acquisitions/Rika Inouye
Vice President of Sales & Marketing/Liza Coppola
Publisher/ Hyoe Narita

In the original Japanese edition, YU-GI-OH!, YU-GI-OH!: DUELIST and
YU-GI-OH!: MILLENNIUM WORLD are known collectively as YU-GI-OH!.
The English YU-GI-OH!: DUELIST was originally volumes 8-31
of the Japanese YU-GI-OH!.

Printed in the U.S.A.

Published by VIZ Media, LLC
P.O. Box 77010
San Francisco, CA 94107

SHONEN JUMP Graphic Novel Edition
10 9 8 7 6 5 4 3 2 1
First printing, November 2005

www.viz.com

PARENTAL ADVISORY
YU-GI-OH!: DUELIST is rated T for Teen
and is recommended for ages 13 and
up. Contains fantasy violence.

THE WORLD'S
MOST POPULAR MANGA

www.shonenjump.com

SHONEN JUMP GRAPHIC NOVEL

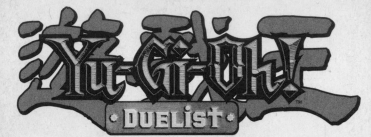

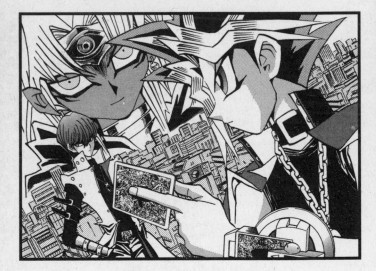

Vol. 11

THE SHADOW OF MARIK

STORY AND ART BY
KAZUKI TAKAHASHI

THE STORY SO FAR...

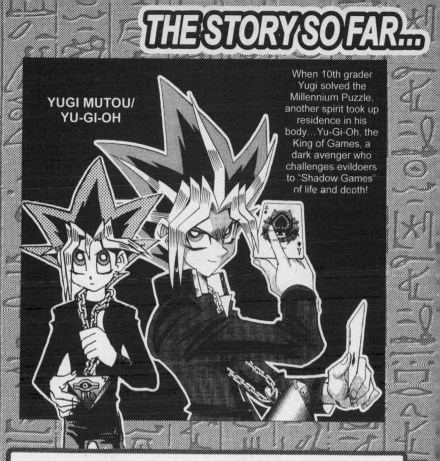

YUGI MUTOU/ YU-GI-OH

When 10th grader Yugi solved the Millennium Puzzle, another spirit took up residence in his body...Yu-Gi-Oh, the King of Games, a dark avenger who challenges evildoers to "Shadow Games" of life and death!

YUGI FACES DEADLY ENEMIES!

Using his gaming skills, Yugi fights ruthless adversaries like Maximillion Pegasus, multimillionaire creator of the collectible card game "Duel Monsters," and Ryo Bakura, whose friendly personality turns evil when he is possessed by the spirit of the Millennium Ring. But Yugi's greatest rival is Seto Kaiba, the world's second-greatest gamer—and the ruthless teenage president of Kaiba Corporation. At first, Kaiba and Yugi are bitter enemies, but after fighting against a common adversary—Pegasus—they come to respect one another. But for all his powers, there is one thing Yu-Gi-Oh cannot do: remember who he is and where he came from.

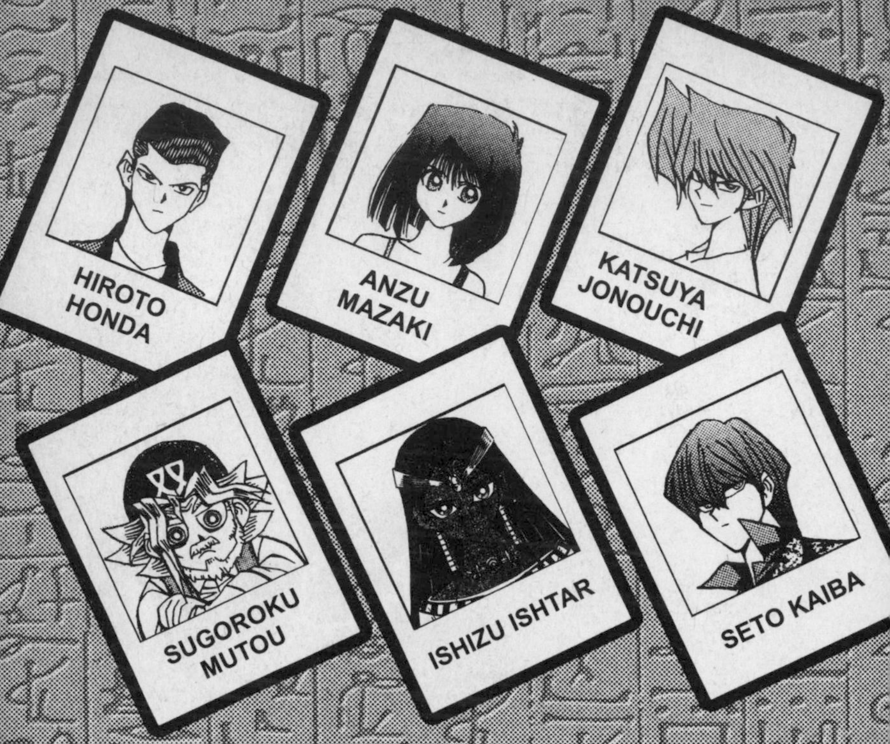

HIROTO HONDA

ANZU MAZAKI

KATSUYA JONOUCHI

SUGOROKU MUTOU

ISHIZU ISHTAR

SETO KAIBA

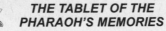

THE TABLET OF THE PHARAOH'S MEMORIES

Then one day, when an Egyptian museum exhibit comes to Japan, Yugi sees an ancient carving of himself as an Egyptian pharaoh! The curator of the exhibit, Ishizu Ishtar, explains that there are seven Millennium Items, which were made to fit into a stone tablet in a hidden shrine in Egypt. According to the legend, when the seven Items are brought together, the pharaoh will regain his memories of his past life.

THE EGYPTIAN GOD CARDS

But Ishizu has a message for Kaiba as well. Ishizu needs Kaiba's help to win back two of three Egyptian God Cards—the rarest cards on Earth—from the clutches of an evil criminal syndicate. In order to draw out the thieves, Kaiba announces "Battle City," an enormous "Duel Monsters" tournament. But Kaiba also wants the power of the Egyptian God Cards for himself...and now that Ishizu has given him the one remaining God Card to use as a weapon, he may be the strongest duelist on Earth!

Yu-Gi-Oh!
·DUELIST·

Vol. 11

CONTENTS

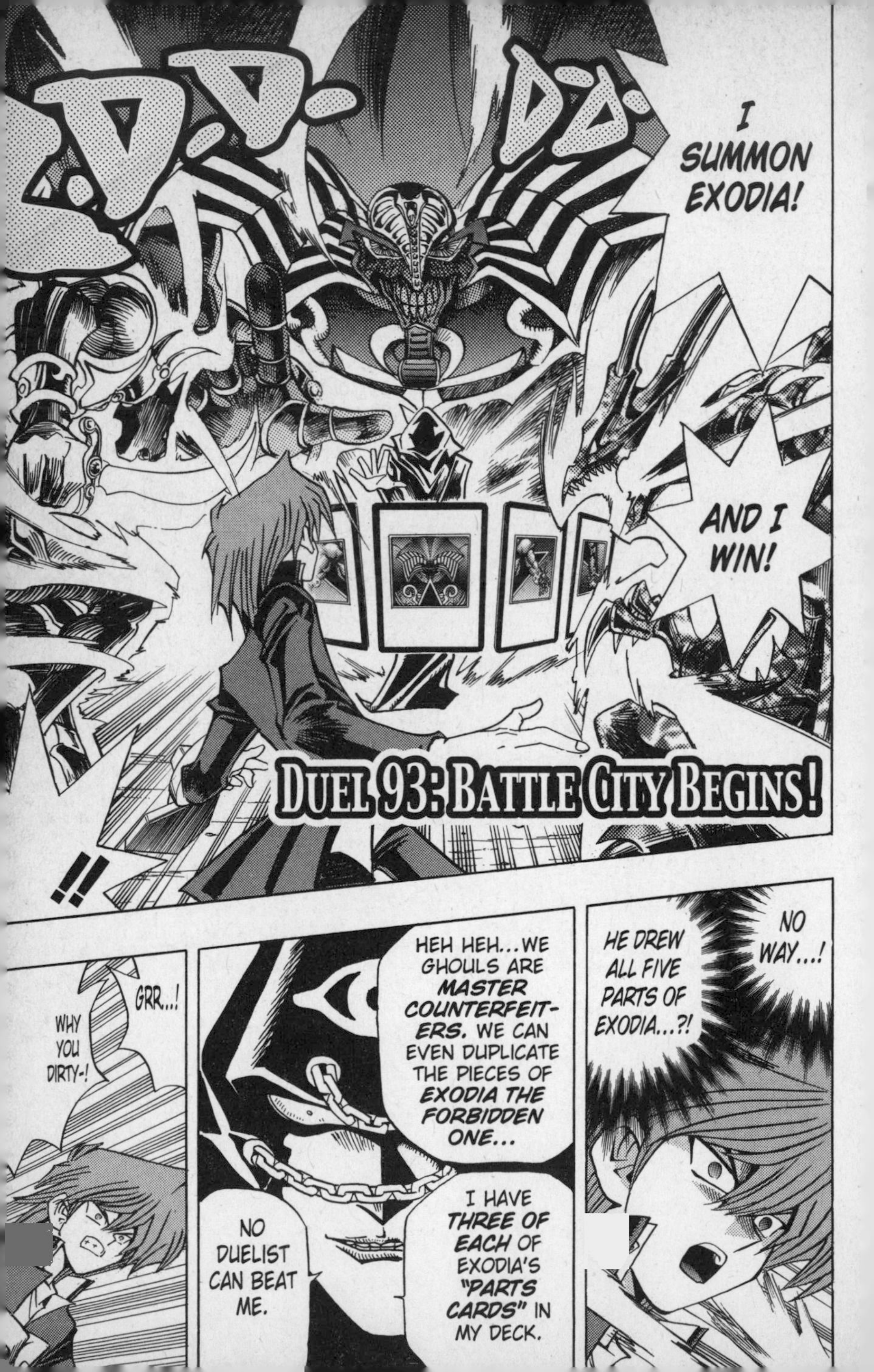
I SUMMON EXODIA!
AND I WIN!
DUEL 93: BATTLE CITY BEGINS!
!!
NO WAY...!
HE DREW ALL FIVE PARTS OF EXODIA...?!
HEH HEH...WE GHOULS ARE MASTER COUNTERFEIT-ERS. WE CAN EVEN DUPLICATE THE PIECES OF EXODIA THE FORBIDDEN ONE...
I HAVE THREE OF EACH OF EXODIA'S "PARTS CARDS" IN MY DECK.
NO DUELIST CAN BEAT ME.
GRR...!
WHY YOU DIRTY-!

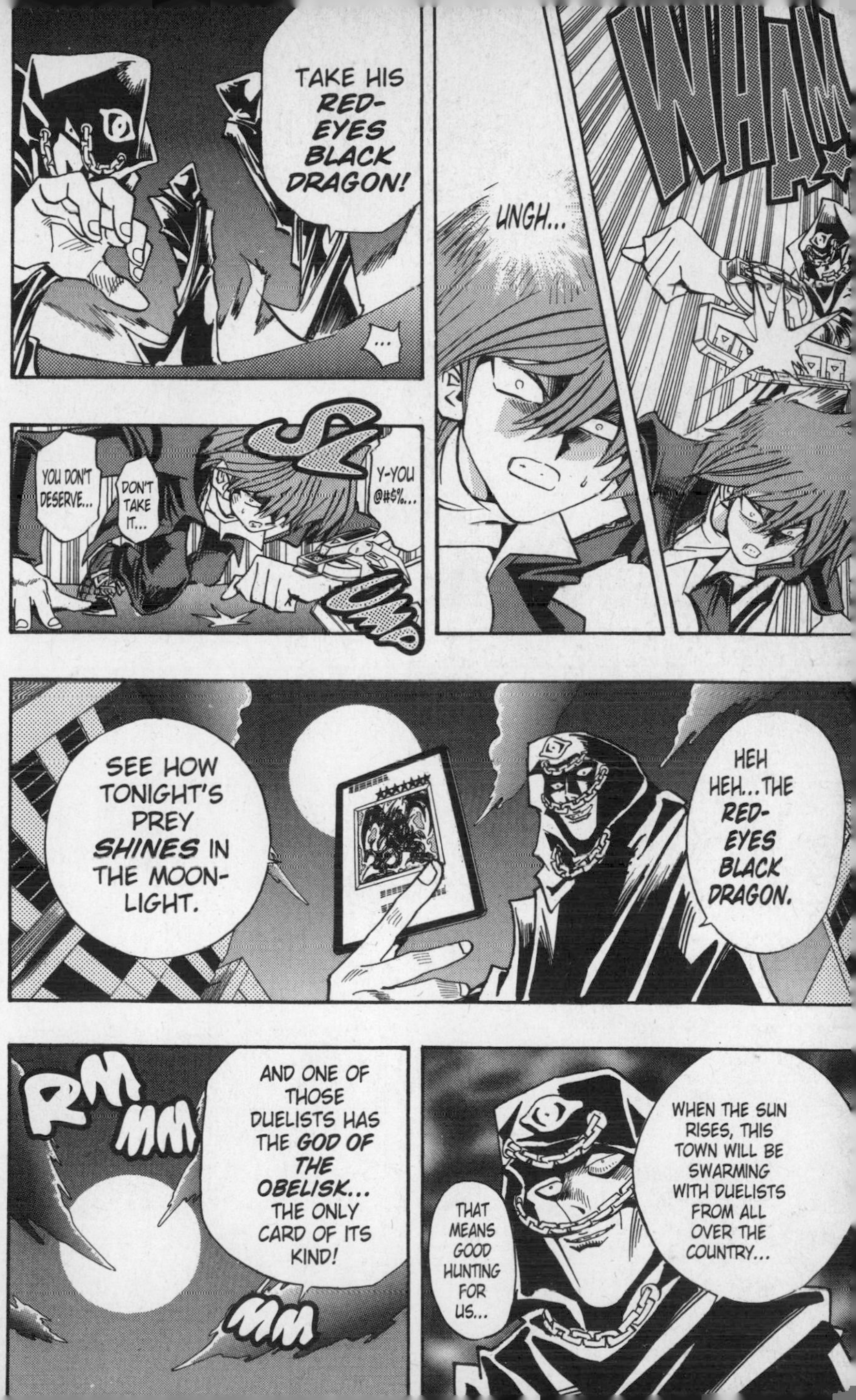
WHAM!
UNGH...
TAKE HIS RED-EYES BLACK DRAGON!
...
Y-YOU @#$%...
DON'T TAKE IT...
YOU DON'T DESERVE...
HEH HEH...THE RED-EYES BLACK DRAGON.
SEE HOW TONIGHT'S PREY SHINES IN THE MOON-LIGHT.
WHEN THE SUN RISES, THIS TOWN WILL BE SWARMING WITH DUELISTS FROM ALL OVER THE COUNTRY...
THAT MEANS GOOD HUNTING FOR US...
RMMMMM
AND ONE OF THOSE DUELISTS HAS THE GOD OF THE OBELISK... THE ONLY CARD OF ITS KIND!

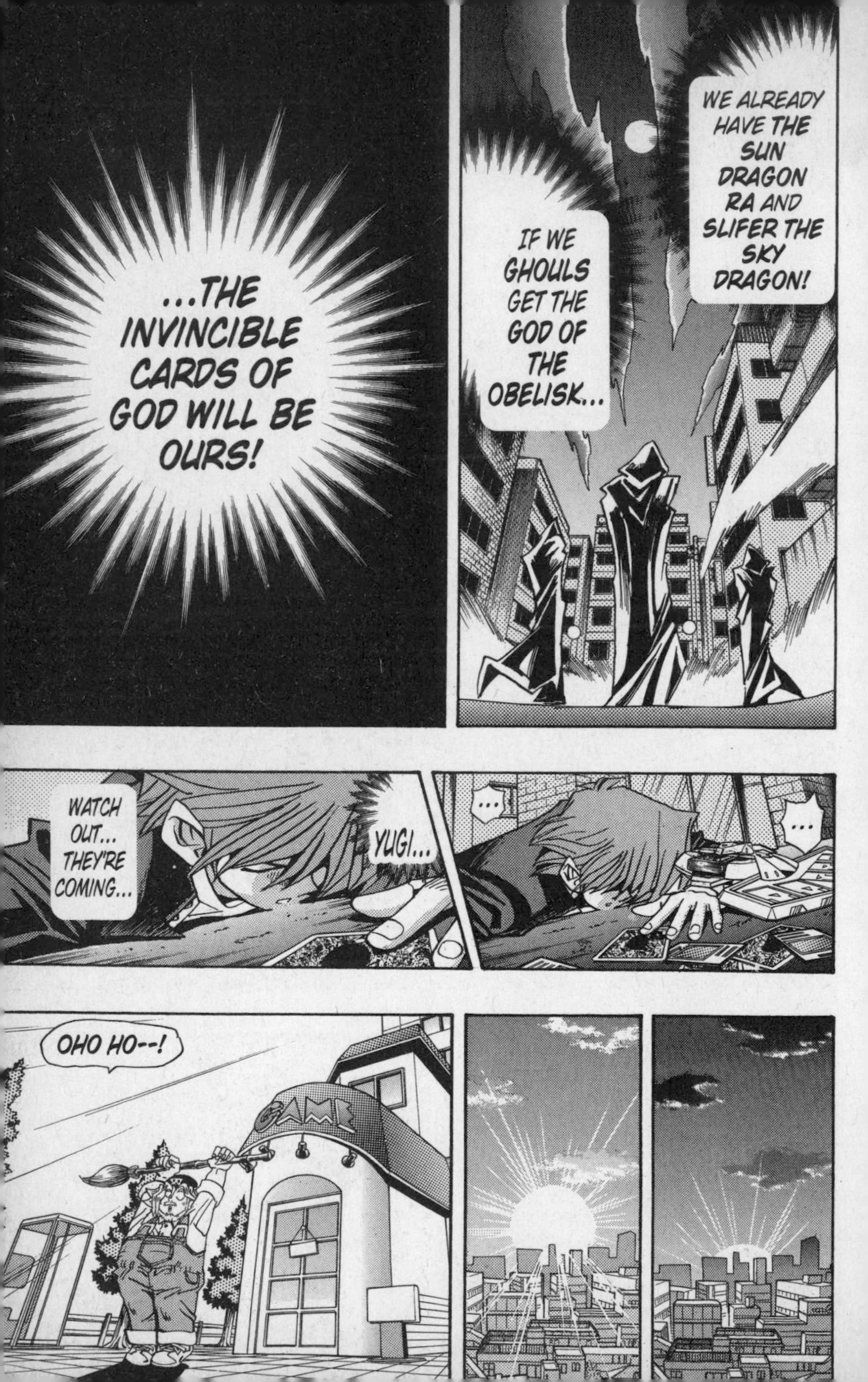
WE ALREADY HAVE THE SUN DRAGON RA AND SLIFER THE SKY DRAGON!
IF WE GHOULS GET THE GOD OF THE OBELISK...
...THE INVINCIBLE CARDS OF GOD WILL BE OURS!
...
...
YUGI...
WATCH OUT... THEY'RE COMING...
GAME
OHO HO--!

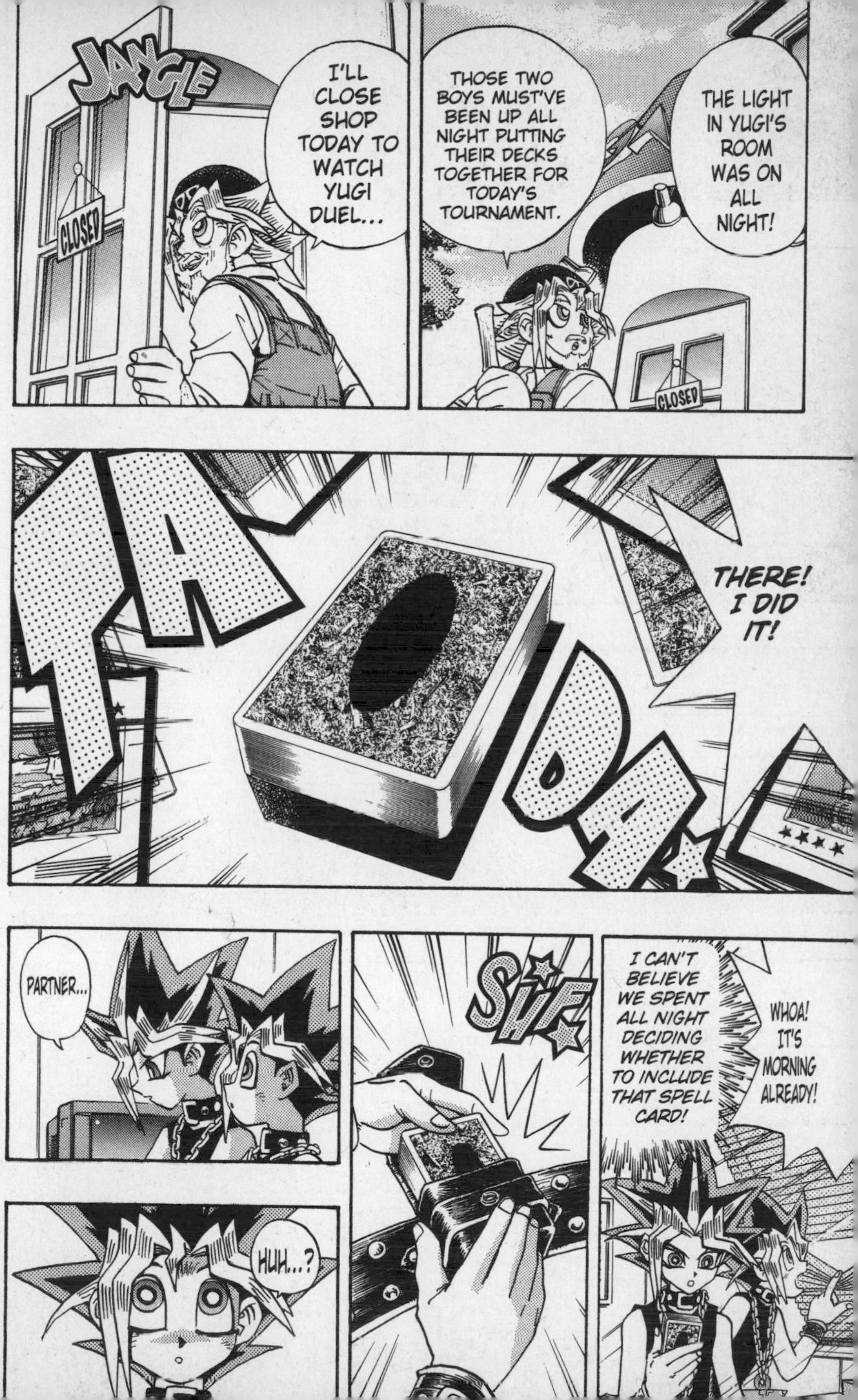
THE LIGHT IN YUGI'S ROOM WAS ON ALL NIGHT!
CLOSED
THOSE TWO BOYS MUST'VE BEEN UP ALL NIGHT PUTTING THEIR DECKS TOGETHER FOR TODAY'S TOURNAMENT.
JANGLE
CLOSED
I'LL CLOSE SHOP TODAY TO WATCH YUGI DUEL...
THERE! I DID IT!
TA
DA
WHOA! IT'S MORNING ALREADY!
I CAN'T BELIEVE WE SPENT ALL NIGHT DECIDING WHETHER TO INCLUDE THAT SPELL CARD!
SHF
PARTNER...
HUH...?

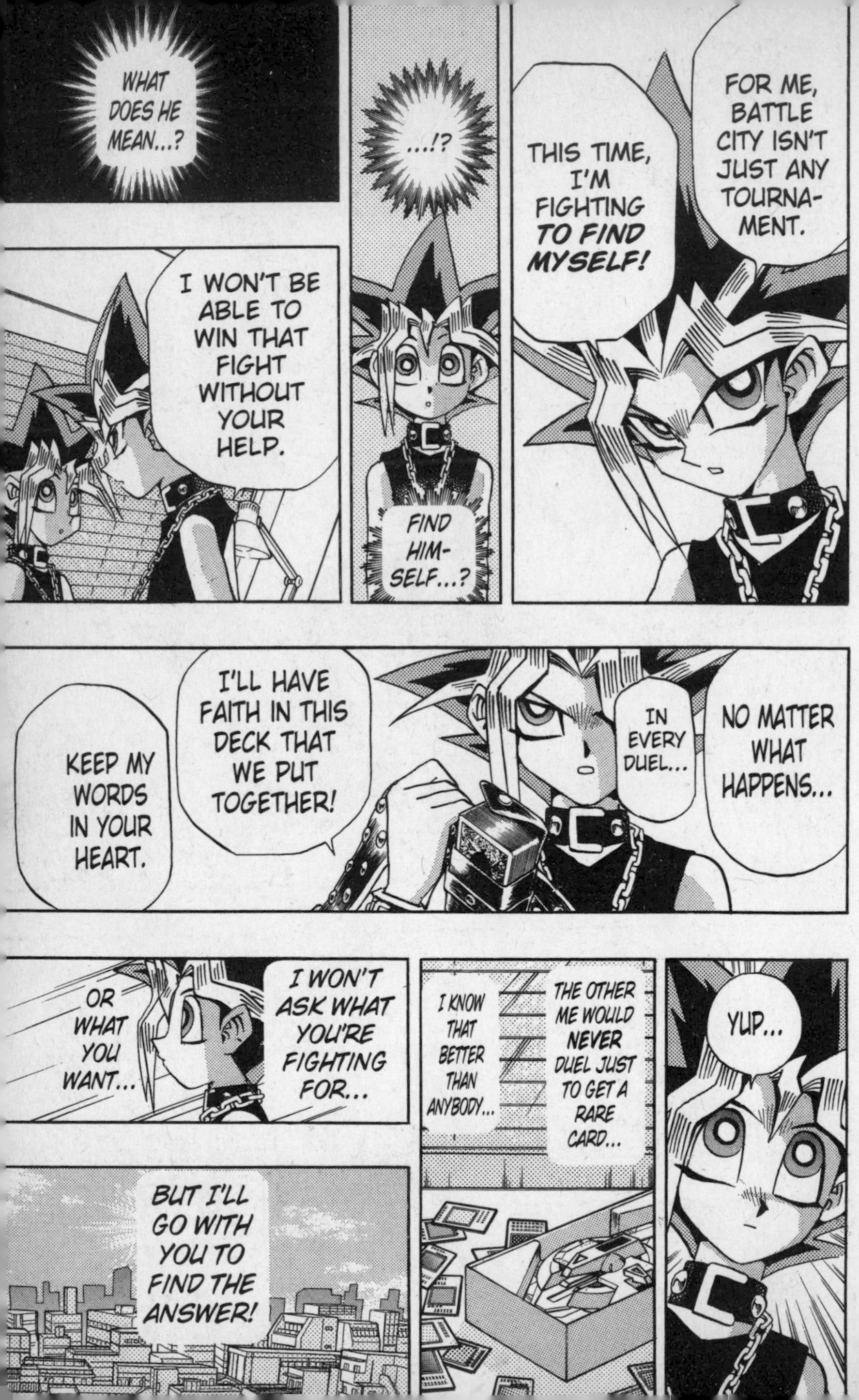
FOR ME, BATTLE CITY ISN'T JUST ANY TOURNAMENT.
THIS TIME, I'M FIGHTING TO FIND MYSELF!
...!?
FIND HIMSELF...?
WHAT DOES HE MEAN...?
I WON'T BE ABLE TO WIN THAT FIGHT WITHOUT YOUR HELP.
NO MATTER WHAT HAPPENS...
IN EVERY DUEL...
I'LL HAVE FAITH IN THIS DECK THAT WE PUT TOGETHER!
KEEP MY WORDS IN YOUR HEART.
YUP...
THE OTHER ME WOULD NEVER DUEL JUST TO GET A RARE CARD...
I KNOW THAT BETTER THAN ANYBODY...
I WON'T ASK WHAT YOU'RE FIGHTING FOR...
OR WHAT YOU WANT...
BUT I'LL GO WITH YOU TO FIND THE ANSWER!

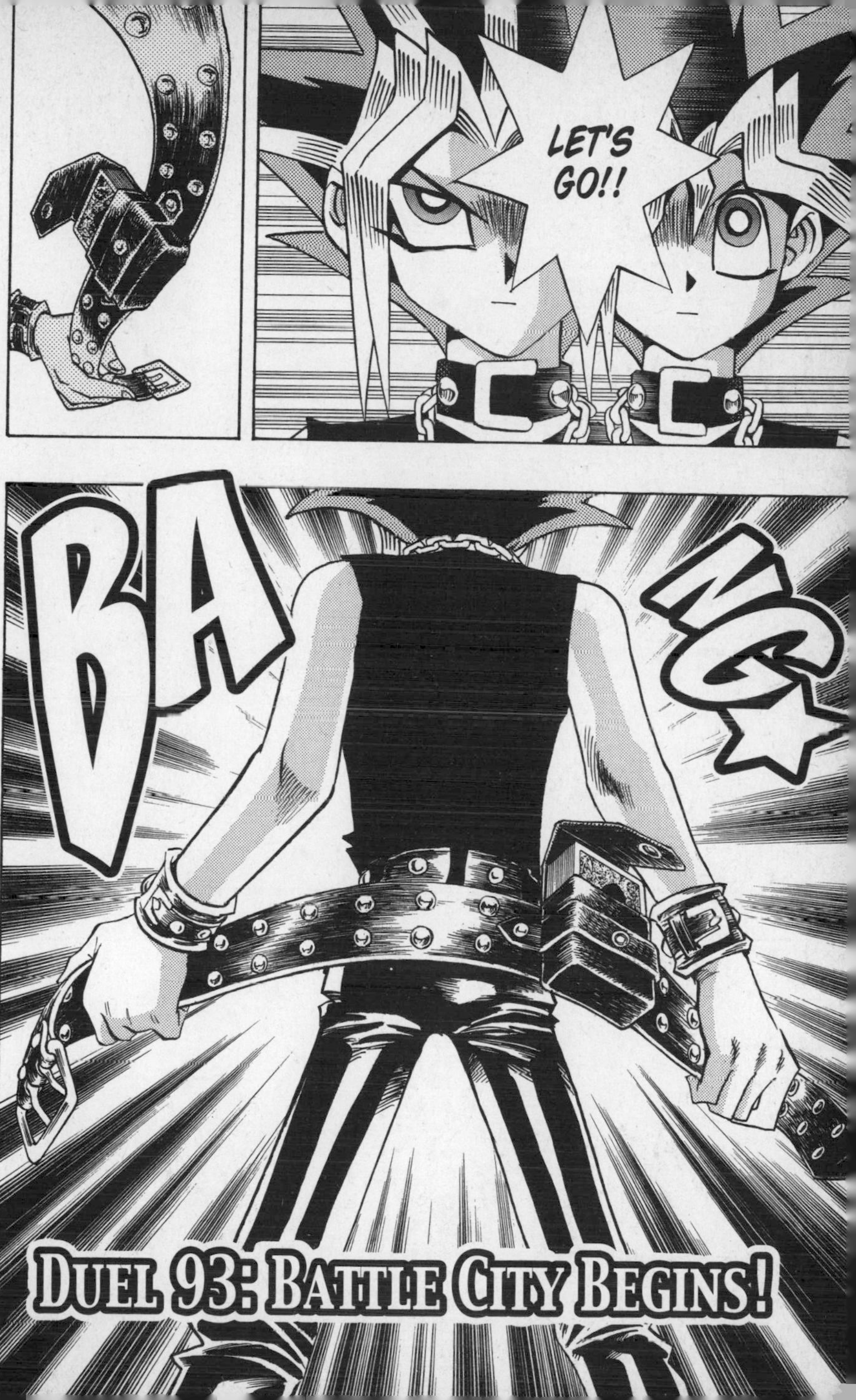
LET'S GO!!
BANG

Duel 93: Battle City Begins!

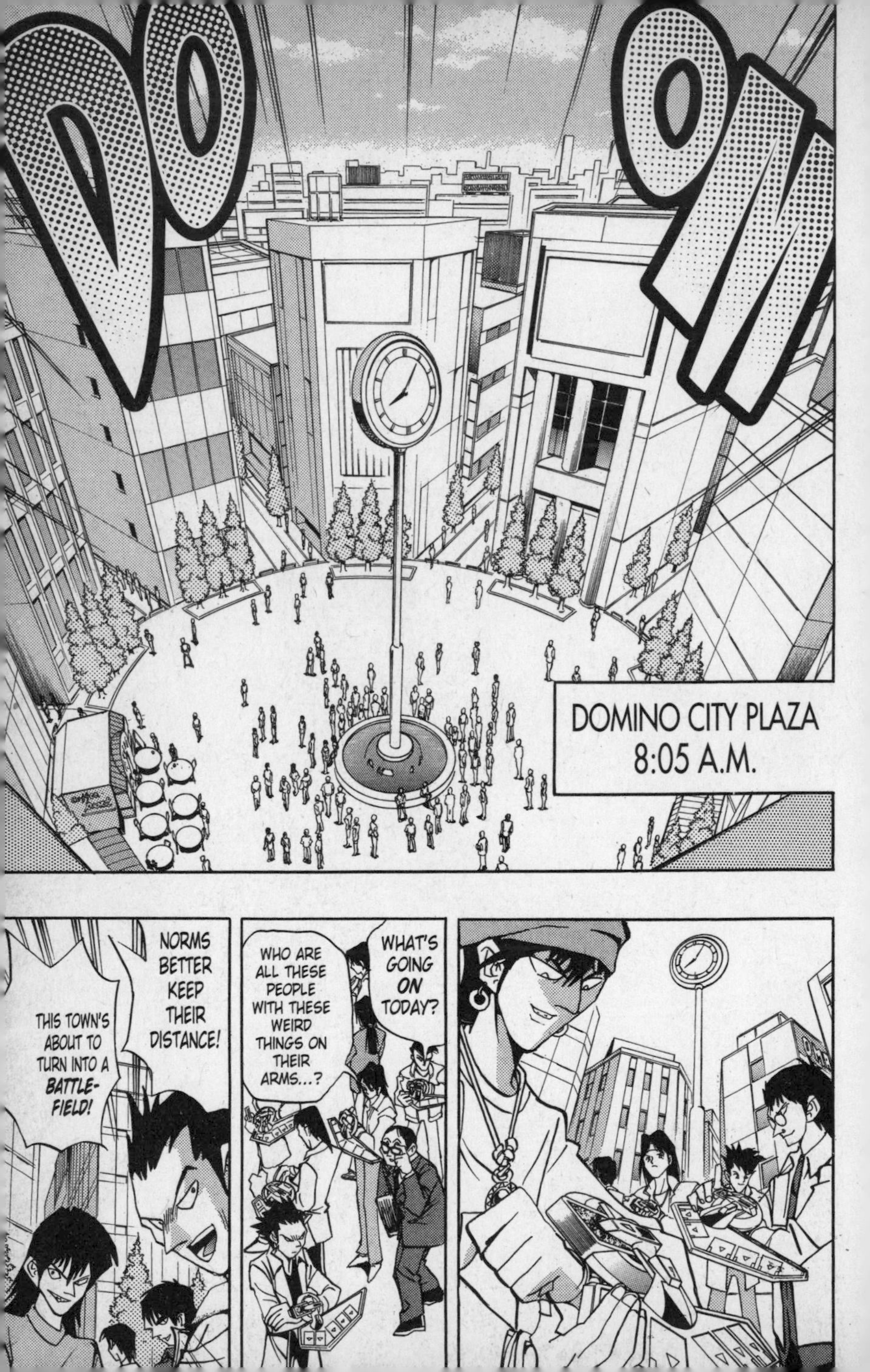
DOMINO CITY PLAZA 8:05 A.M.
WHAT'S GOING ON TODAY?
WHO ARE ALL THESE PEOPLE WITH THESE WEIRD THINGS ON THEIR ARMS...?
NORMS BETTER KEEP THEIR DISTANCE!
THIS TOWN'S ABOUT TO TURN INTO A BATTLE-FIELD!

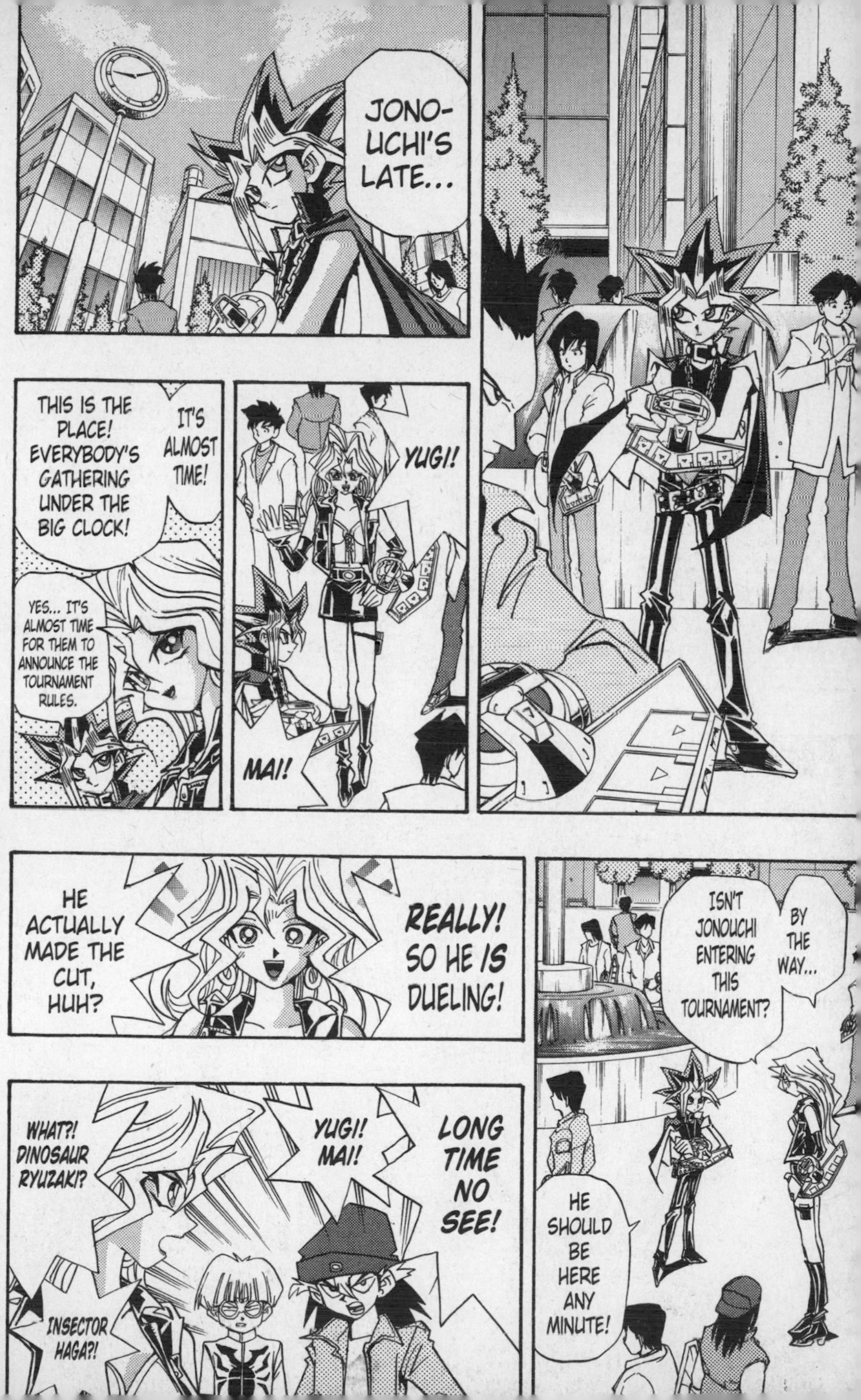
JONO-UCHI'S LATE...
YUGI!
MAI!
IT'S ALMOST TIME!
THIS IS THE PLACE! EVERYBODY'S GATHERING UNDER THE BIG CLOCK!
YES... IT'S ALMOST TIME FOR THEM TO ANNOUNCE THE TOURNAMENT RULES.
BY THE WAY...
ISN'T JONOUCHI ENTERING THIS TOURNAMENT?
HE SHOULD BE HERE ANY MINUTE!
REALLY! SO HE *IS* DUELING!
HE ACTUALLY MADE THE CUT, HUH?
LONG TIME NO SEE!
YUGI! MAI!
WHAT?! DINOSAUR RYUZAKI?
INSECTOR HAGA?!

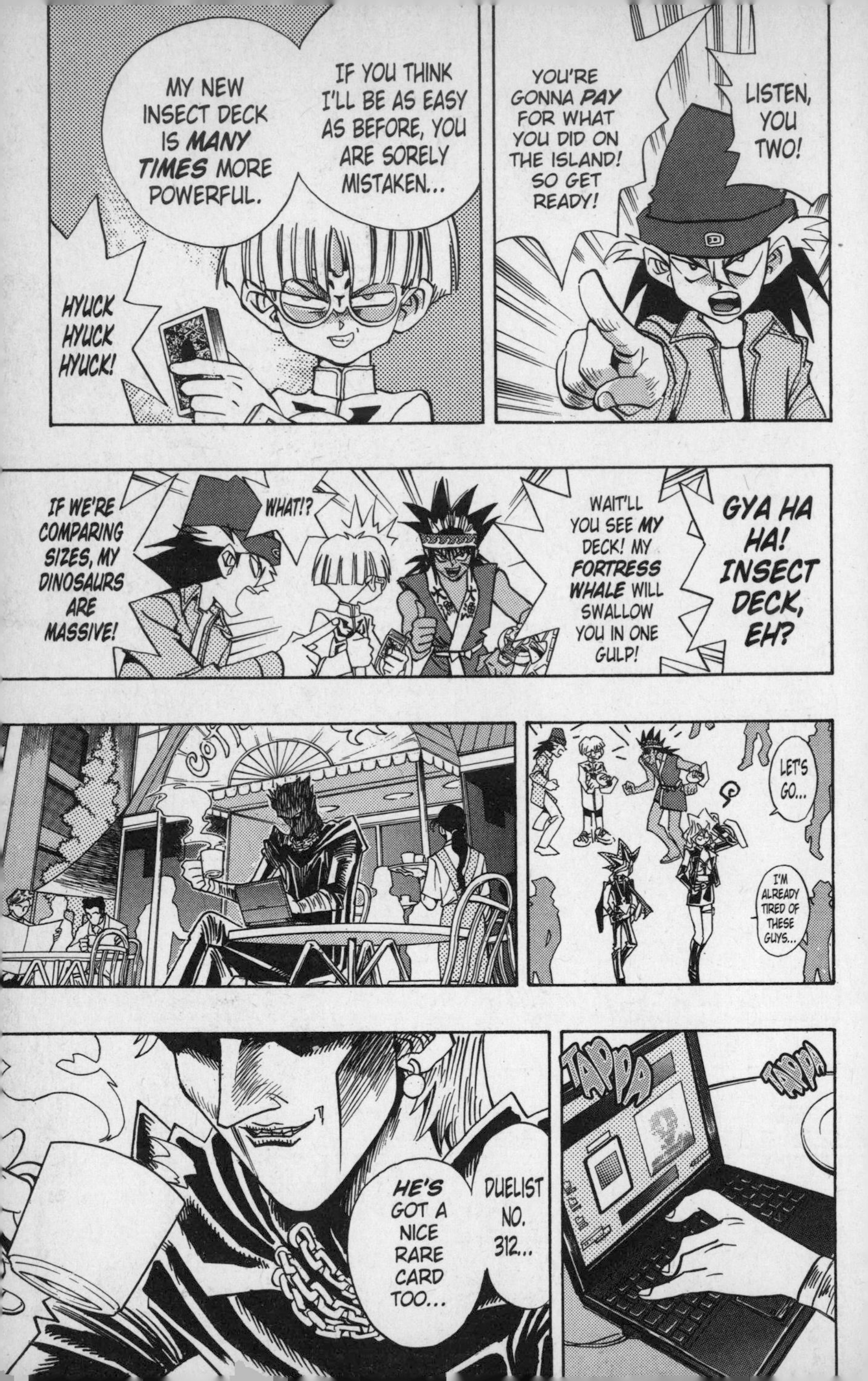
LISTEN, YOU TWO!
YOU'RE GONNA **PAY** FOR WHAT YOU DID ON THE ISLAND! SO GET READY!
IF YOU THINK I'LL BE AS EASY AS BEFORE, YOU ARE SORELY MISTAKEN...
MY NEW INSECT DECK IS **MANY TIMES** MORE POWERFUL.
HYUCK HYUCK HYUCK!
GYA HA HA! INSECT DECK, EH?
WAIT'LL YOU SEE **MY** DECK! MY **FORTRESS WHALE** WILL SWALLOW YOU IN ONE GULP!
WHAT!?
IF WE'RE COMPARING SIZES, MY DINOSAURS ARE MASSIVE!
LET'S GO...
I'M ALREADY TIRED OF THESE GUYS...
TAPPA
TAPPA
DUELIST NO. 312...
HE'S GOT A NICE RARE CARD TOO...

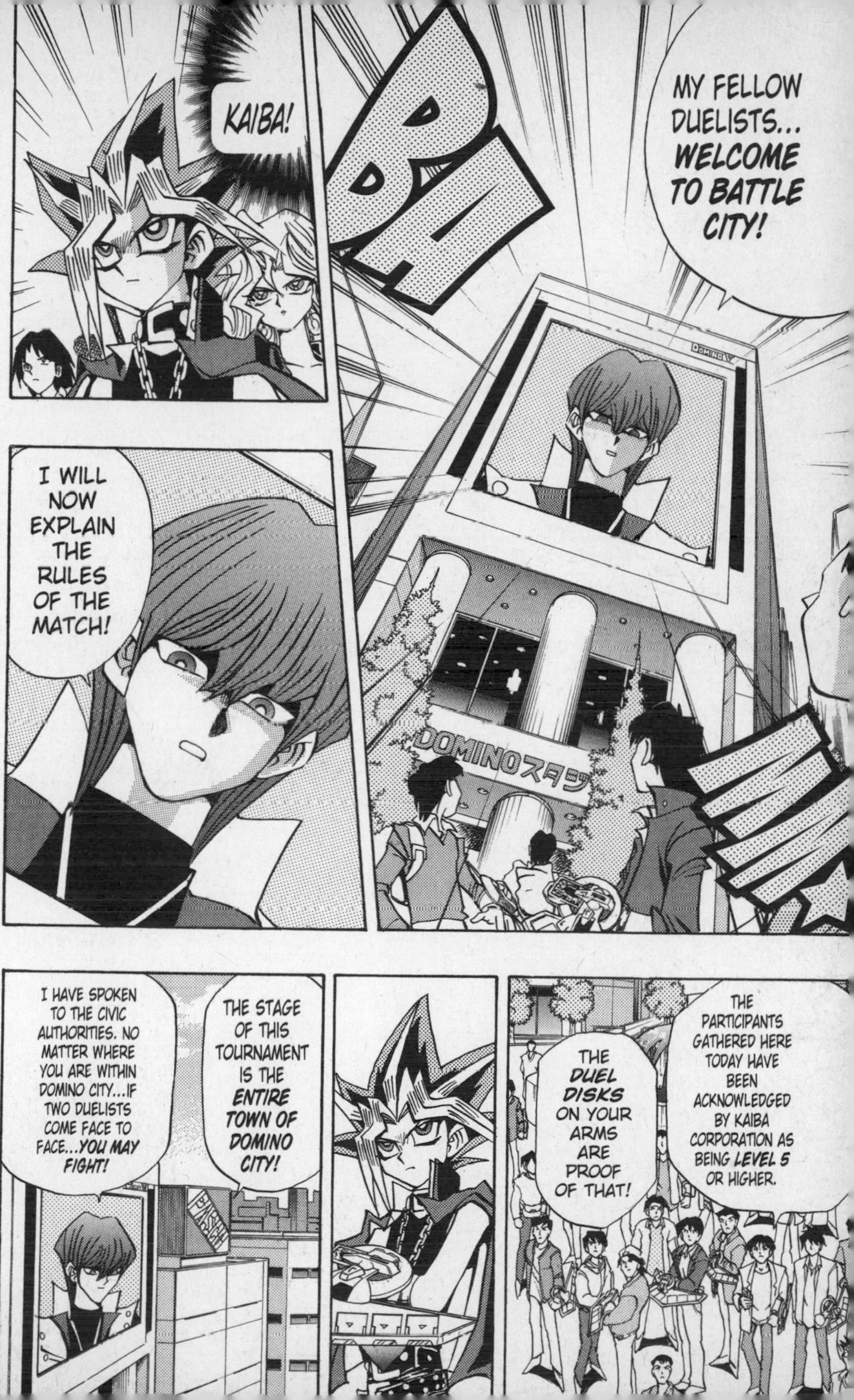
MY FELLOW DUELISTS... WELCOME TO BATTLE CITY!
KAIBA!
I WILL NOW EXPLAIN THE RULES OF THE MATCH!
THE PARTICIPANTS GATHERED HERE TODAY HAVE BEEN ACKNOWLEDGED BY KAIBA CORPORATION AS BEING LEVEL 5 OR HIGHER.
THE DUEL DISKS ON YOUR ARMS ARE PROOF OF THAT!
THE STAGE OF THIS TOURNAMENT IS THE ENTIRE TOWN OF DOMINO CITY!
I HAVE SPOKEN TO THE CIVIC AUTHORITIES. NO MATTER WHERE YOU ARE WITHIN DOMINO CITY...IF TWO DUELISTS COME FACE TO FACE...YOU MAY FIGHT!

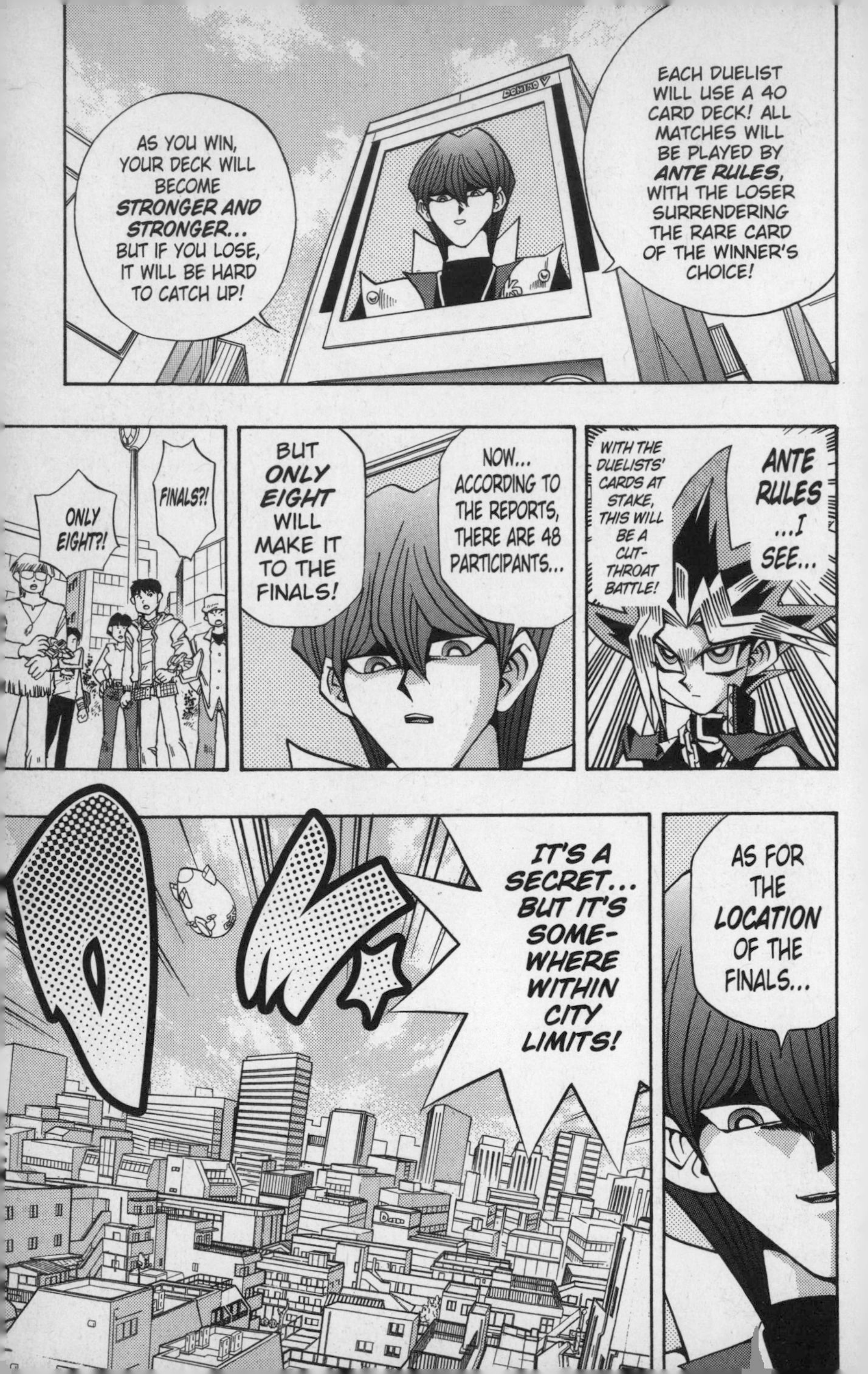
EACH DUELIST WILL USE A 40 CARD DECK! ALL MATCHES WILL BE PLAYED BY ANTE RULES, WITH THE LOSER SURRENDERING THE RARE CARD OF THE WINNER'S CHOICE!
AS YOU WIN, YOUR DECK WILL BECOME STRONGER AND STRONGER... BUT IF YOU LOSE, IT WILL BE HARD TO CATCH UP!
ANTE RULES ...I SEE...
WITH THE DUELISTS' CARDS AT STAKE, THIS WILL BE A CUT-THROAT BATTLE!
NOW... ACCORDING TO THE REPORTS, THERE ARE 48 PARTICIPANTS...
BUT ONLY EIGHT WILL MAKE IT TO THE FINALS!
FINALS?!
ONLY EIGHT?!
AS FOR THE LOCATION OF THE FINALS...
IT'S A SECRET... BUT IT'S SOME-WHERE WITHIN CITY LIMITS!

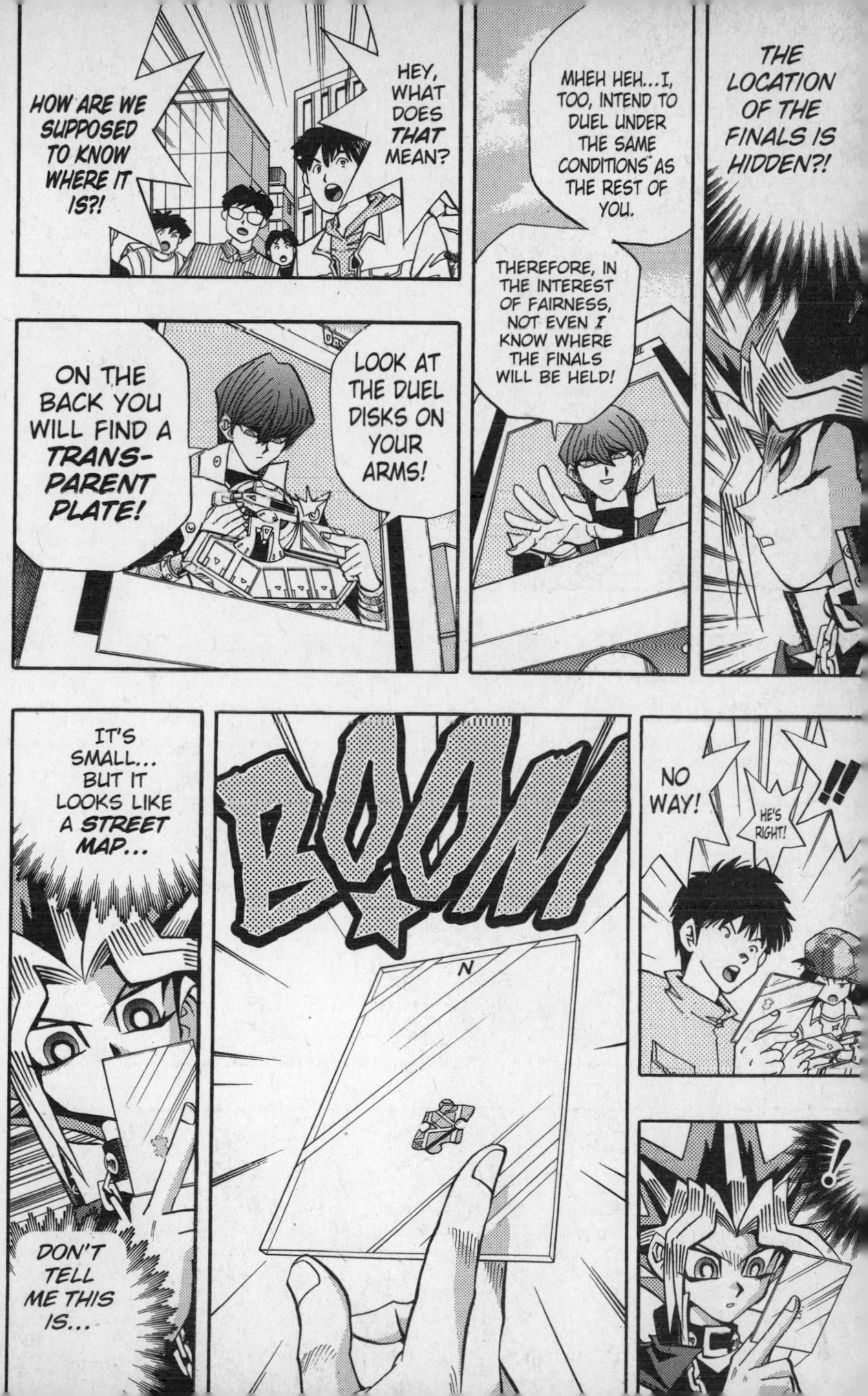
THE LOCATION OF THE FINALS IS HIDDEN?!
MHEH HEH...I, TOO, INTEND TO DUEL UNDER THE SAME CONDITIONS AS THE REST OF YOU.
THEREFORE, IN THE INTEREST OF FAIRNESS, NOT EVEN I KNOW WHERE THE FINALS WILL BE HELD!
HEY, WHAT DOES THAT MEAN?
HOW ARE WE SUPPOSED TO KNOW WHERE IT IS?!
LOOK AT THE DUEL DISKS ON YOUR ARMS!
ON THE BACK YOU WILL FIND A TRANS-PARENT PLATE!
!!
NO WAY!
HE'S RIGHT!
!
BOOM
N
IT'S SMALL... BUT IT LOOKS LIKE A STREET MAP...
DON'T TELL ME THIS IS...

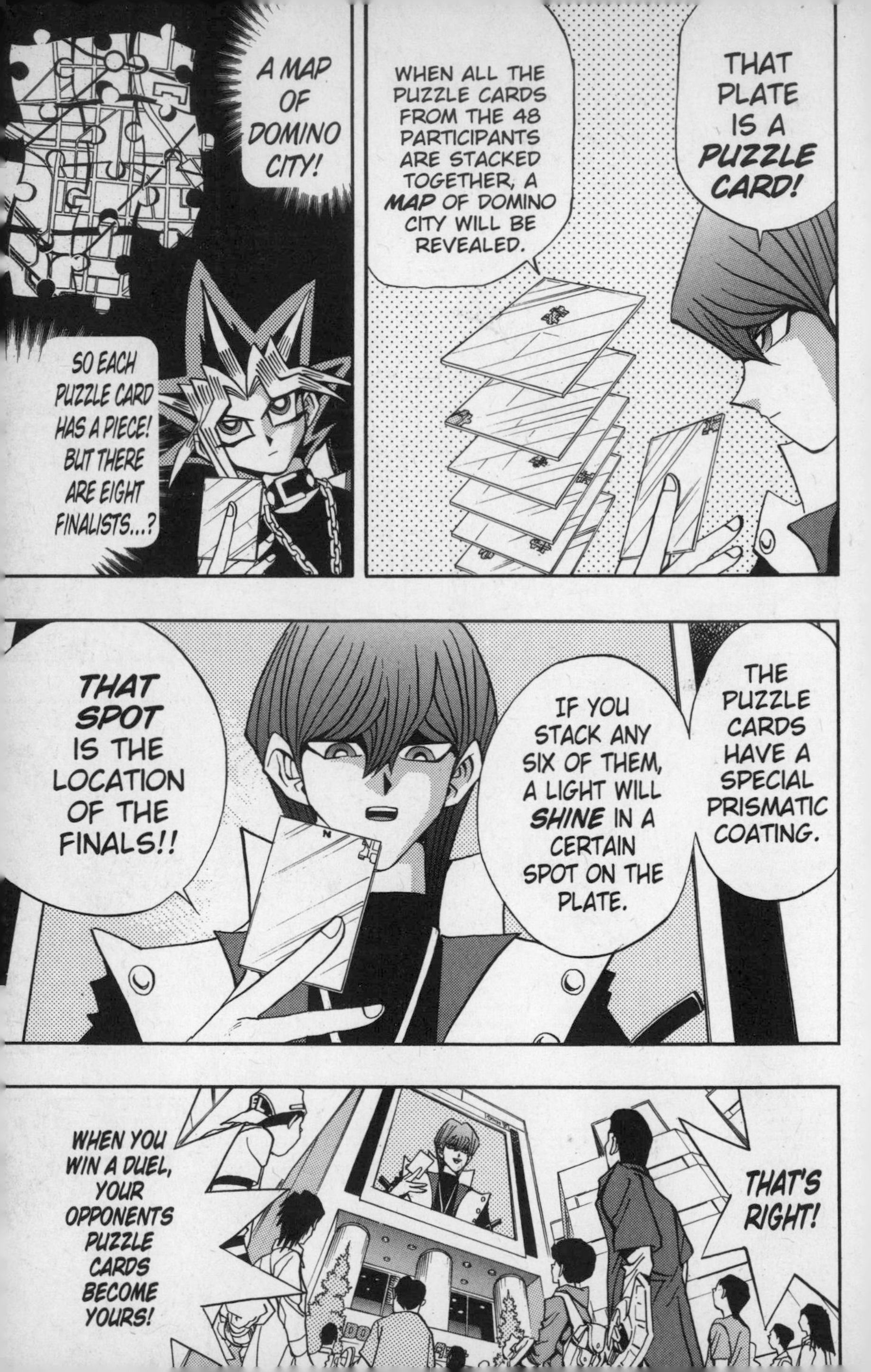

THAT PLATE IS A PUZZLE CARD!
WHEN ALL THE PUZZLE CARDS FROM THE 48 PARTICIPANTS ARE STACKED TOGETHER, A MAP OF DOMINO CITY WILL BE REVEALED.
A MAP OF DOMINO CITY!
SO EACH PUZZLE CARD HAS A PIECE! BUT THERE ARE EIGHT FINALISTS...?
THE PUZZLE CARDS HAVE A SPECIAL PRISMATIC COATING.
IF YOU STACK ANY SIX OF THEM, A LIGHT WILL SHINE IN A CERTAIN SPOT ON THE PLATE.
THAT SPOT IS THE LOCATION OF THE FINALS!!
THAT'S RIGHT!
WHEN YOU WIN A DUEL, YOUR OPPONENTS PUZZLE CARDS BECOME YOURS!

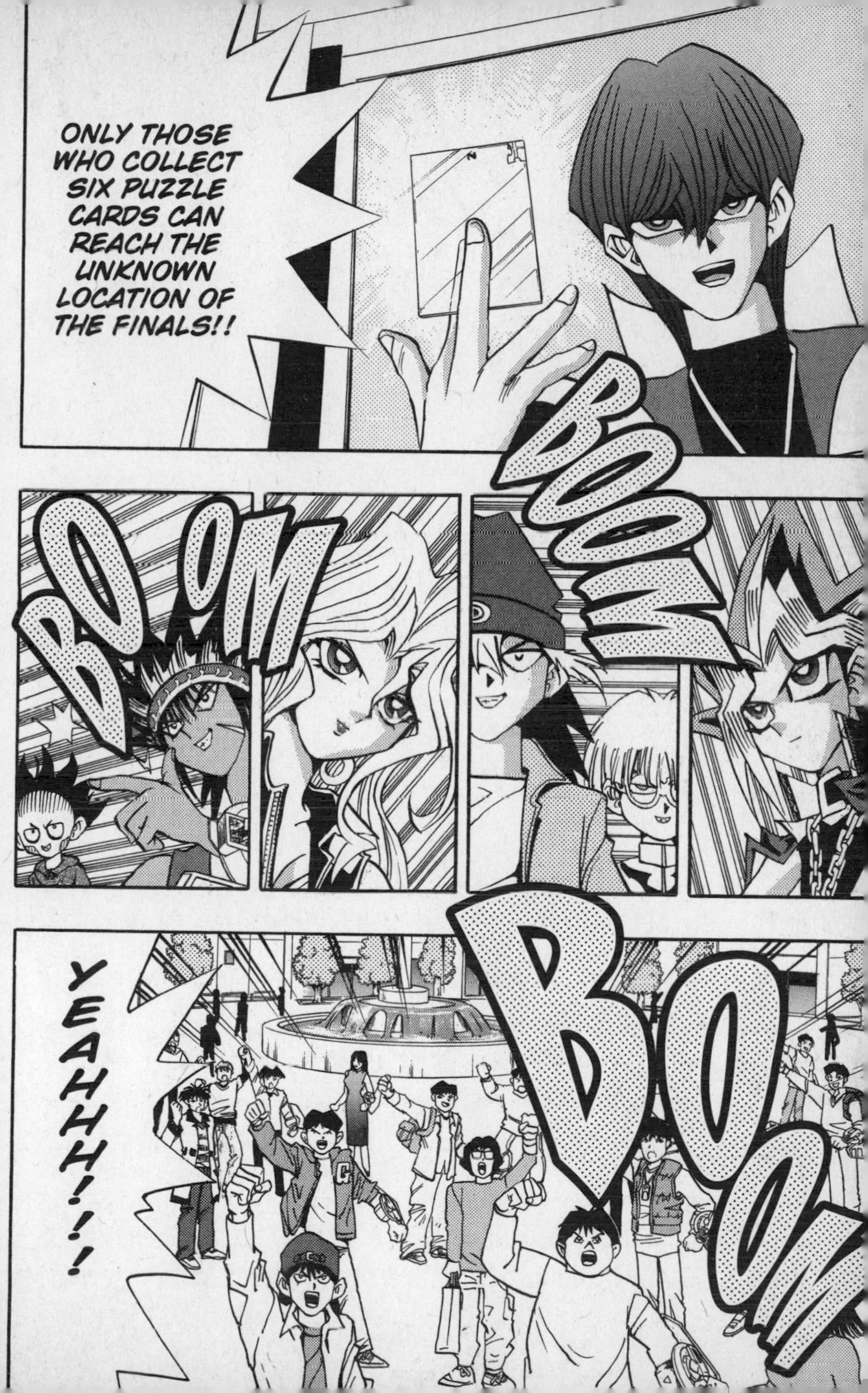
ONLY THOSE WHO COLLECT SIX PUZZLE CARDS CAN REACH THE UNKNOWN LOCATION OF THE FINALS!!
BOOOM!
BOOM
BOOO
YEAHHH!!!

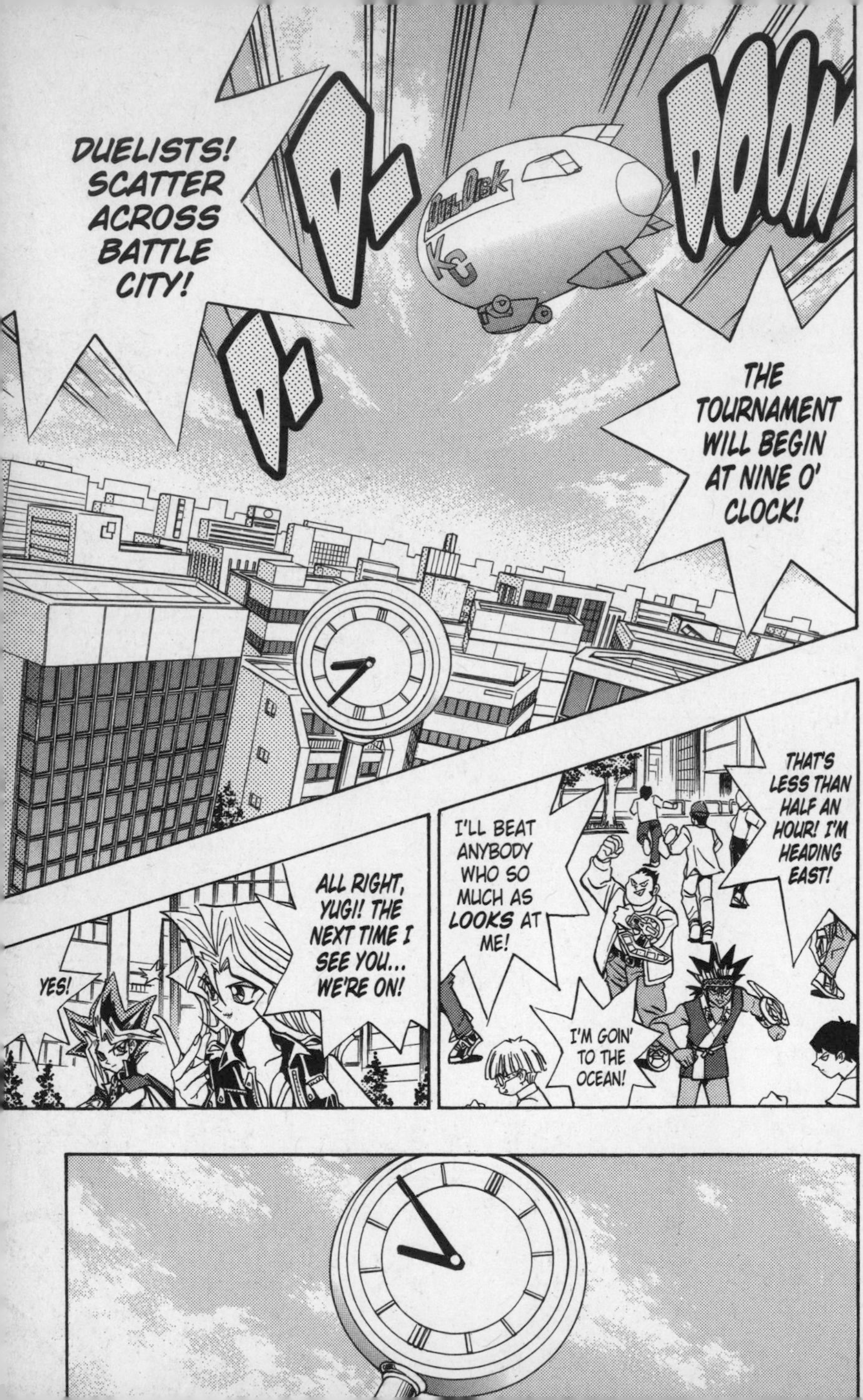
D-D-DOOM
THE TOURNAMENT WILL BEGIN AT NINE O' CLOCK!
DUELISTS! SCATTER ACROSS BATTLE CITY!
THAT'S LESS THAN HALF AN HOUR! I'M HEADING EAST!
I'LL BEAT ANYBODY WHO SO MUCH AS *LOOKS* AT ME!
I'M GOIN' TO THE OCEAN!
ALL RIGHT, YUGI! THE NEXT TIME I SEE YOU... WE'RE ON!
YES!

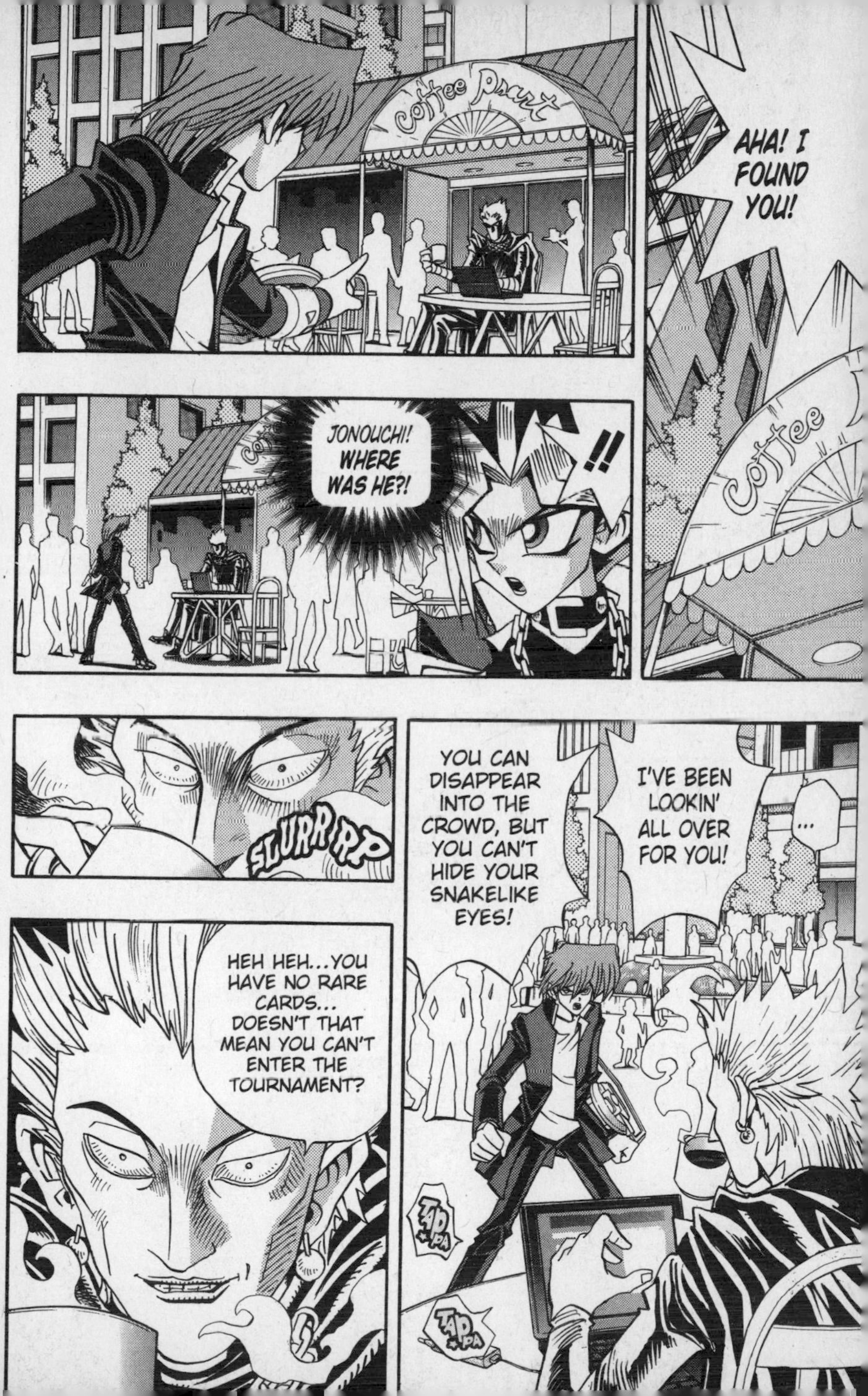
AHA! I FOUND YOU!
JONOUCHI! WHERE WAS HE?!
!!
...
I'VE BEEN LOOKIN' ALL OVER FOR YOU!
YOU CAN DISAPPEAR INTO THE CROWD, BUT YOU CAN'T HIDE YOUR SNAKELIKE EYES!
TAPPA
TAPPA
SLURRRP
HEH HEH...YOU HAVE NO RARE CARDS... DOESN'T THAT MEAN YOU CAN'T ENTER THE TOURNAMENT?

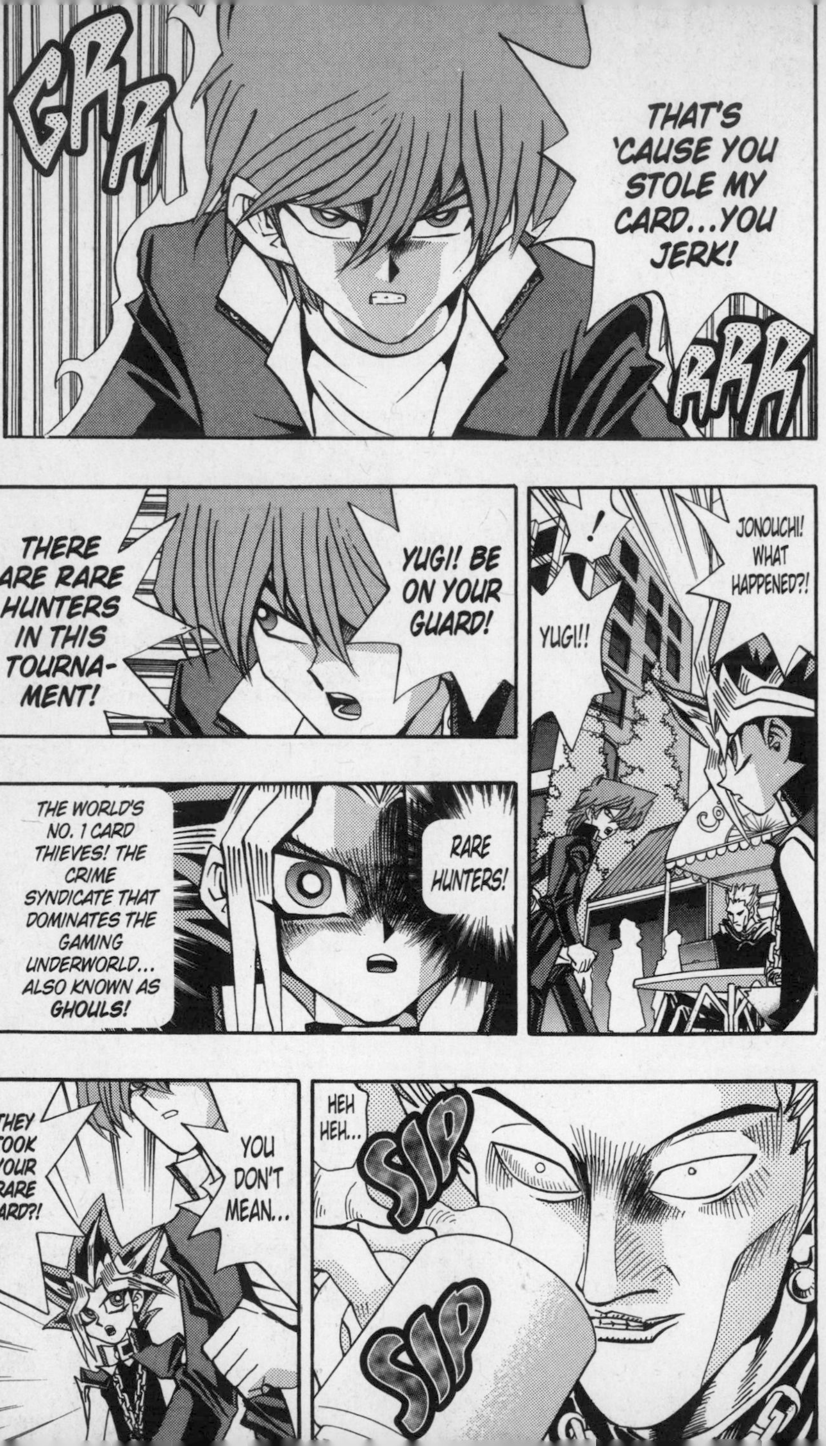
THAT'S 'CAUSE YOU STOLE MY CARD...YOU JERK!
GRR
RRR
JONOUCHI! WHAT HAPPENED?!
!
YUGI!!
YUGI! BE ON YOUR GUARD!
THERE ARE RARE HUNTERS IN THIS TOURNA-MENT!
RARE HUNTERS!
THE WORLD'S NO. 1 CARD THIEVES! THE CRIME SYNDICATE THAT DOMINATES THE GAMING UNDERWORLD... ALSO KNOWN AS GHOULS!
HEH HEH...
SIP
SIP
YOU DON'T MEAN...
THEY TOOK YOUR RARE CARD?!

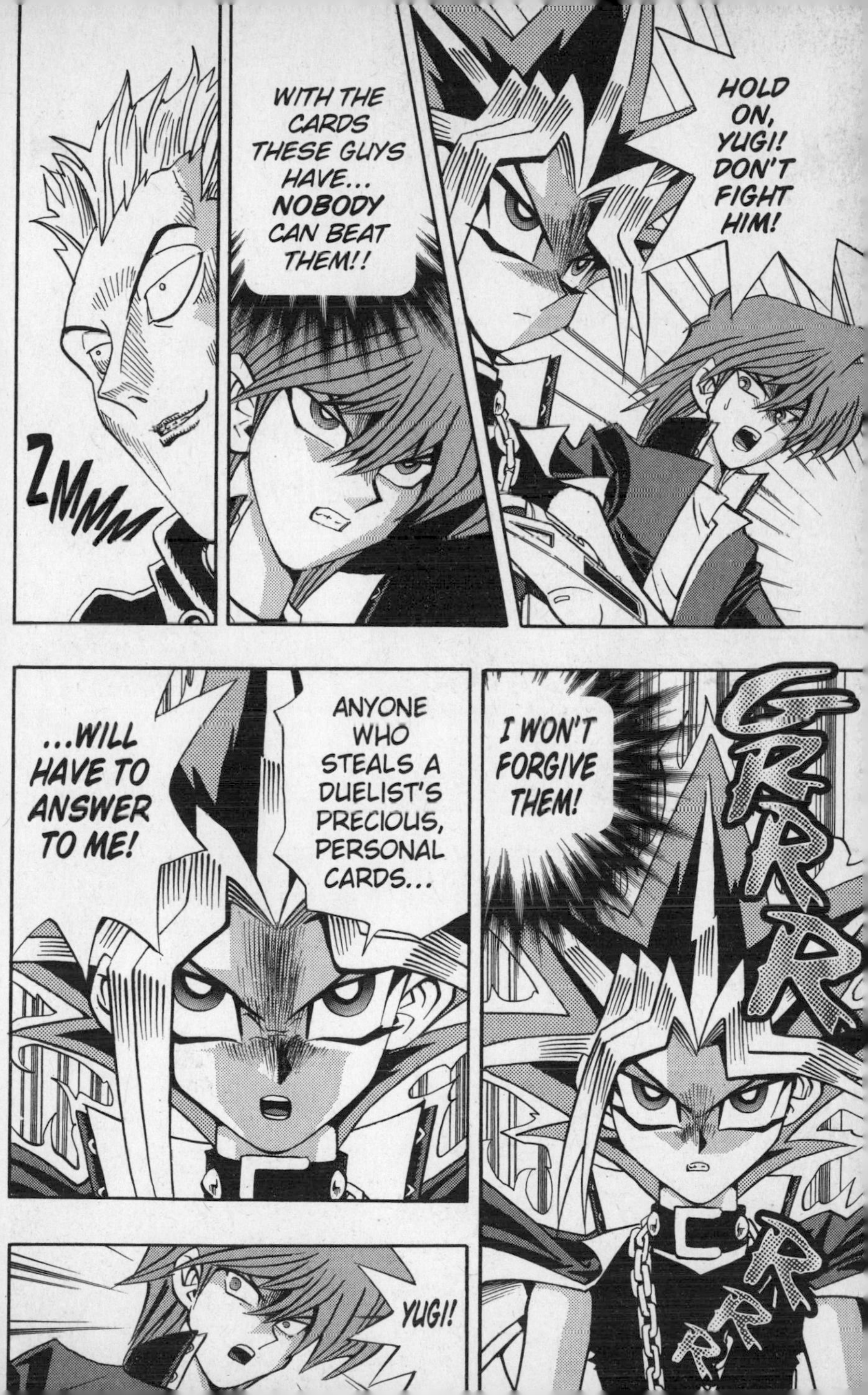
HOLD ON, YUGI! DON'T FIGHT HIM!
WITH THE CARDS THESE GUYS HAVE... NOBODY CAN BEAT THEM!!
ZMMM
GRRR
I WON'T FORGIVE THEM!
RRRR
ANYONE WHO STEALS A DUELIST'S PRECIOUS, PERSONAL CARDS...
...WILL HAVE TO ANSWER TO ME!
YUGI!

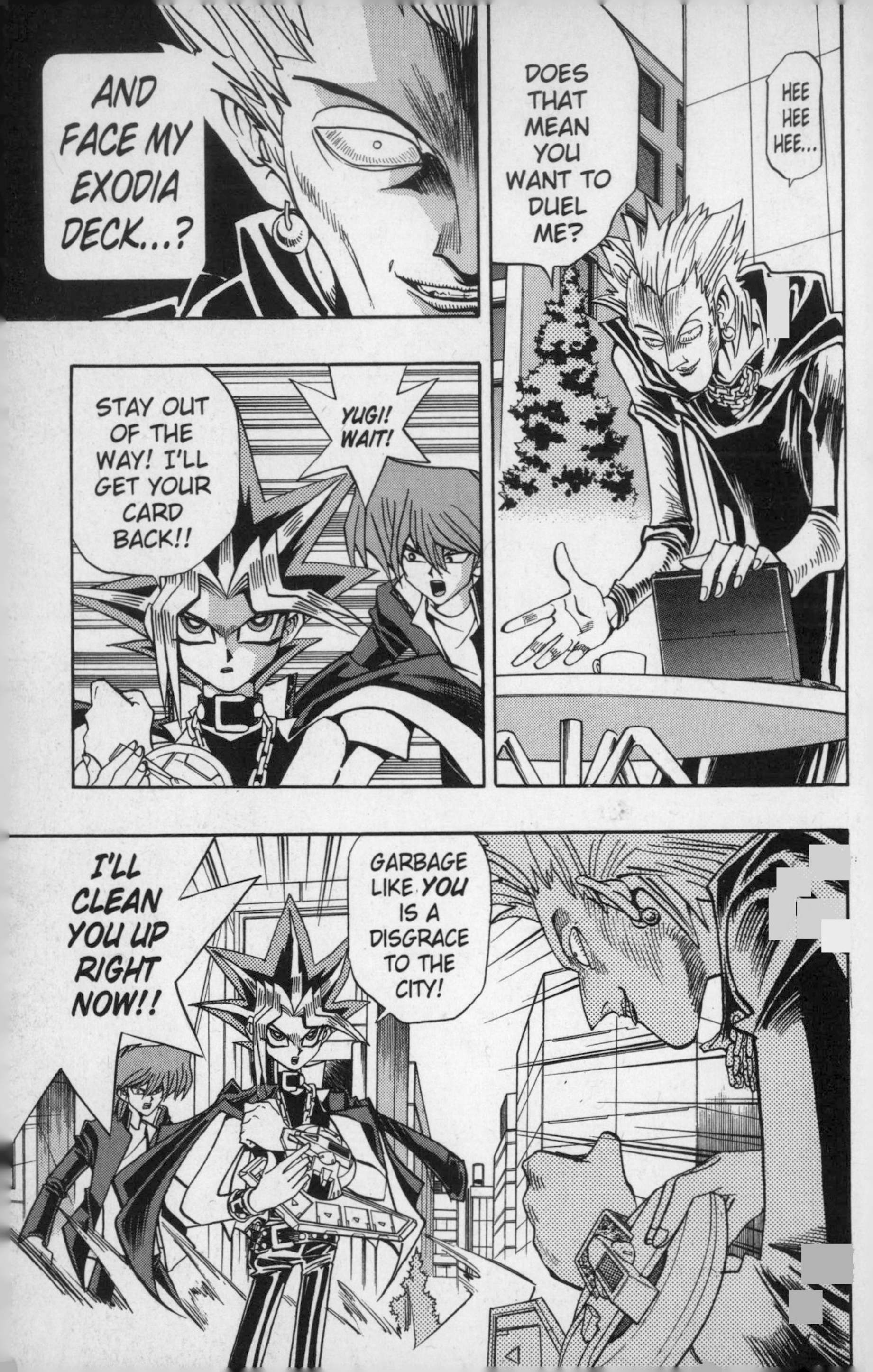
HEE HEE HEE...
DOES THAT MEAN YOU WANT TO DUEL ME?
AND FACE MY EXODIA DECK...?
YUGI! WAIT!
STAY OUT OF THE WAY! I'LL GET YOUR CARD BACK!!
GARBAGE LIKE YOU IS A DISGRACE TO THE CITY!
I'LL CLEAN YOU UP RIGHT NOW!!

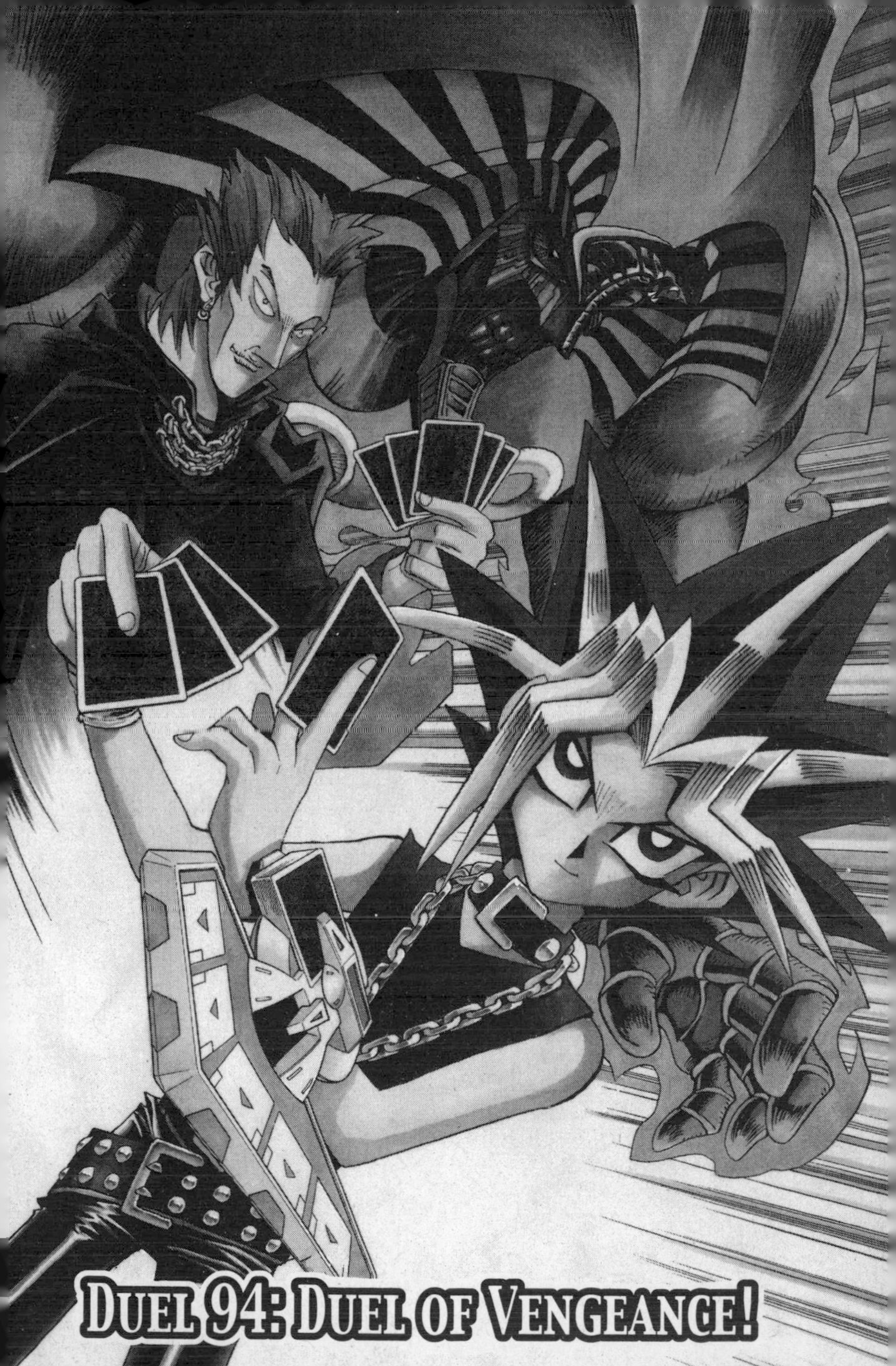

Duel 94: Duel of Vengeance!

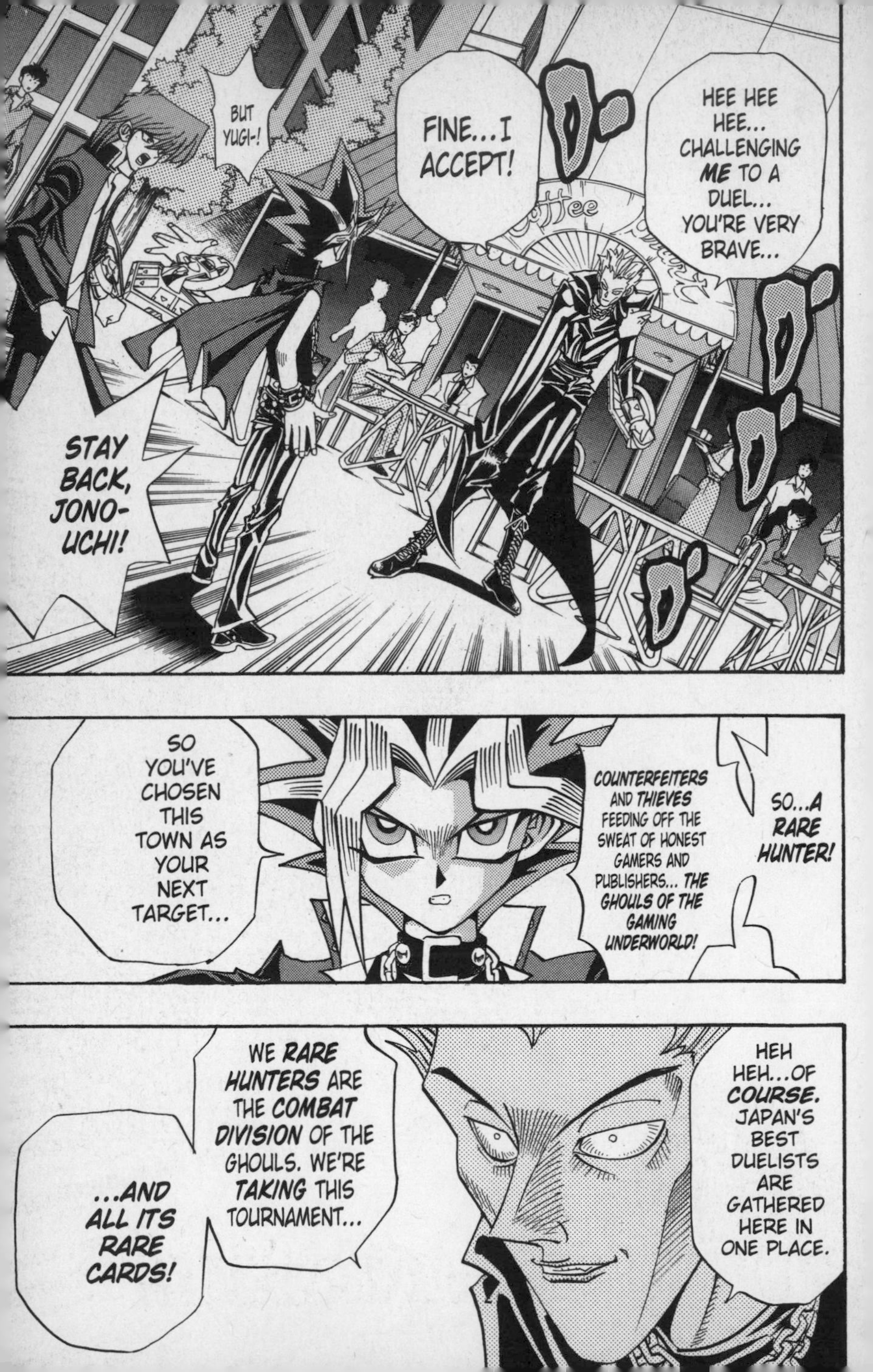
HEE HEE HEE... CHALLENGING ME TO A DUEL... YOU'RE VERY BRAVE...
FINE...I ACCEPT!
BUT YUGI-!
STAY BACK, JONO-UCHI!
SO...A RARE HUNTER!
COUNTERFEITERS AND THIEVES FEEDING OFF THE SWEAT OF HONEST GAMERS AND PUBLISHERS... THE GHOULS OF THE GAMING UNDERWORLD!
SO YOU'VE CHOSEN THIS TOWN AS YOUR NEXT TARGET...
HEH HEH...OF COURSE. JAPAN'S BEST DUELISTS ARE GATHERED HERE IN ONE PLACE.
WE RARE HUNTERS ARE THE COMBAT DIVISION OF THE GHOULS. WE'RE TAKING THIS TOURNAMENT...
...AND ALL ITS RARE CARDS!

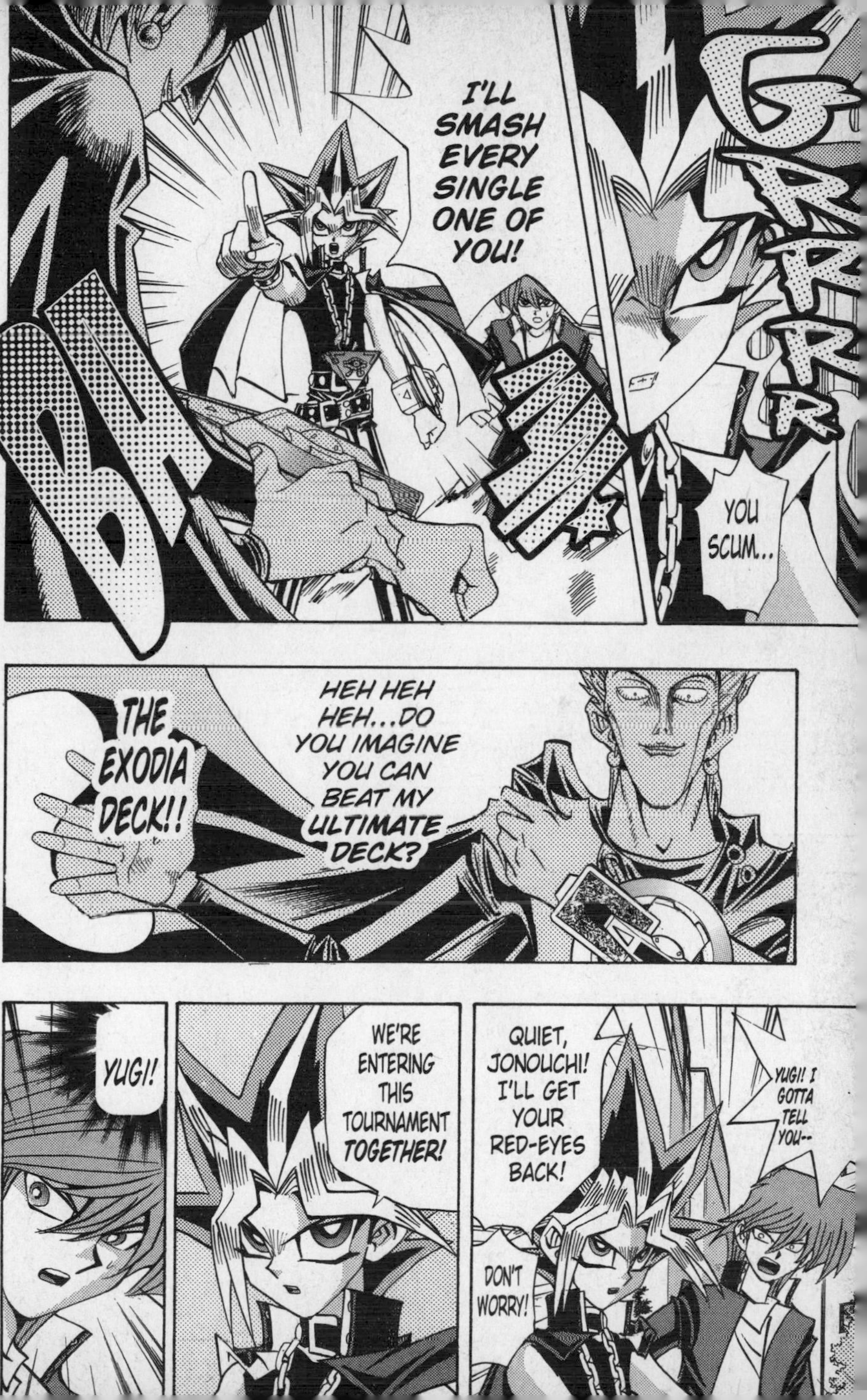
YOU SCUM...
I'LL SMASH EVERY SINGLE ONE OF YOU!
HEH HEH HEH...DO YOU IMAGINE YOU CAN BEAT MY ULTIMATE DECK?
THE EXODIA DECK!!
YUGI! I GOTTA TELL YOU--
QUIET, JONOUCHI! I'LL GET YOUR RED-EYES BACK!
DON'T WORRY!
WE'RE ENTERING THIS TOURNAMENT TOGETHER!
YUGI!

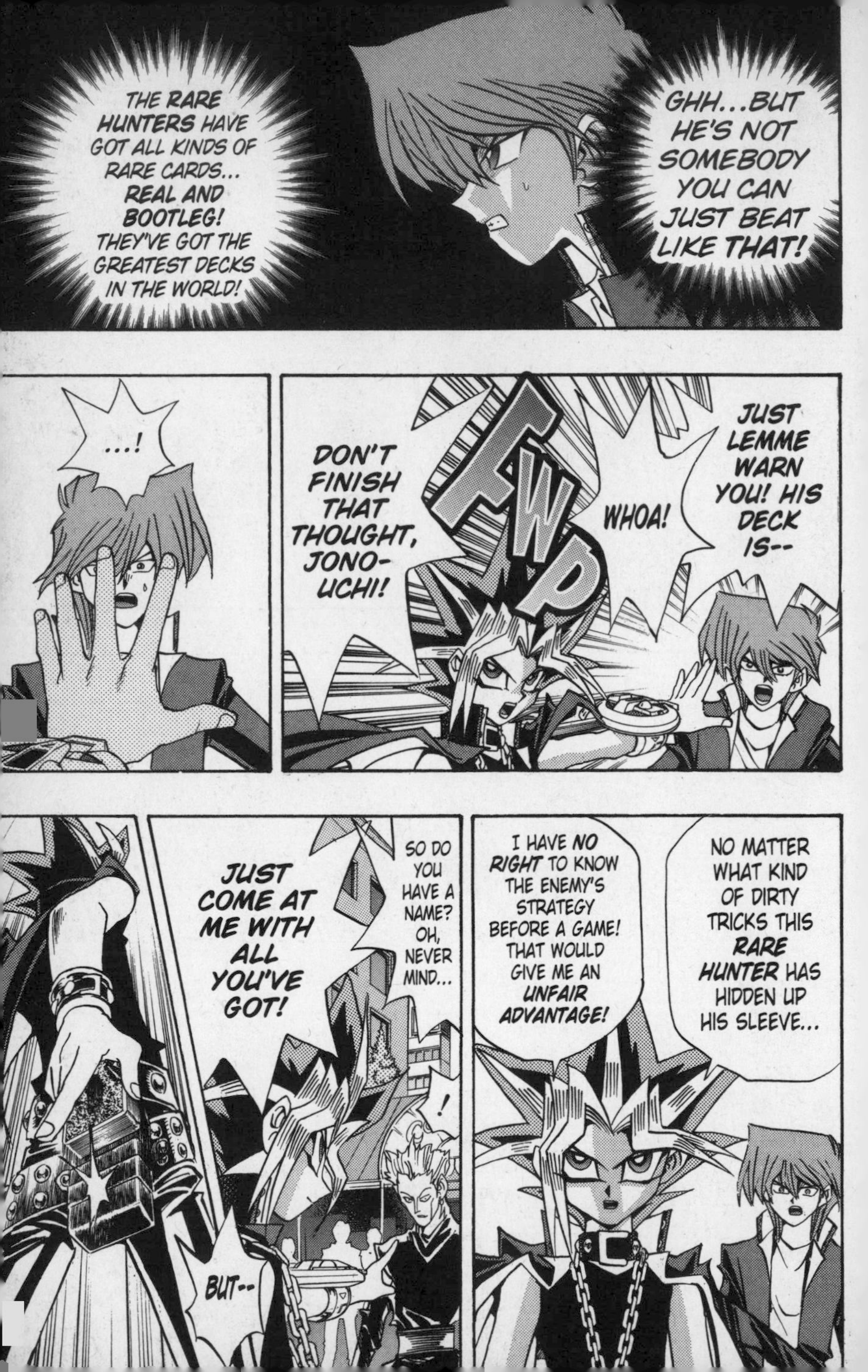
GHH...BUT HE'S NOT SOMEBODY YOU CAN JUST BEAT LIKE THAT!
THE RARE HUNTERS HAVE GOT ALL KINDS OF RARE CARDS... REAL AND BOOTLEG! THEY'VE GOT THE GREATEST DECKS IN THE WORLD!
JUST LEMME WARN YOU! HIS DECK IS--
WHOA!
FWP
DON'T FINISH THAT THOUGHT, JONO-UCHI!
...!
NO MATTER WHAT KIND OF DIRTY TRICKS THIS RARE HUNTER HAS HIDDEN UP HIS SLEEVE...
I HAVE NO RIGHT TO KNOW THE ENEMY'S STRATEGY BEFORE A GAME! THAT WOULD GIVE ME AN UNFAIR ADVANTAGE!
SO DO YOU HAVE A NAME? OH, NEVER MIND...
JUST COME AT ME WITH ALL YOU'VE GOT!
!
BUT--

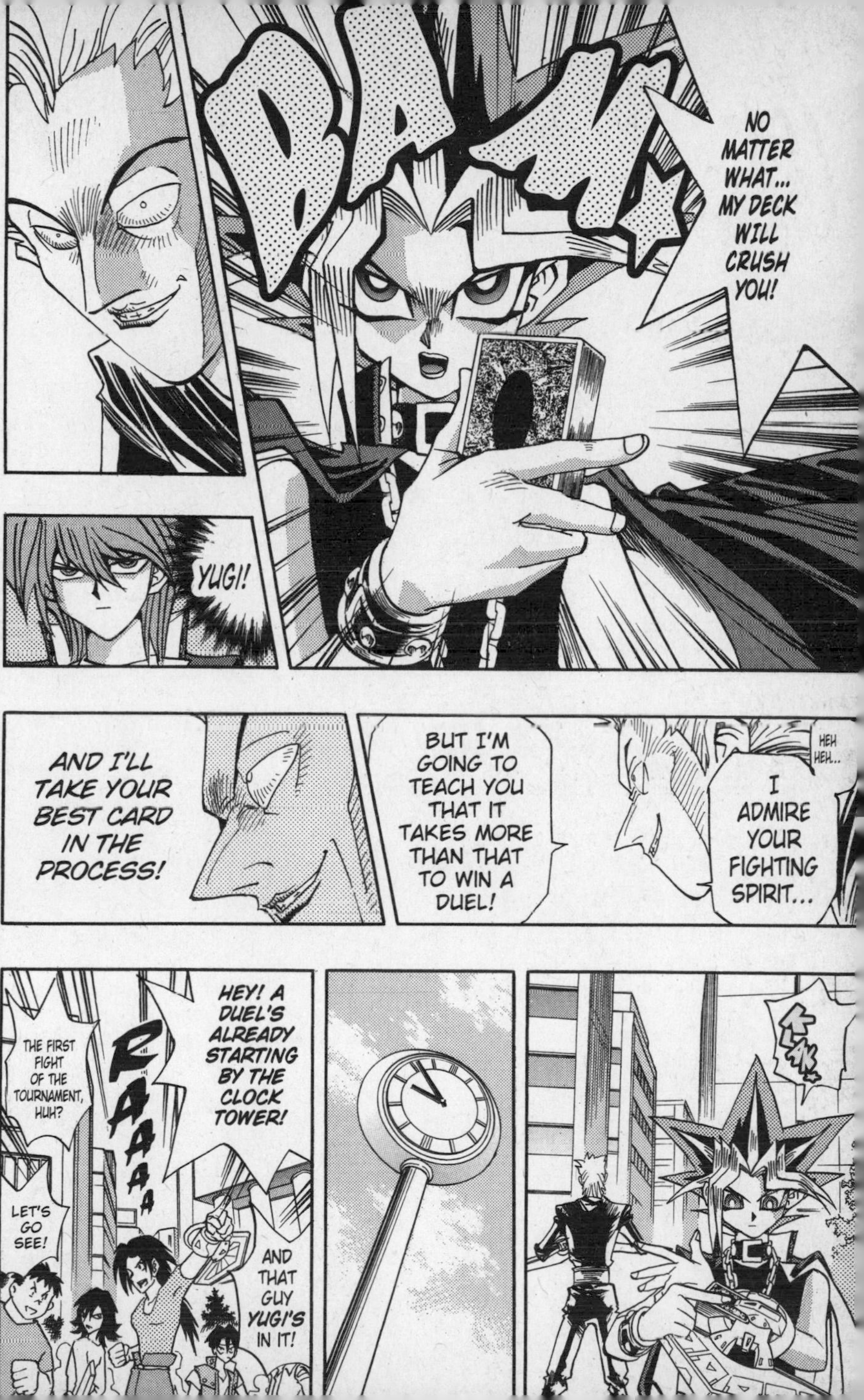
BAM
NO MATTER WHAT... MY DECK WILL CRUSH YOU!
YUGI!
HEH HEH...
I ADMIRE YOUR FIGHTING SPIRIT...
BUT I'M GOING TO TEACH YOU THAT IT TAKES MORE THAN THAT TO WIN A DUEL!
AND I'LL TAKE YOUR BEST CARD IN THE PROCESS!
KLAK
HEY! A DUEL'S ALREADY STARTING BY THE CLOCK TOWER!
THE FIRST FIGHT OF THE TOURNAMENT, HUH?
RAAAA
AND THAT GUY YUGI'S IN IT!
LET'S GO SEE!

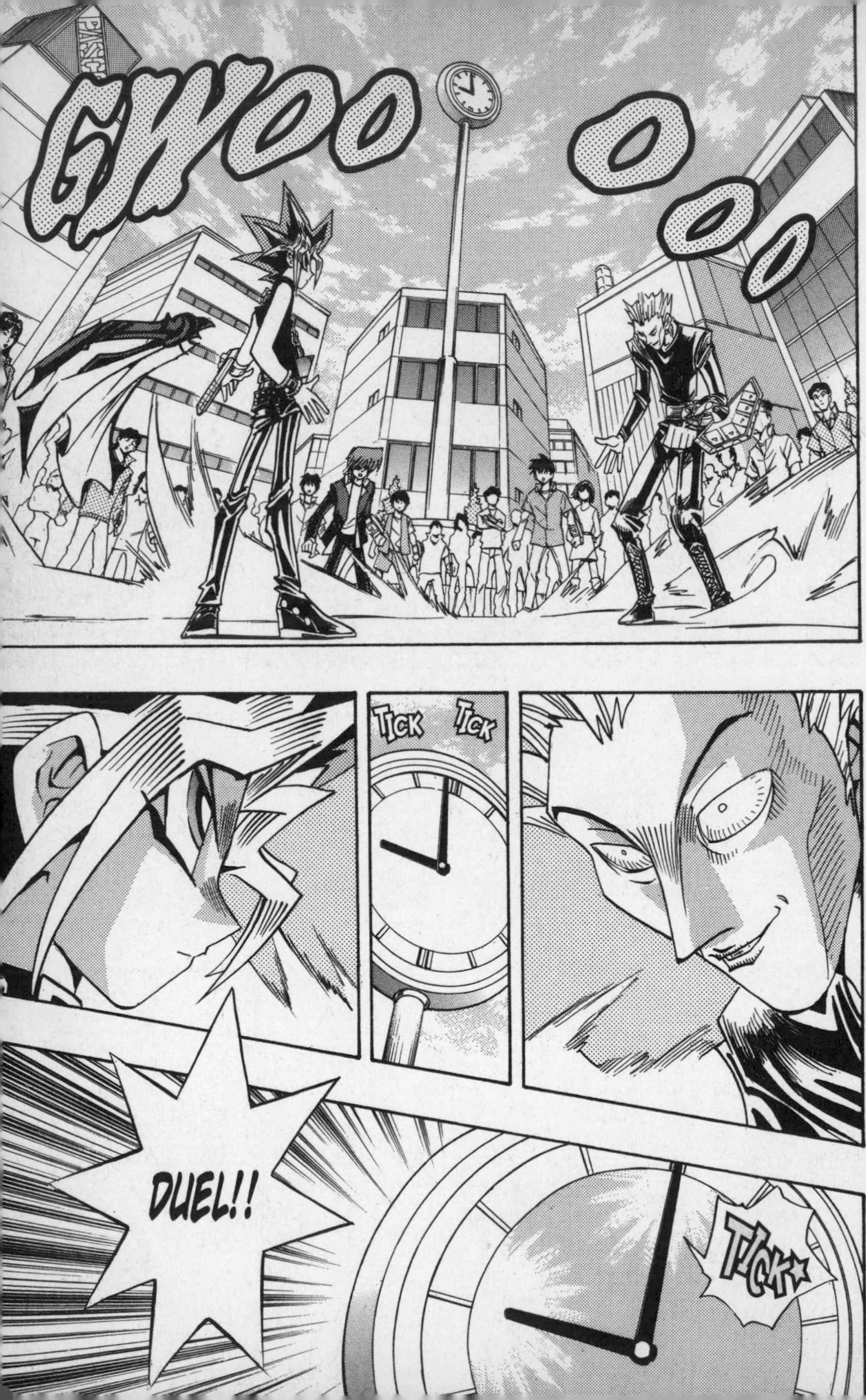
GWOO O O O
TICK TICK
TICK
DUEL!!

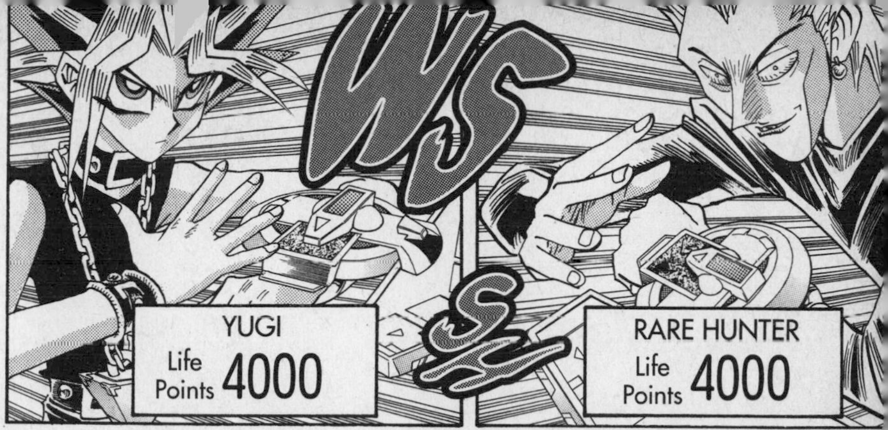
RARE HUNTER
Life Points 4000
YUGI
Life Points 4000

BATTLE CITY DUEL MONSTERS TOURNAMENT

The tournament uses the special "Duel Monsters Super Expert Rules." All participants must use Duel Disks.

• Each player starts with 4000 life points.
• Each player's deck must contain a minimum of 40 cards. (Any less will result in disqualification.)
• Order of play is determined randomly. When the game begins, each player draws five cards from their deck. (A player's hand may have a maximum of seven cards at any time.)
• On their turn, each player may play one card: either a Monster Card, Spell Card, or Trap Card.

Conditions of Victory

• When a player's life points reach zero, that player loses.
• When a player cannot draw a card on their turn, that player loses.

Monster Card Battle

• Monster Cards may be played in either Attack or Defense Mode.
Attack Mode is indicated by the card being face-up and vertical.
• Defense Mode is indicated by the card being face-down and horizontal. When the card is attacked by an opponent, or switches to Attack Mode, it is turned face-up and vertical.

Attack vs. Attack

• The monster with higher ATK (Attack Points) wins. The losing monster is destroyed and the difference in points is subtracted from the losing player's Life Points.

Attack vs. Defense

• If the attacker's ATK is higher than the defender's DEF (Defense Points), the defending monster is destroyed. The defending player's Life Points are unaffected.
• If the attacker's ATK is lower than the defender's DEF, the attacking monster is destroyed. The difference in points is subtracted from the attacking player's Life Points.

• In Super Expert Rules, monsters may directly attack the enemy player if the player has no monsters to defend with.
• Monsters with five or more stars may only be summoned by sacrificing one of the player's other monsters.
• Monsters with seven or more stars may only be summoned by sacrificing two of the player's other monsters.

Spell Cards

• Spell Cards may be played face-down or kept in the player's hand. If played face-down, they may be activated at any time. If kept in the player's hand, they may only be used on the player's turn.

Trap Cards

• Trap Cards must be played face-down before activation. The trigger for activation is indicated on the card.

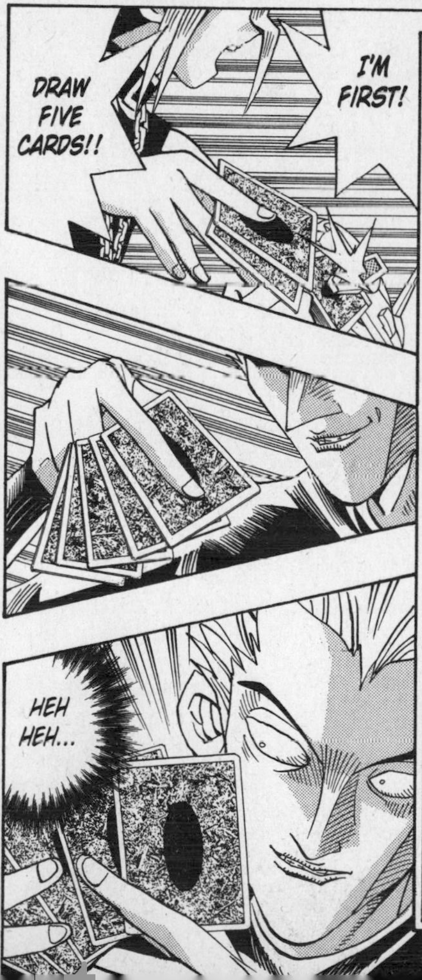
I'M FIRST!
DRAW FIVE CARDS!!
HEH HEH...

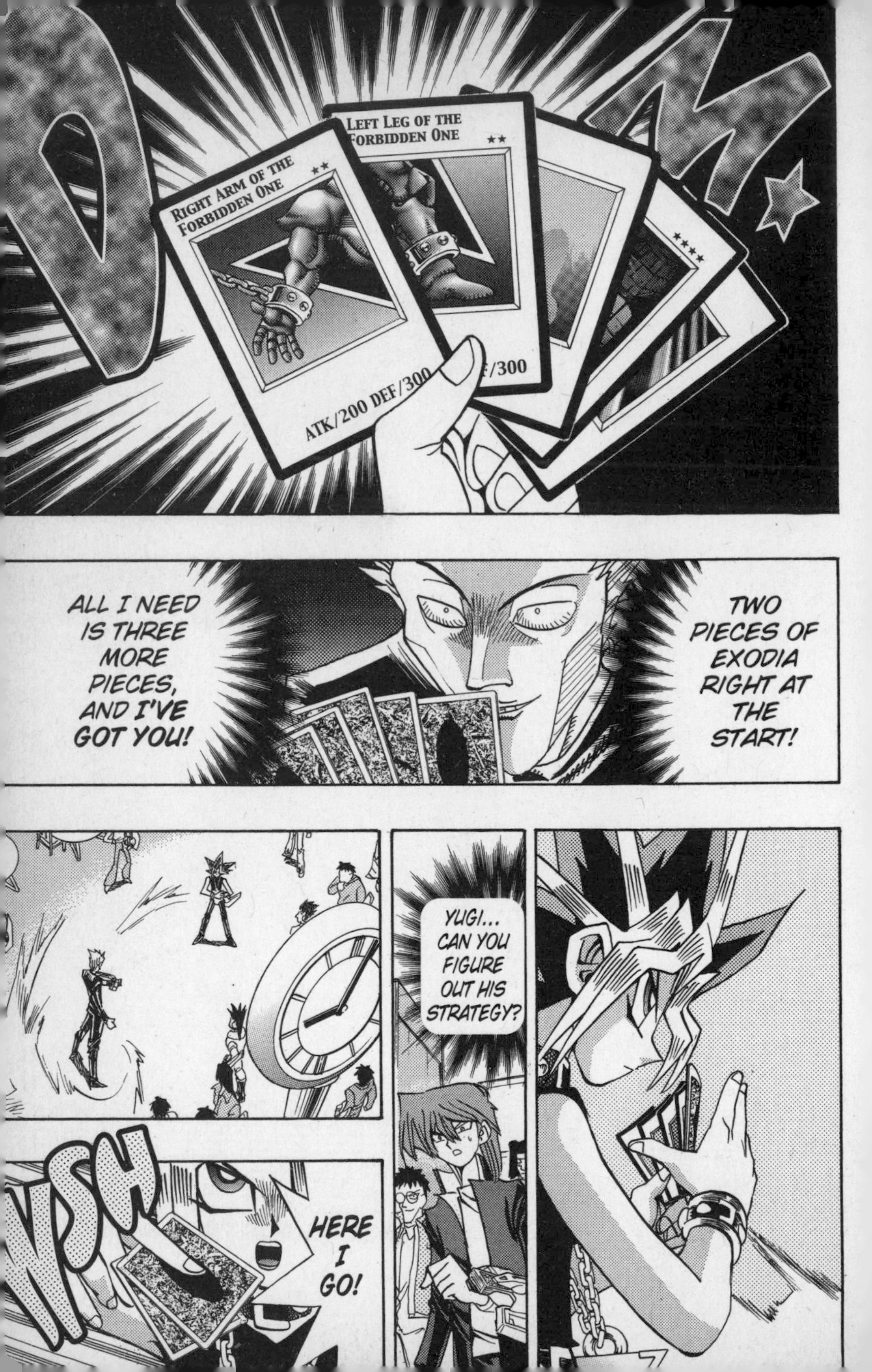
RIGHT ARM OF THE FORBIDDEN ONE
ATK/200 DEF/300
LEFT LEG OF THE FORBIDDEN ONE
TWO PIECES OF EXODIA RIGHT AT THE START!
ALL I NEED IS THREE MORE PIECES, AND I'VE GOT YOU!
YUGI... CAN YOU FIGURE OUT HIS STRATEGY?
HERE I GO!

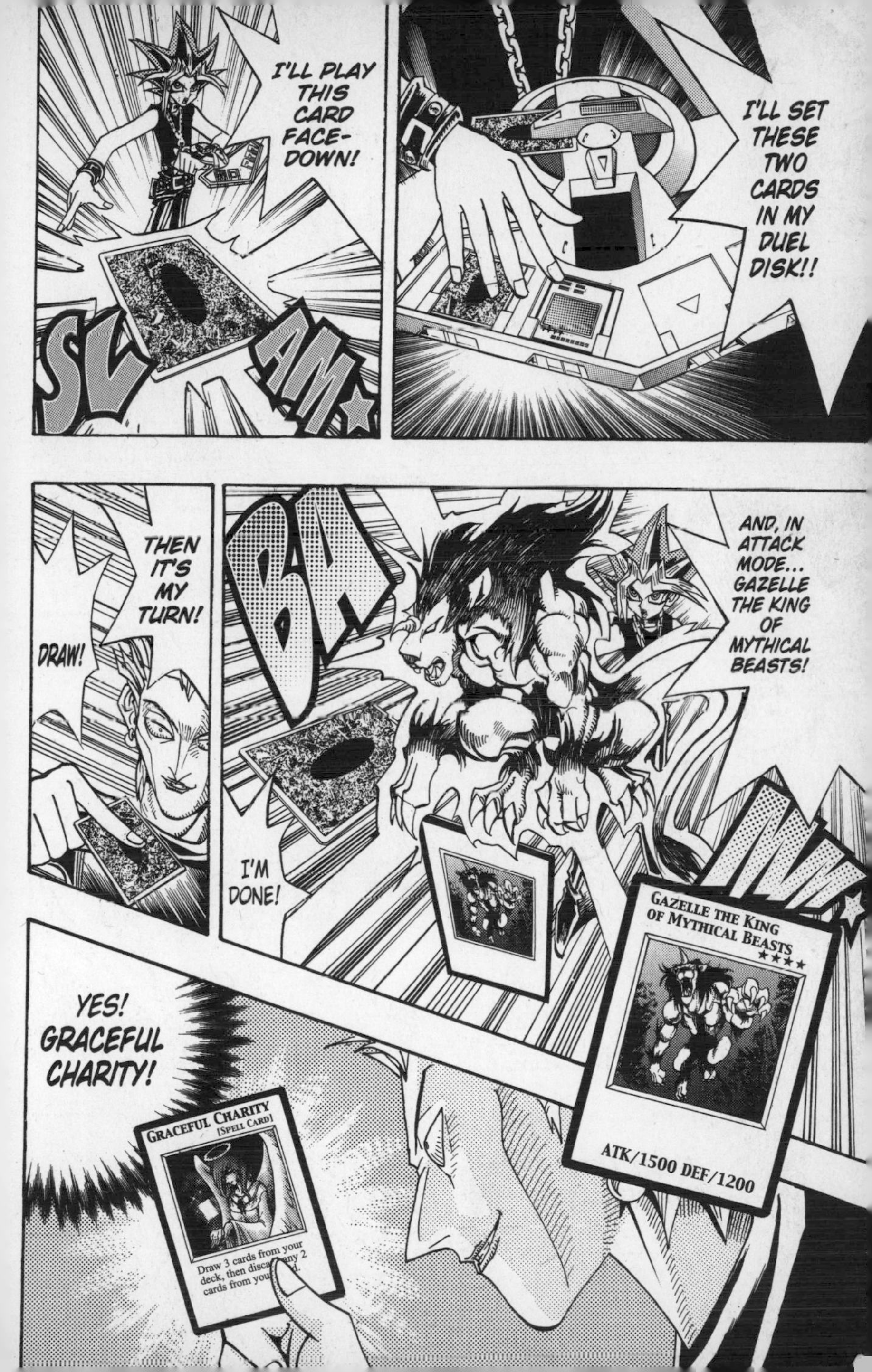
I'LL SET THESE TWO CARDS IN MY DUEL DISK!!
I'LL PLAY THIS CARD FACE-DOWN!
SLAM
AND, IN ATTACK MODE... GAZELLE THE KING OF MYTHICAL BEASTS!
GAZELLE THE KING OF MYTHICAL BEASTS
ATK/1500 DEF/1200
I'M DONE!
THEN IT'S MY TURN!
DRAW!
YES! GRACEFUL CHARITY!
GRACEFUL CHARITY
[SPELL CARD]

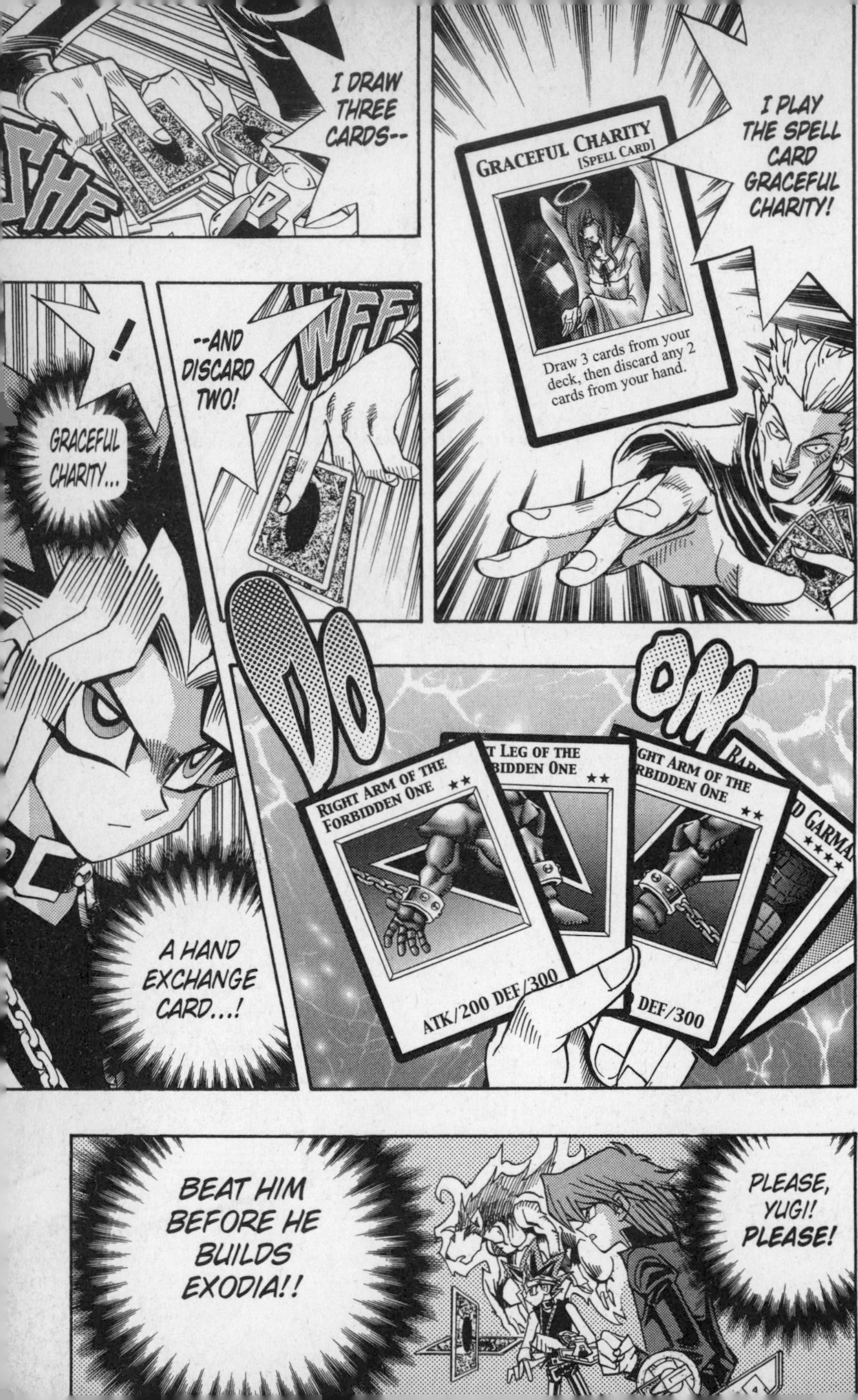
GRACEFUL CHARITY [SPELL CARD]
Draw 3 cards from your deck, then discard any 2 cards from your hand.
I PLAY THE SPELL CARD GRACEFUL CHARITY!
I DRAW THREE CARDS--
SHF
WFF
--AND DISCARD TWO!
!
GRACEFUL CHARITY...
DOOM
RIGHT ARM OF THE FORBIDDEN ONE
ATK/200 DEF/300
DEF/300
A HAND EXCHANGE CARD...!
PLEASE, YUGI! PLEASE!
BEAT HIM BEFORE HE BUILDS EXODIA!!

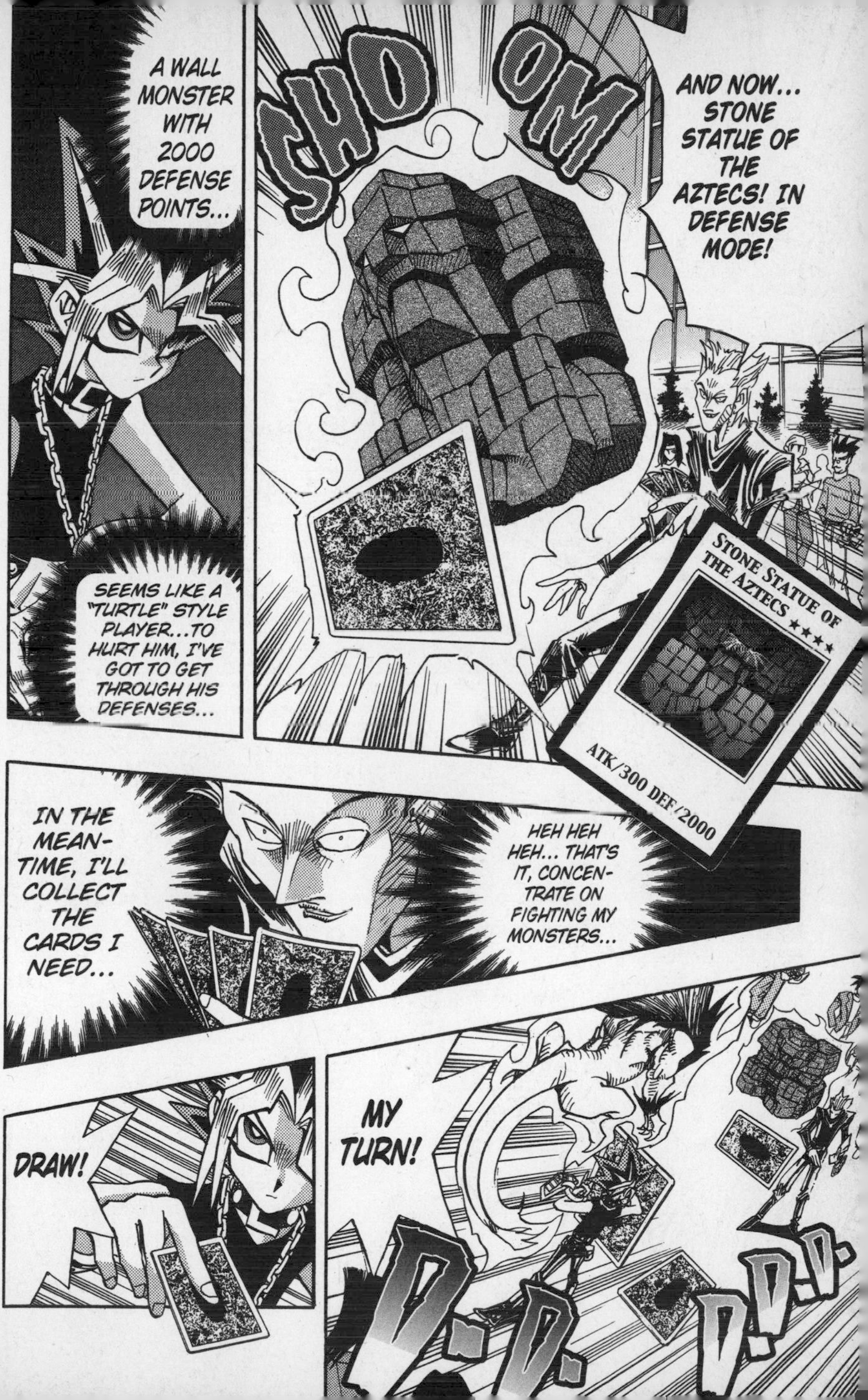
SHO OM
AND NOW... STONE STATUE OF THE AZTECS! IN DEFENSE MODE!
STONE STATUE OF THE AZTECS ★★★★
ATK/300 DEF/2000
A WALL MONSTER WITH 2000 DEFENSE POINTS...
SEEMS LIKE A "TURTLE" STYLE PLAYER...TO HURT HIM, I'VE GOT TO GET THROUGH HIS DEFENSES...
HEH HEH HEH... THAT'S IT, CONCEN-TRATE ON FIGHTING MY MONSTERS...
IN THE MEAN-TIME, I'LL COLLECT THE CARDS I NEED...
MY TURN!
D-D- D-D-D-
DRAW!

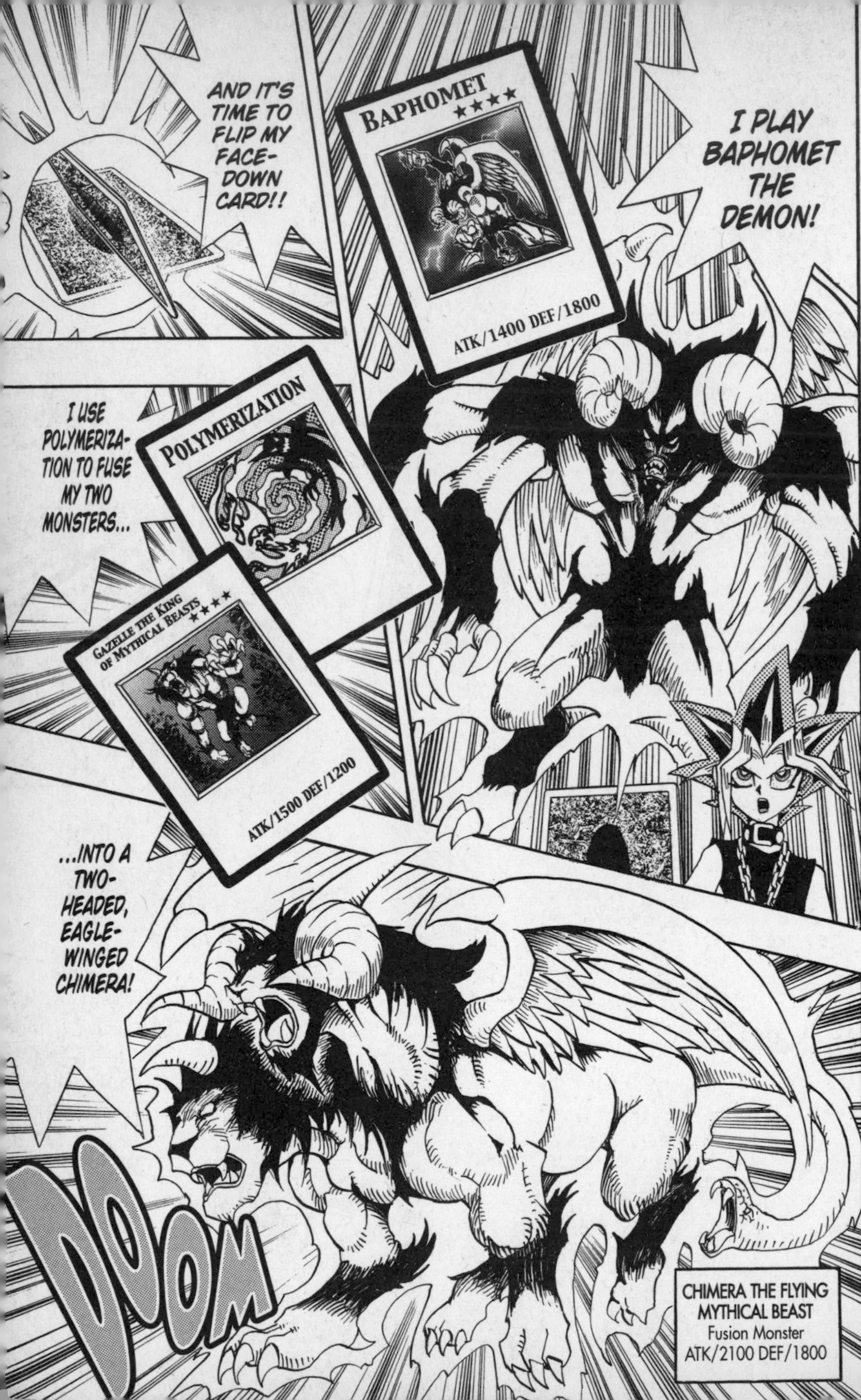
BAPHOMET
ATK/1400 DEF/1800
I PLAY BAPHOMET THE DEMON!
AND IT'S TIME TO FLIP MY FACE-DOWN CARD!!
POLYMERIZATION
I USE POLYMERIZATION TO FUSE MY TWO MONSTERS...
GAZELLE THE KING OF MYTHICAL BEASTS
ATK/1500 DEF/1200
...INTO A TWO-HEADED, EAGLE-WINGED CHIMERA!
DOOM
CHIMERA THE FLYING MYTHICAL BEAST
Fusion Monster
ATK/2100 DEF/1800

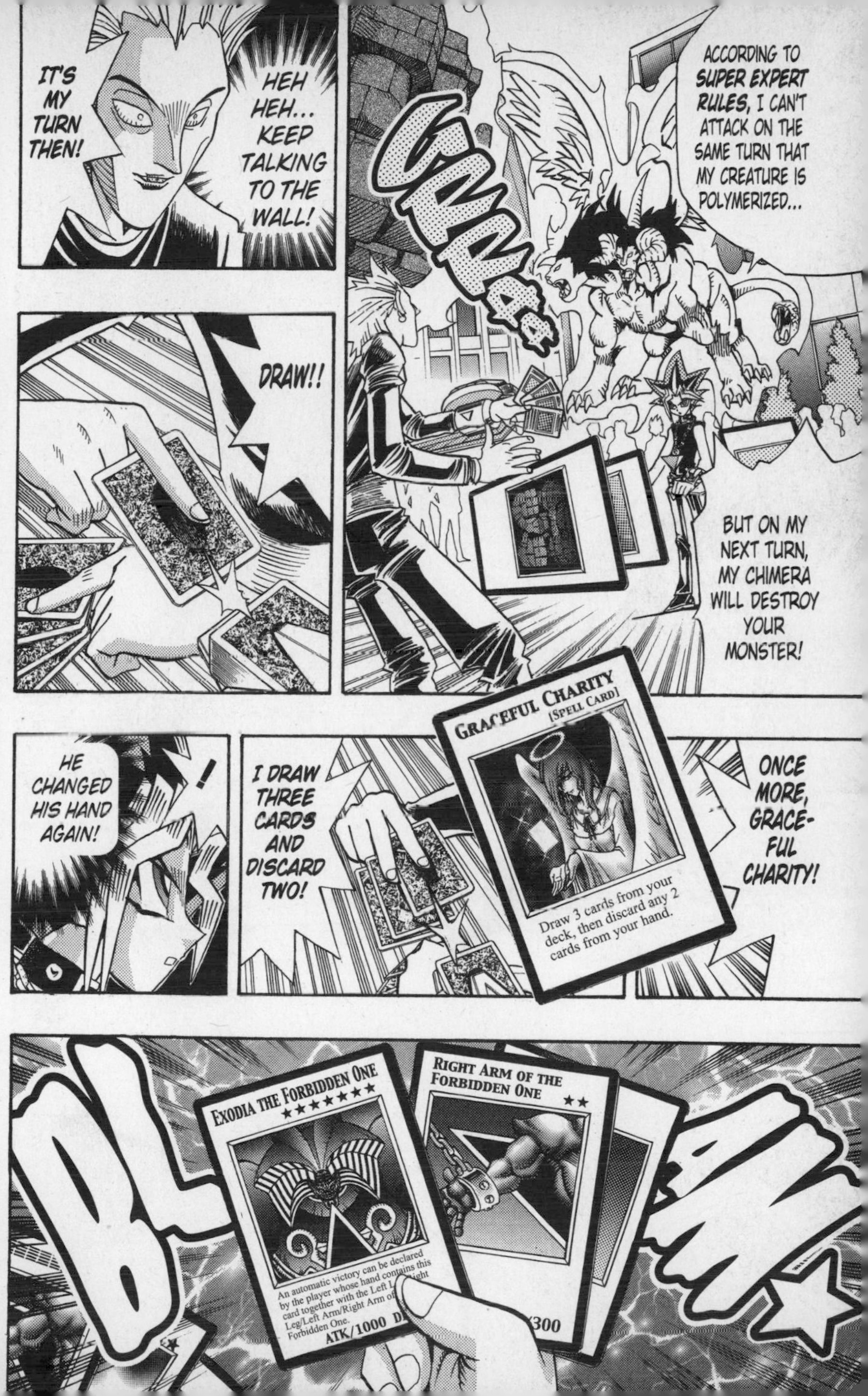
ACCORDING TO SUPER EXPERT RULES, I CAN'T ATTACK ON THE SAME TURN THAT MY CREATURE IS POLYMERIZED...
BUT ON MY NEXT TURN, MY CHIMERA WILL DESTROY YOUR MONSTER!
HEH HEH... KEEP TALKING TO THE WALL!
IT'S MY TURN THEN!
DRAW!!
ONCE MORE, GRACE-FUL CHARITY!
GRACEFUL CHARITY
[SPELL CARD]
Draw 3 cards from your deck, then discard any 2 cards from your hand.
I DRAW THREE CARDS AND DISCARD TWO!
HE CHANGED HIS HAND AGAIN!
!
EXODIA THE FORBIDDEN ONE
RIGHT ARM OF THE FORBIDDEN ONE
ATK/1000

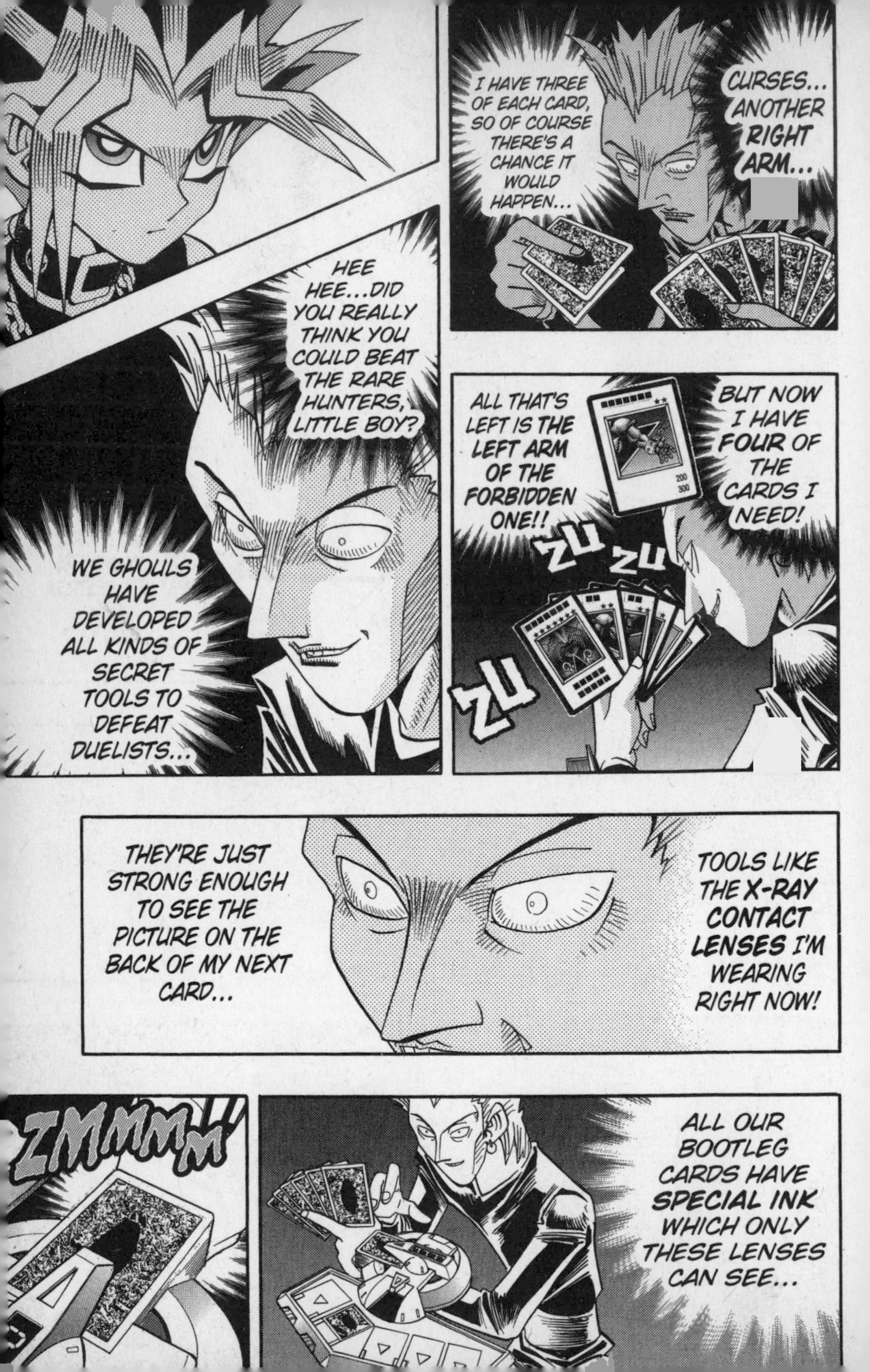
CURSES... ANOTHER RIGHT ARM...
I HAVE THREE OF EACH CARD, SO OF COURSE THERE'S A CHANCE IT WOULD HAPPEN...
BUT NOW I HAVE FOUR OF THE CARDS I NEED!
ALL THAT'S LEFT IS THE LEFT ARM OF THE FORBIDDEN ONE!!
ZU
ZU
ZU
HEE HEE...DID YOU REALLY THINK YOU COULD BEAT THE RARE HUNTERS, LITTLE BOY?
WE GHOULS HAVE DEVELOPED ALL KINDS OF SECRET TOOLS TO DEFEAT DUELISTS...
TOOLS LIKE THE X-RAY CONTACT LENSES I'M WEARING RIGHT NOW!
THEY'RE JUST STRONG ENOUGH TO SEE THE PICTURE ON THE BACK OF MY NEXT CARD...
ALL OUR BOOTLEG CARDS HAVE SPECIAL INK WHICH ONLY THESE LENSES CAN SEE...
ZMMMM

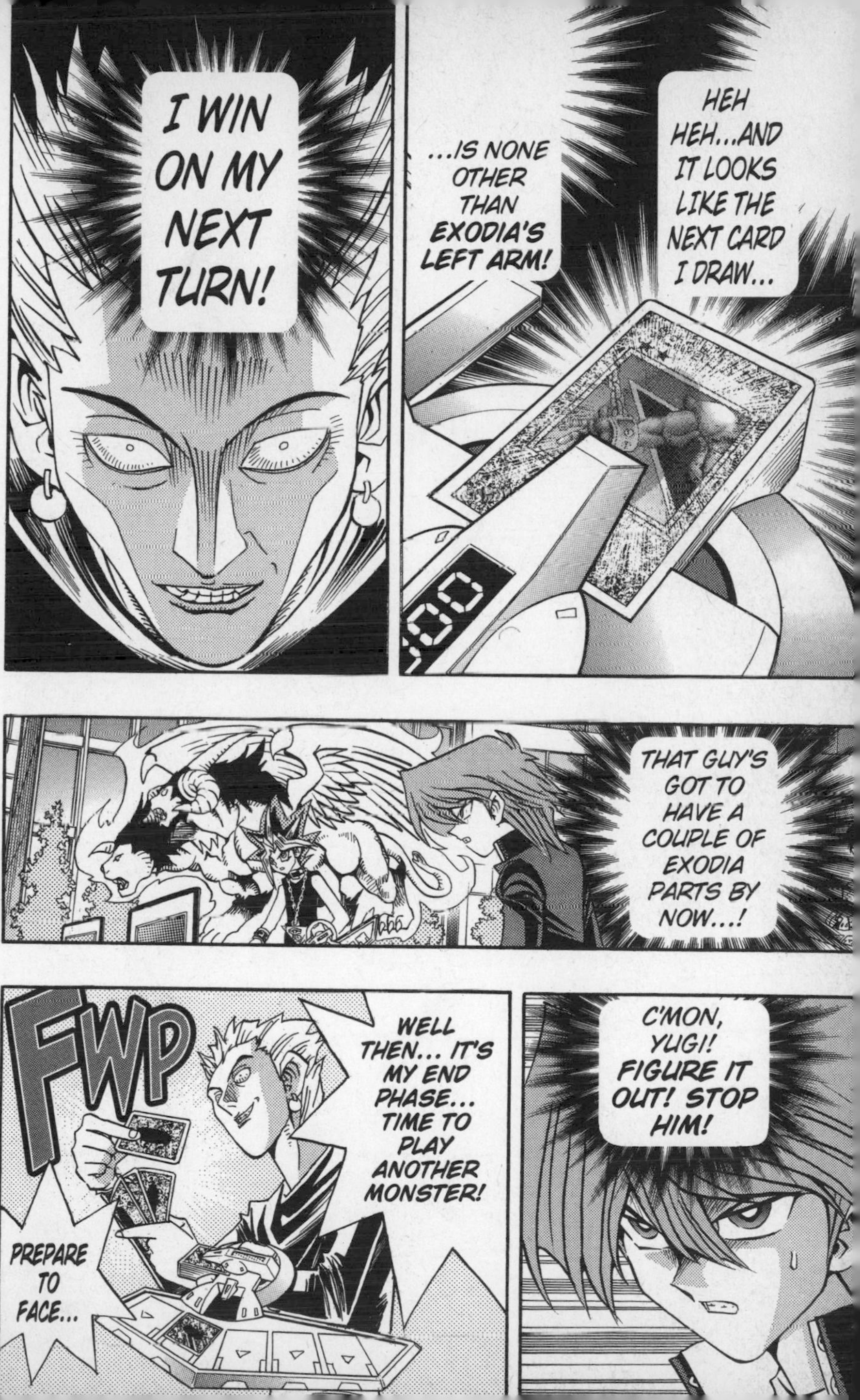
HEH HEH...AND IT LOOKS LIKE THE NEXT CARD I DRAW...
...IS NONE OTHER THAN EXODIA'S LEFT ARM!
I WIN ON MY NEXT TURN!
THAT GUY'S GOT TO HAVE A COUPLE OF EXODIA PARTS BY NOW...!
C'MON, YUGI! FIGURE IT OUT! STOP HIM!
FWP
WELL THEN... IT'S MY END PHASE... TIME TO PLAY ANOTHER MONSTER!
PREPARE TO FACE...

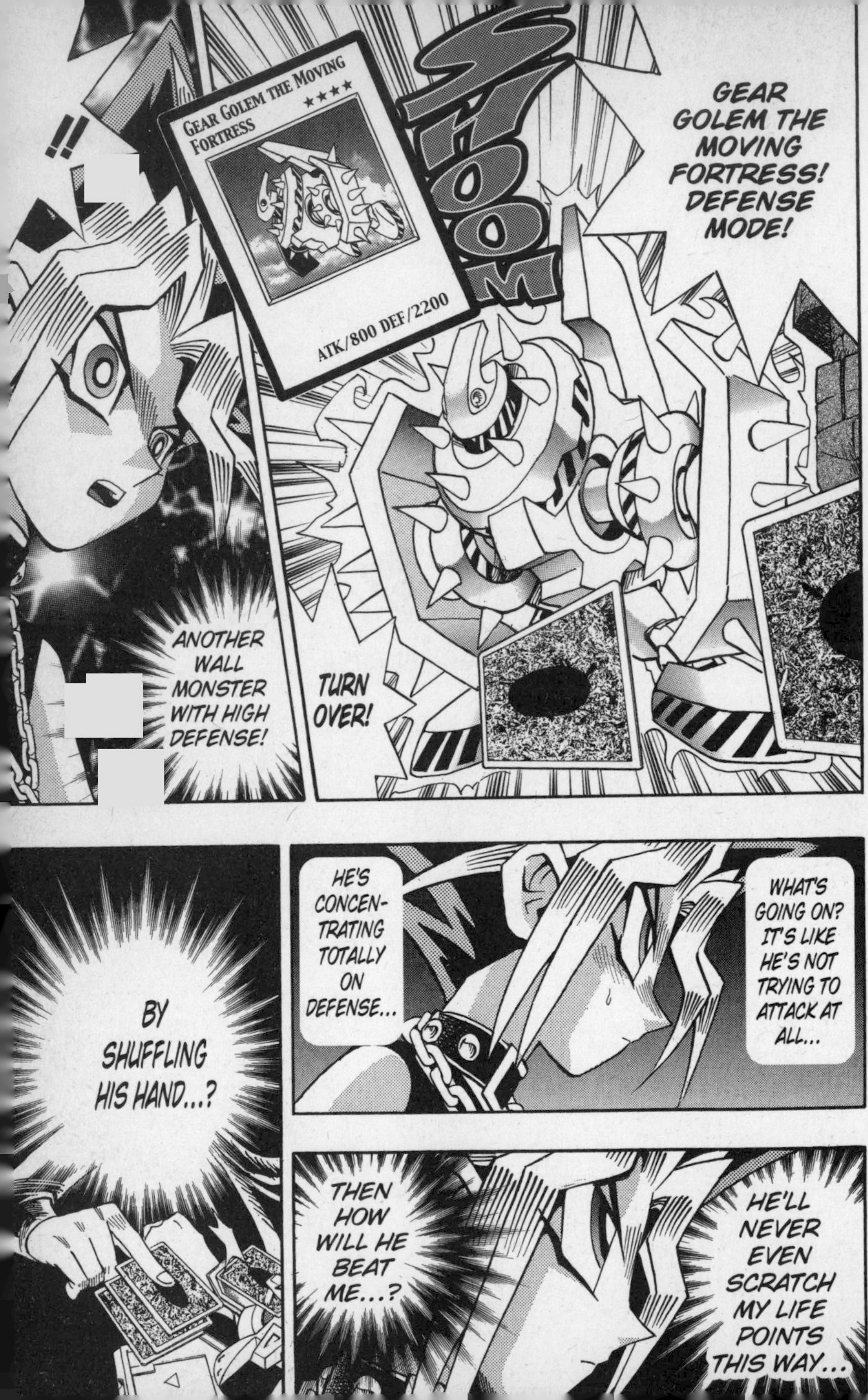
GEAR GOLEM THE MOVING FORTRESS! DEFENSE MODE!
SHOOM
GEAR GOLEM THE MOVING FORTRESS
ATK/800 DEF/2200
TURN OVER!
!!
ANOTHER WALL MONSTER WITH HIGH DEFENSE!
WHAT'S GOING ON? IT'S LIKE HE'S NOT TRYING TO ATTACK AT ALL...
HE'S CONCEN-TRATING TOTALLY ON DEFENSE...
HE'LL NEVER EVEN SCRATCH MY LIFE POINTS THIS WAY...
THEN HOW WILL HE BEAT ME...?
BY SHUFFLING HIS HAND...?

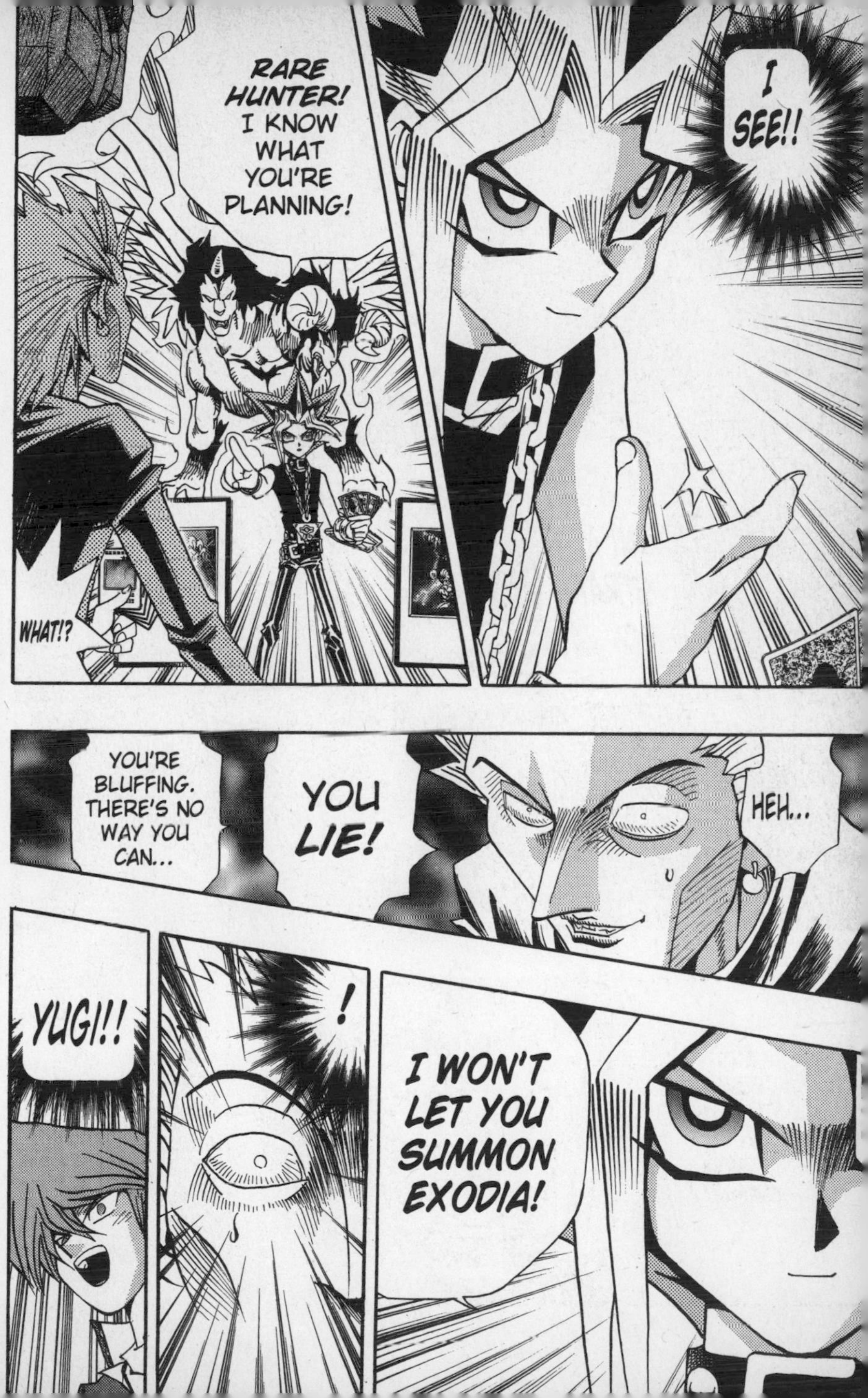
I SEE!!
RARE HUNTER! I KNOW WHAT YOU'RE PLANNING!
WHAT!?
HEH...
YOU LIE!
YOU'RE BLUFFING. THERE'S NO WAY YOU CAN...
I WON'T LET YOU SUMMON EXODIA!
!
YUGI!!

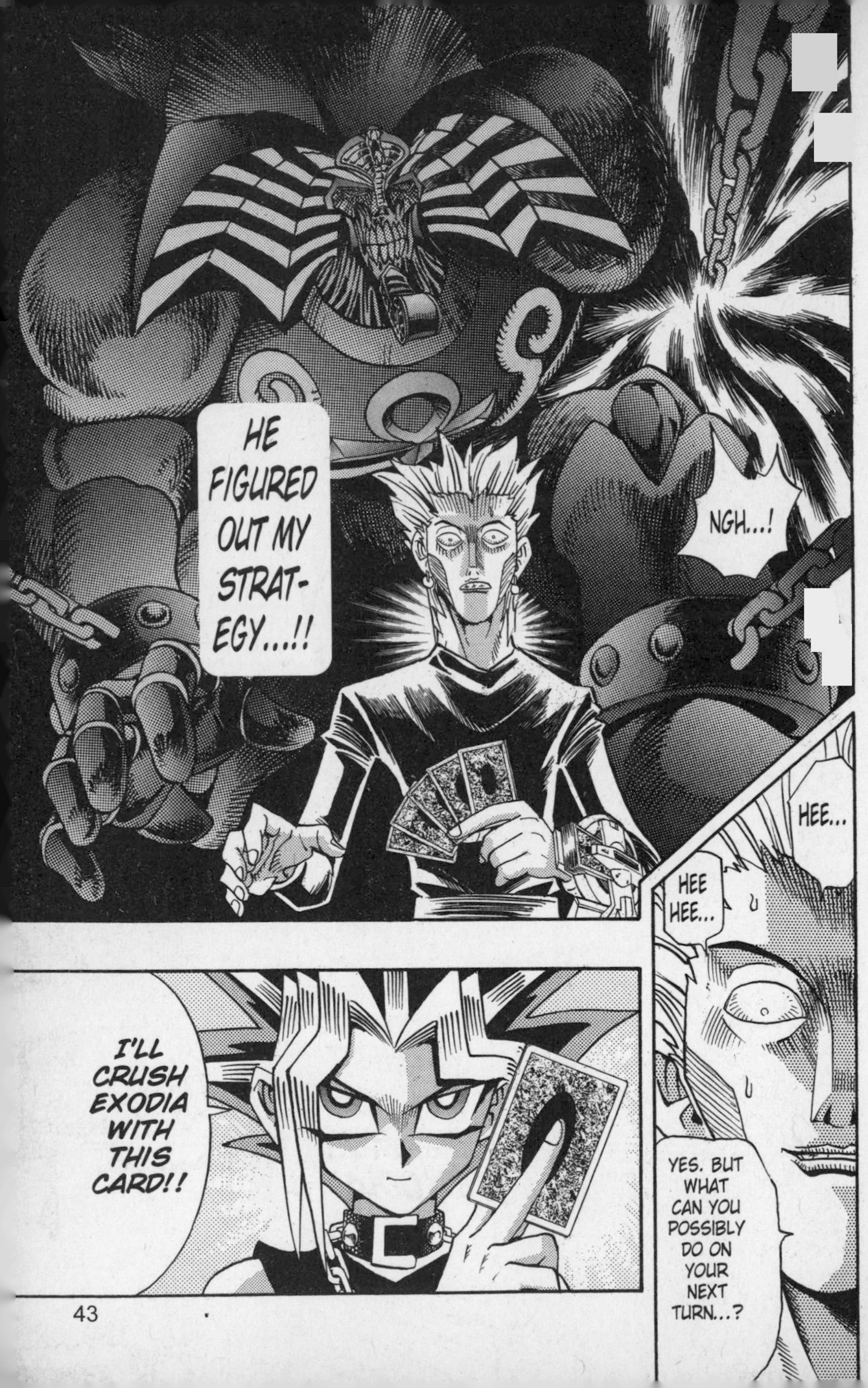
NGH...!
HE FIGURED OUT MY STRAT-EGY...!!
HEE...
HEE HEE...
YES. BUT WHAT CAN YOU POSSIBLY DO ON YOUR NEXT TURN...?
I'LL CRUSH EXODIA WITH THIS CARD!!

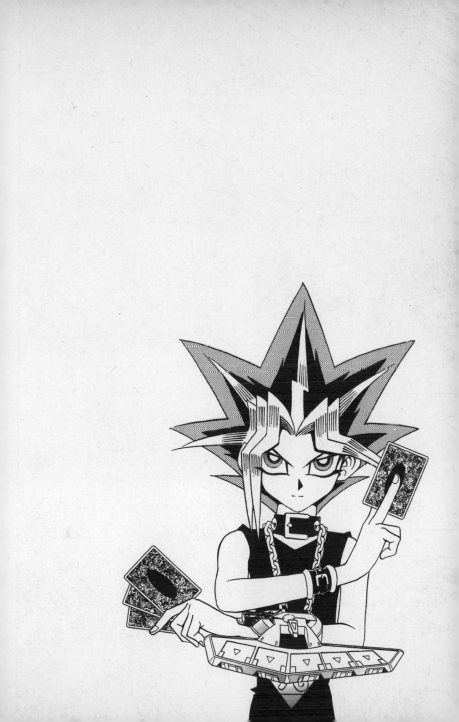

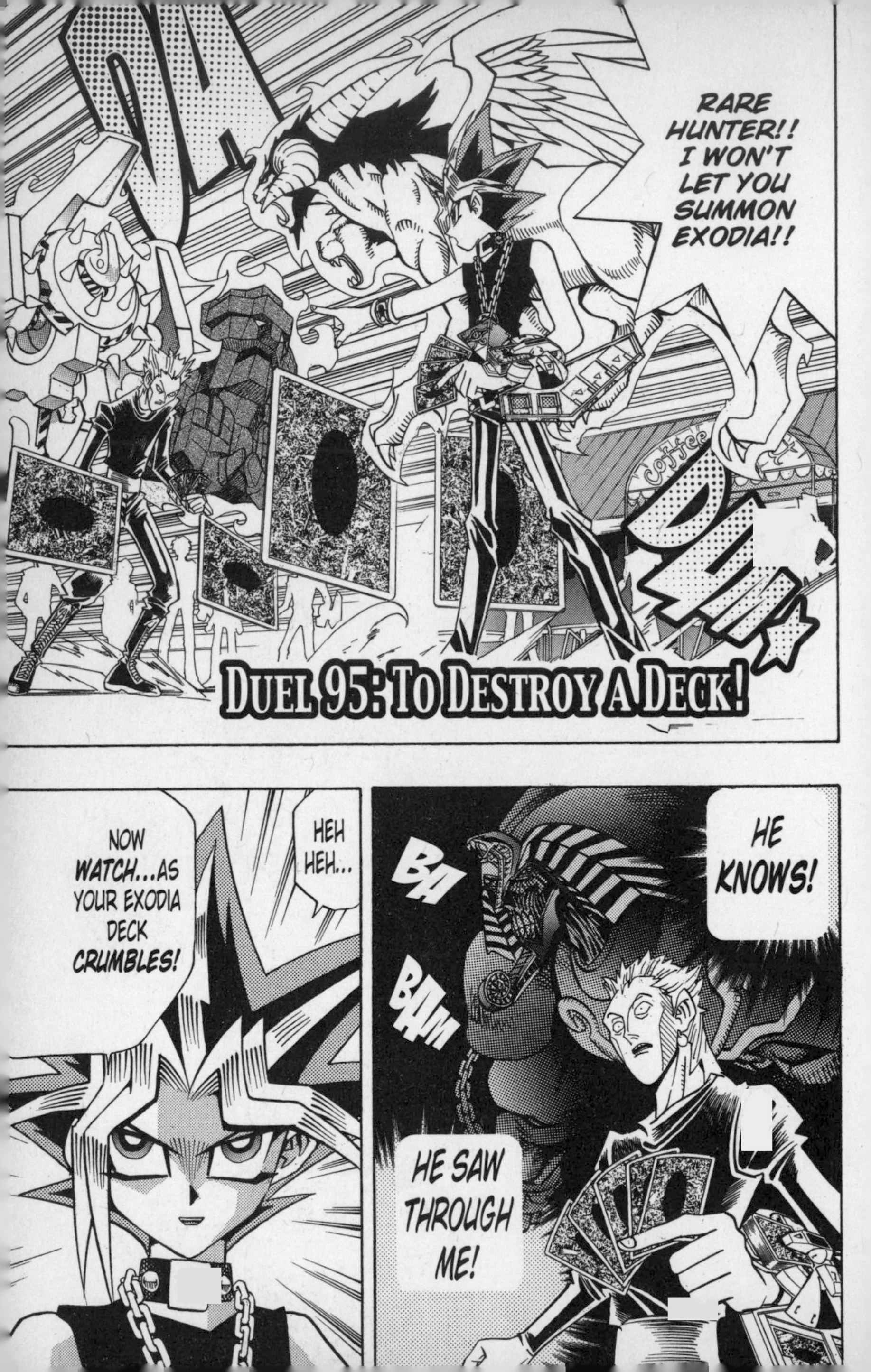
RARE HUNTER!! I WON'T LET YOU SUMMON EXODIA!!
DUEL 95: TO DESTROY A DECK!
HE KNOWS!
BA
BAM
HE SAW THROUGH ME!
HEH HEH...
NOW WATCH...AS YOUR EXODIA DECK CRUMBLES!

Duel 95: To Destroy a Deck!

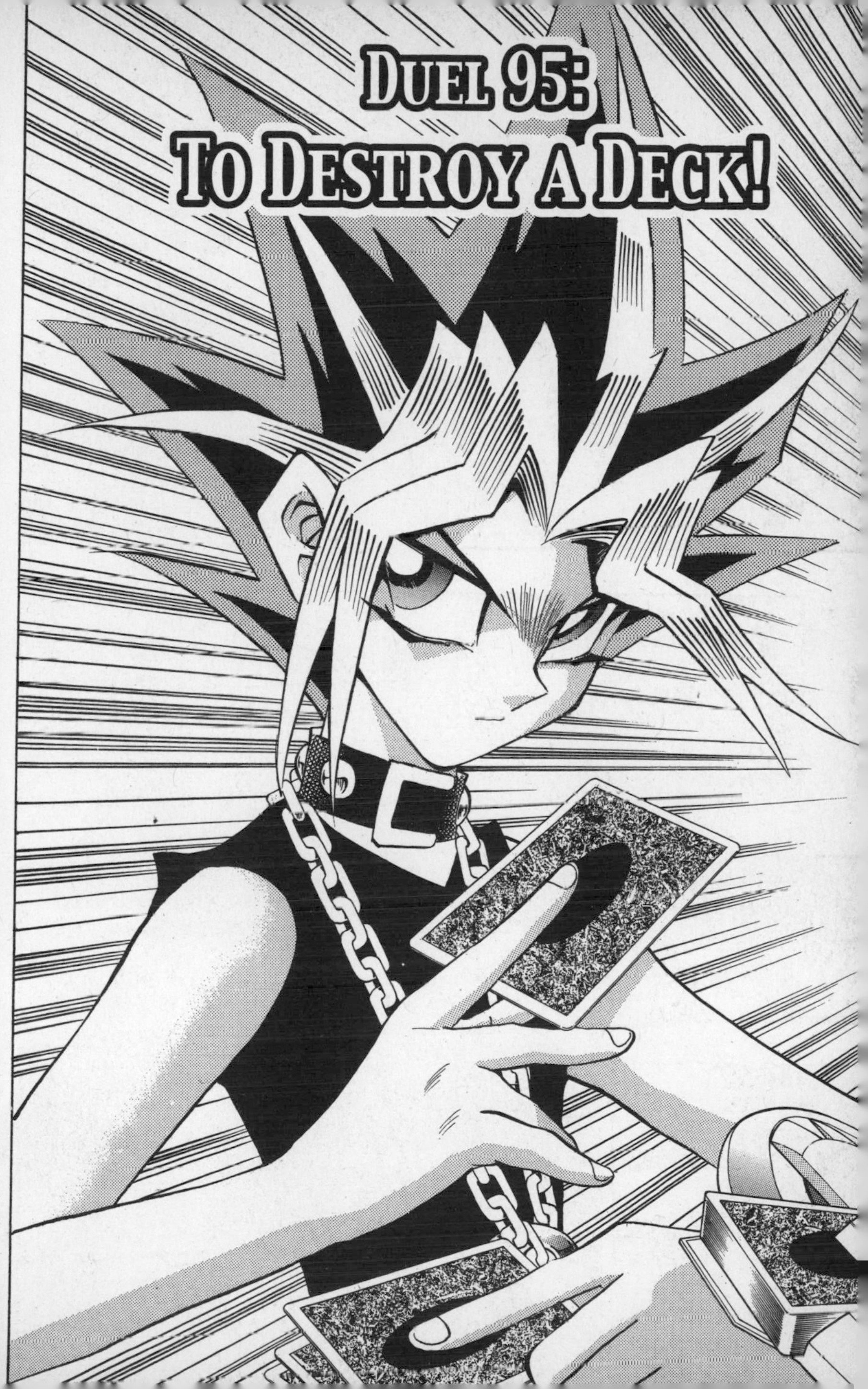

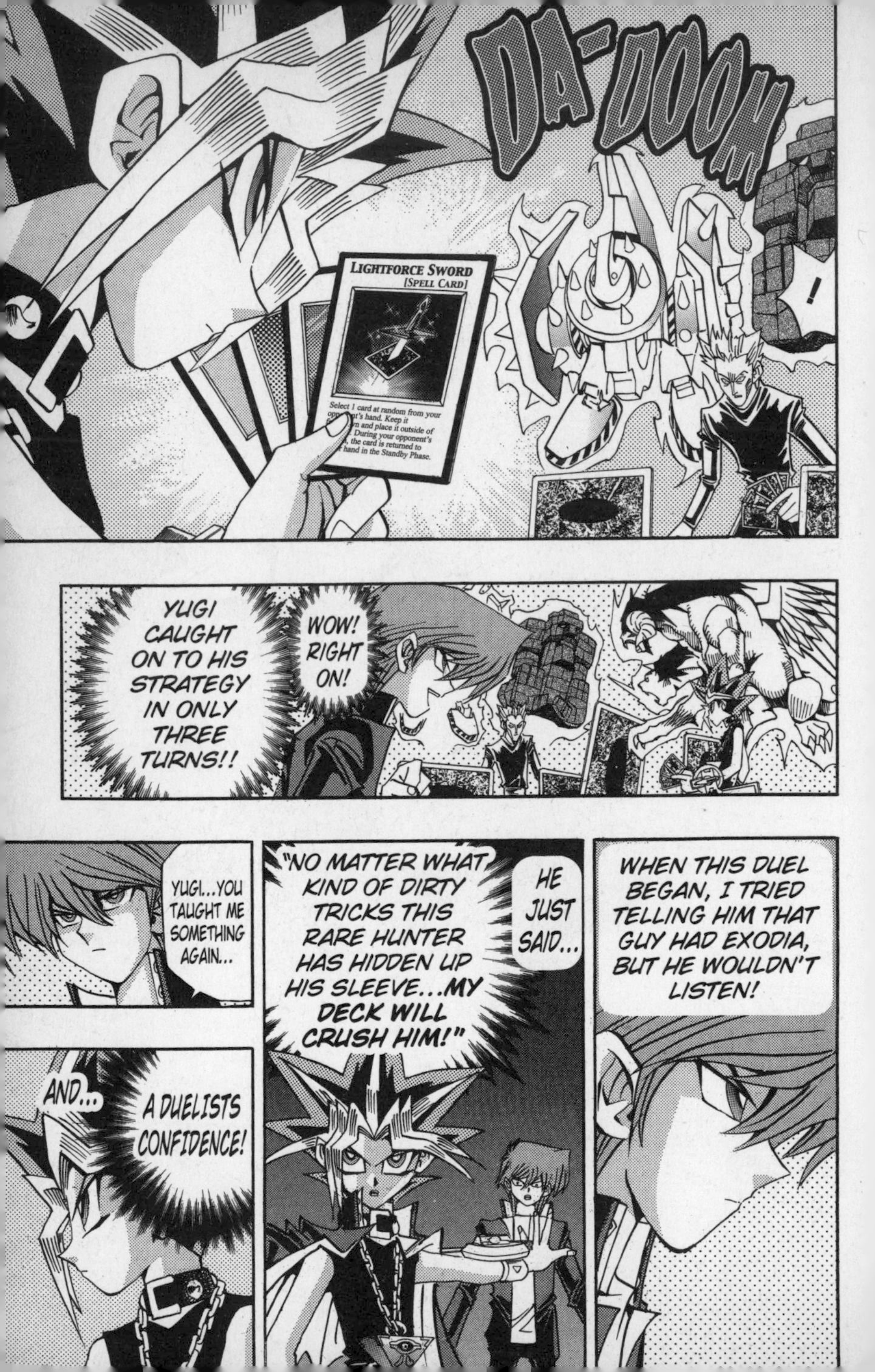
DA-DOOM
LIGHTFORCE SWORD
[SPELL CARD]
!
WOW! RIGHT ON!
YUGI CAUGHT ON TO HIS STRATEGY IN ONLY THREE TURNS!!
WHEN THIS DUEL BEGAN, I TRIED TELLING HIM THAT GUY HAD EXODIA, BUT HE WOULDN'T LISTEN!
HE JUST SAID...
"NO MATTER WHAT KIND OF DIRTY TRICKS THIS RARE HUNTER HAS HIDDEN UP HIS SLEEVE...MY DECK WILL CRUSH HIM!"
YUGI...YOU TAUGHT ME SOMETHING AGAIN...
AND...
A DUELISTS CONFIDENCE!

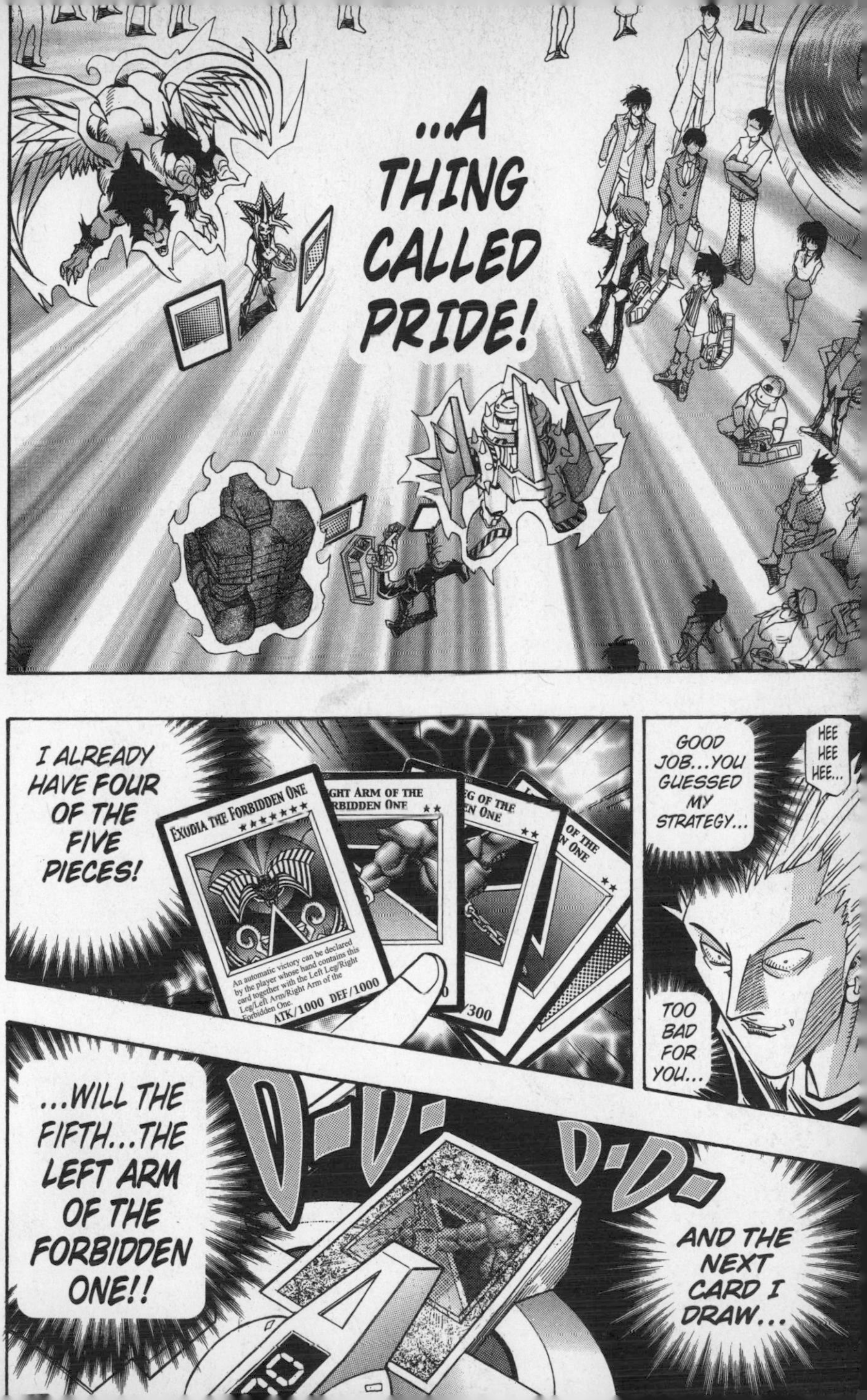
...A THING CALLED PRIDE!
HEE HEE HEE...
GOOD JOB...YOU GUESSED MY STRATEGY...
TOO BAD FOR YOU...
I ALREADY HAVE FOUR OF THE FIVE PIECES!
EXODIA THE FORBIDDEN ONE
An automatic victory can be declared by the player whose hand contains this card together with the Left Leg/Right Leg/Left Arm/Right Arm of the Forbidden One.
ATK/1000 DEF/1000
AND THE NEXT CARD I DRAW...
D-D- D-D-
...WILL THE FIFTH...THE LEFT ARM OF THE FORBIDDEN ONE!!

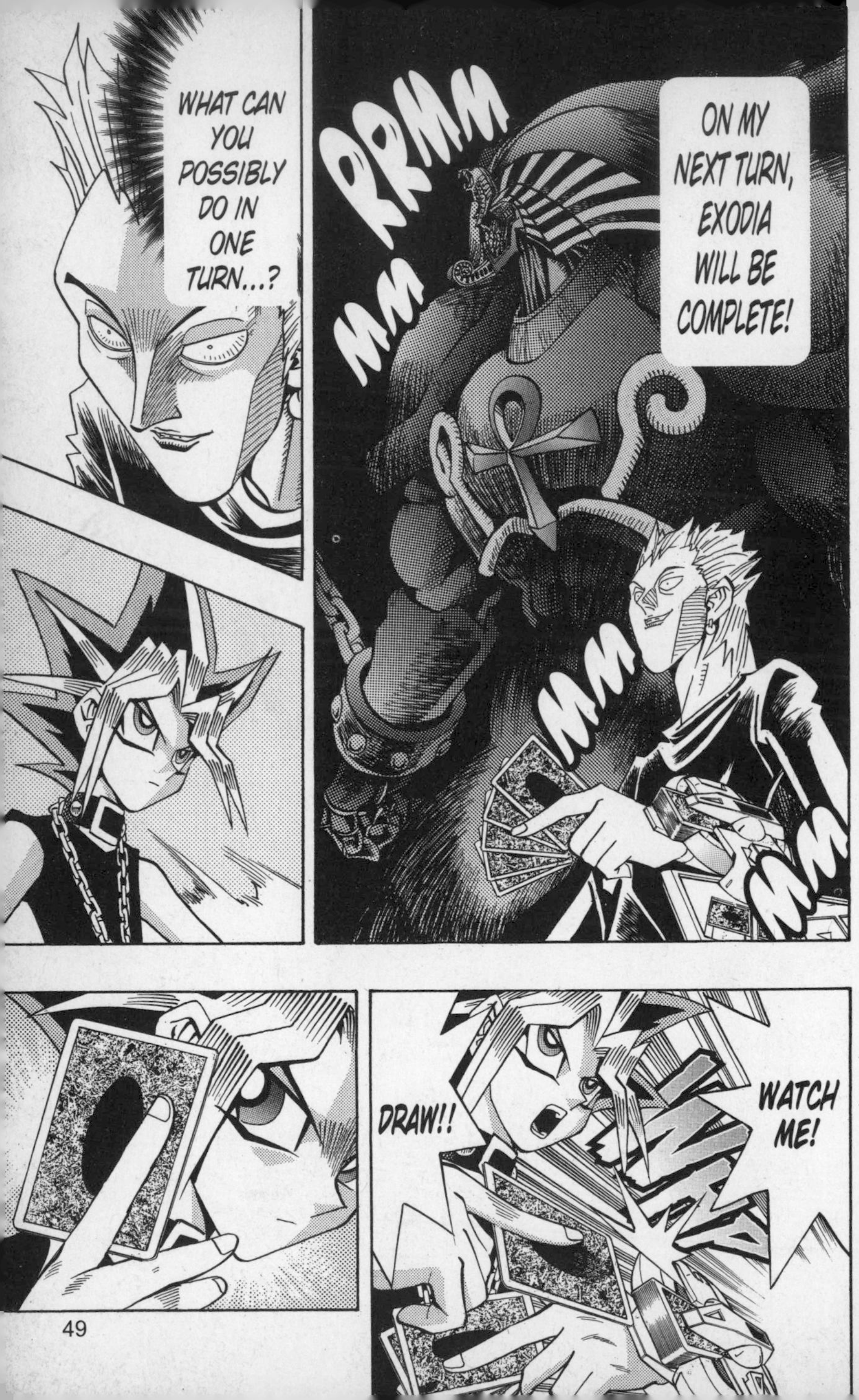

RRMM
MM
ON MY NEXT TURN, EXODIA WILL BE COMPLETE!
MM
MM
WHAT CAN YOU POSSIBLY DO IN ONE TURN...?
WATCH ME!
DRAW!!

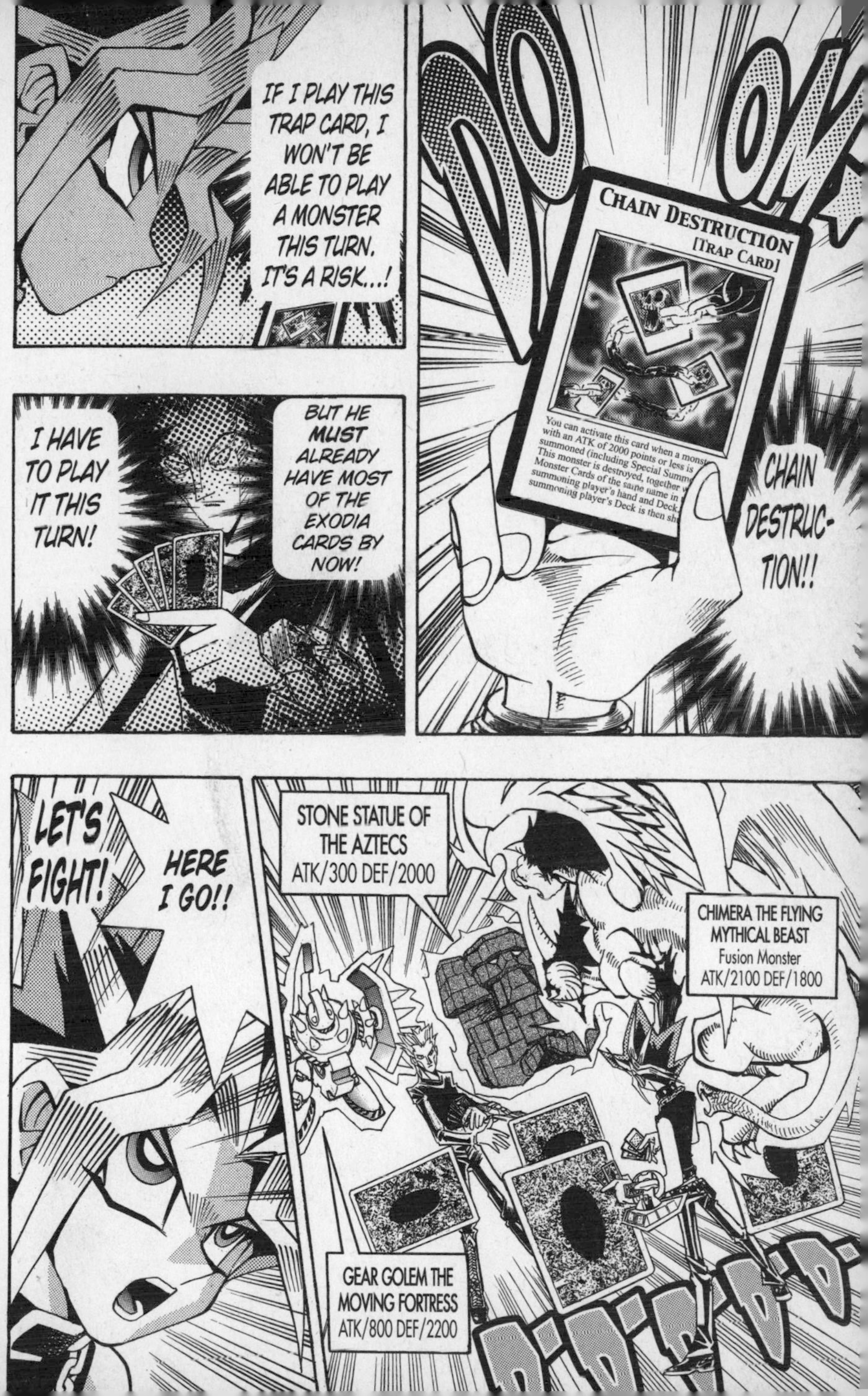
CHAIN DESTRUCTION
[TRAP CARD]
CHAIN DESTRUCTION!!
IF I PLAY THIS TRAP CARD, I WON'T BE ABLE TO PLAY A MONSTER THIS TURN. IT'S A RISK...!
BUT HE MUST ALREADY HAVE MOST OF THE EXODIA CARDS BY NOW!
I HAVE TO PLAY IT THIS TURN!
CHIMERA THE FLYING MYTHICAL BEAST
Fusion Monster
ATK/2100 DEF/1800
STONE STATUE OF THE AZTECS
ATK/300 DEF/2000
GEAR GOLEM THE MOVING FORTRESS
ATK/800 DEF/2200
HERE I GO!!
LET'S FIGHT!

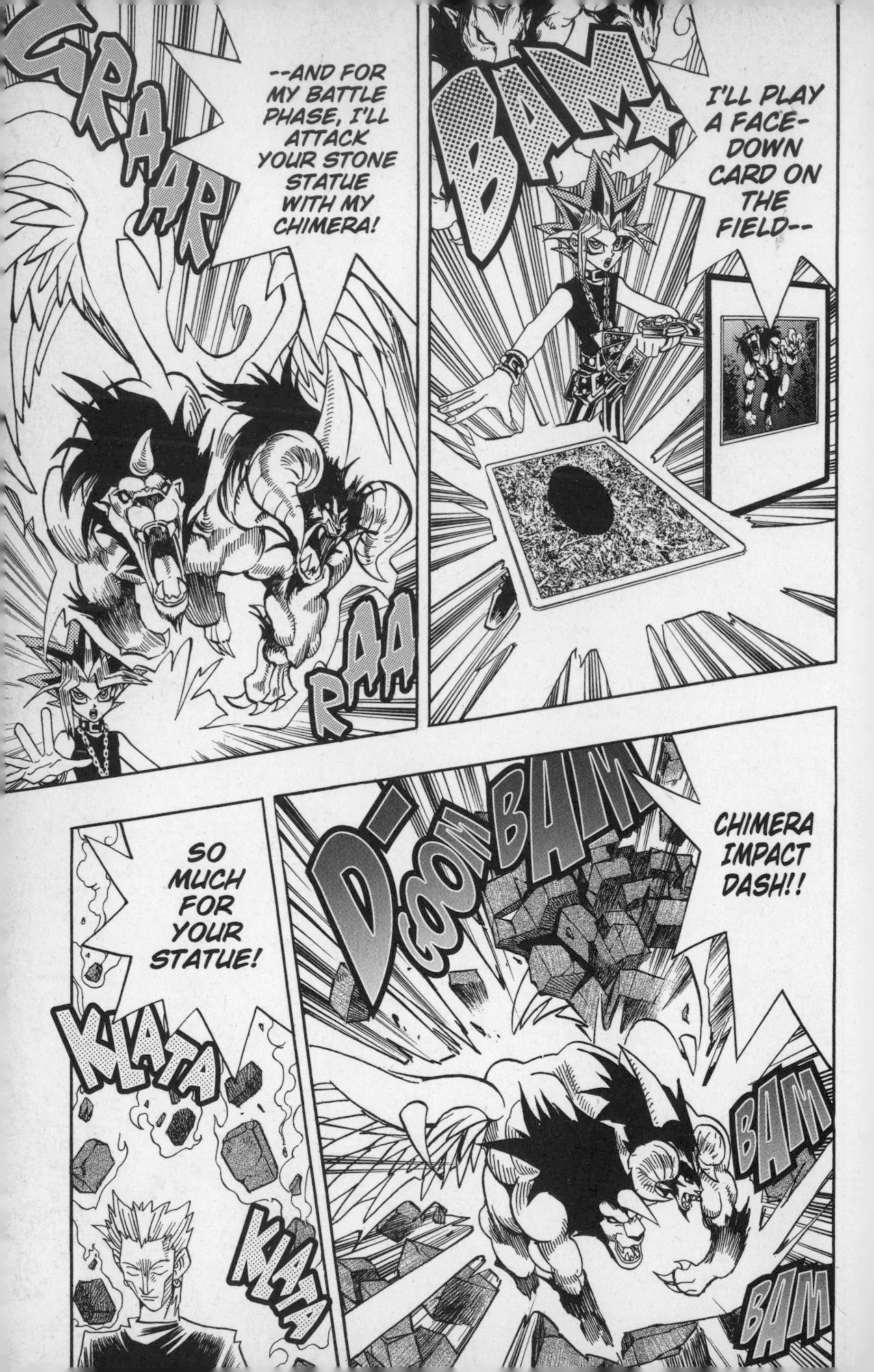
BAM
I'LL PLAY A FACE-DOWN CARD ON THE FIELD--
GRAAR
--AND FOR MY BATTLE PHASE, I'LL ATTACK YOUR STONE STATUE WITH MY CHIMERA!
RAAA
CHIMERA IMPACT DASH!!
D'GOOM BAM
BAM
BAM
SO MUCH FOR YOUR STATUE!
KLATA
KLATA

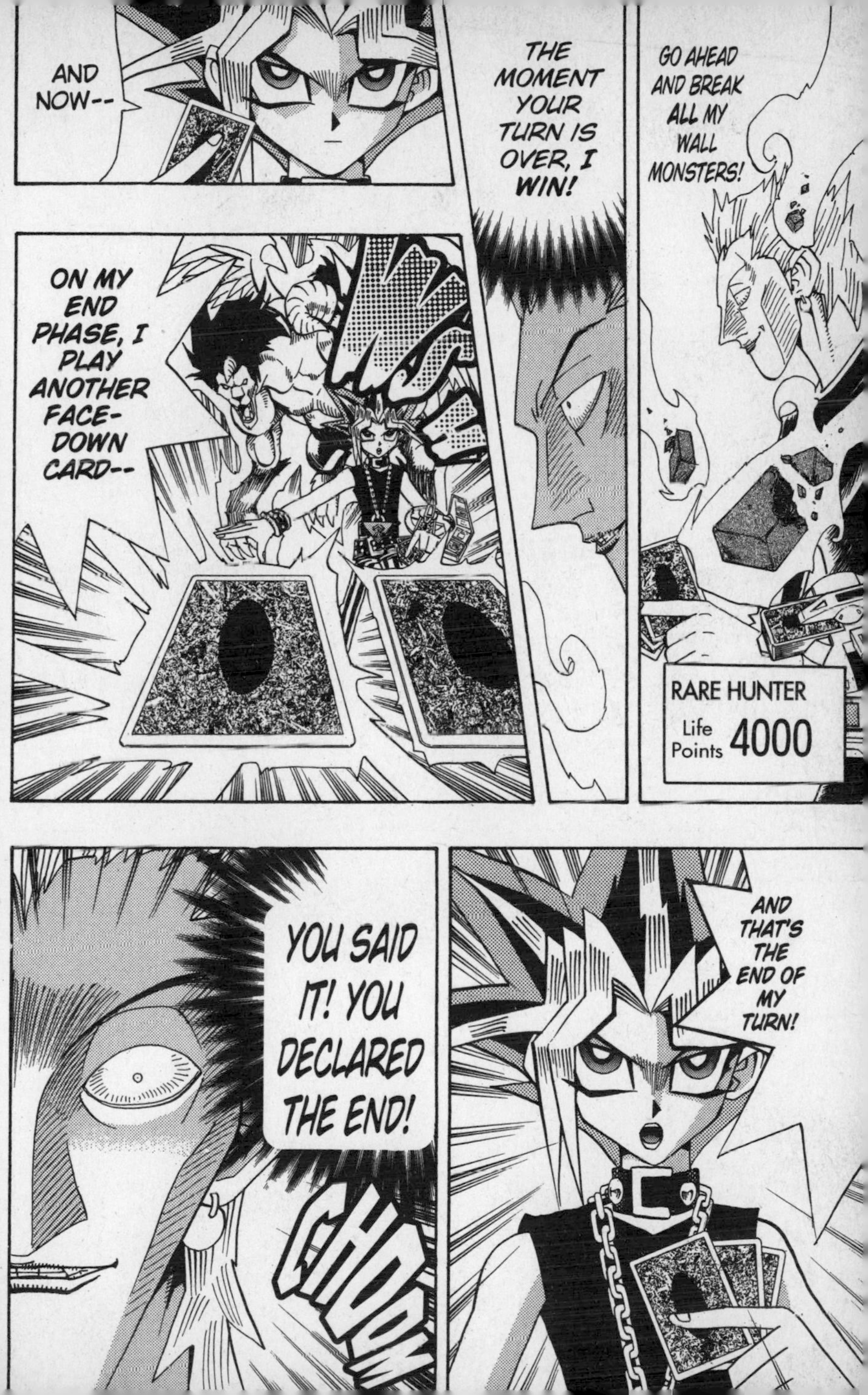
GO AHEAD AND BREAK ALL MY WALL MONSTERS!
RARE HUNTER Life Points 4000
THE MOMENT YOUR TURN IS OVER, I WIN!
AND NOW--
ON MY END PHASE, I PLAY ANOTHER FACE-DOWN CARD--
AND THAT'S THE END OF MY TURN!
YOU SAID IT! YOU DECLARED THE END!

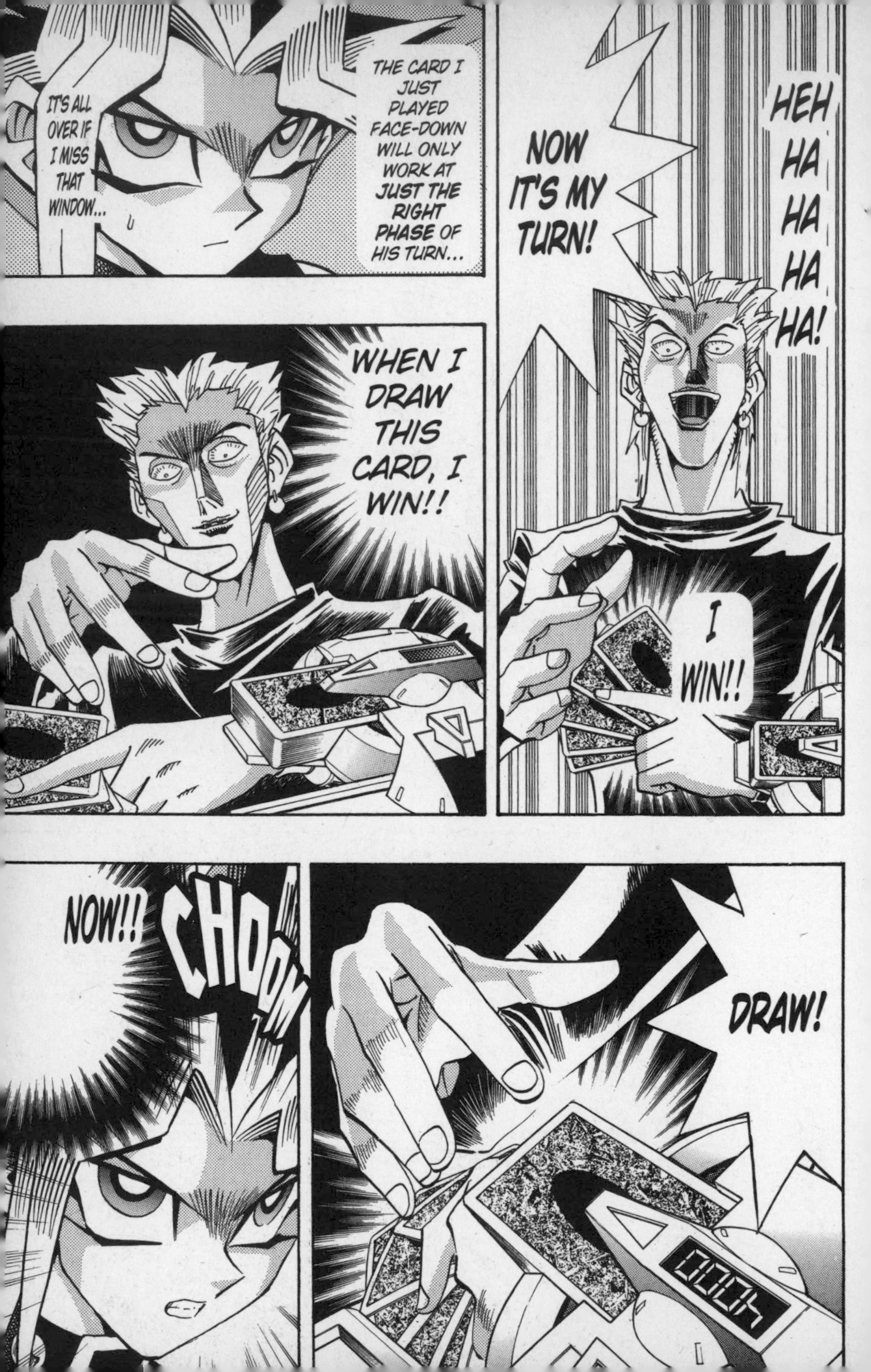
HEH HA HA HA HA!
NOW IT'S MY TURN!
I WIN!!
THE CARD I JUST PLAYED FACE-DOWN WILL ONLY WORK AT JUST THE RIGHT PHASE OF HIS TURN...
IT'S ALL OVER IF I MISS THAT WINDOW...
WHEN I DRAW THIS CARD, I WIN!!
DRAW!
CHOOM
NOW!!

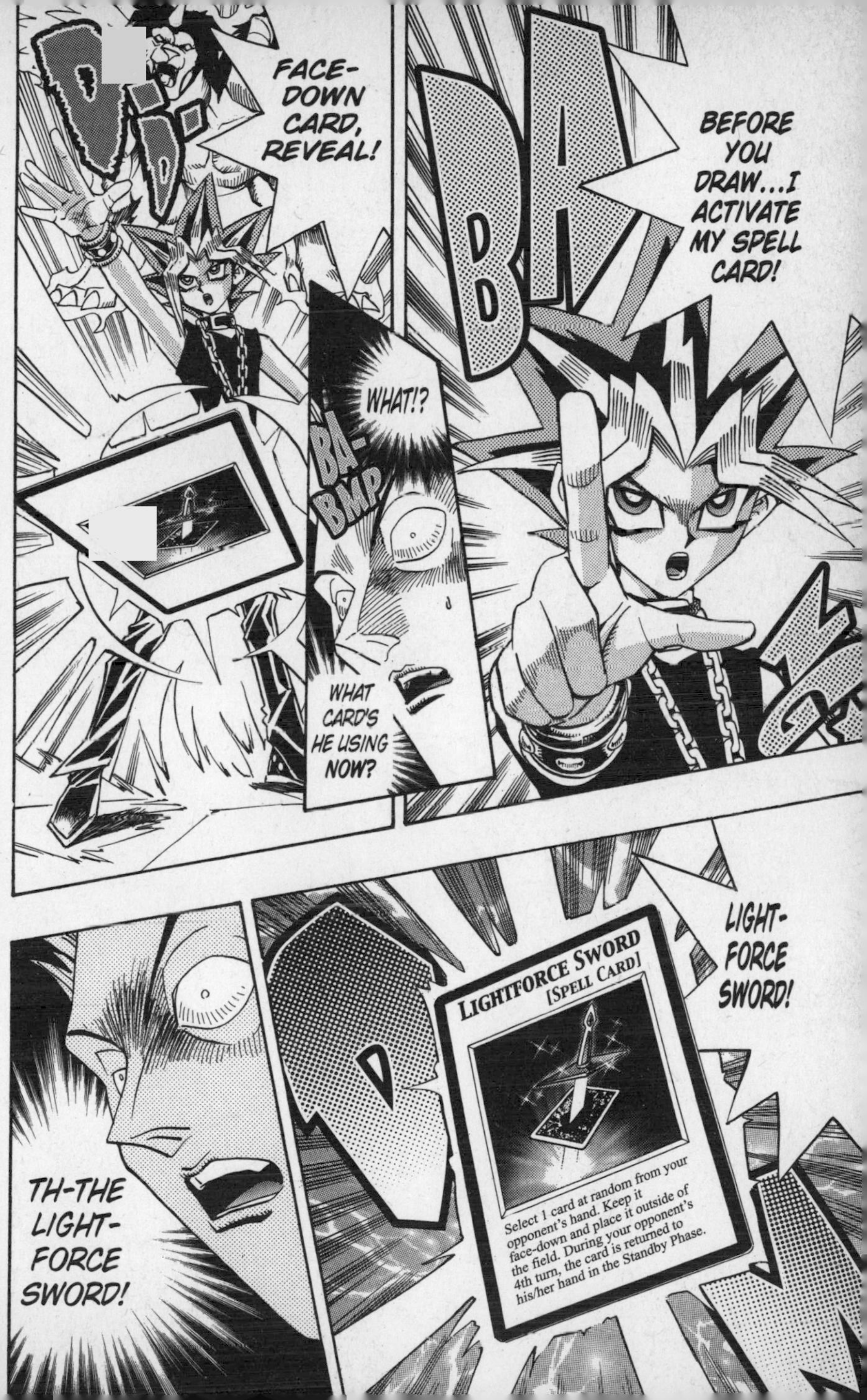
BEFORE YOU DRAW...I ACTIVATE MY SPELL CARD!
BA
WHAT!?
BA-BMP
WHAT CARD'S HE USING NOW?
FACE-DOWN CARD, REVEAL!
LIGHT-FORCE SWORD!
LIGHTFORCE SWORD
[SPELL CARD]
Select 1 card at random from your opponent's hand. Keep it face-down and place it outside of the field. During your opponent's 4th turn, the card is returned to his/her hand in the Standby Phase.
TH-THE LIGHT-FORCE SWORD!

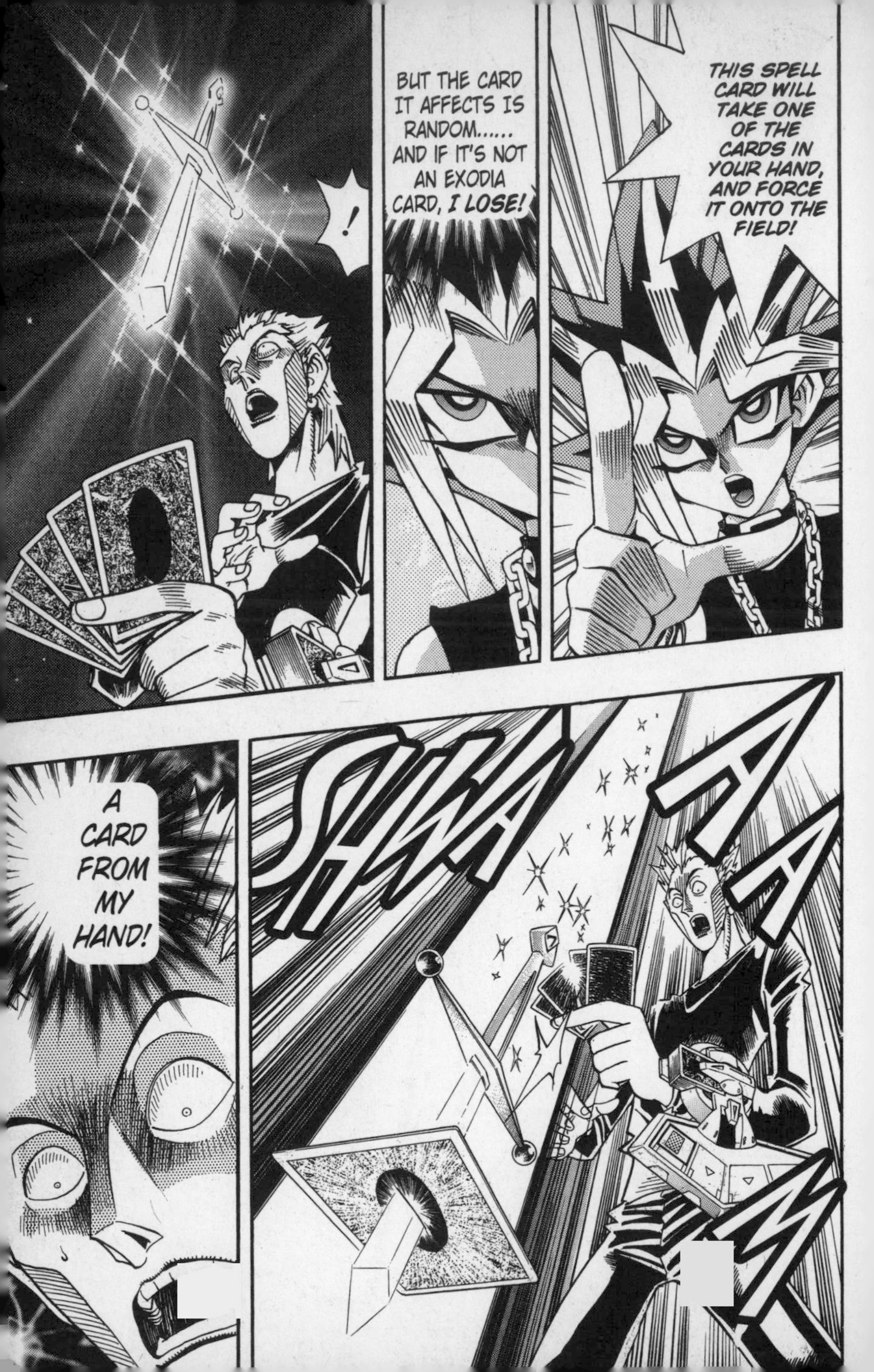
THIS SPELL CARD WILL TAKE ONE OF THE CARDS IN YOUR HAND, AND FORCE IT ONTO THE FIELD!
BUT THE CARD IT AFFECTS IS RANDOM...... AND IF IT'S NOT AN EXODIA CARD, I LOSE!
!
SHWAAA
A CARD FROM MY HAND!

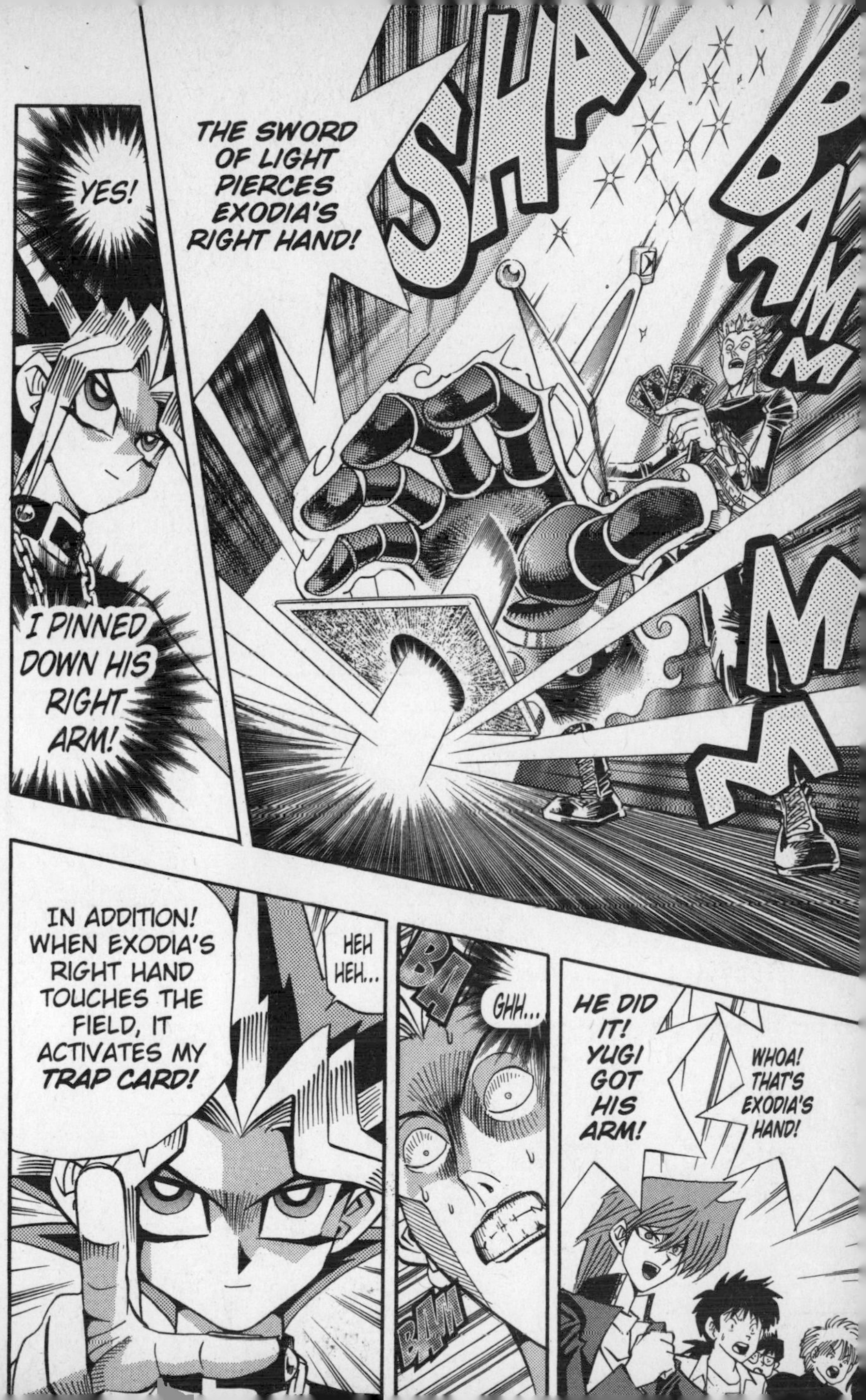
SHP
BAMMMM
THE SWORD OF LIGHT PIERCES EXODIA'S RIGHT HAND!
YES!
I PINNED DOWN HIS RIGHT ARM!
WHOA! THAT'S EXODIA'S HAND!
HE DID IT! YUGI GOT HIS ARM!
BA
GHH...
BAM
IN ADDITION! WHEN EXODIA'S RIGHT HAND TOUCHES THE FIELD, IT ACTIVATES MY *TRAP CARD!*
HEH HEH...

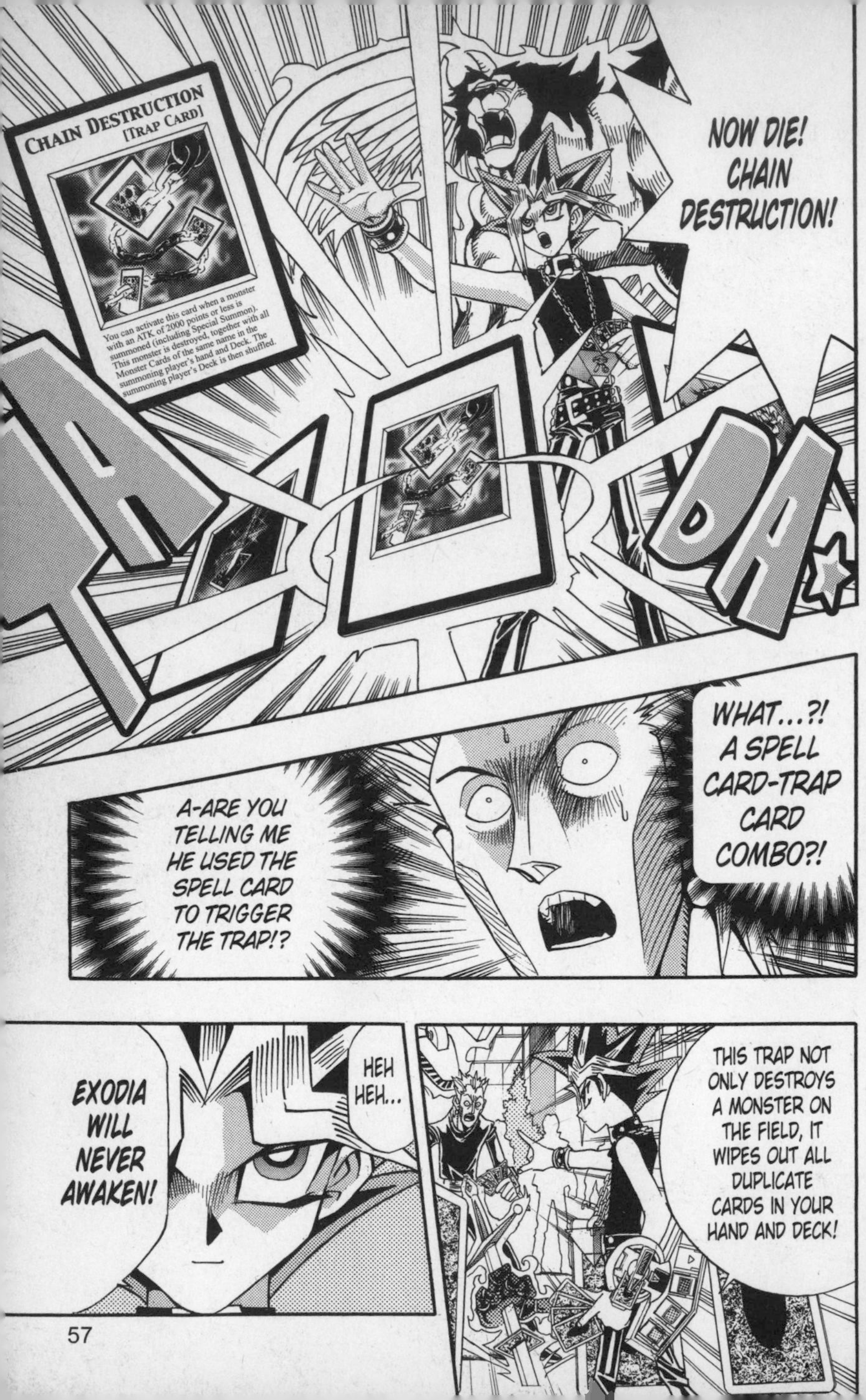
NOW DIE! CHAIN DESTRUCTION!
CHAIN DESTRUCTION [TRAP CARD]
You can activate this card when a monster with an ATK of 2000 points or less is summoned (including Special Summon). This monster is destroyed, together with all Monster Cards of the same name in the summoning player's hand and Deck. The summoning player's Deck is then shuffled.
TA DA
WHAT...?! A SPELL CARD-TRAP CARD COMBO?!
A-ARE YOU TELLING ME HE USED THE SPELL CARD TO TRIGGER THE TRAP!?
THIS TRAP NOT ONLY DESTROYS A MONSTER ON THE FIELD, IT WIPES OUT ALL DUPLICATE CARDS IN YOUR HAND AND DECK!
HEH HEH...
EXODIA WILL NEVER AWAKEN!

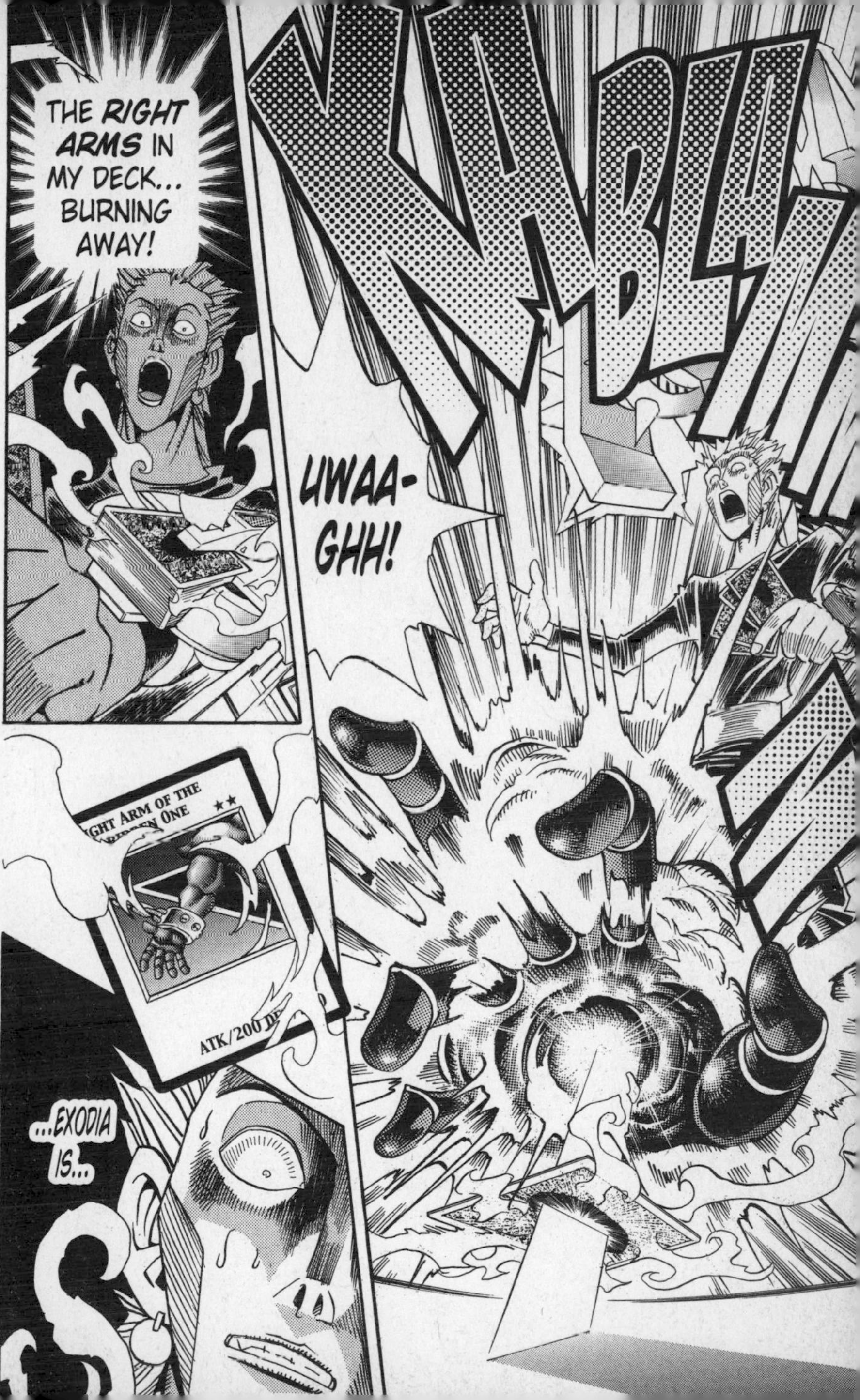
WHABLAM
UWAA-GHH!
THE RIGHT ARMS IN MY DECK... BURNING AWAY!
...EXODIA IS...

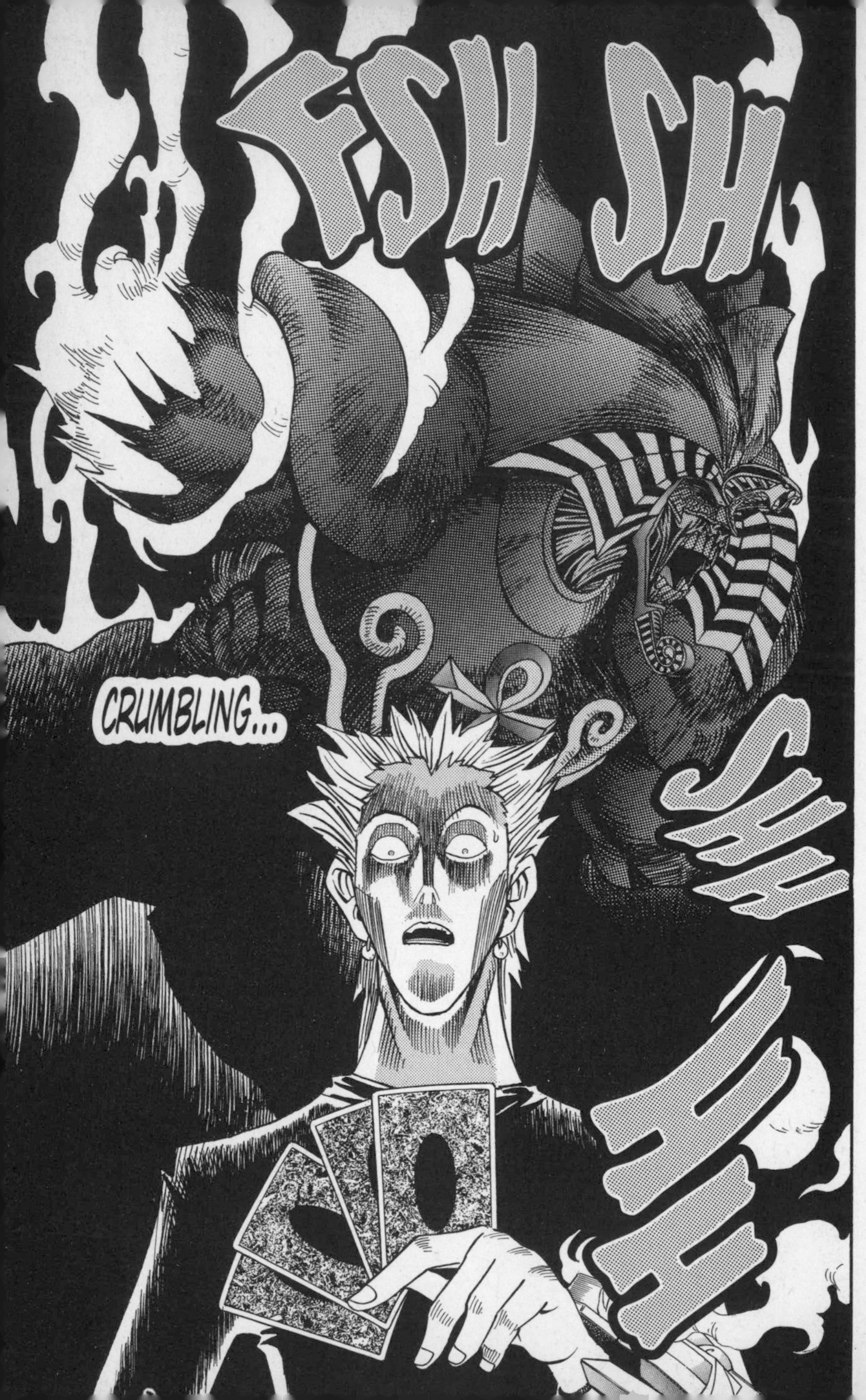
FSH SH
SHH
CRUMBLING...

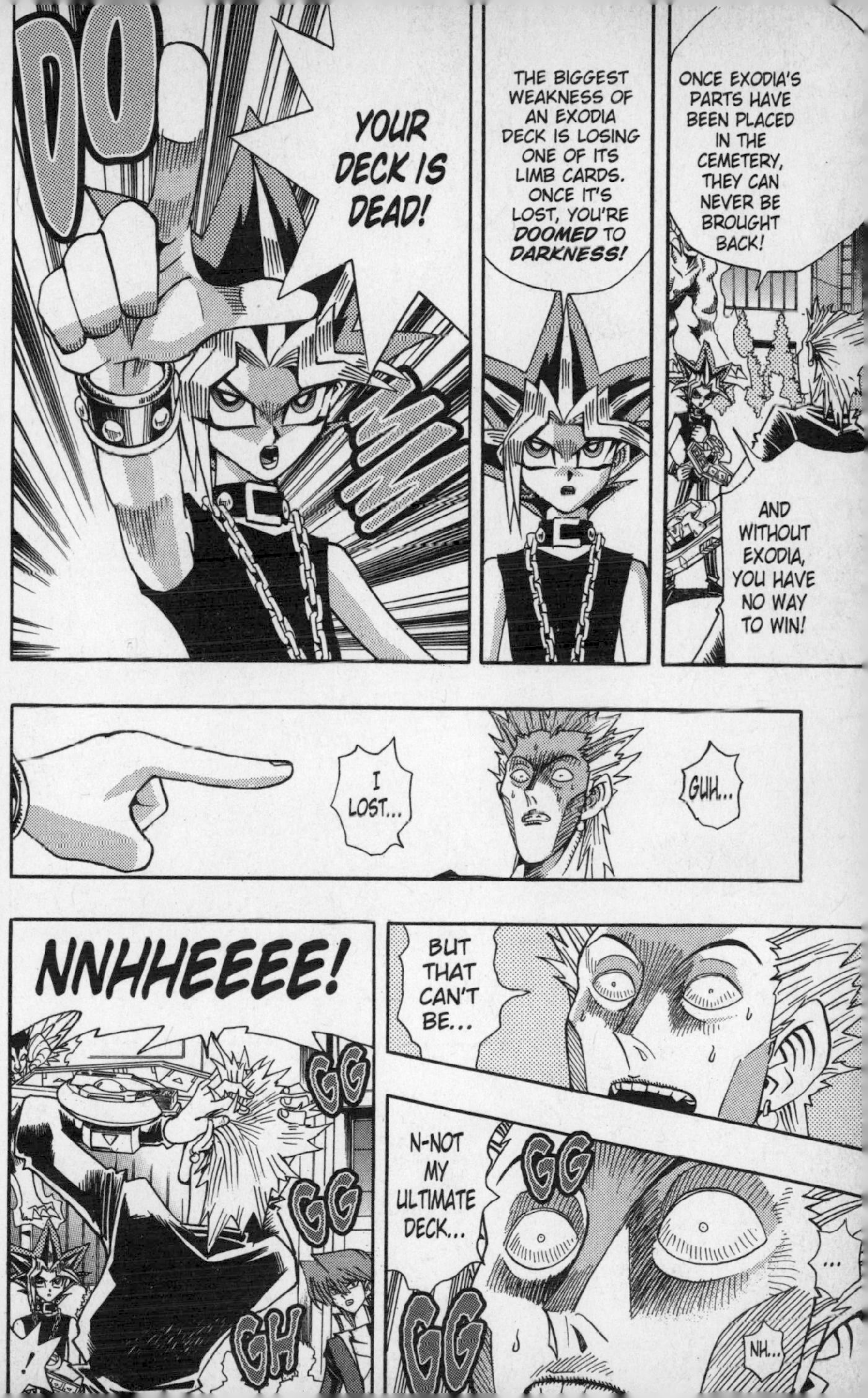
ONCE EXODIA'S PARTS HAVE BEEN PLACED IN THE CEMETERY, THEY CAN NEVER BE BROUGHT BACK!
AND WITHOUT EXODIA, YOU HAVE NO WAY TO WIN!
THE BIGGEST WEAKNESS OF AN EXODIA DECK IS LOSING ONE OF ITS LIMB CARDS. ONCE IT'S LOST, YOU'RE *DOOMED* TO *DARKNESS!*
YOUR DECK IS DEAD!
GUH...
I LOST...
BUT THAT CAN'T BE...
...
NH...
N-NOT MY ULTIMATE DECK...
GG
GG
NNHEEEEE!
GG
GG
GH

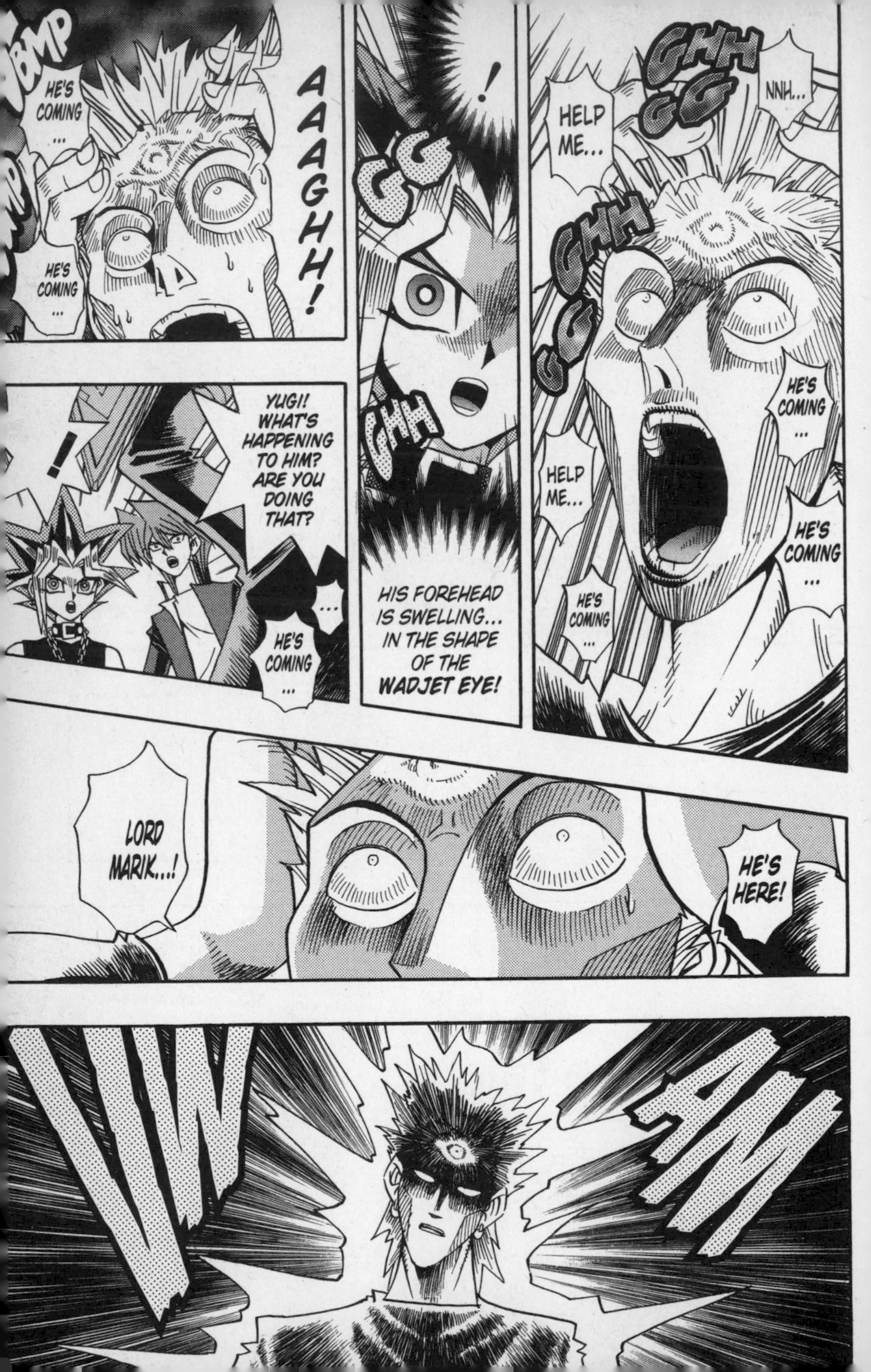
GHH
GG
NNH...
HELP ME...
GHH
GG
HE'S COMING ...
HELP ME...
HE'S COMING ...
HE'S COMING ...
!
GG
GHH
HIS FOREHEAD IS SWELLING... IN THE SHAPE OF THE WADJET EYE!
HE'S COMING ...
HE'S COMING ...
AAAAGHH!
YUGI! WHAT'S HAPPENING TO HIM? ARE YOU DOING THAT?
!
...
HE'S COMING ...
HE'S HERE!
LORD MARIK...!

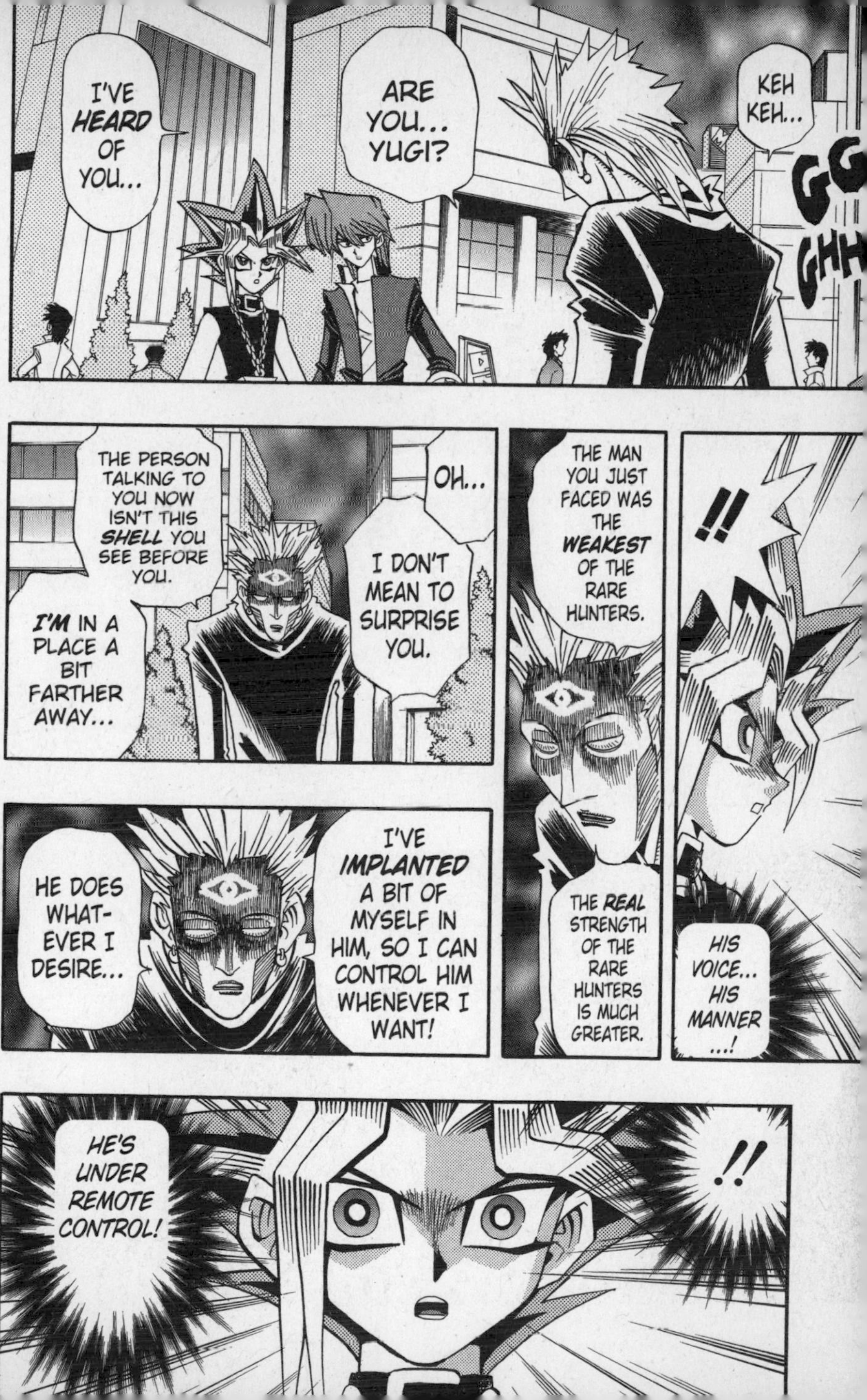
KEH KEH...
GG GHH
ARE YOU... YUGI?
I'VE HEARD OF YOU...
!!
HIS VOICE... HIS MANNER ...!
THE MAN YOU JUST FACED WAS THE WEAKEST OF THE RARE HUNTERS.
THE REAL STRENGTH OF THE RARE HUNTERS IS MUCH GREATER.
OH...
I DON'T MEAN TO SURPRISE YOU.
THE PERSON TALKING TO YOU NOW ISN'T THIS SHELL YOU SEE BEFORE YOU.
I'M IN A PLACE A BIT FARTHER AWAY...
I'VE IMPLANTED A BIT OF MYSELF IN HIM, SO I CAN CONTROL HIM WHENEVER I WANT!
HE DOES WHATEVER I DESIRE...
!!
HE'S UNDER REMOTE CONTROL!

READ THIS WAY

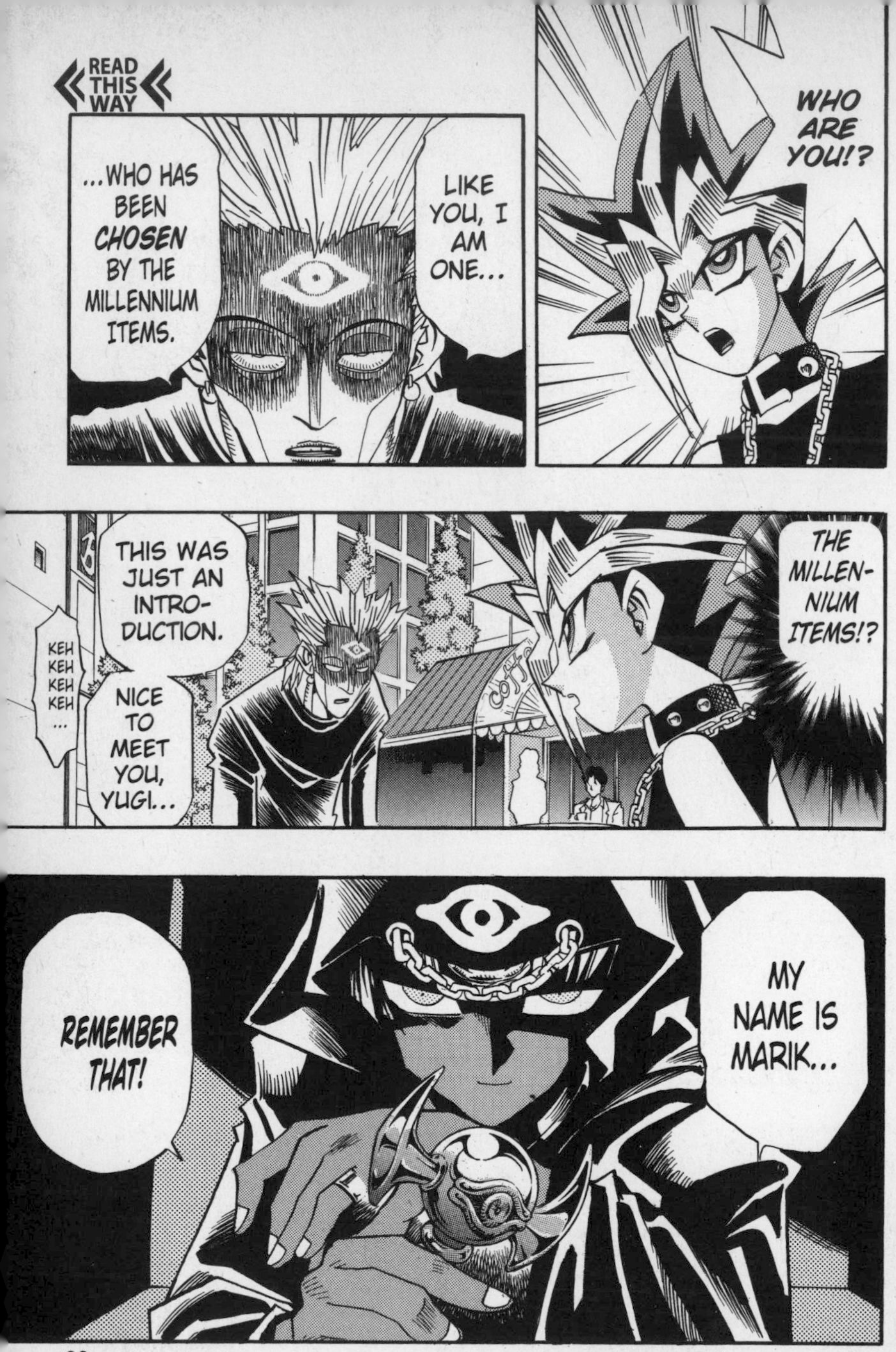
WHO ARE YOU!?
LIKE YOU, I AM ONE...
...WHO HAS BEEN CHOSEN BY THE MILLENNIUM ITEMS.
THE MILLEN-NIUM ITEMS!?
THIS WAS JUST AN INTRO-DUCTION.
NICE TO MEET YOU, YUGI...
KEH KEH KEH KEH ...
MY NAME IS MARIK...
REMEMBER THAT!

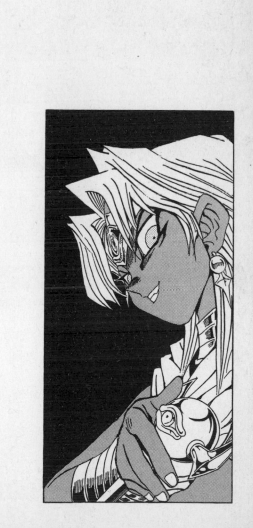

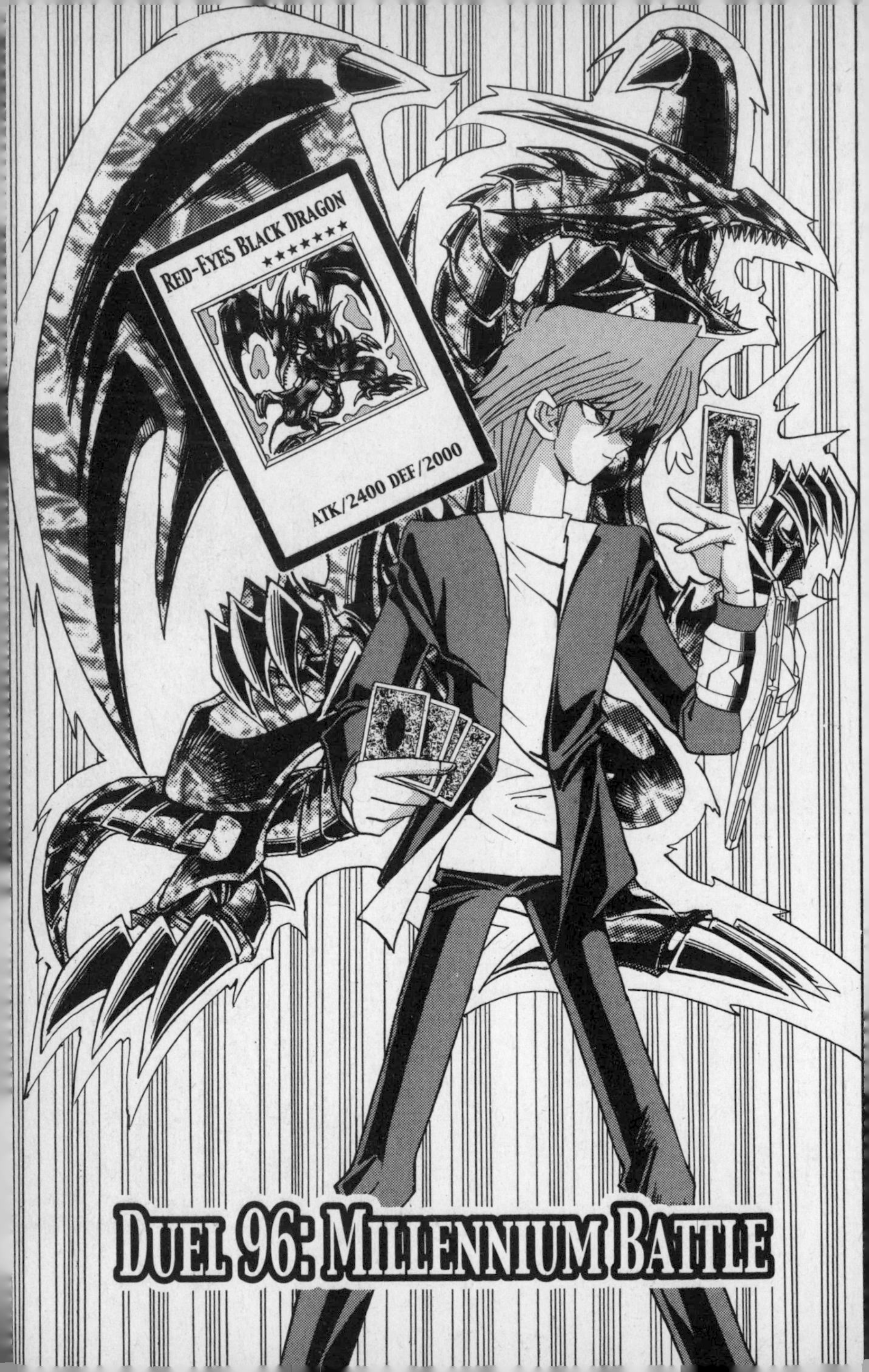
RED-EYES BLACK DRAGON
★★★★★★★
ATK/2400 DEF/2000

DUEL 96: MILLENNIUM BATTLE

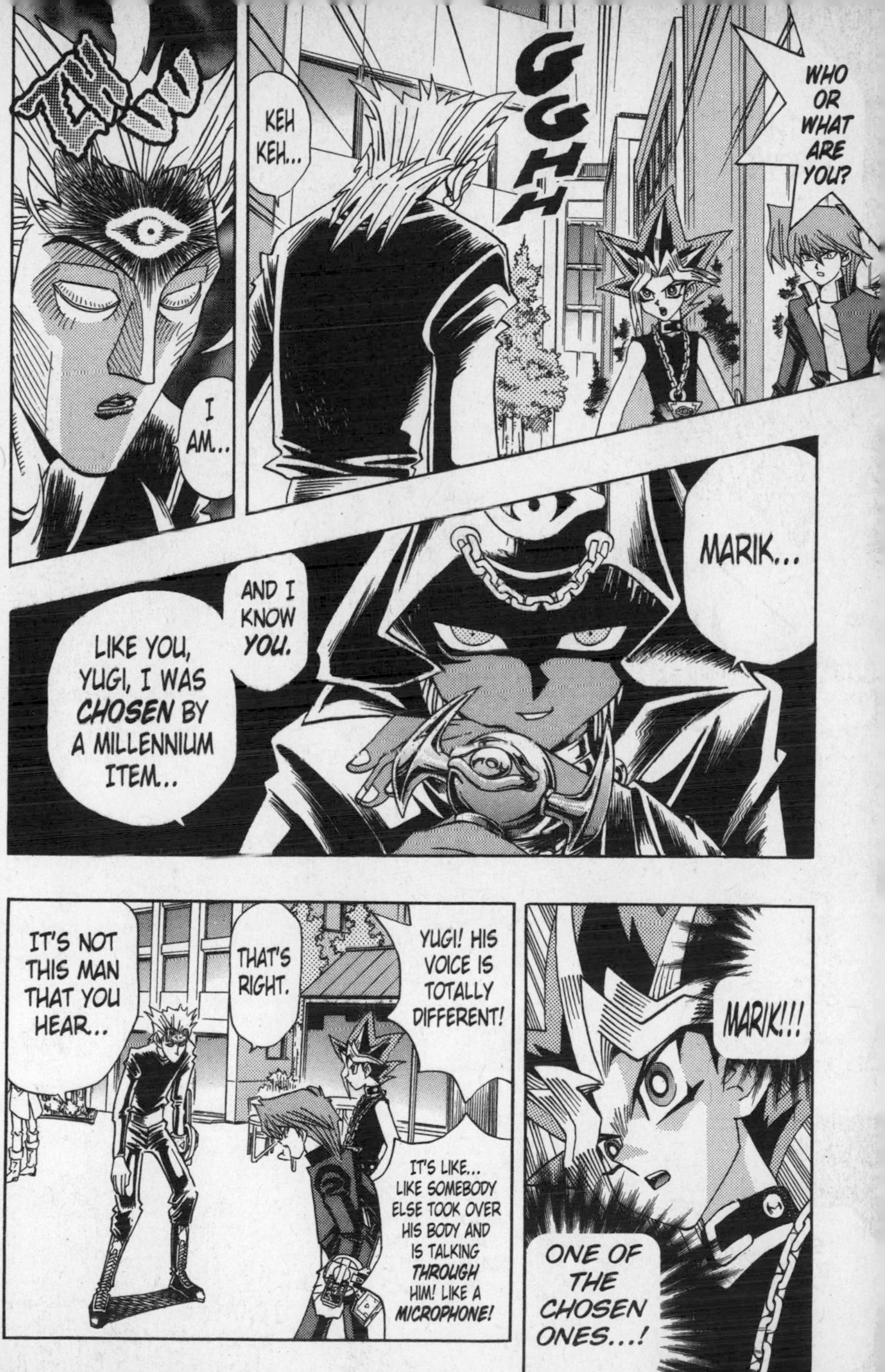
WHO OR WHAT ARE YOU?
GGHH
KEH KEH...
I AM...
MARIK...
AND I KNOW YOU.
LIKE YOU, YUGI, I WAS CHOSEN BY A MILLENNIUM ITEM...
MARIK!!!
ONE OF THE CHOSEN ONES...!
YUGI! HIS VOICE IS TOTALLY DIFFERENT!
IT'S LIKE... LIKE SOMEBODY ELSE TOOK OVER HIS BODY AND IS TALKING THROUGH HIM! LIKE A MICROPHONE!
THAT'S RIGHT.
IT'S NOT THIS MAN THAT YOU HEAR...

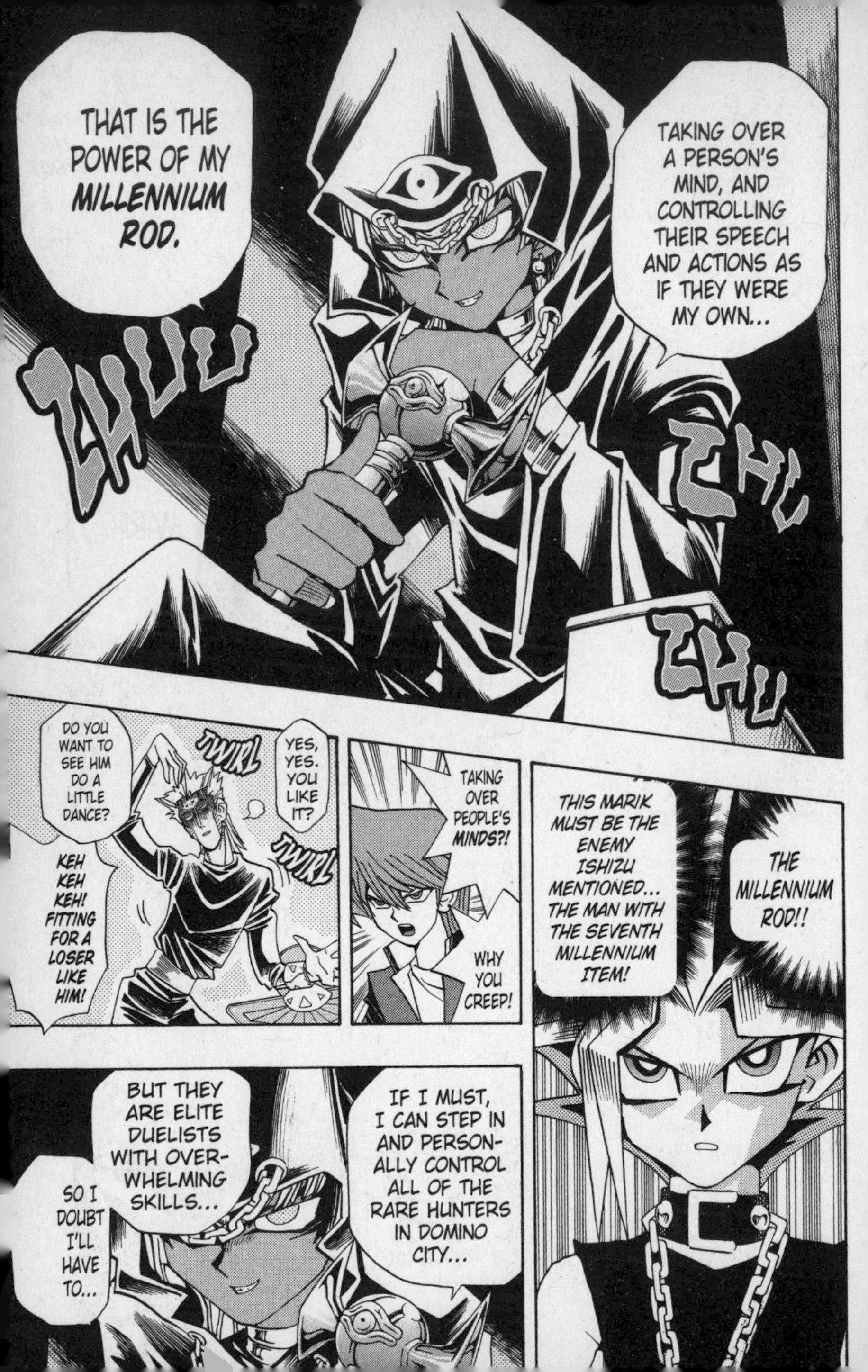
TAKING OVER A PERSON'S MIND, AND CONTROLLING THEIR SPEECH AND ACTIONS AS IF THEY WERE MY OWN...
THAT IS THE POWER OF MY MILLENNIUM ROD.
ZHU
ZHU
ZHUUU
THE MILLENNIUM ROD!!
THIS MARIK MUST BE THE ENEMY ISHIZU MENTIONED... THE MAN WITH THE SEVENTH MILLENNIUM ITEM!
TAKING OVER PEOPLE'S MINDS?!
WHY YOU CREEP!
YES, YES. YOU LIKE IT?
TWIRL
DO YOU WANT TO SEE HIM DO A LITTLE DANCE?
TWIRL
KEH KEH KEH! FITTING FOR A LOSER LIKE HIM!
IF I MUST, I CAN STEP IN AND PERSON-ALLY CONTROL ALL OF THE RARE HUNTERS IN DOMINO CITY...
BUT THEY ARE ELITE DUELISTS WITH OVER-WHELMING SKILLS...
SO I DOUBT I'LL HAVE TO...

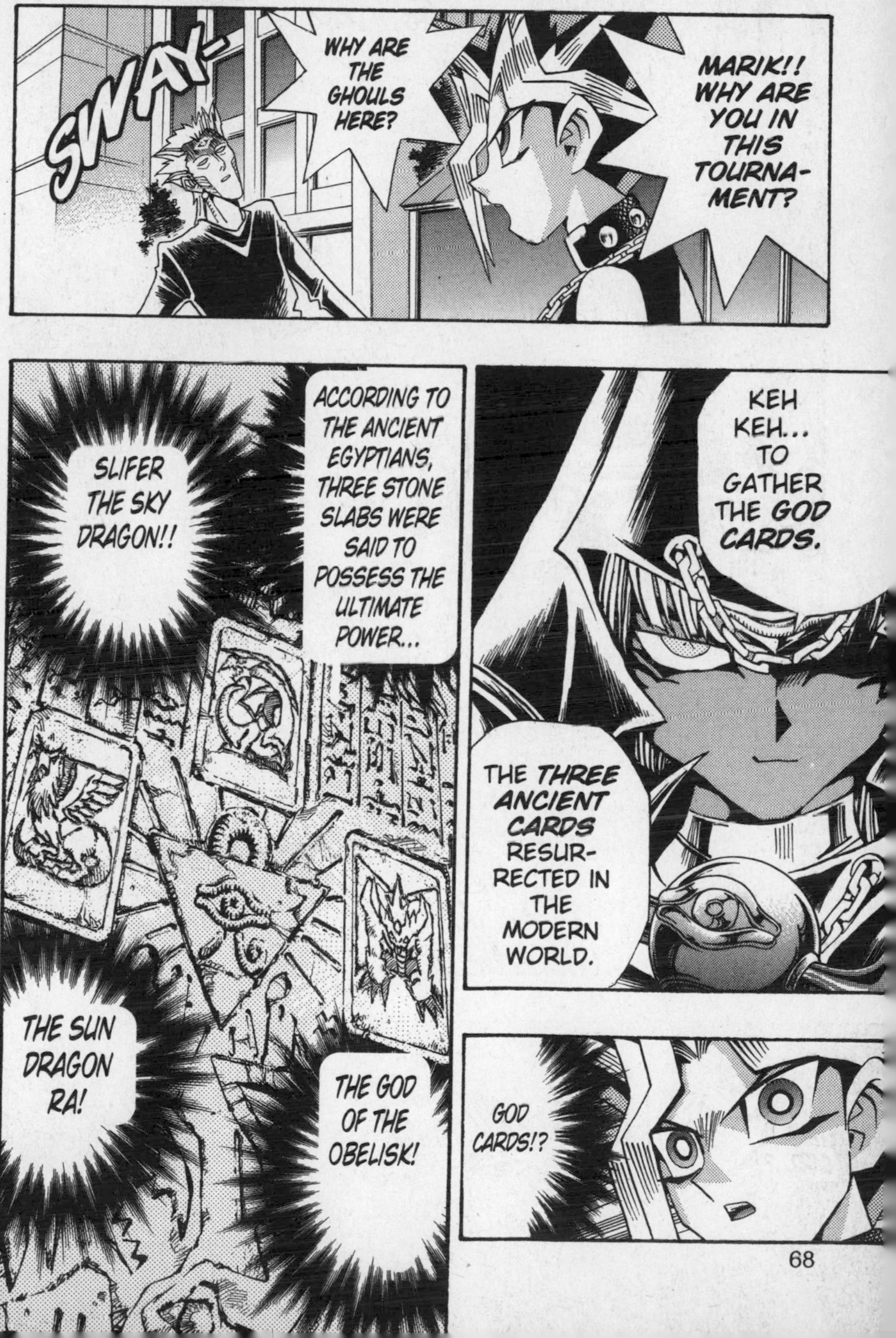
MARIK!! WHY ARE YOU IN THIS TOURNAMENT?
WHY ARE THE GHOULS HERE?
SWAY-
KEH KEH... TO GATHER THE *GOD CARDS*.
THE *THREE ANCIENT CARDS* RESURRECTED IN THE MODERN WORLD.
GOD CARDS!?
ACCORDING TO THE ANCIENT EGYPTIANS, THREE STONE SLABS WERE SAID TO POSSESS THE ULTIMATE POWER...
SLIFER THE SKY DRAGON!!
THE GOD OF THE OBELISK!
THE SUN DRAGON RA!

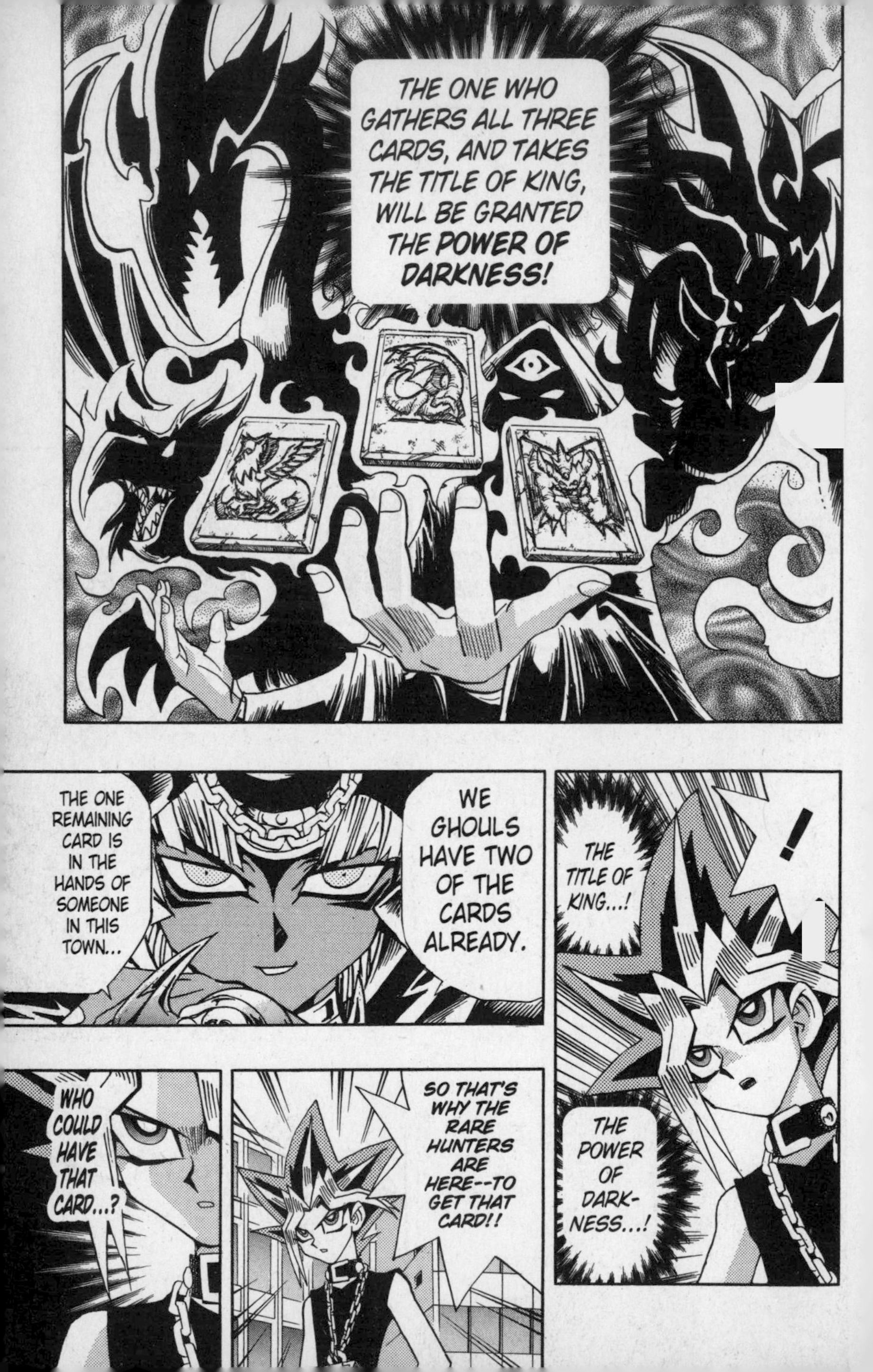
THE ONE WHO GATHERS ALL THREE CARDS, AND TAKES THE TITLE OF KING, WILL BE GRANTED THE POWER OF DARKNESS!
!
THE TITLE OF KING...!
THE POWER OF DARK-NESS...!
WE GHOULS HAVE TWO OF THE CARDS ALREADY.
THE ONE REMAINING CARD IS IN THE HANDS OF SOMEONE IN THIS TOWN...
SO THAT'S WHY THE RARE HUNTERS ARE HERE--TO GET THAT CARD!!
WHO COULD HAVE THAT CARD...?

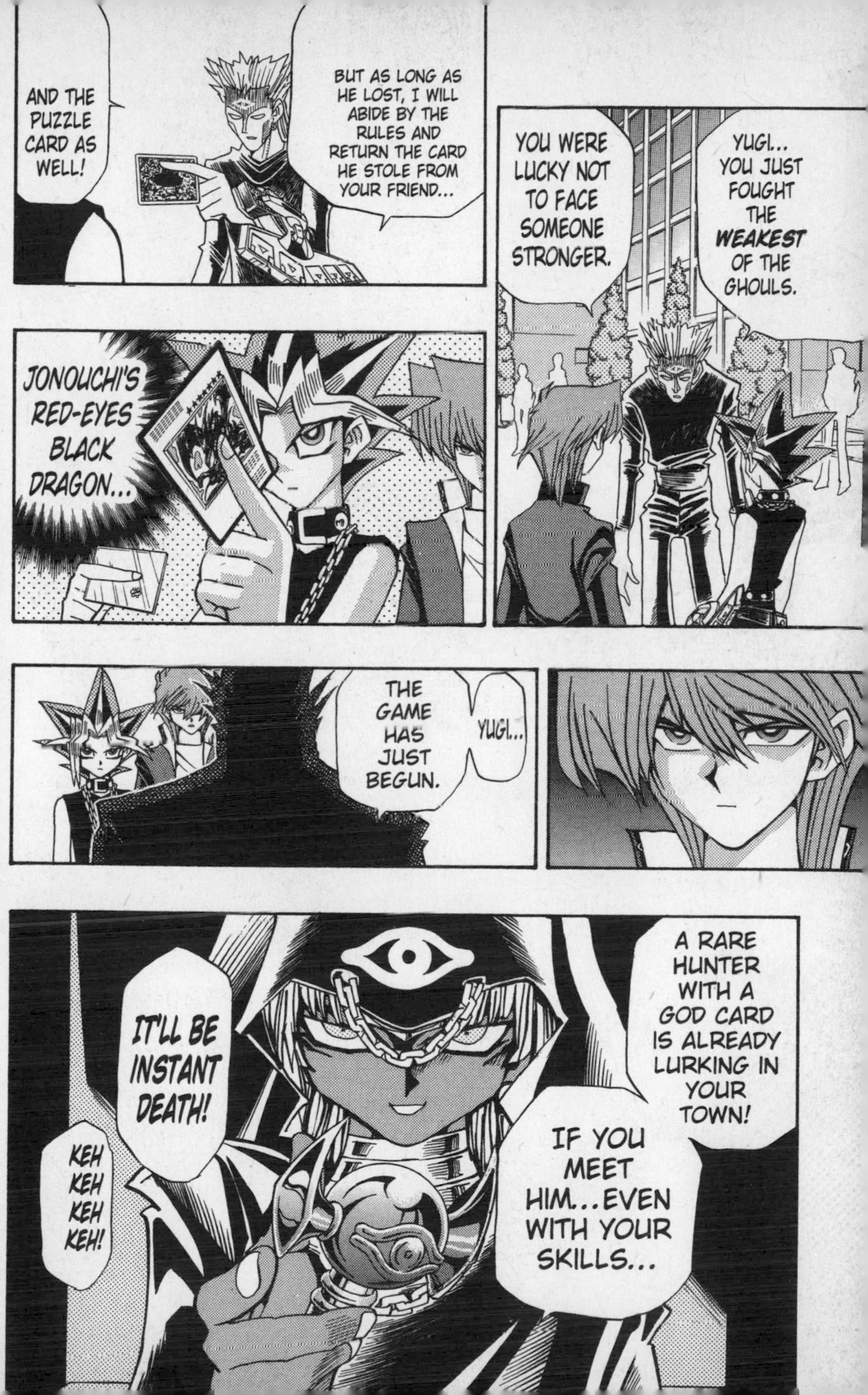
BUT AS LONG AS HE LOST, I WILL ABIDE BY THE RULES AND RETURN THE CARD HE STOLE FROM YOUR FRIEND...
AND THE PUZZLE CARD AS WELL!
JONOUCHI'S RED-EYES BLACK DRAGON...
YUGI... YOU JUST FOUGHT THE **WEAKEST** OF THE GHOULS.
YOU WERE LUCKY NOT TO FACE SOMEONE STRONGER.
YUGI...
THE GAME HAS JUST BEGUN.
A RARE HUNTER WITH A GOD CARD IS ALREADY LURKING IN YOUR TOWN!
IF YOU MEET HIM...EVEN WITH YOUR SKILLS...
IT'LL BE INSTANT DEATH!
KEH KEH KEH KEH!

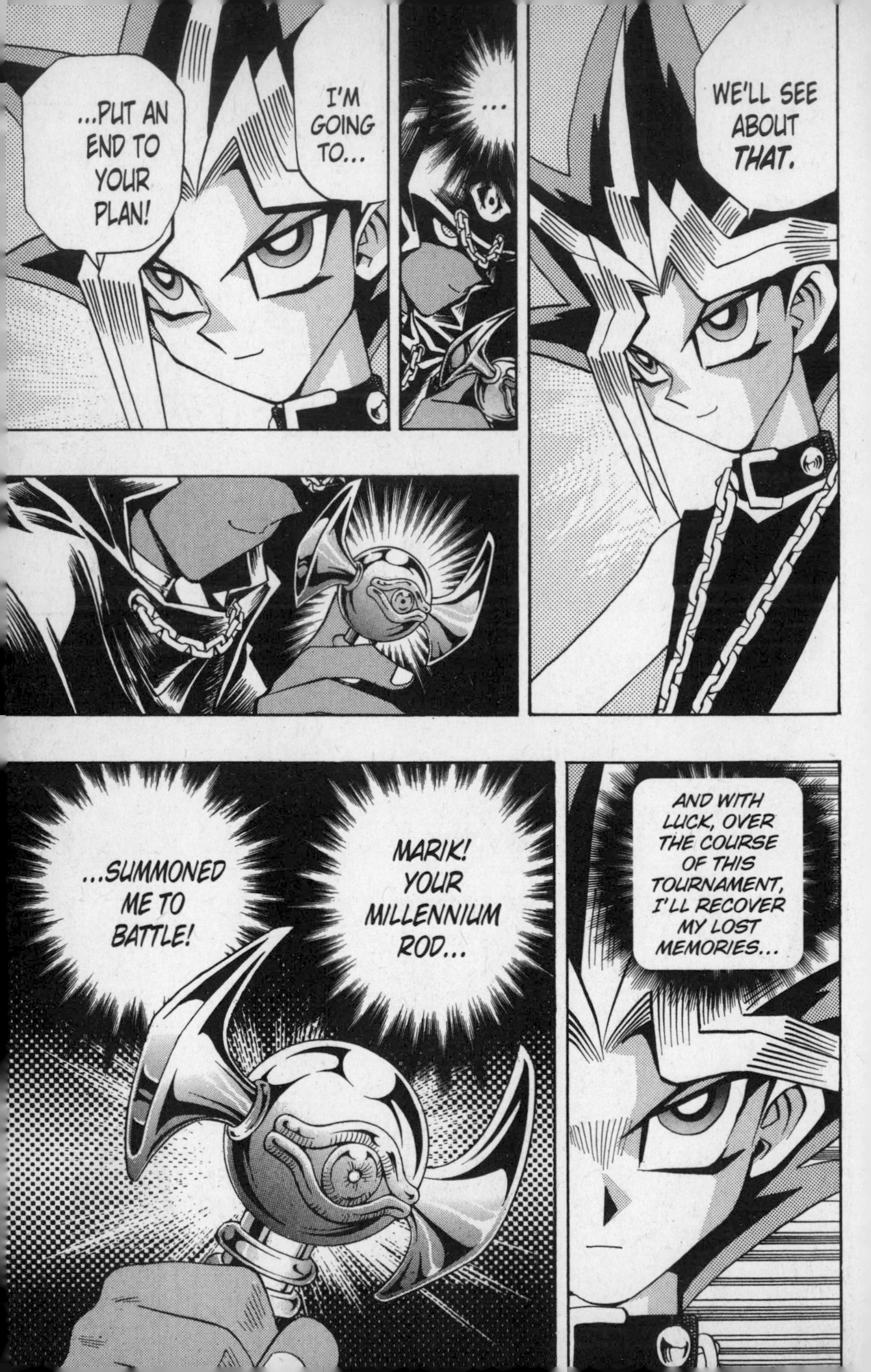
WE'LL SEE ABOUT THAT.
...
I'M GOING TO...
...PUT AN END TO YOUR PLAN!
AND WITH LUCK, OVER THE COURSE OF THIS TOURNAMENT, I'LL RECOVER MY LOST MEMORIES...
MARIK! YOUR MILLENNIUM ROD...
...SUMMONED ME TO BATTLE!

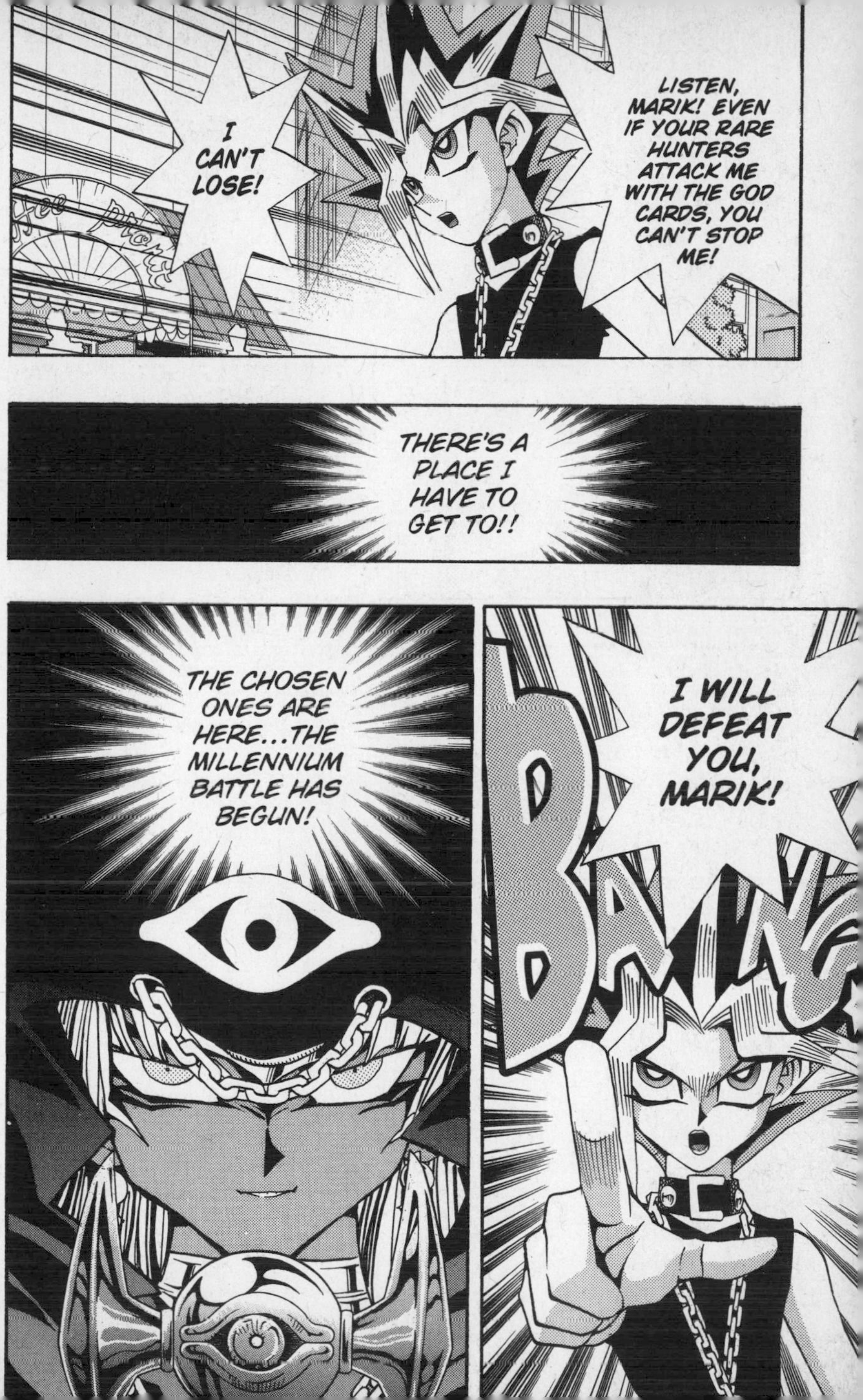
LISTEN, MARIK! EVEN IF YOUR RARE HUNTERS ATTACK ME WITH THE GOD CARDS, YOU CAN'T STOP ME!
I CAN'T LOSE!
THERE'S A PLACE I HAVE TO GET TO!!
I WILL DEFEAT YOU, MARIK!
THE CHOSEN ONES ARE HERE...THE MILLENNIUM BATTLE HAS BEGUN!

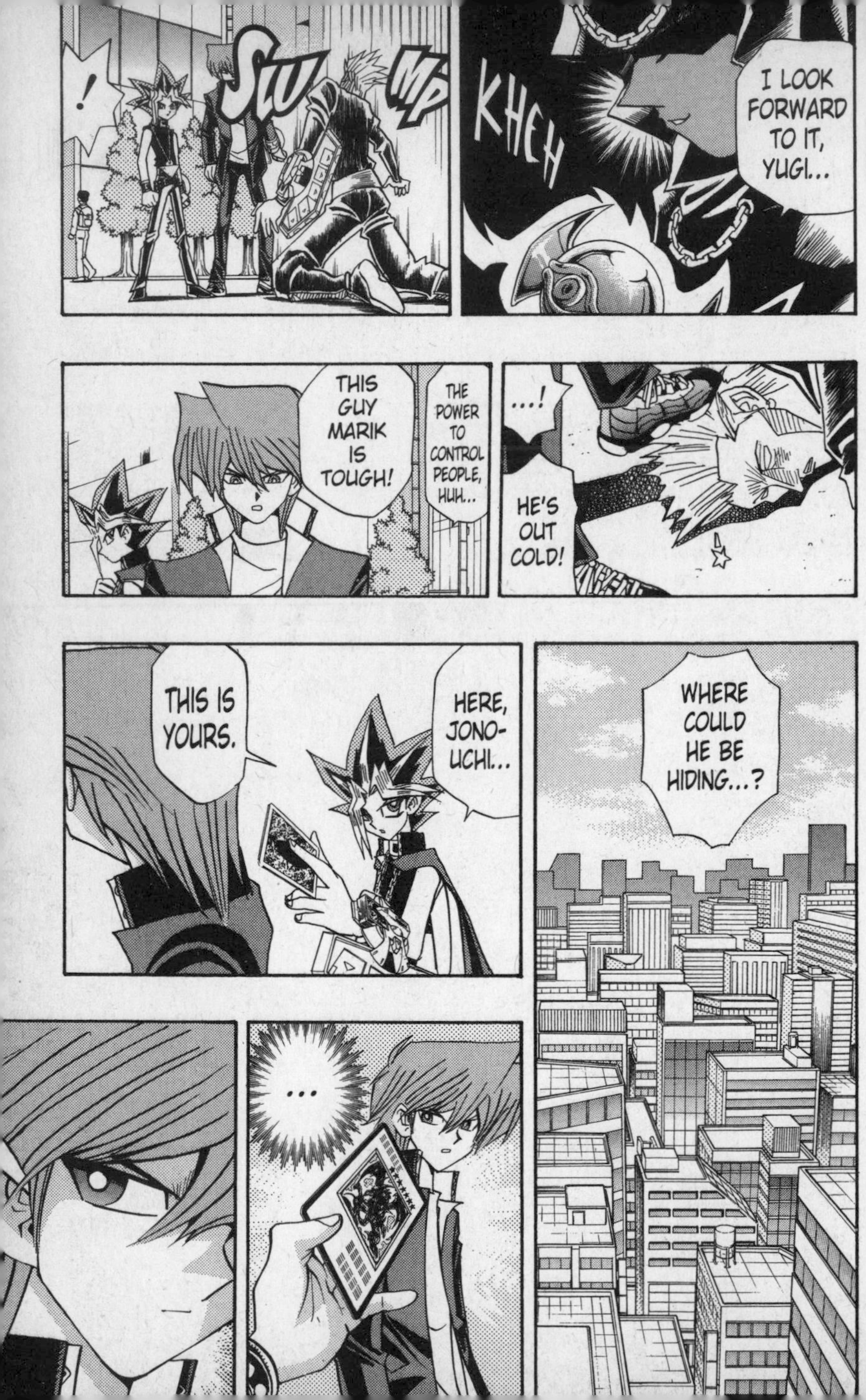
I LOOK FORWARD TO IT, YUGI...
KHEH
!
SLUMP
...!
HE'S OUT COLD!
THE POWER TO CONTROL PEOPLE, HUH...
THIS GUY MARIK IS TOUGH!
WHERE COULD HE BE HIDING...?
HERE, JONOUCHI...
THIS IS YOURS.
...

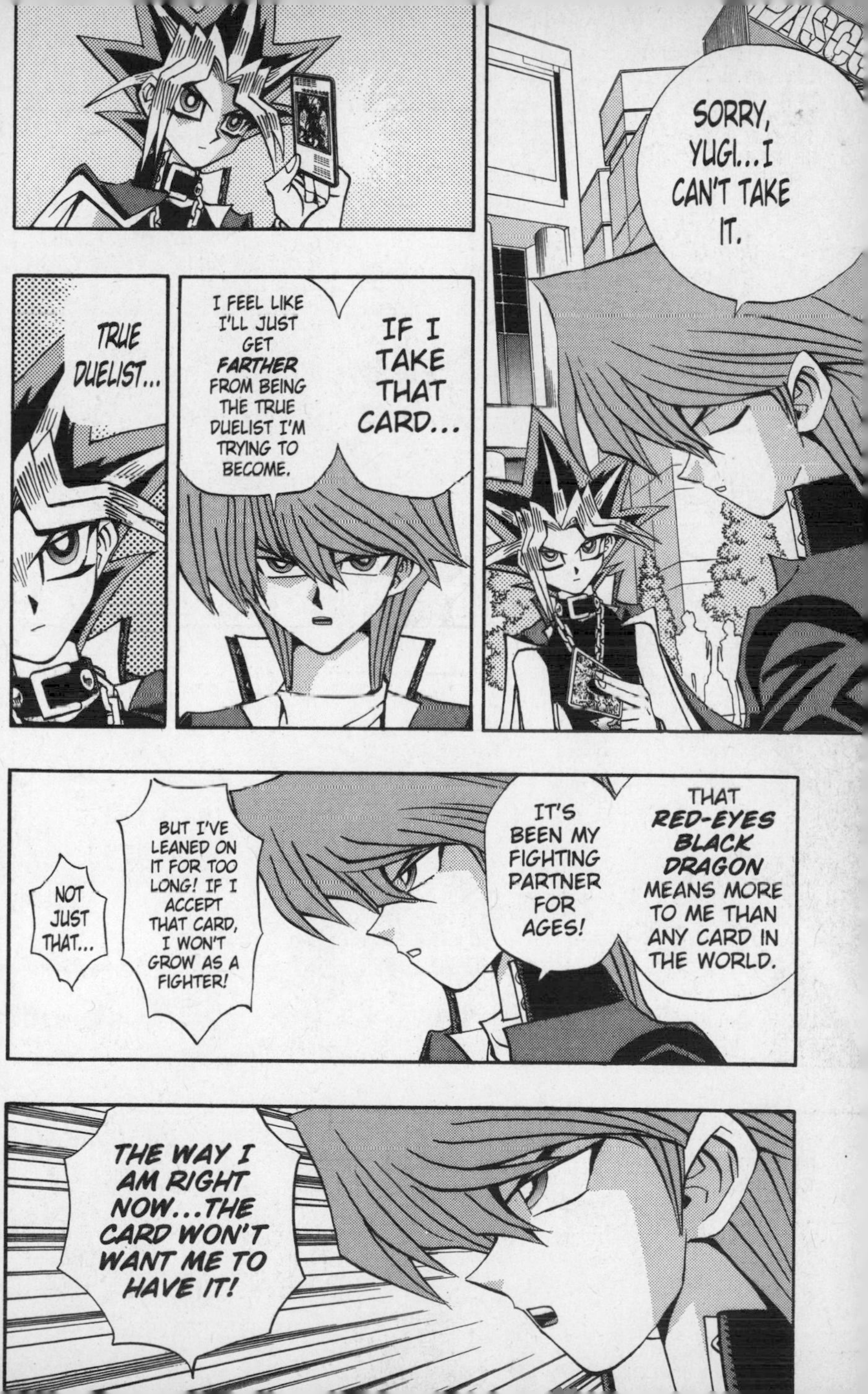
SORRY, YUGI...I CAN'T TAKE IT.
IF I TAKE THAT CARD...
I FEEL LIKE I'LL JUST GET FARTHER FROM BEING THE TRUE DUELIST I'M TRYING TO BECOME.
TRUE DUELIST...
THAT RED-EYES BLACK DRAGON MEANS MORE TO ME THAN ANY CARD IN THE WORLD.
IT'S BEEN MY FIGHTING PARTNER FOR AGES!
BUT I'VE LEANED ON IT FOR TOO LONG! IF I ACCEPT THAT CARD, I WON'T GROW AS A FIGHTER!
NOT JUST THAT...
THE WAY I AM RIGHT NOW...THE CARD WON'T WANT ME TO HAVE IT!

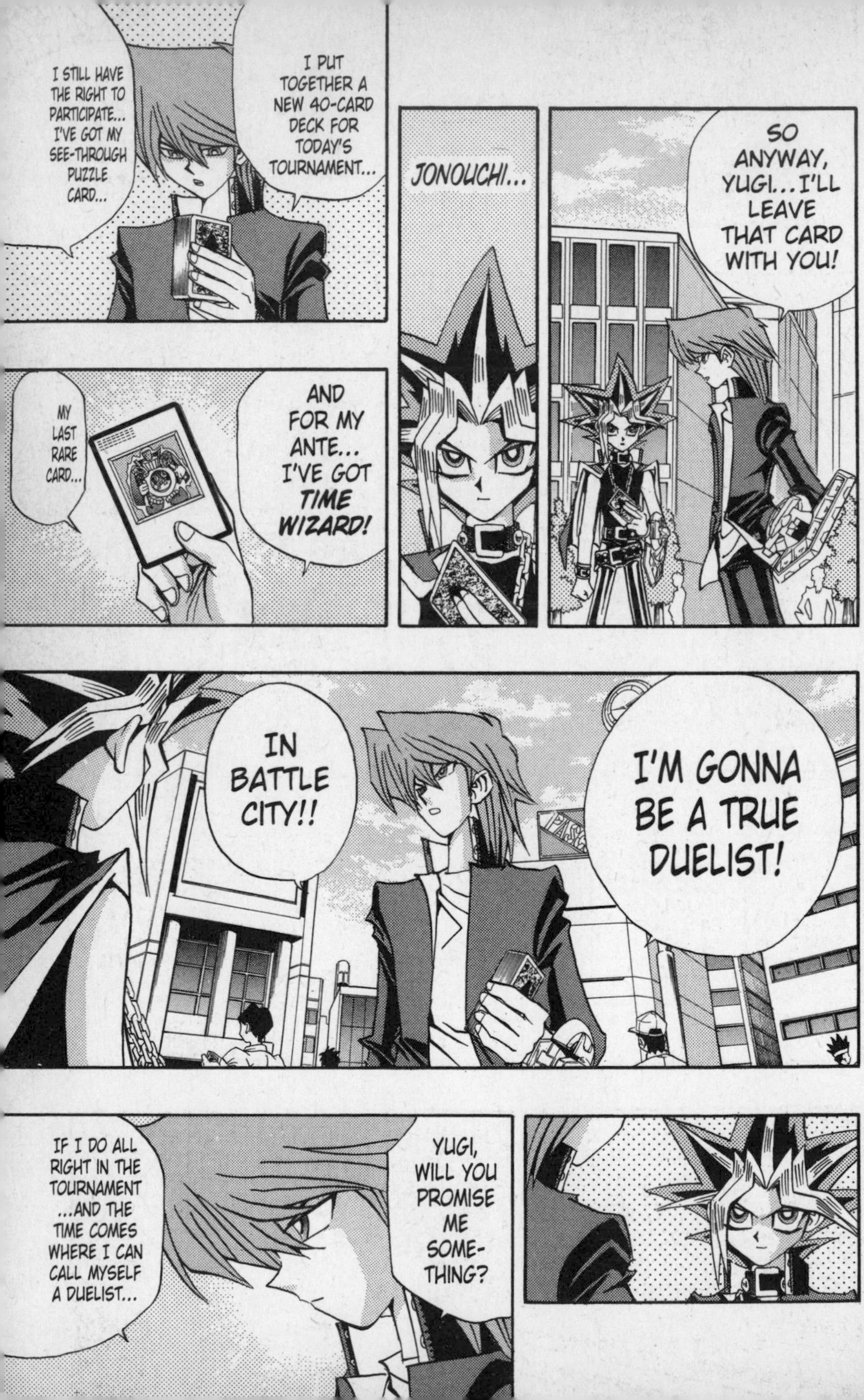
SO ANYWAY, YUGI...I'LL LEAVE THAT CARD WITH YOU!
JONOUCHI...
I PUT TOGETHER A NEW 40-CARD DECK FOR TODAY'S TOURNAMENT...
I STILL HAVE THE RIGHT TO PARTICIPATE... I'VE GOT MY SEE-THROUGH PUZZLE CARD...
AND FOR MY ANTE... I'VE GOT *TIME WIZARD!*
MY LAST RARE CARD...
I'M GONNA BE A TRUE DUELIST!
IN BATTLE CITY!!
YUGI, WILL YOU PROMISE ME SOME-THING?
IF I DO ALL RIGHT IN THE TOURNAMENT ...AND THE TIME COMES WHERE I CAN CALL MYSELF A DUELIST...

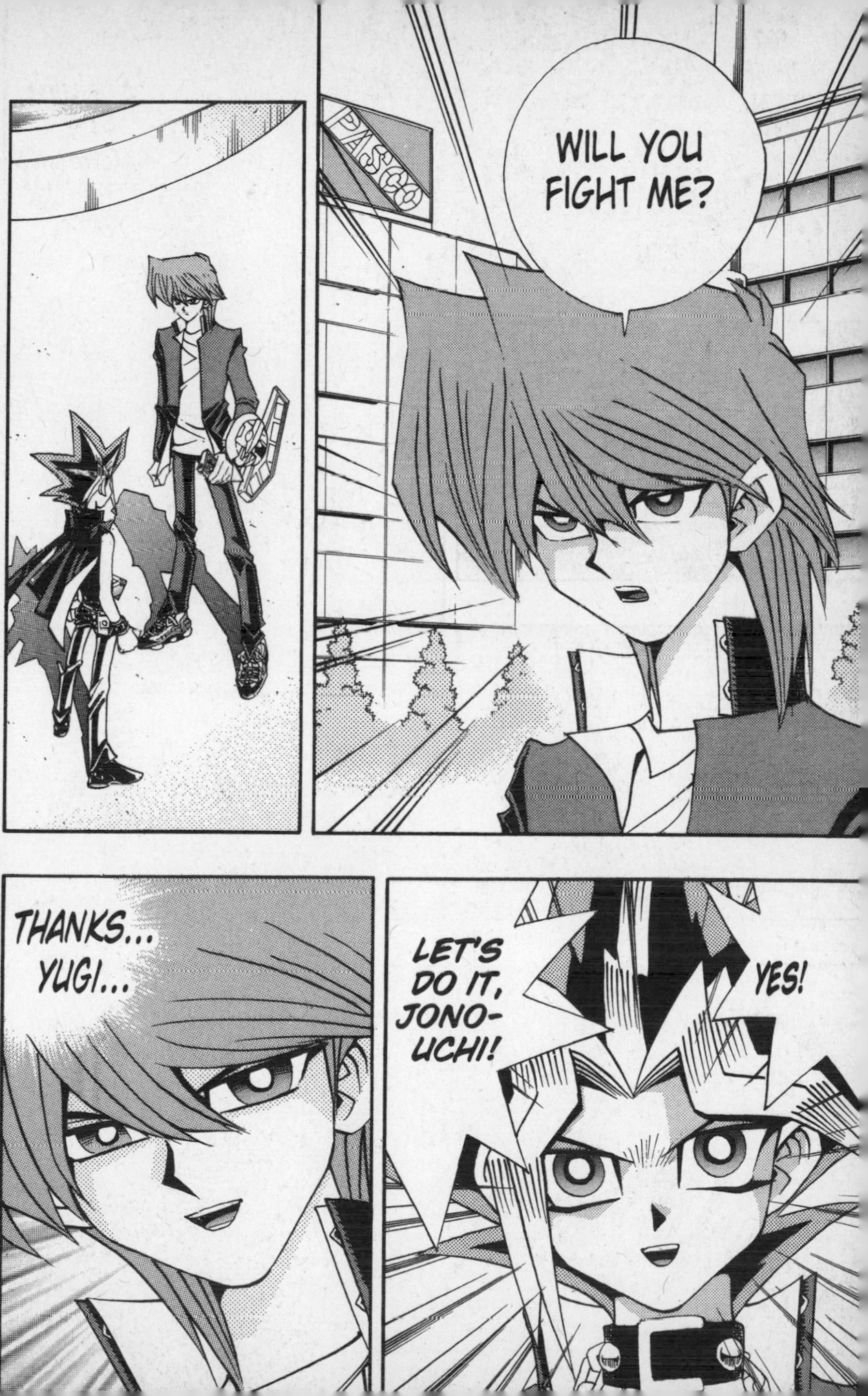
PASCO
WILL YOU FIGHT ME?
YES!
LET'S DO IT, JONOUCHI!
THANKS... YUGI...

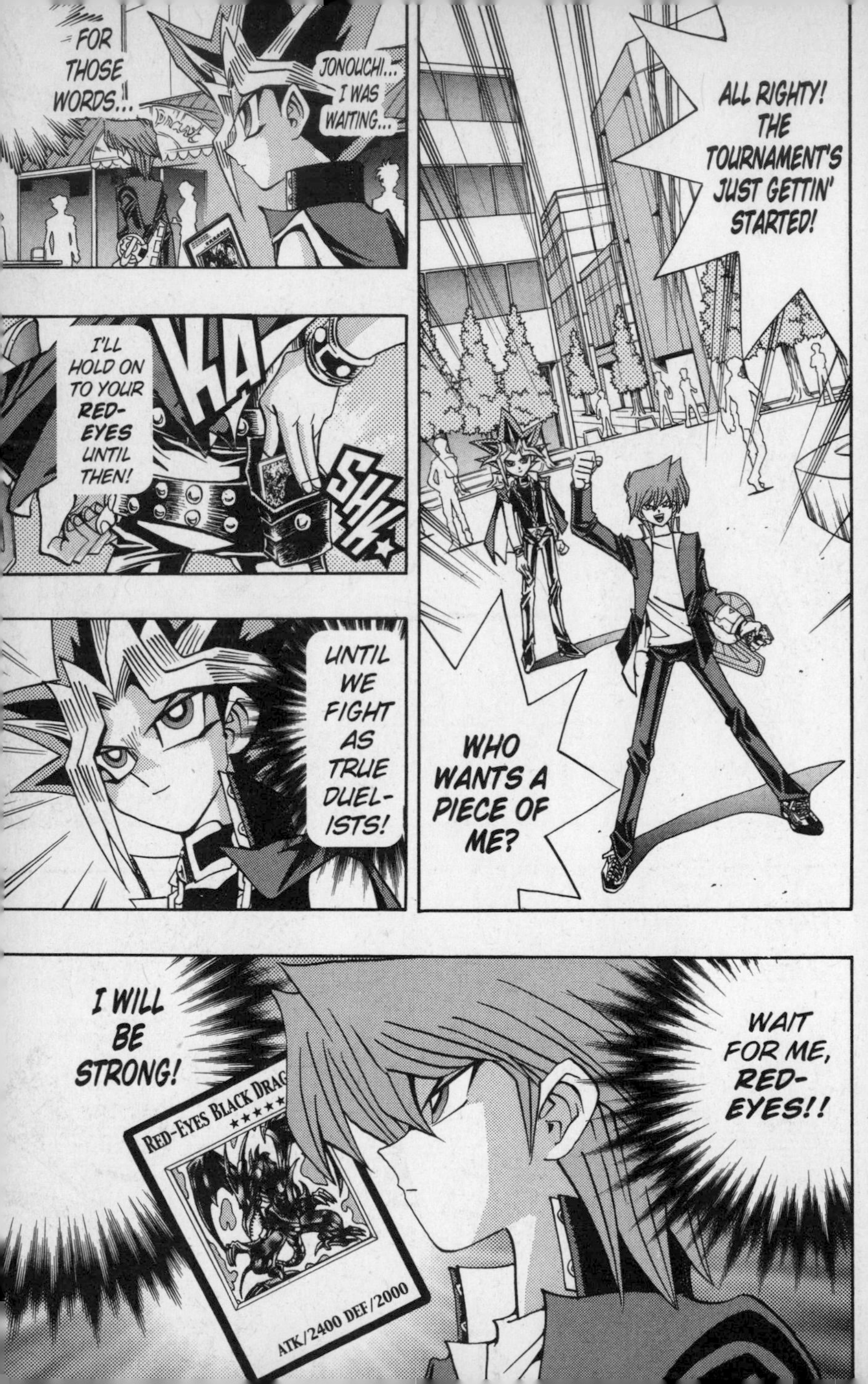
ALL RIGHTY! THE TOURNAMENT'S JUST GETTIN' STARTED!
WHO WANTS A PIECE OF ME?
JONOUCHI... I WAS WAITING...
FOR THOSE WORDS...
KA
SHK☆
I'LL HOLD ON TO YOUR RED-EYES UNTIL THEN!
UNTIL WE FIGHT AS TRUE DUEL-ISTS!
WAIT FOR ME, RED-EYES!!
I WILL BE STRONG!
RED-EYES BLACK DRAG
ATK/2400 DEF/2000

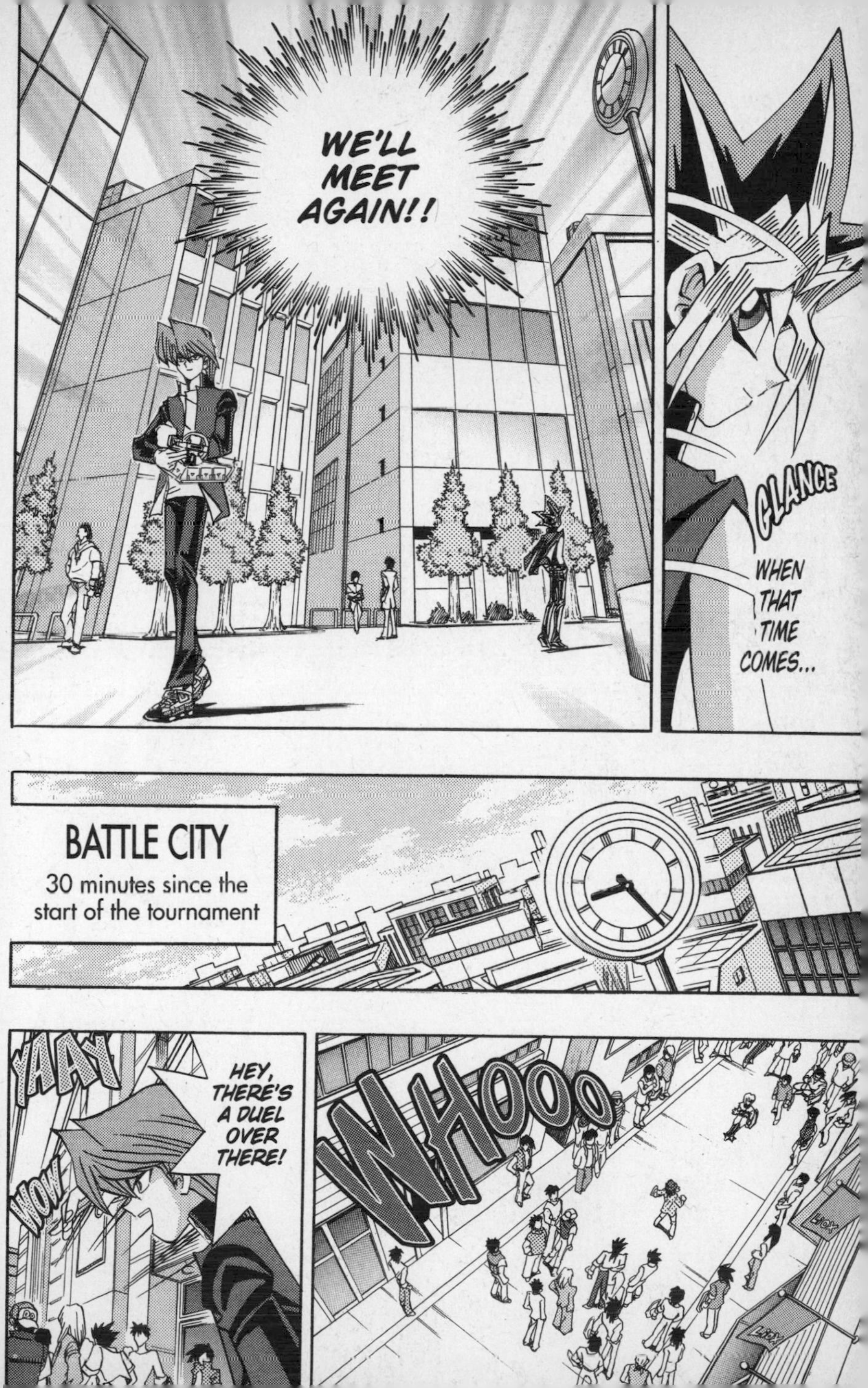
GLANCE
WHEN THAT TIME COMES...
WE'LL MEET AGAIN!!
BATTLE CITY
30 minutes since the start of the tournament
WHOOO
YAAAY
HEY, THERE'S A DUEL OVER THERE!
WOW

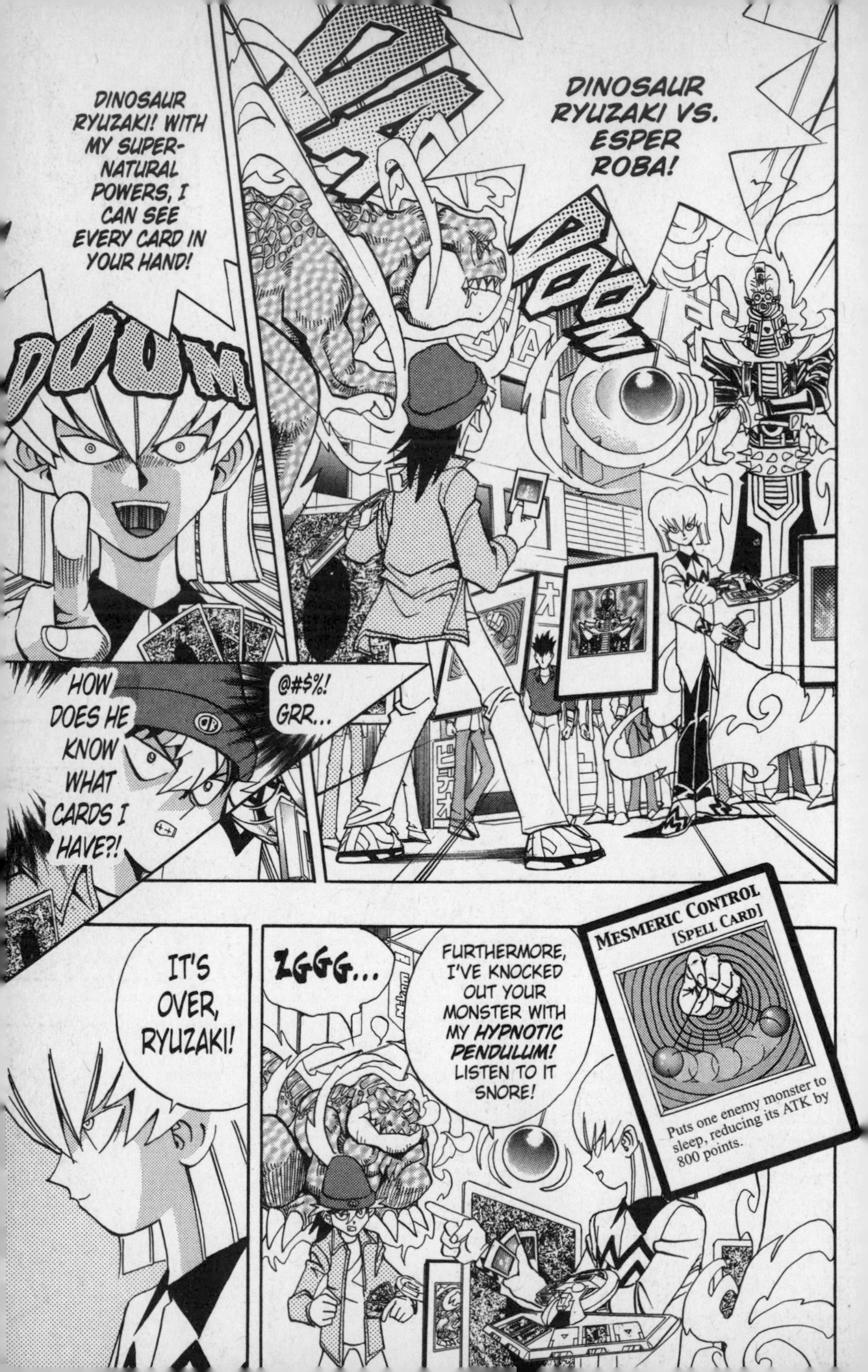
DINOSAUR RYUZAKI VS. ESPER ROBA!
VROOM
DINOSAUR RYUZAKI! WITH MY SUPER-NATURAL POWERS, I CAN SEE EVERY CARD IN YOUR HAND!
DOOM
@#$%! GRR...
HOW DOES HE KNOW WHAT CARDS I HAVE?!
FURTHERMORE, I'VE KNOCKED OUT YOUR MONSTER WITH MY *HYPNOTIC PENDULUM!* LISTEN TO IT SNORE!
ZGGG...
MESMERIC CONTROL [SPELL CARD]
Puts one enemy monster to sleep, reducing its ATK by 800 points.
IT'S OVER, RYUZAKI!

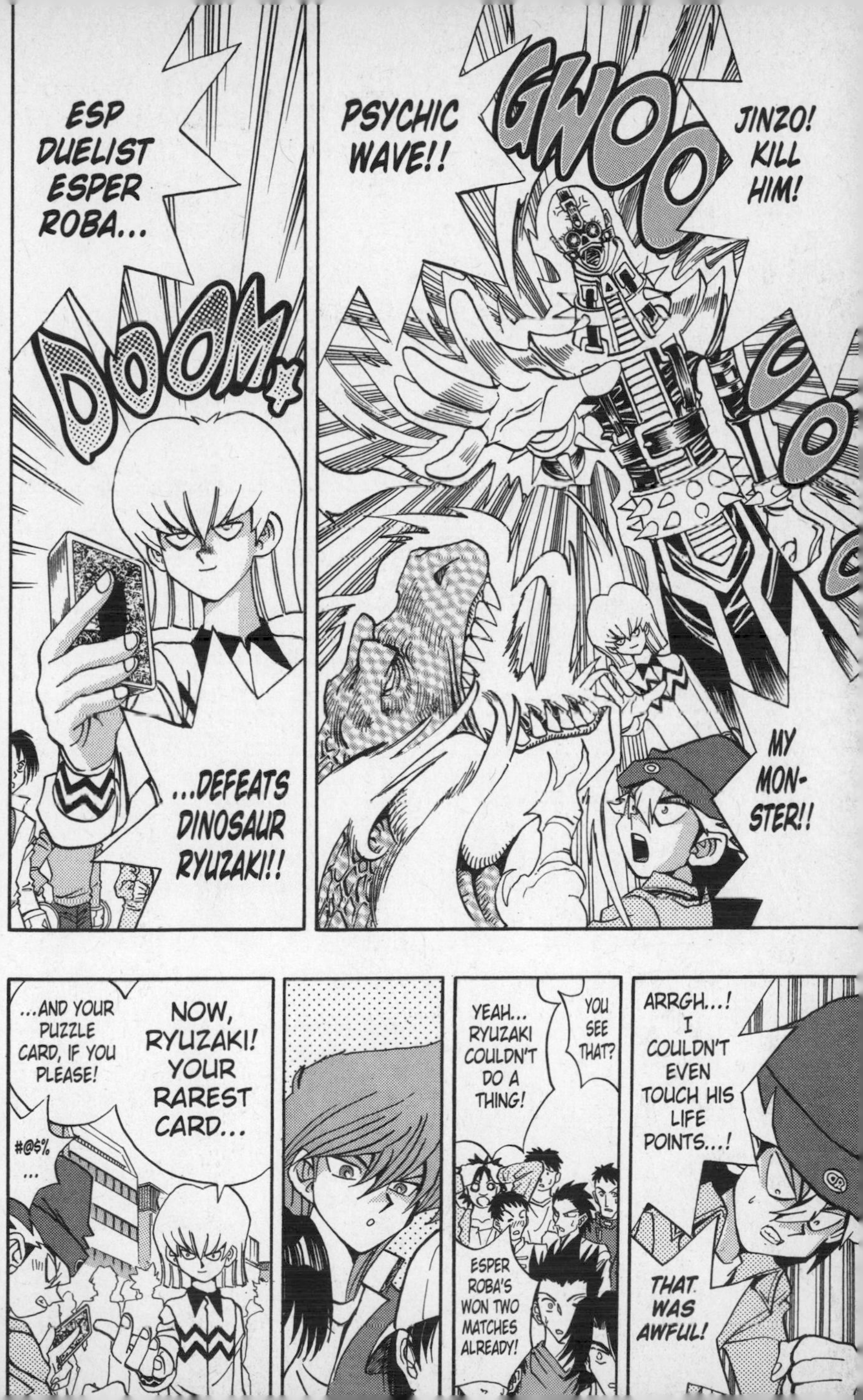
JINZO! KILL HIM!
GWOOOOOO
PSYCHIC WAVE!!
MY MON-STER!!
ESP DUELIST ESPER ROBA...
DOOM
...DEFEATS DINOSAUR RYUZAKI!!!
ARRGH...! I COULDN'T EVEN TOUCH HIS LIFE POINTS...!
THAT WAS AWFUL!
YOU SEE THAT?
YEAH... RYUZAKI COULDN'T DO A THING!
ESPER ROBA'S WON TWO MATCHES ALREADY!
NOW, RYUZAKI! YOUR RAREST CARD...
...AND YOUR PUZZLE CARD, IF YOU PLEASE!
#@$% ...

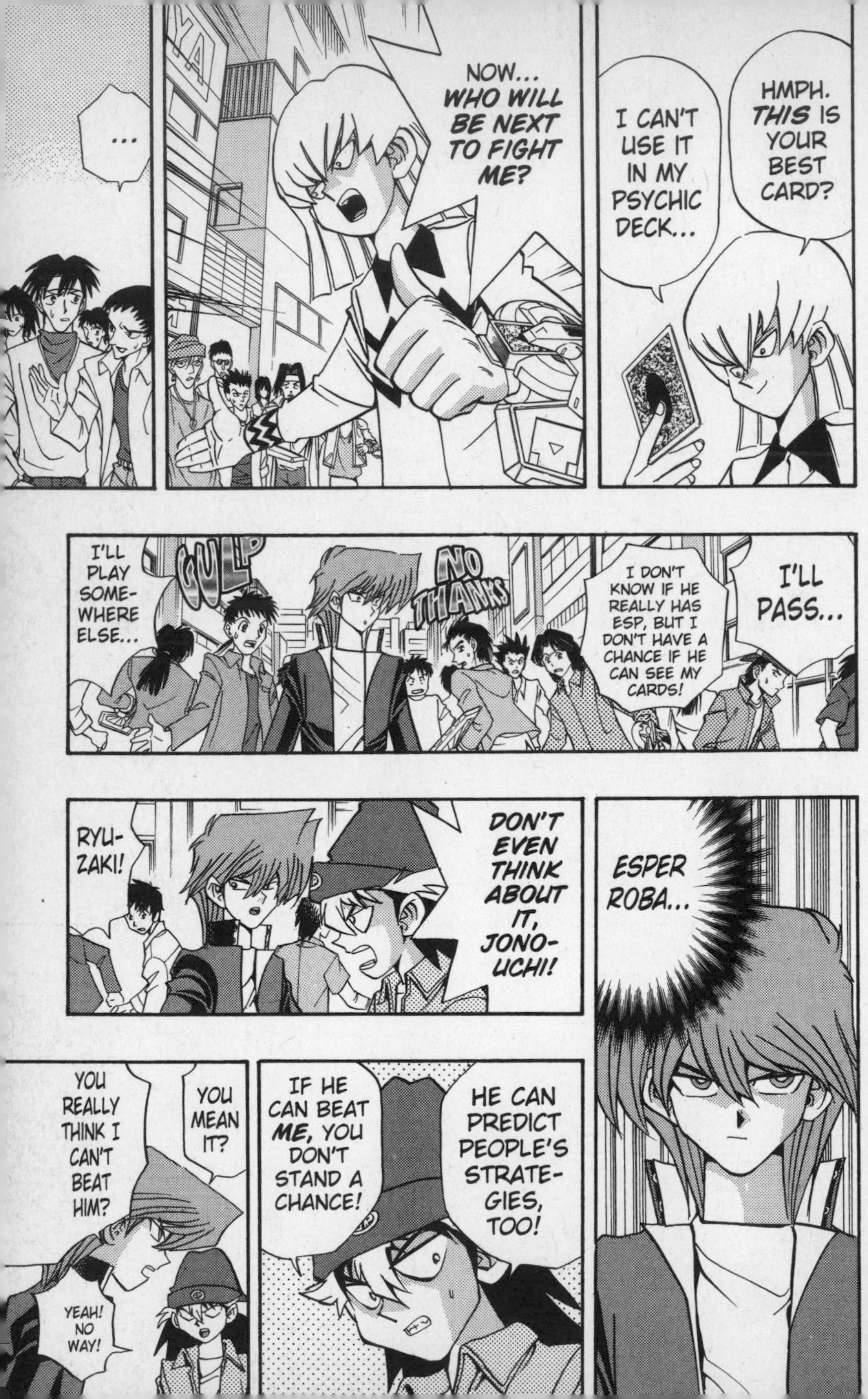
HMPH. THIS IS YOUR BEST CARD?
I CAN'T USE IT IN MY PSYCHIC DECK...
NOW... WHO WILL BE NEXT TO FIGHT ME?
...
I'LL PASS...
I DON'T KNOW IF HE REALLY HAS ESP, BUT I DON'T HAVE A CHANCE IF HE CAN SEE MY CARDS!
NO THANKS
GULP
I'LL PLAY SOME-WHERE ELSE...
ESPER ROBA...
DON'T EVEN THINK ABOUT IT, JONO-UCHI!
RYU-ZAKI!
HE CAN PREDICT PEOPLE'S STRATE-GIES, TOO!
IF HE CAN BEAT ME, YOU DON'T STAND A CHANCE!
YOU MEAN IT?
YOU REALLY THINK I CAN'T BEAT HIM?
YEAH! NO WAY!

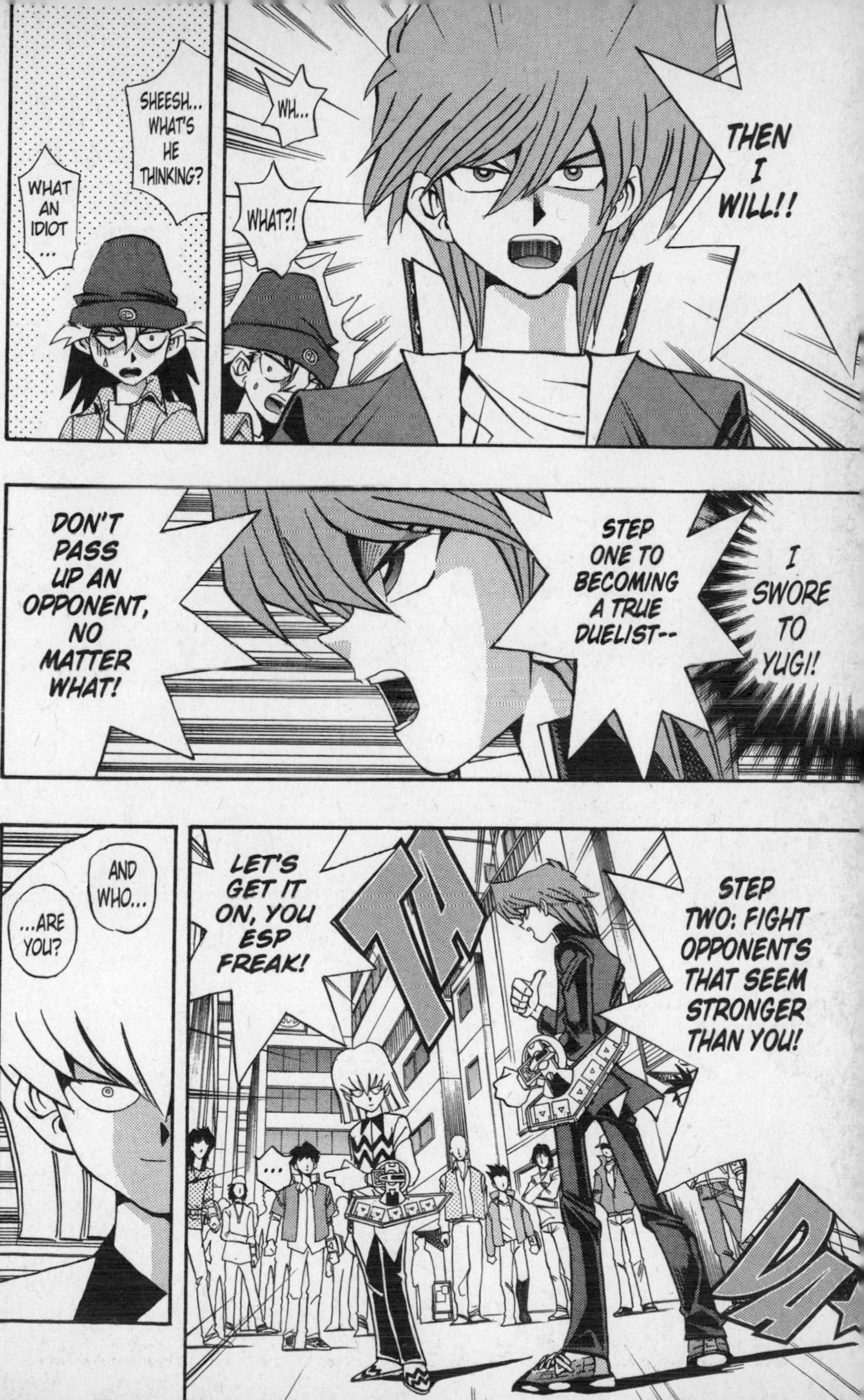
THEN I WILL!!
WH...
WHAT?!
SHEESH... WHAT'S HE THINKING?
WHAT AN IDIOT ...
I SWORE TO YUGI!
STEP ONE TO BECOMING A TRUE DUELIST--
DON'T PASS UP AN OPPONENT, NO MATTER WHAT!
STEP TWO: FIGHT OPPONENTS THAT SEEM STRONGER THAN YOU!
LET'S GET IT ON, YOU ESP FREAK!
...
AND WHO...
...ARE YOU?

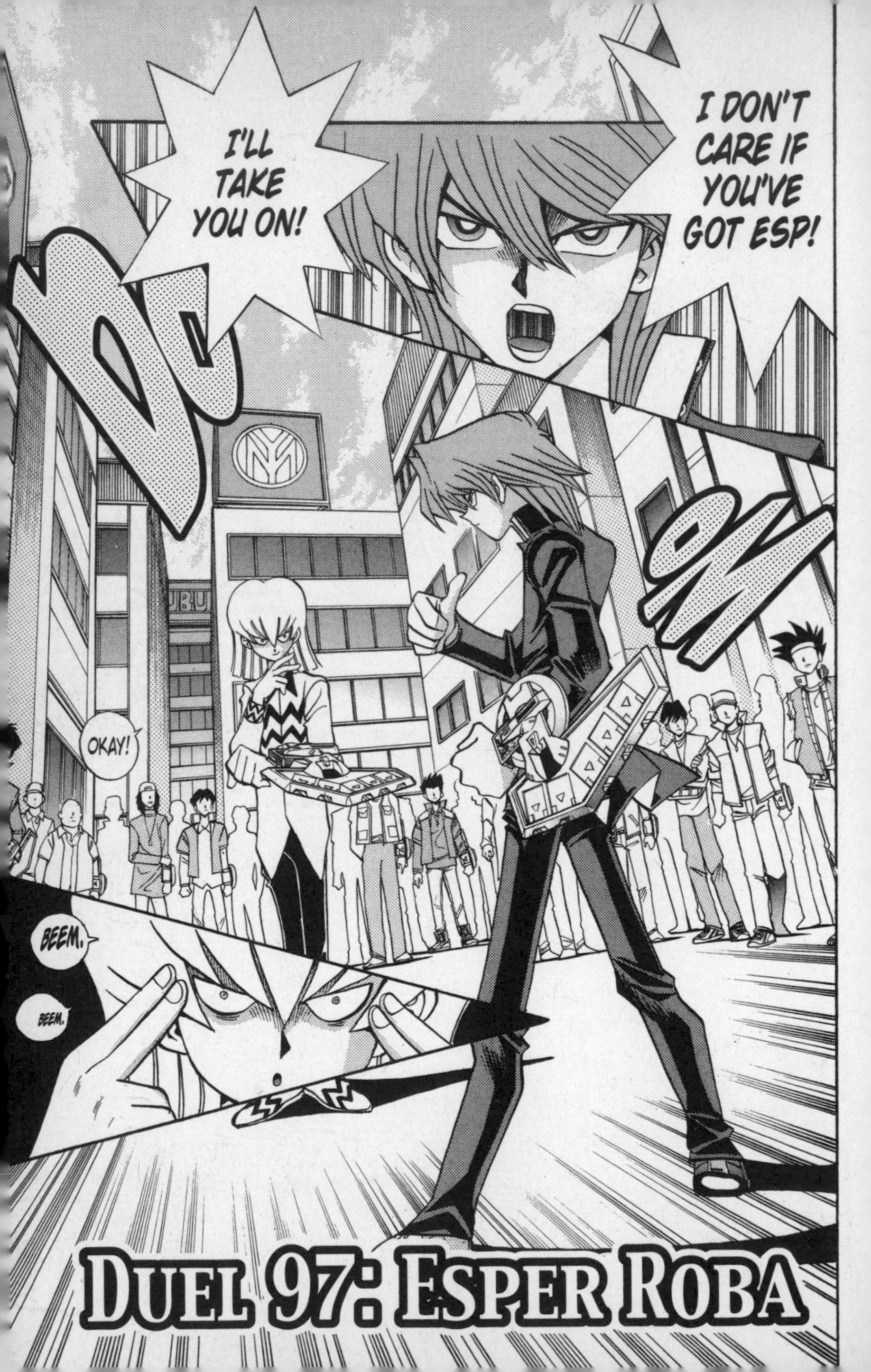
I DON'T CARE IF YOU'VE GOT ESP!
I'LL TAKE YOU ON!
OKAY!
BEEM.
BEEM.

Duel 97: Esper Roba

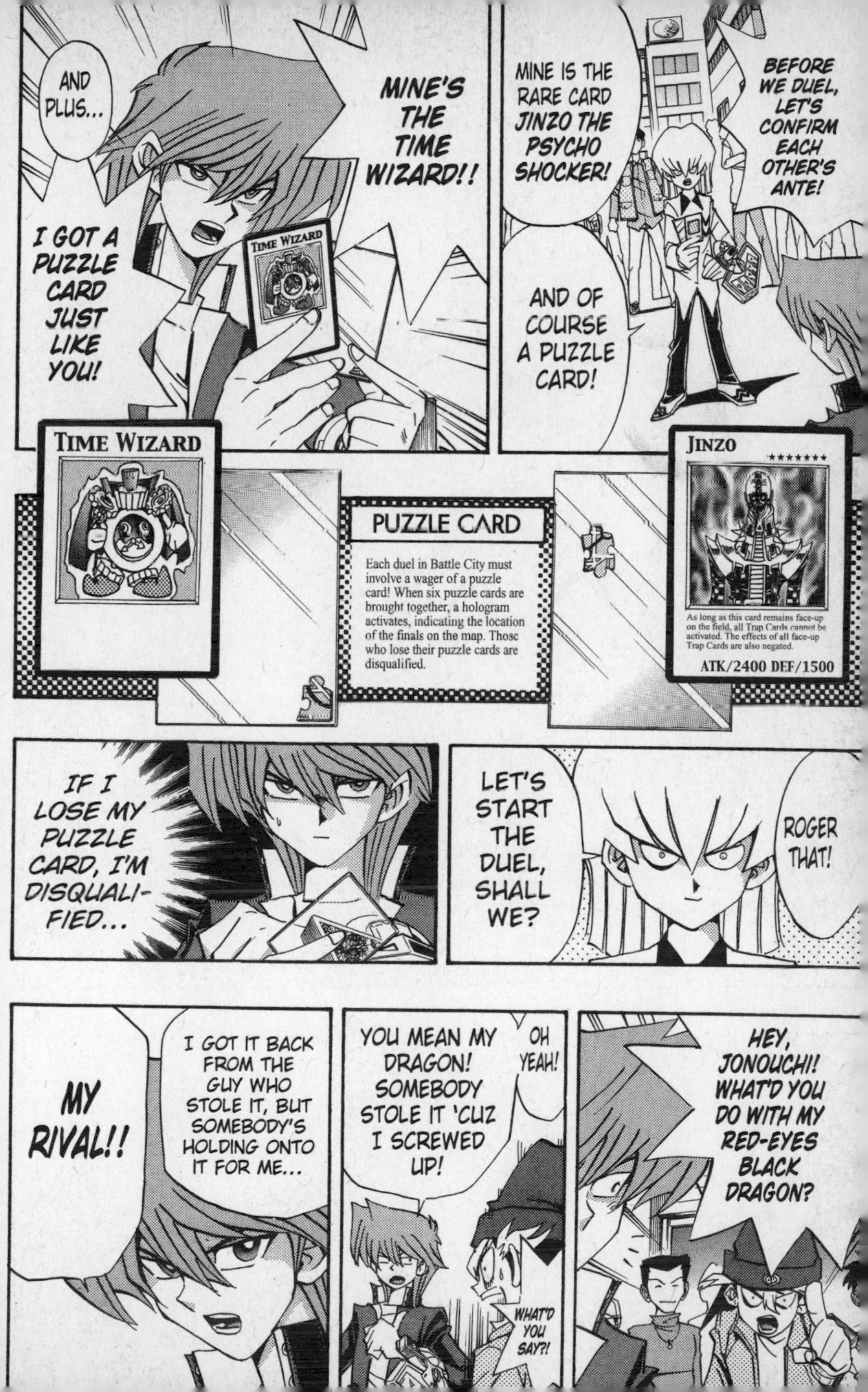
BEFORE WE DUEL, LET'S CONFIRM EACH OTHER'S ANTE!
MINE IS THE RARE CARD JINZO THE PSYCHO SHOCKER!
AND OF COURSE A PUZZLE CARD!
MINE'S THE TIME WIZARD!!
AND PLUS...
I GOT A PUZZLE CARD JUST LIKE YOU!
TIME WIZARD
JINZO
★★★★★★★
As long as this card remains face-up on the field, all Trap Cards cannot be activated. The effects of all face-up Trap Cards are also negated.
ATK/2400 DEF/1500
PUZZLE CARD
Each duel in Battle City must involve a wager of a puzzle card! When six puzzle cards are brought together, a hologram activates, indicating the location of the finals on the map. Those who lose their puzzle cards are disqualified.
TIME WIZARD
LET'S START THE DUEL, SHALL WE?
ROGER THAT!
IF I LOSE MY PUZZLE CARD, I'M DISQUALIFIED...
HEY, JONOUCHI! WHAT'D YOU DO WITH MY RED-EYES BLACK DRAGON?
OH YEAH!
YOU MEAN MY DRAGON! SOMEBODY STOLE IT 'CUZ I SCREWED UP!
WHAT'D YOU SAY?!
I GOT IT BACK FROM THE GUY WHO STOLE IT, BUT SOMEBODY'S HOLDING ONTO IT FOR ME...
MY RIVAL!!

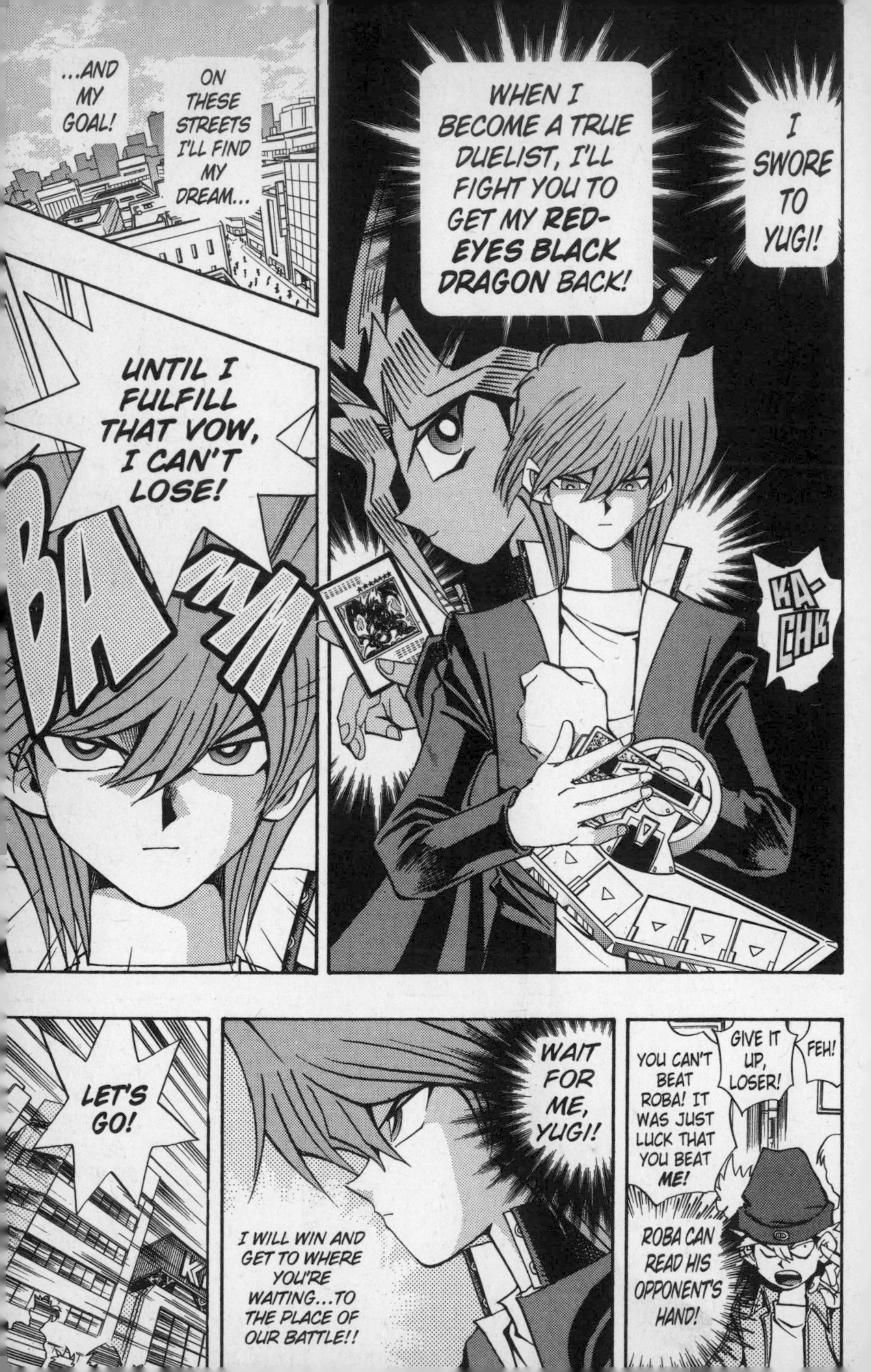
I SWORE TO YUGI!
WHEN I BECOME A TRUE DUELIST, I'LL FIGHT YOU TO GET MY RED-EYES BLACK DRAGON BACK!
KA-CHK
ON THESE STREETS I'LL FIND MY DREAM...
...AND MY GOAL!
UNTIL I FULFILL THAT VOW, I CAN'T LOSE!
BAMM
FEH!
GIVE IT UP, LOSER!
YOU CAN'T BEAT ROBA! IT WAS JUST LUCK THAT YOU BEAT ME!
ROBA CAN READ HIS OPPONENT'S HAND!
WAIT FOR ME, YUGI!
I WILL WIN AND GET TO WHERE YOU'RE WAITING...TO THE PLACE OF OUR BATTLE!!
LET'S GO!

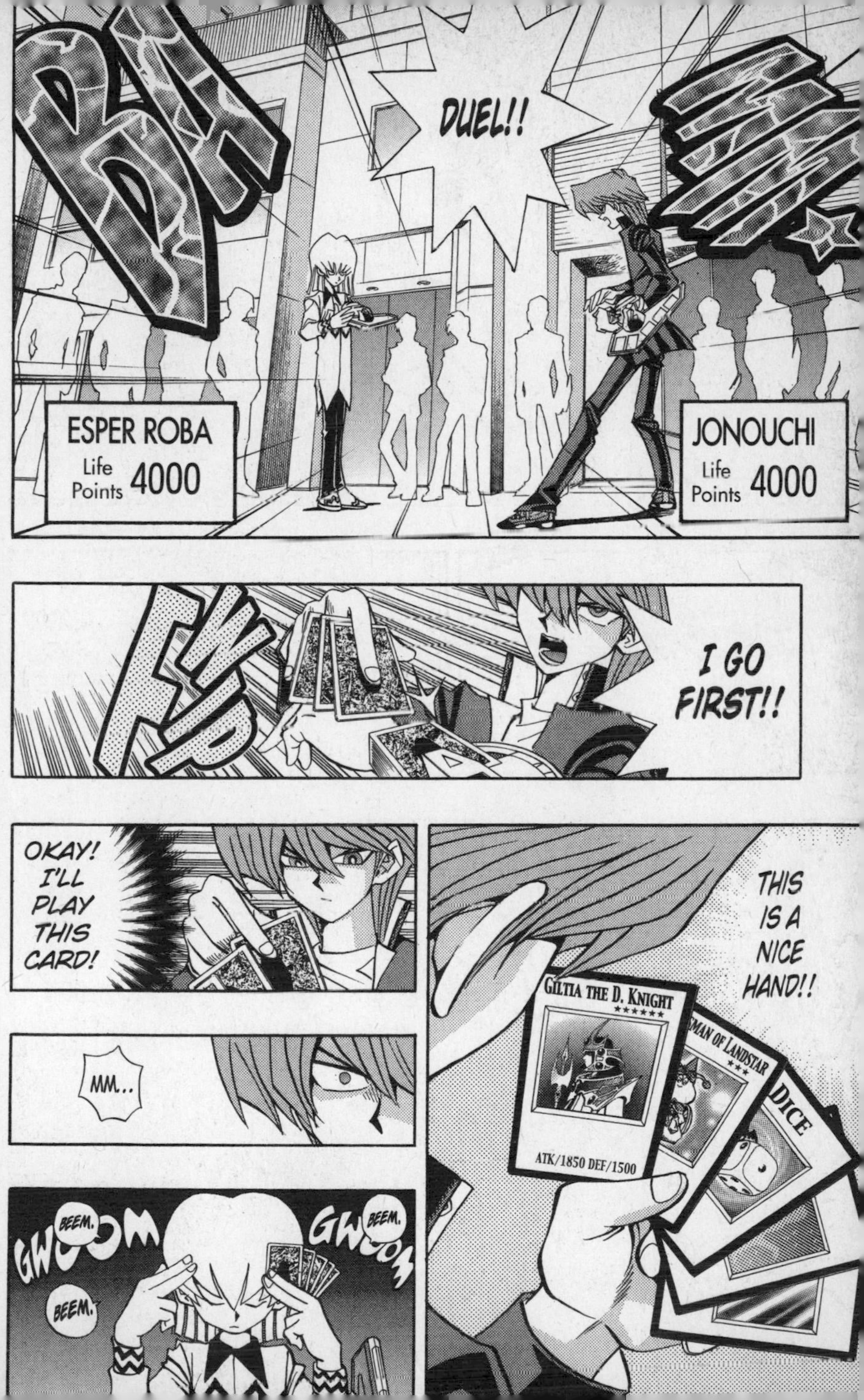
DUEL!!
JONOUCHI
Life Points 4000
ESPER ROBA
Life Points 4000
I GO FIRST!!
FWIP
THIS IS A NICE HAND!!
GILTIA THE D. KNIGHT
ATK/1850 DEF/1500
DICE
OKAY! I'LL PLAY THIS CARD!
MM...
GWOOM
BEEM.
GWOOM
BEEM.
BEEM.

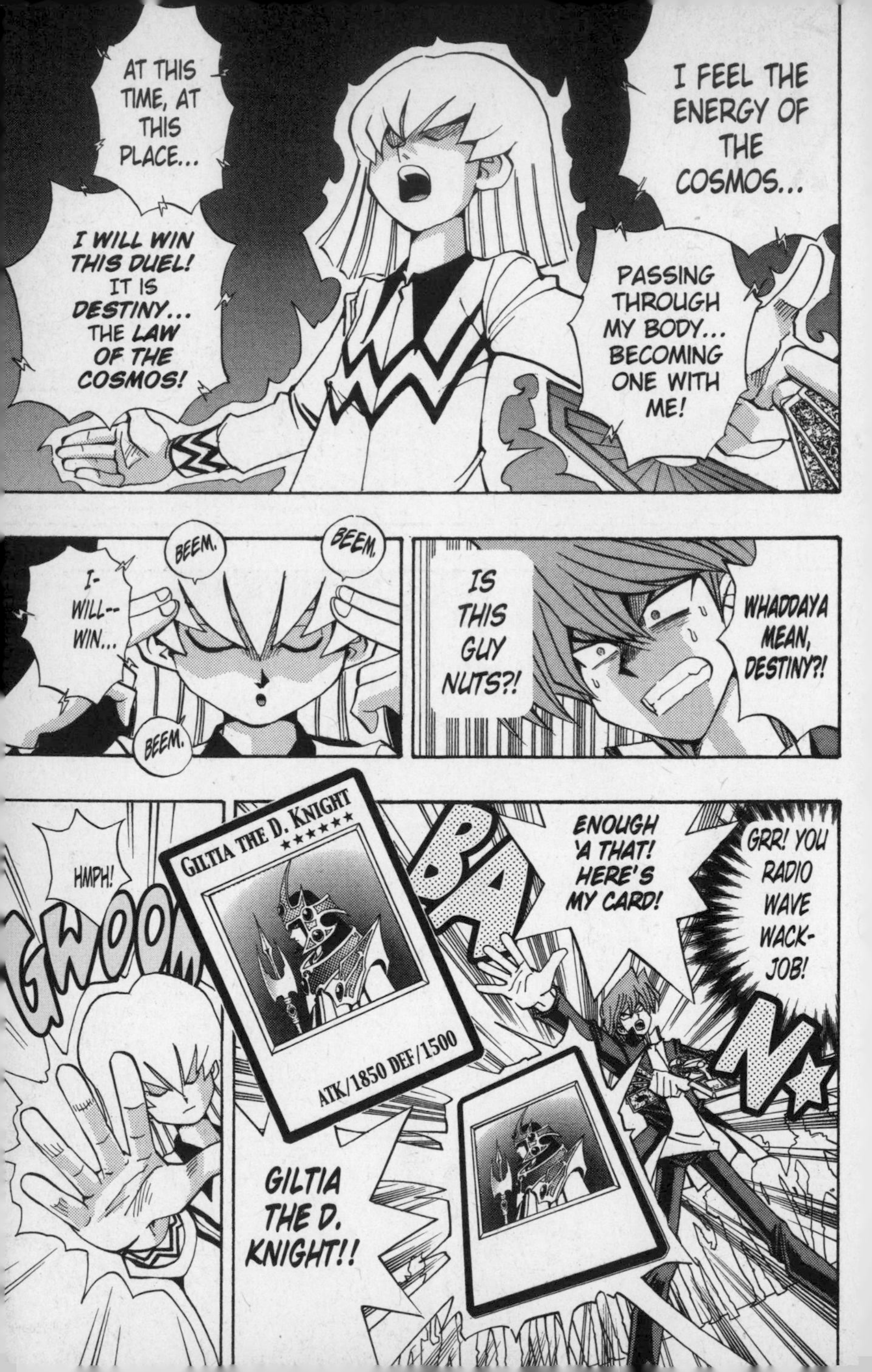
I FEEL THE ENERGY OF THE COSMOS...
PASSING THROUGH MY BODY... BECOMING ONE WITH ME!
AT THIS TIME, AT THIS PLACE...
I WILL WIN THIS DUEL! IT IS DESTINY... THE LAW OF THE COSMOS!
WHADDAYA MEAN, DESTINY?!
IS THIS GUY NUTS?!
BEEM.
BEEM.
I- WILL-- WIN...
BEEM.
GRR! YOU RADIO WAVE WACK-JOB!
ENOUGH 'A THAT! HERE'S MY CARD!
BAN
GILTIA THE D. KNIGHT
ATK/1850 DEF/1500
GILTIA THE D. KNIGHT!!
HMPH!
GWOO

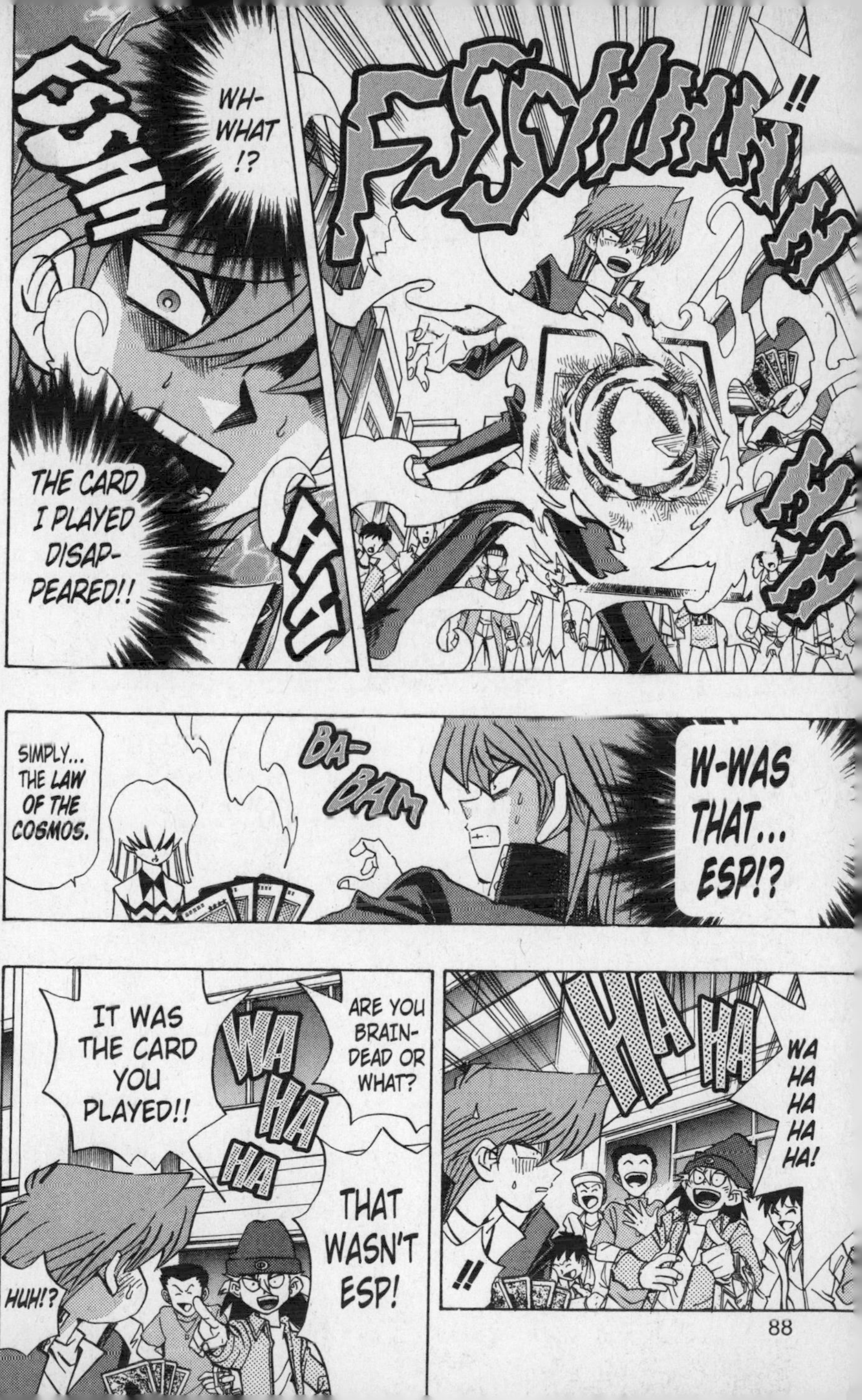
WH-WHAT!?
THE CARD I PLAYED DISAP-PEARED!!
W-WAS THAT... ESP!?
BA-BAM
SIMPLY... THE LAW OF THE COSMOS.
HA HA
WA HA HA HA HA HA!
!!
ARE YOU BRAIN-DEAD OR WHAT?
WA HA HA HA
IT WAS THE CARD YOU PLAYED!!
THAT WASN'T ESP!
HUH!?

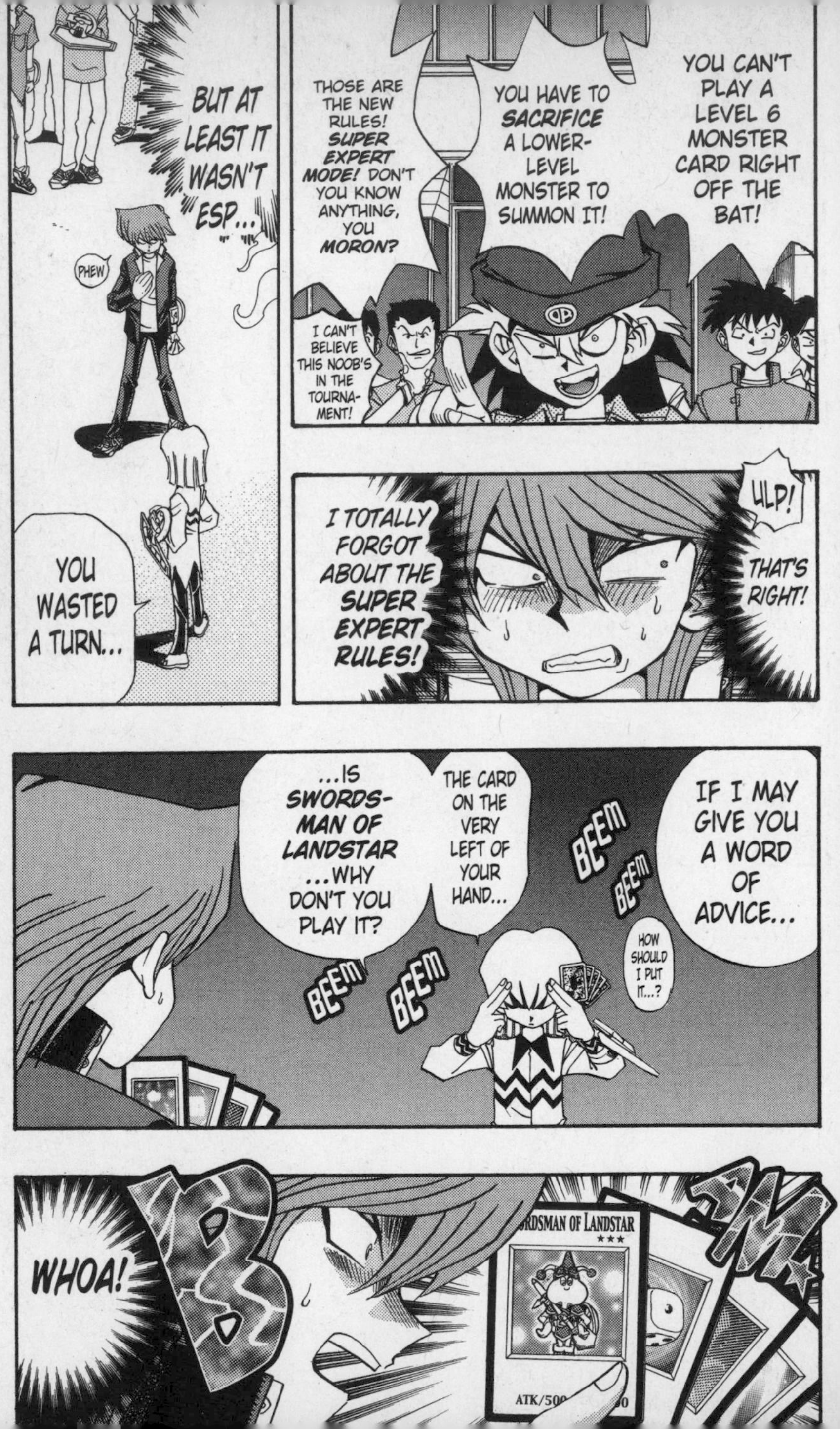

YOU CAN'T PLAY A LEVEL 6 MONSTER CARD RIGHT OFF THE BAT!
YOU HAVE TO SACRIFICE A LOWER-LEVEL MONSTER TO SUMMON IT!
THOSE ARE THE NEW RULES! SUPER EXPERT MODE! DON'T YOU KNOW ANYTHING, YOU MORON?
I CAN'T BELIEVE THIS NOOB'S IN THE TOURNAMENT!
ULP!
THAT'S RIGHT!
I TOTALLY FORGOT ABOUT THE SUPER EXPERT RULES!
BUT AT LEAST IT WASN'T ESP...
PHEW
YOU WASTED A TURN...
IF I MAY GIVE YOU A WORD OF ADVICE...
BEEM
BEEM
HOW SHOULD I PUT IT...?
THE CARD ON THE VERY LEFT OF YOUR HAND...
...IS SWORDSMAN OF LANDSTAR ...WHY DON'T YOU PLAY IT?
BEEM
BEEM
ATK/500
WHOA!

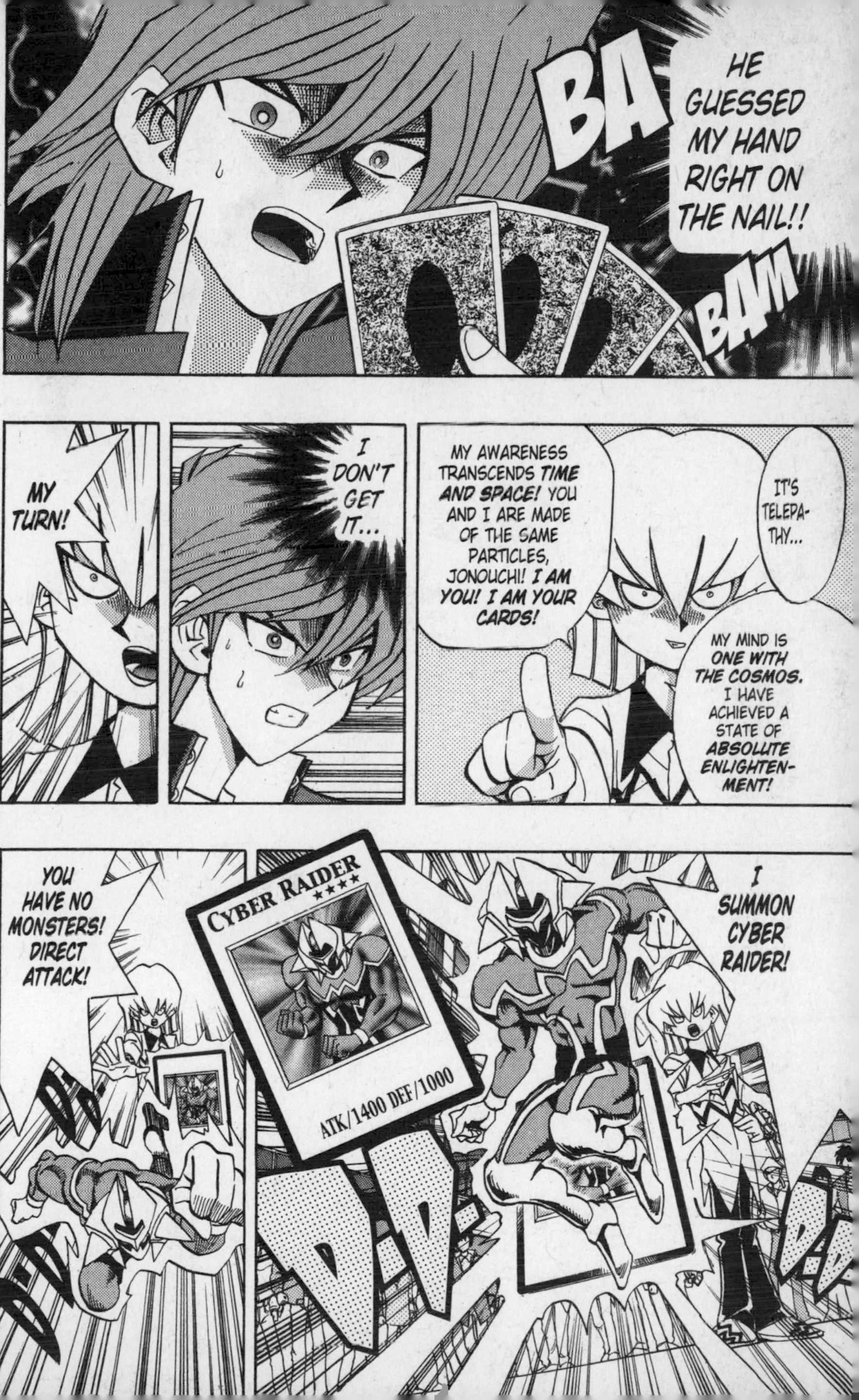
HE GUESSED MY HAND RIGHT ON THE NAIL!!
BA
BAM
IT'S TELEPATHY...
MY AWARENESS TRANSCENDS TIME AND SPACE! YOU AND I ARE MADE OF THE SAME PARTICLES, JONOUCHI! I AM YOU! I AM YOUR CARDS!
MY MIND IS ONE WITH THE COSMOS. I HAVE ACHIEVED A STATE OF ABSOLUTE ENLIGHTENMENT!
I DON'T GET IT...
MY TURN!
I SUMMON CYBER RAIDER!
CYBER RAIDER
ATK/1400 DEF/1000
YOU HAVE NO MONSTERS! DIRECT ATTACK!

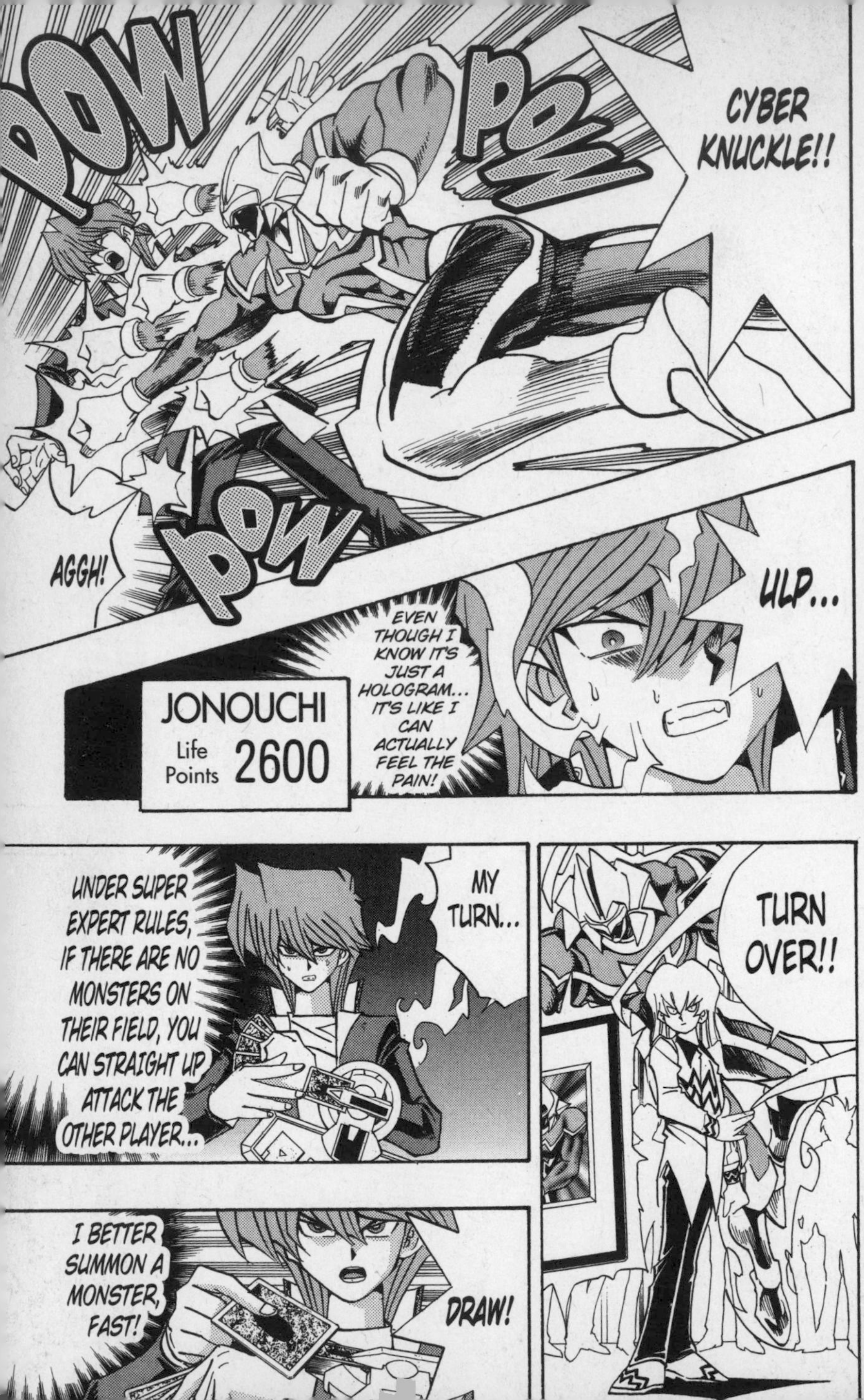
CYBER KNUCKLE!!
POW
POW
AGGH!
POW
ULP...
EVEN THOUGH I KNOW IT'S JUST A HOLOGRAM... IT'S LIKE I CAN ACTUALLY FEEL THE PAIN!
JONOUCHI
Life Points 2600
TURN OVER!!
MY TURN...
UNDER SUPER EXPERT RULES, IF THERE ARE NO MONSTERS ON THEIR FIELD, YOU CAN STRAIGHT UP ATTACK THE OTHER PLAYER...
DRAW!
I BETTER SUMMON A MONSTER, FAST!

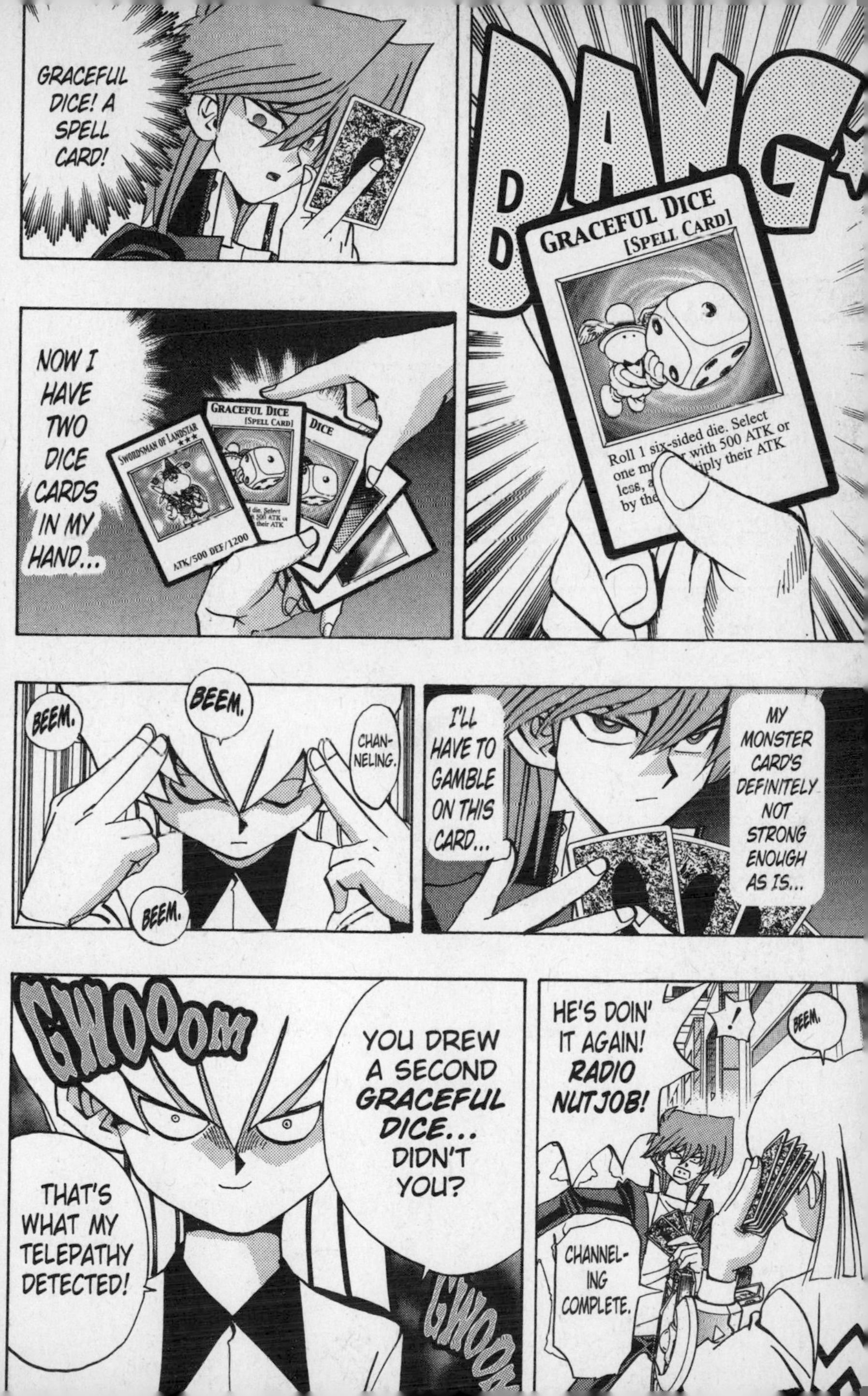
DANG
D
D
GRACEFUL DICE
[SPELL CARD]
Roll 1 six-sided die. Select
GRACEFUL DICE! A SPELL CARD!
NOW I HAVE TWO DICE CARDS IN MY HAND...
GRACEFUL DICE
[SPELL CARD]
SWORDSMAN OF LANDSTAR
ATK/500 DEF/1200
MY MONSTER CARD'S DEFINITELY NOT STRONG ENOUGH AS IS...
I'LL HAVE TO GAMBLE ON THIS CARD...
CHAN-NELING.
BEEM.
BEEM.
BEEM.
BEEM.
!
HE'S DOIN' IT AGAIN! RADIO NUTJOB!
CHANNEL-ING COMPLETE.
GWOOOM
YOU DREW A SECOND GRACEFUL DICE... DIDN'T YOU?
THAT'S WHAT MY TELEPATHY DETECTED!

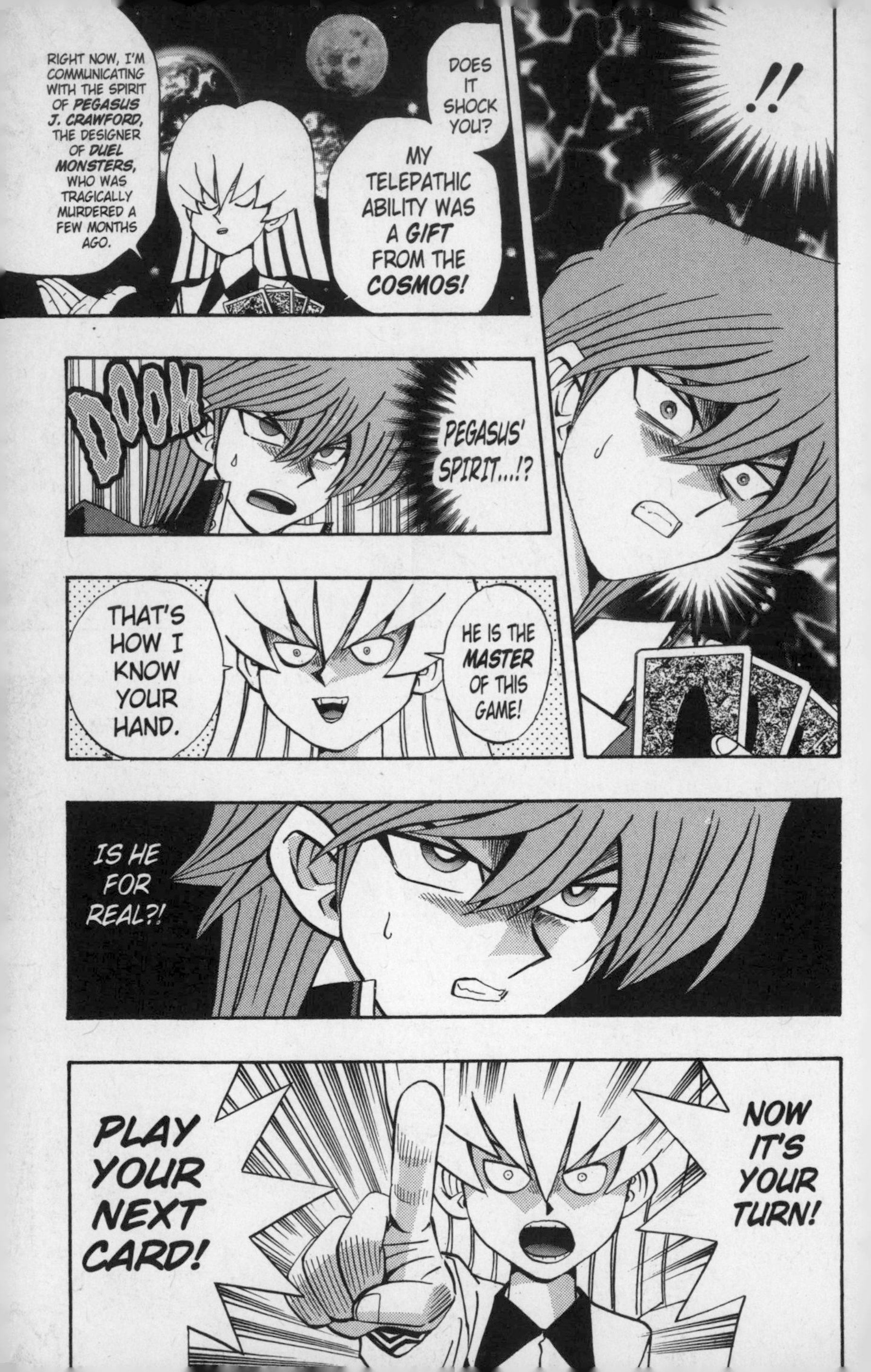
!!
DOES IT SHOCK YOU?
MY TELEPATHIC ABILITY WAS A GIFT FROM THE COSMOS!
RIGHT NOW, I'M COMMUNICATING WITH THE SPIRIT OF PEGASUS J. CRAWFORD, THE DESIGNER OF DUEL MONSTERS, WHO WAS TRAGICALLY MURDERED A FEW MONTHS AGO.
PEGASUS' SPIRIT...!?
DOOM
HE IS THE MASTER OF THIS GAME!
THAT'S HOW I KNOW YOUR HAND.
IS HE FOR REAL?!
NOW IT'S YOUR TURN!
PLAY YOUR NEXT CARD!

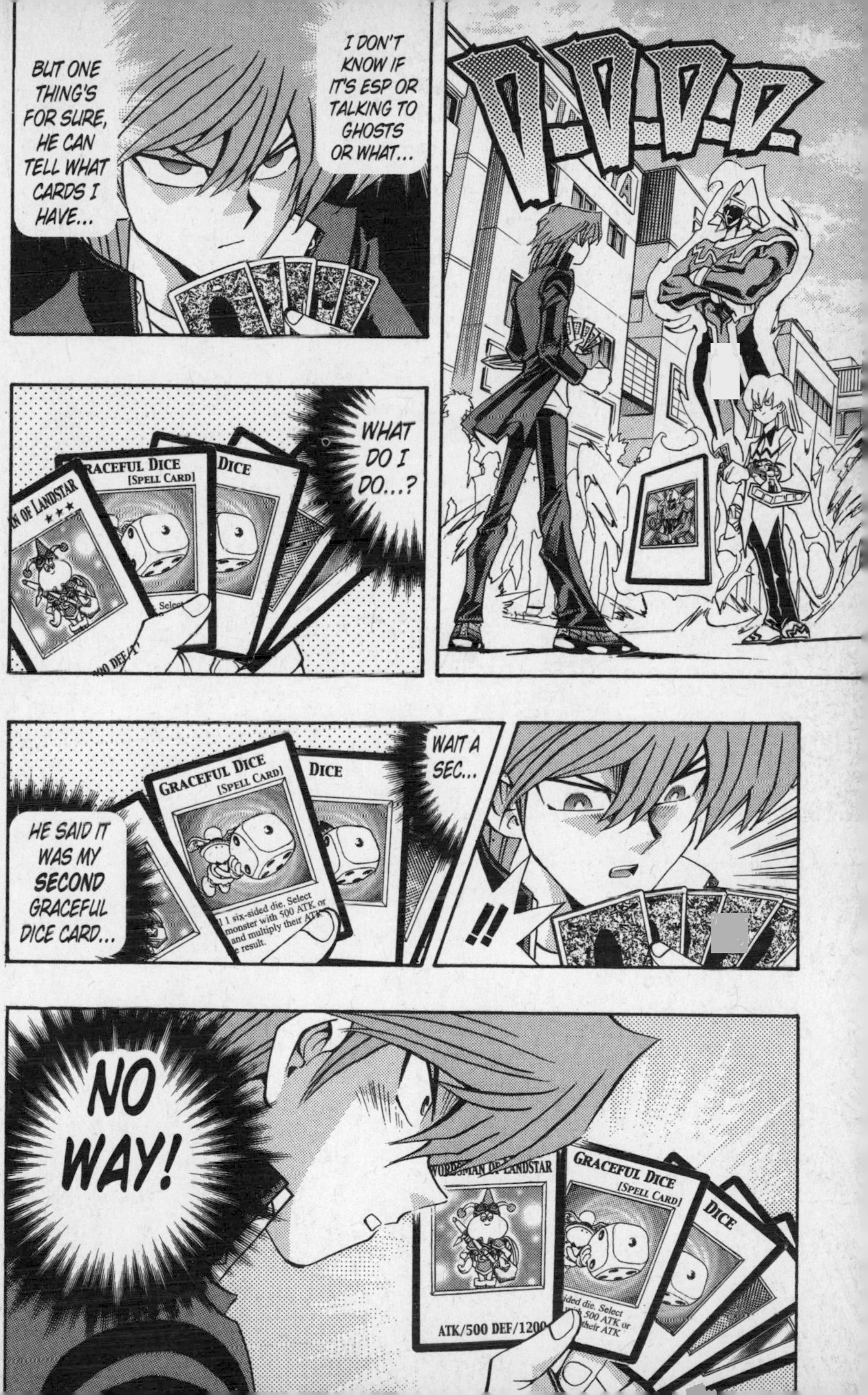
D-D-D-D
I DON'T KNOW IF IT'S ESP OR TALKING TO GHOSTS OR WHAT...
BUT ONE THING'S FOR SURE, HE CAN TELL WHAT CARDS I HAVE...
WHAT DO I DO...?
WAIT A SEC...
!!
HE SAID IT WAS MY SECOND GRACEFUL DICE CARD...
GRACEFUL DICE
[SPELL CARD]
NO WAY!
GRACEFUL DICE
[SPELL CARD]
ATK/500 DEF/1200

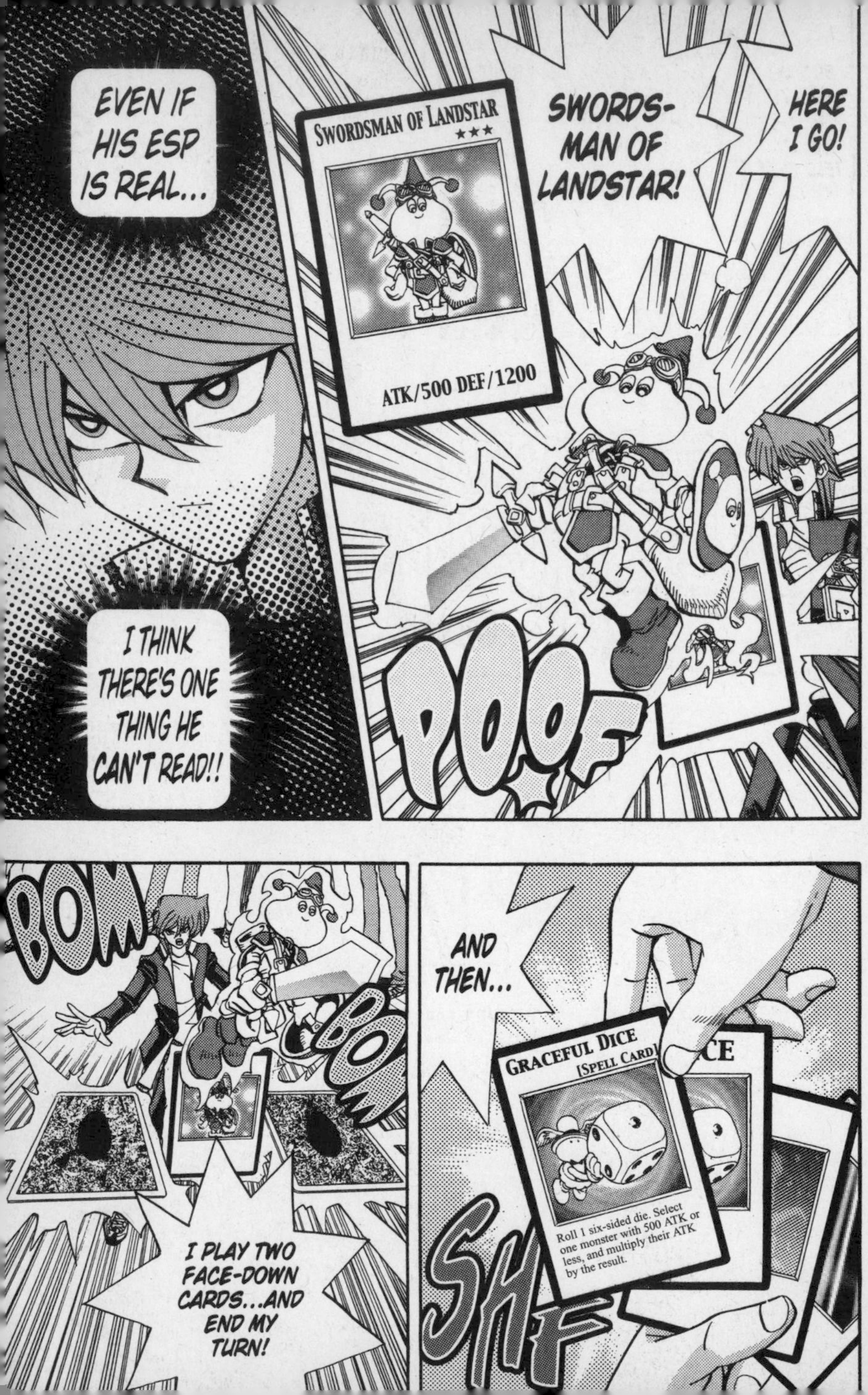
HERE I GO!
SWORDSMAN OF LANDSTAR!
SWORDSMAN OF LANDSTAR
★★★
ATK/500 DEF/1200
POOF
EVEN IF HIS ESP IS REAL...
I THINK THERE'S ONE THING HE CAN'T READ!!
AND THEN...
GRACEFUL DICE
[SPELL CARD]
Roll 1 six-sided die. Select one monster with 500 ATK or less, and multiply their ATK by the result.
SHF
BOM
BOM
I PLAY TWO FACE-DOWN CARDS...AND END MY TURN!

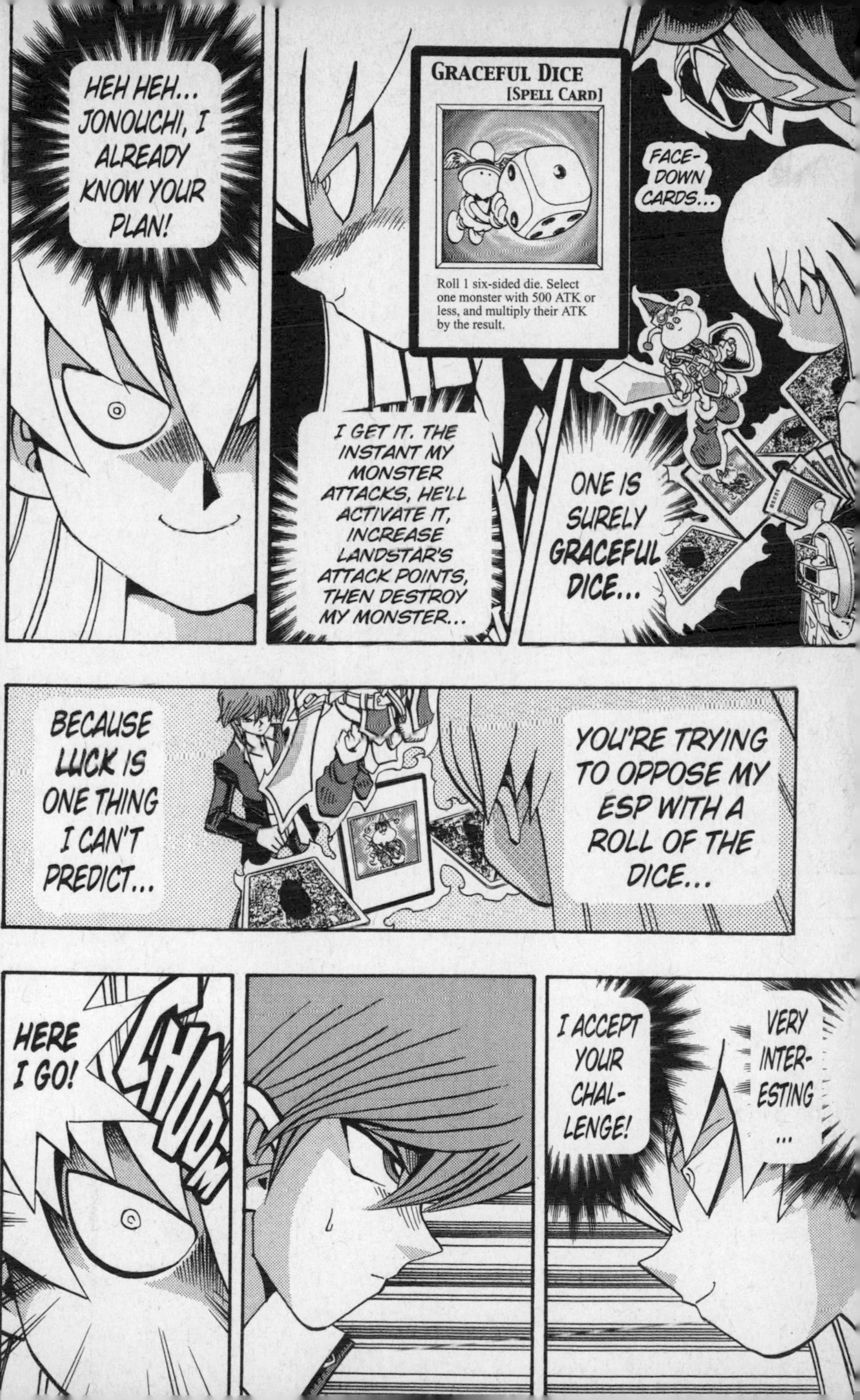
FACE-DOWN CARDS...
ONE IS SURELY GRACEFUL DICE...
GRACEFUL DICE
[SPELL CARD]
Roll 1 six-sided die. Select one monster with 500 ATK or less, and multiply their ATK by the result.
I GET IT. THE INSTANT MY MONSTER ATTACKS, HE'LL ACTIVATE IT, INCREASE LANDSTAR'S ATTACK POINTS, THEN DESTROY MY MONSTER...
HEH HEH... JONOUCHI, I ALREADY KNOW YOUR PLAN!
YOU'RE TRYING TO OPPOSE MY ESP WITH A ROLL OF THE DICE...
BECAUSE LUCK IS ONE THING I CAN'T PREDICT...
VERY INTER-ESTING...
I ACCEPT YOUR CHAL-LENGE!
CHOOM
HERE I GO!

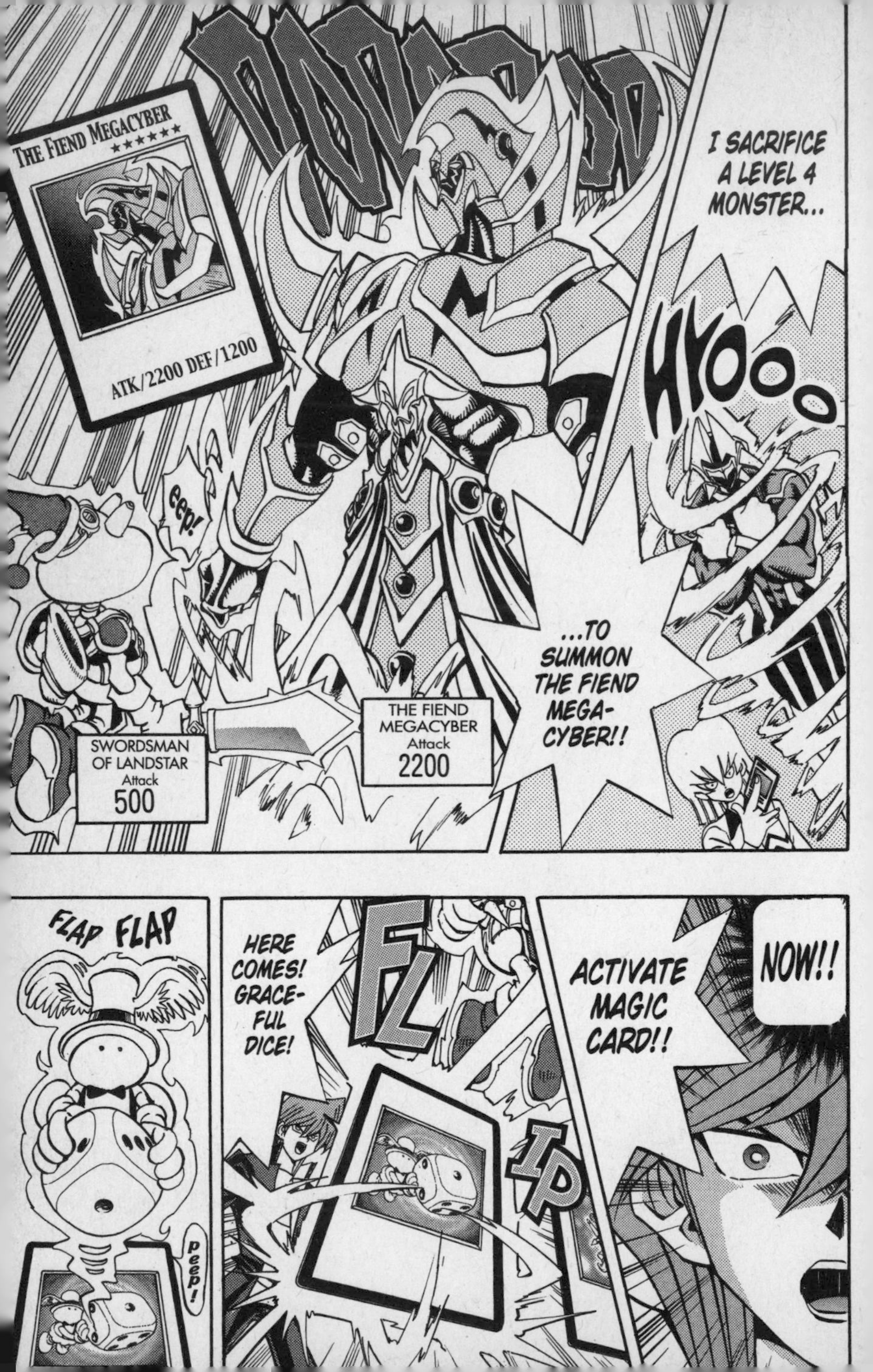
I SACRIFICE A LEVEL 4 MONSTER...
HYOOO
...TO SUMMON THE FIEND MEGA-CYBER!!
THE FIEND MEGACYBER
ATK/2200 DEF/1200
eep!
THE FIEND MEGACYBER Attack 2200
SWORDSMAN OF LANDSTAR Attack 500
NOW!!
ACTIVATE MAGIC CARD!!
FL
IP
HERE COMES! GRACE-FUL DICE!
FLAP FLAP
peep!

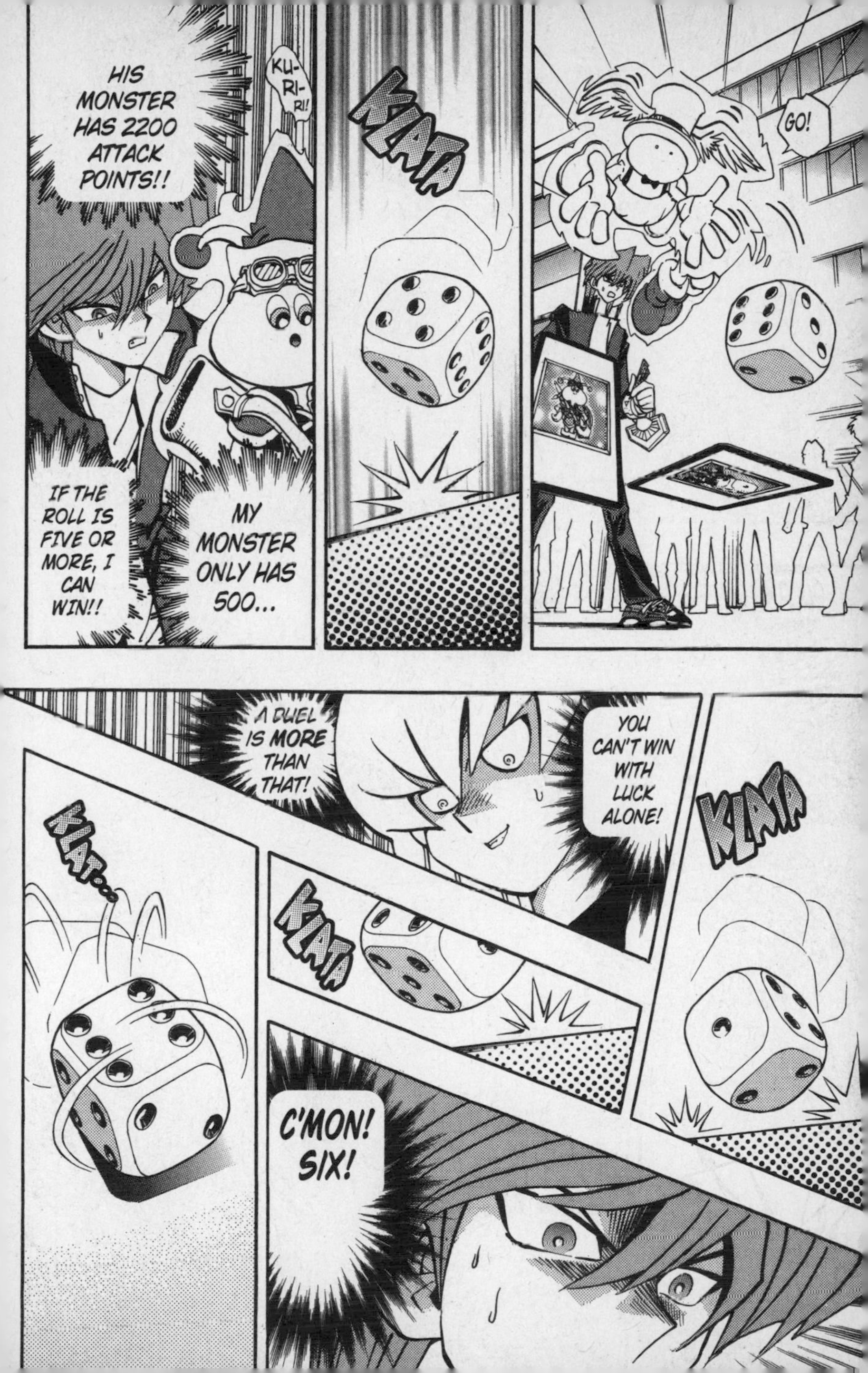
GO!
KLATA
KU-RI-RI!
HIS MONSTER HAS 2200 ATTACK POINTS!!
MY MONSTER ONLY HAS 500...
IF THE ROLL IS FIVE OR MORE, I CAN WIN!!
YOU CAN'T WIN WITH LUCK ALONE!
A DUEL IS MORE THAN THAT!
KLATA
KLATA
KLAT...
C'MON! SIX!

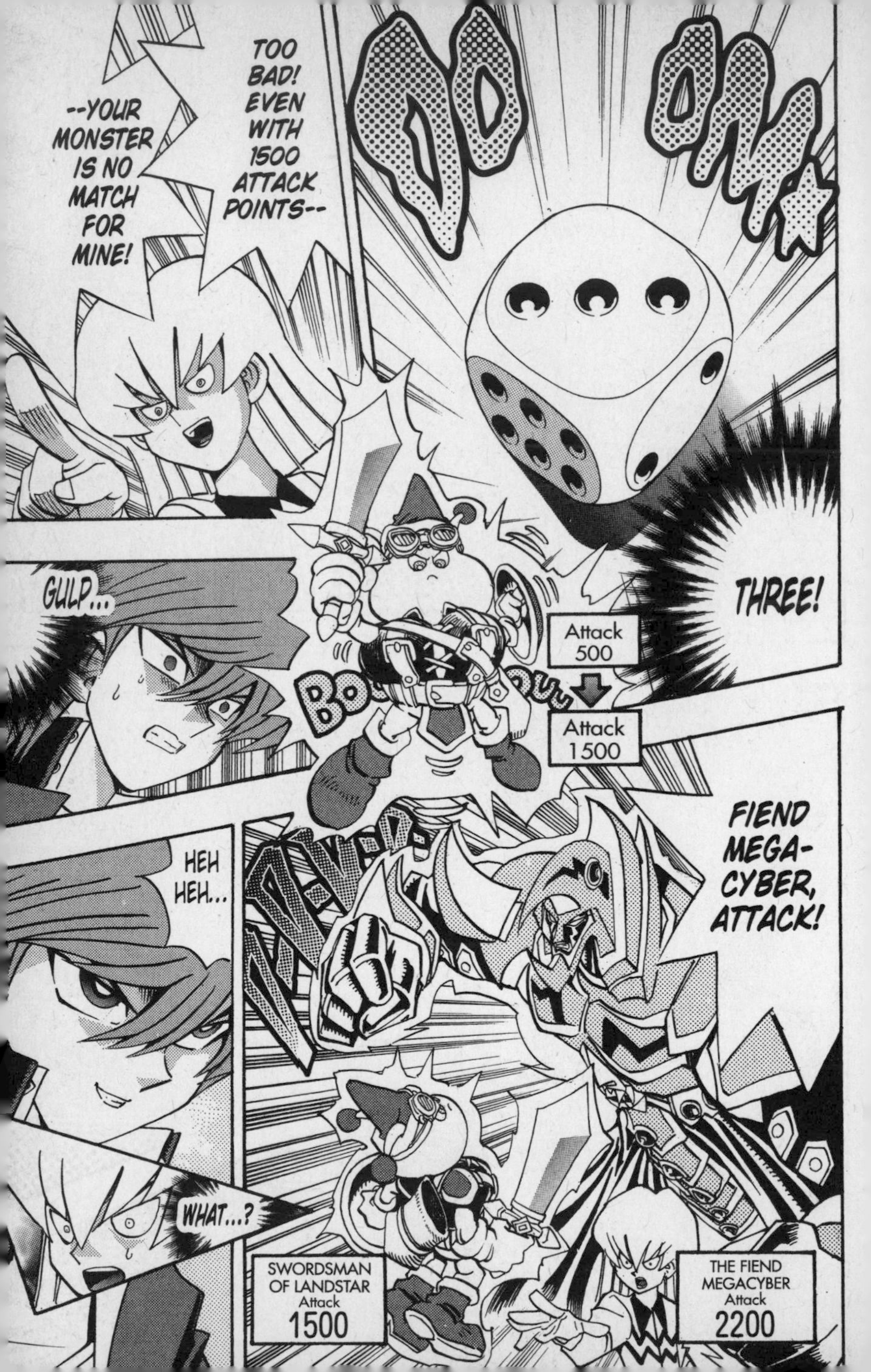
THREE!
TOO BAD! EVEN WITH 1500 ATTACK POINTS--
--YOUR MONSTER IS NO MATCH FOR MINE!
Attack 500
Attack 1500
GULP...
FIEND MEGA-CYBER, ATTACK!
THE FIEND MEGACYBER Attack 2200
SWORDSMAN OF LANDSTAR Attack 1500
HEH HEH...
WHAT...?

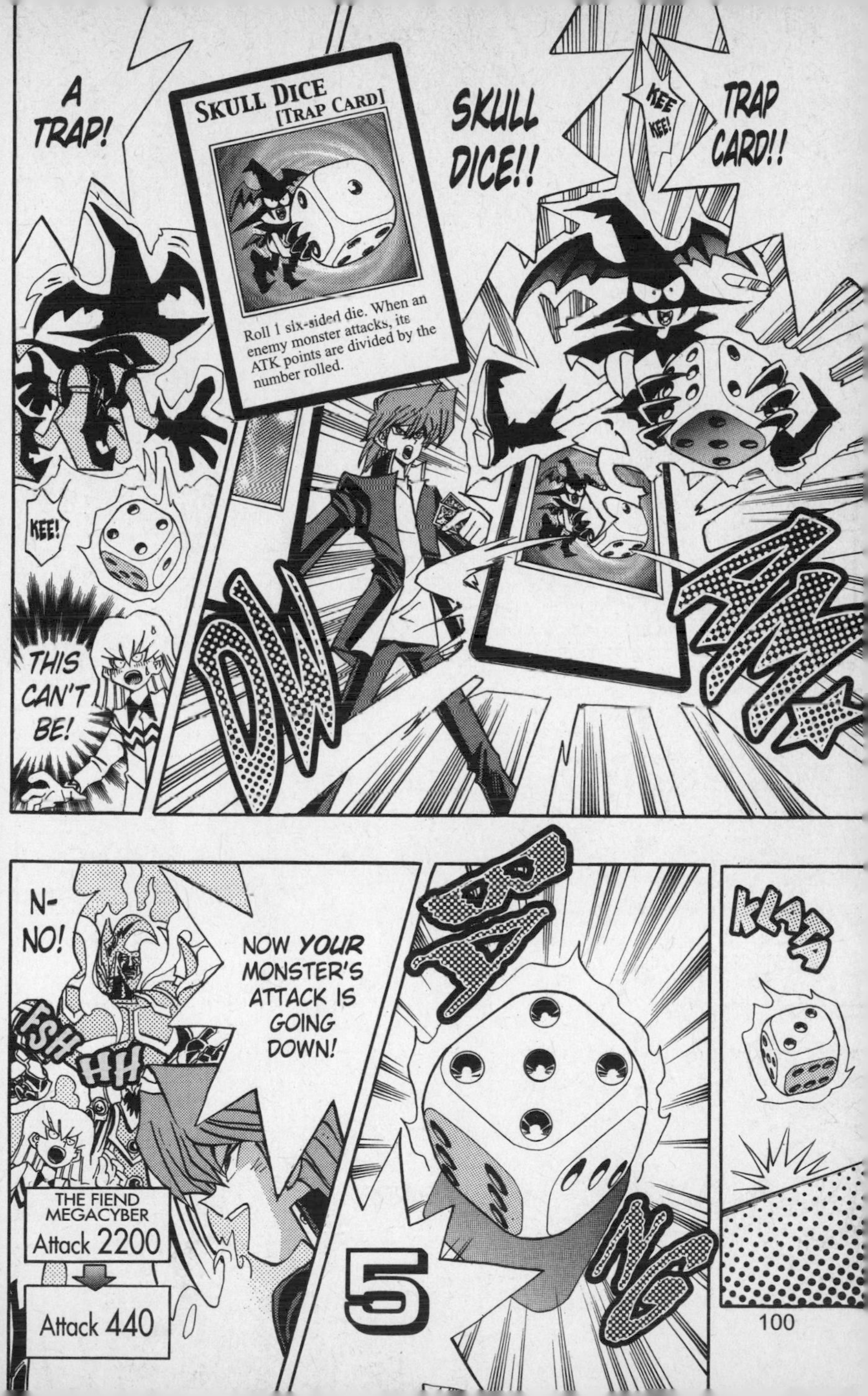
TRAP CARD!!
KEE KEE!
SKULL DICE!!
SKULL DICE [TRAP CARD]
Roll 1 six-sided die. When an enemy monster attacks, its ATK points are divided by the number rolled.
A TRAP!
KEE!
THIS CAN'T BE!
5
NOW YOUR MONSTER'S ATTACK IS GOING DOWN!
N- NO!
THE FIEND MEGACYBER
Attack 2200
Attack 440

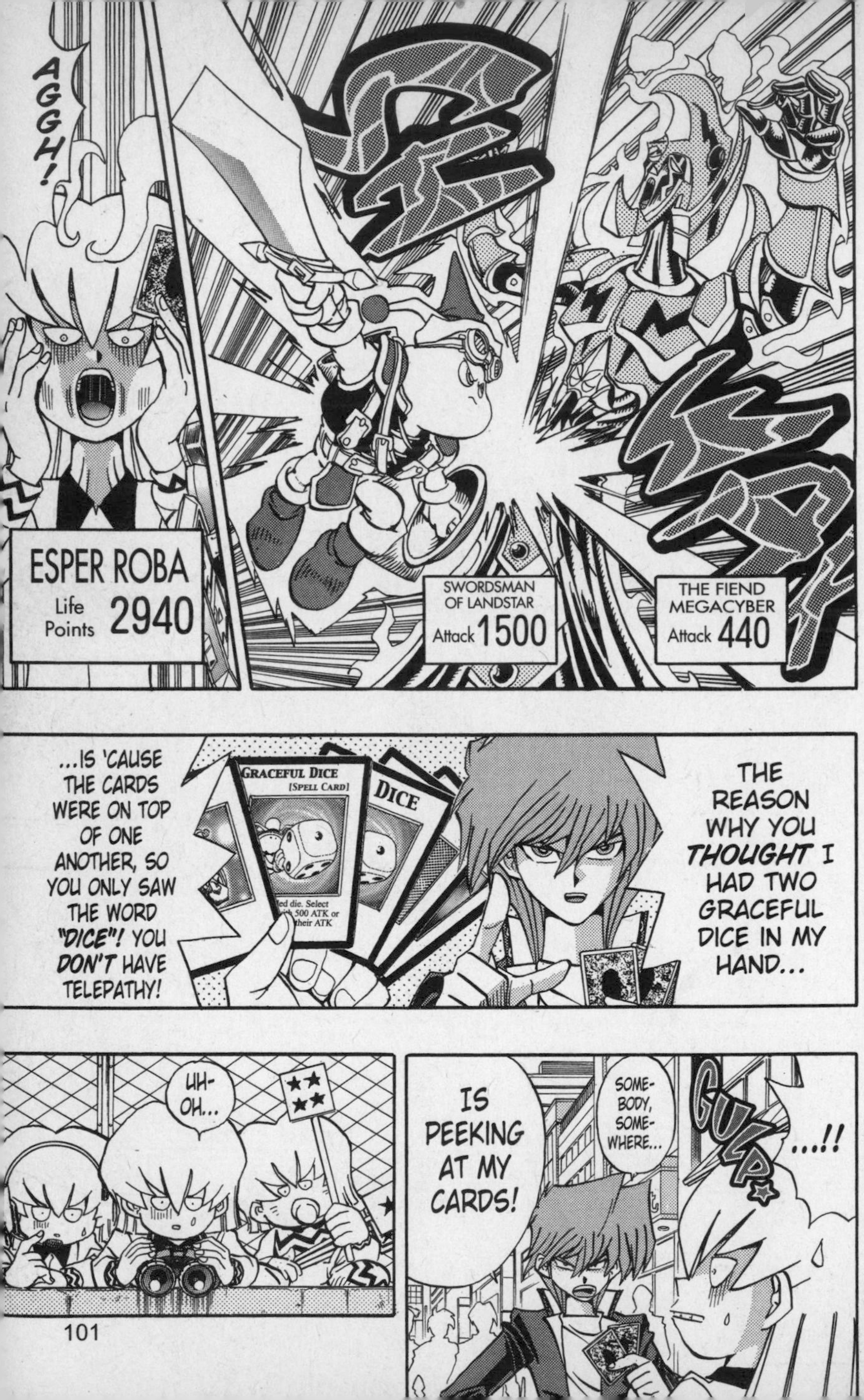
THE FIEND MEGACYBER Attack 440
SWORDSMAN OF LANDSTAR Attack 1500
ESPER ROBA Life Points 2940
AGGH!
THE REASON WHY YOU *THOUGHT* I HAD TWO GRACEFUL DICE IN MY HAND...
GRACEFUL DICE [SPELL CARD]
DICE
...IS 'CAUSE THE CARDS WERE ON TOP OF ONE ANOTHER, SO YOU ONLY SAW THE WORD *"DICE"*! YOU *DON'T* HAVE TELEPATHY!
...!!
GULP
SOME-BODY, SOME-WHERE...
IS PEEKING AT MY CARDS!
UH-OH...

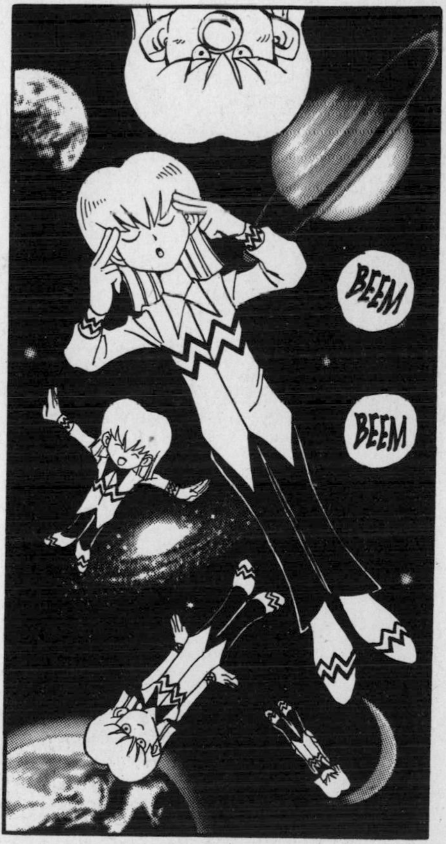
BEEM
BEEM

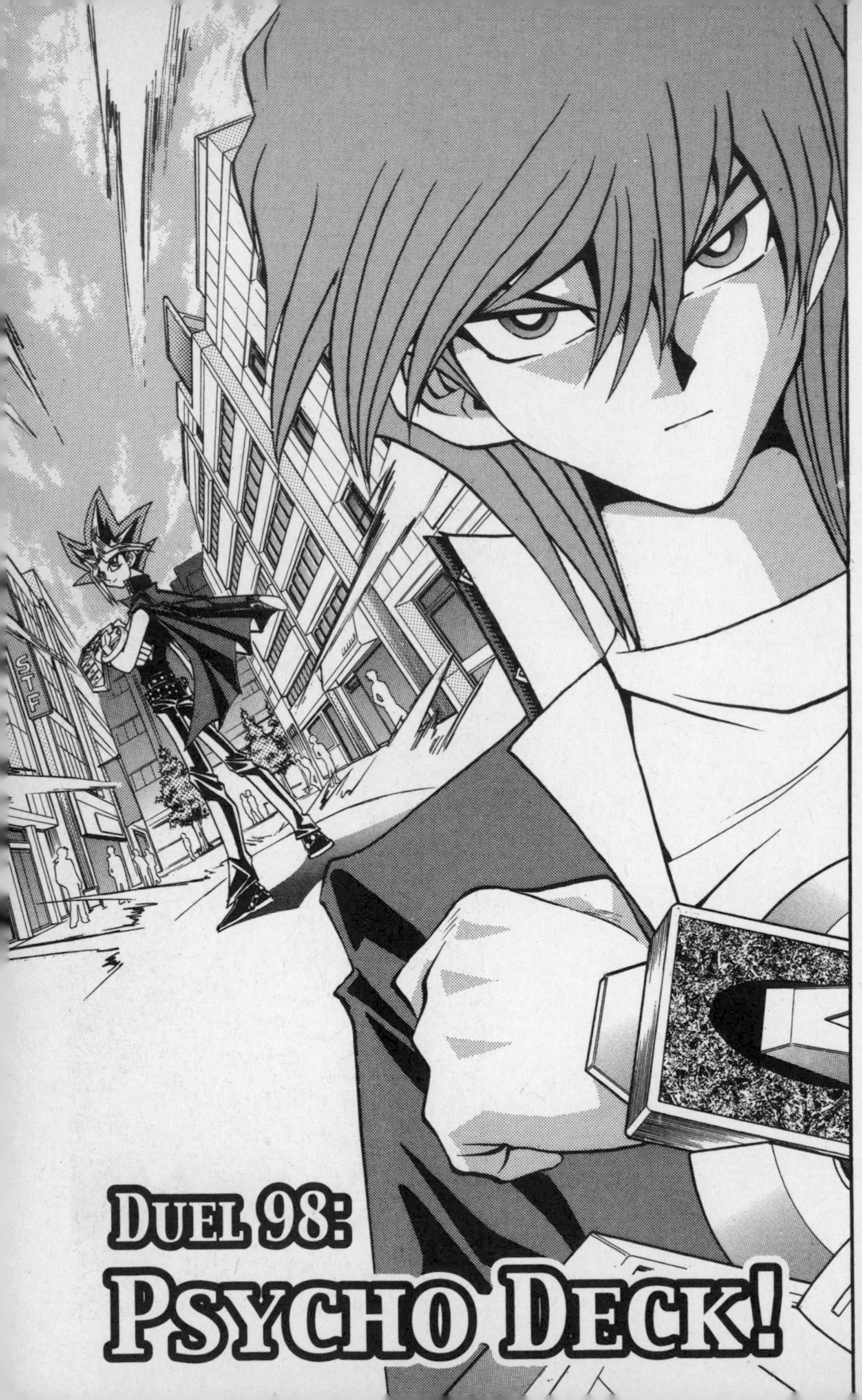
STF

Duel 98: Psycho Deck!

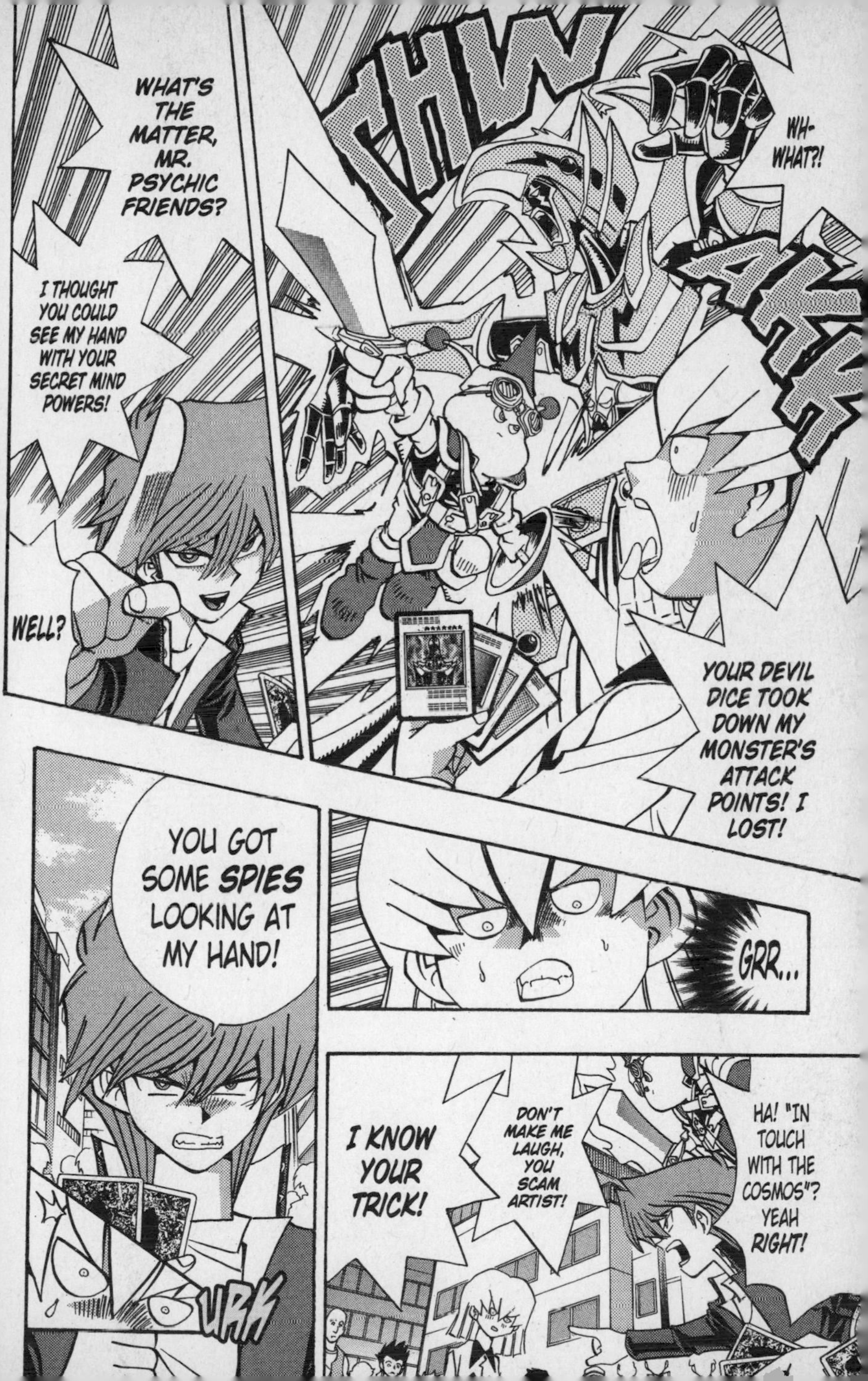
THWAK
WH-WHAT?!
YOUR DEVIL DICE TOOK DOWN MY MONSTER'S ATTACK POINTS! I LOST!
WHAT'S THE MATTER, MR. PSYCHIC FRIENDS?
I THOUGHT YOU COULD SEE MY HAND WITH YOUR SECRET MIND POWERS!
WELL?
GRR...
HA! "IN TOUCH WITH THE COSMOS"? YEAH RIGHT!
DON'T MAKE ME LAUGH, YOU SCAM ARTIST!
I KNOW YOUR TRICK!
YOU GOT SOME SPIES LOOKING AT MY HAND!
URK

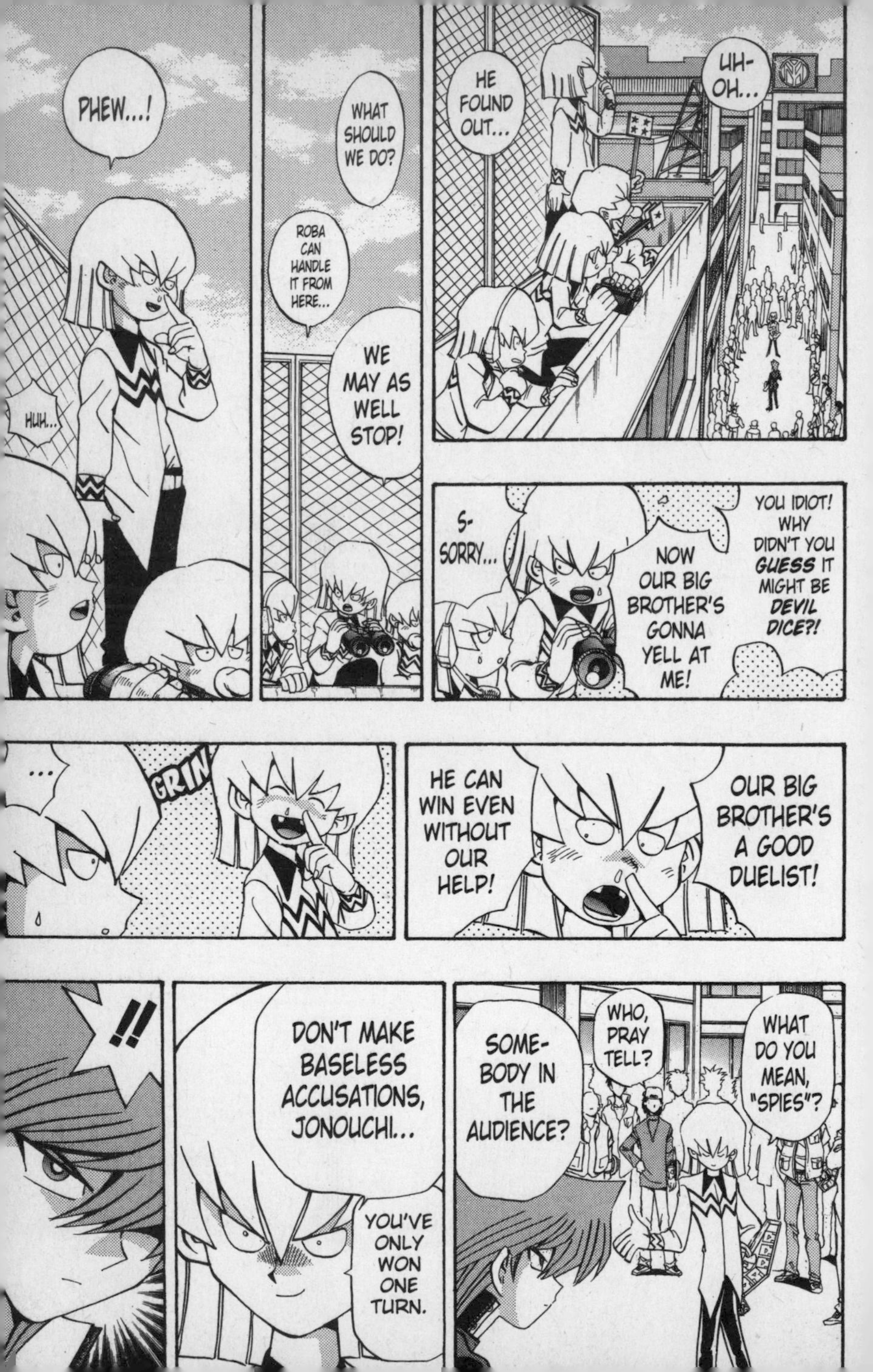
UH-OH...
HE FOUND OUT...
YOU IDIOT! WHY DIDN'T YOU GUESS IT MIGHT BE DEVIL DICE?!
NOW OUR BIG BROTHER'S GONNA YELL AT ME!
S-SORRY...
WHAT SHOULD WE DO?
ROBA CAN HANDLE IT FROM HERE...
WE MAY AS WELL STOP!
PHEW...!
HUH...
OUR BIG BROTHER'S A GOOD DUELIST!
HE CAN WIN EVEN WITHOUT OUR HELP!
GRIN
...
WHAT DO YOU MEAN, "SPIES"?
WHO, PRAY TELL?
SOME-BODY IN THE AUDIENCE?
DON'T MAKE BASELESS ACCUSATIONS, JONOUCHI...
YOU'VE ONLY WON ONE TURN.
!!

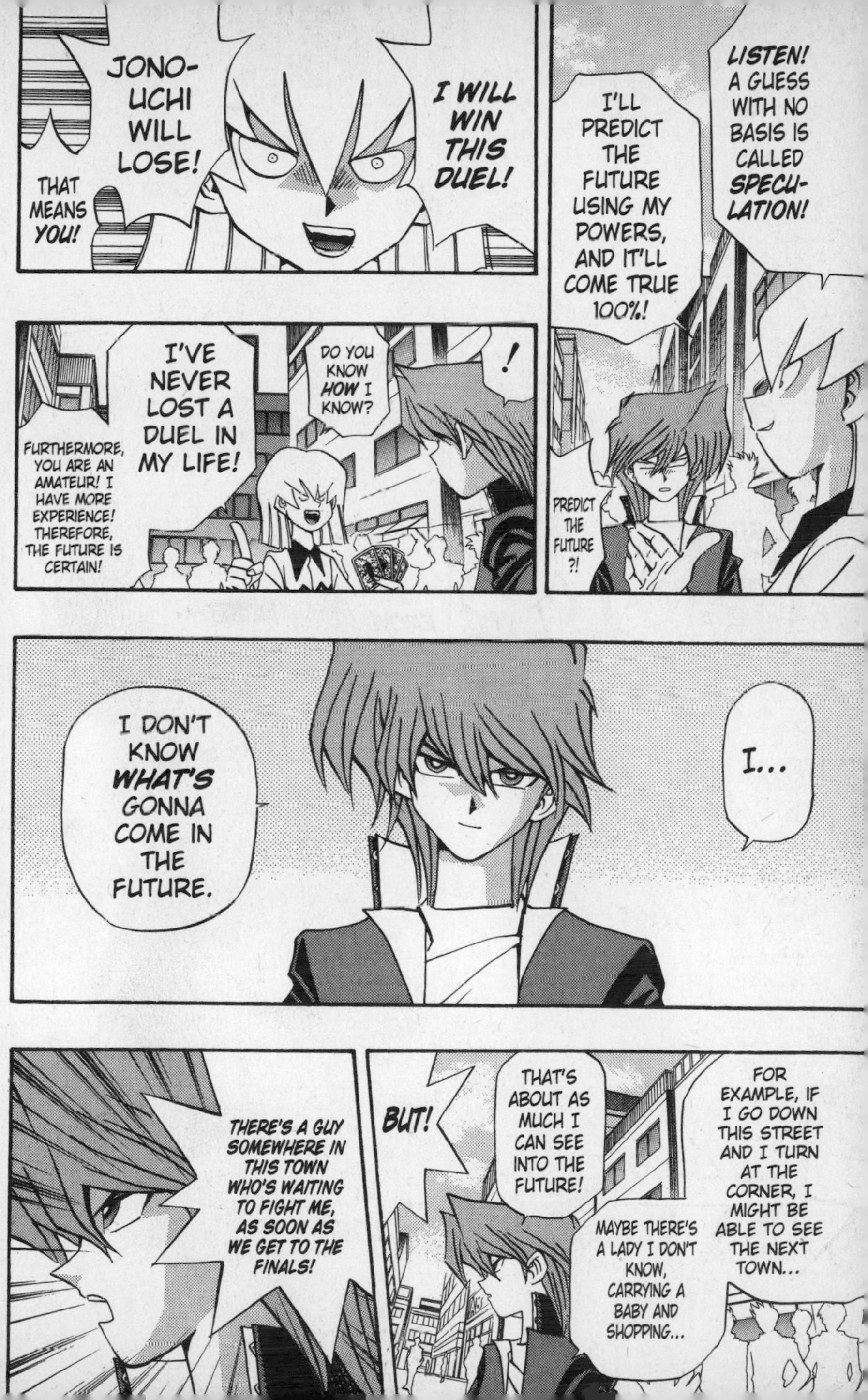
LISTEN! A GUESS WITH NO BASIS IS CALLED SPECULATION!
I'LL PREDICT THE FUTURE USING MY POWERS, AND IT'LL COME TRUE 100%!
PREDICT THE FUTURE ?!
I WILL WIN THIS DUEL!
JONOUCHI WILL LOSE!
THAT MEANS YOU!
!
DO YOU KNOW HOW I KNOW?
I'VE NEVER LOST A DUEL IN MY LIFE!
FURTHERMORE, YOU ARE AN AMATEUR! I HAVE MORE EXPERIENCE! THEREFORE, THE FUTURE IS CERTAIN!
I...
I DON'T KNOW WHAT'S GONNA COME IN THE FUTURE.
FOR EXAMPLE, IF I GO DOWN THIS STREET AND I TURN AT THE CORNER, I MIGHT BE ABLE TO SEE THE NEXT TOWN...
MAYBE THERE'S A LADY I DON'T KNOW, CARRYING A BABY AND SHOPPING...
THAT'S ABOUT AS MUCH I CAN SEE INTO THE FUTURE!
BUT!
THERE'S A GUY SOMEWHERE IN THIS TOWN WHO'S WAITING TO FIGHT ME, AS SOON AS WE GET TO THE FINALS!

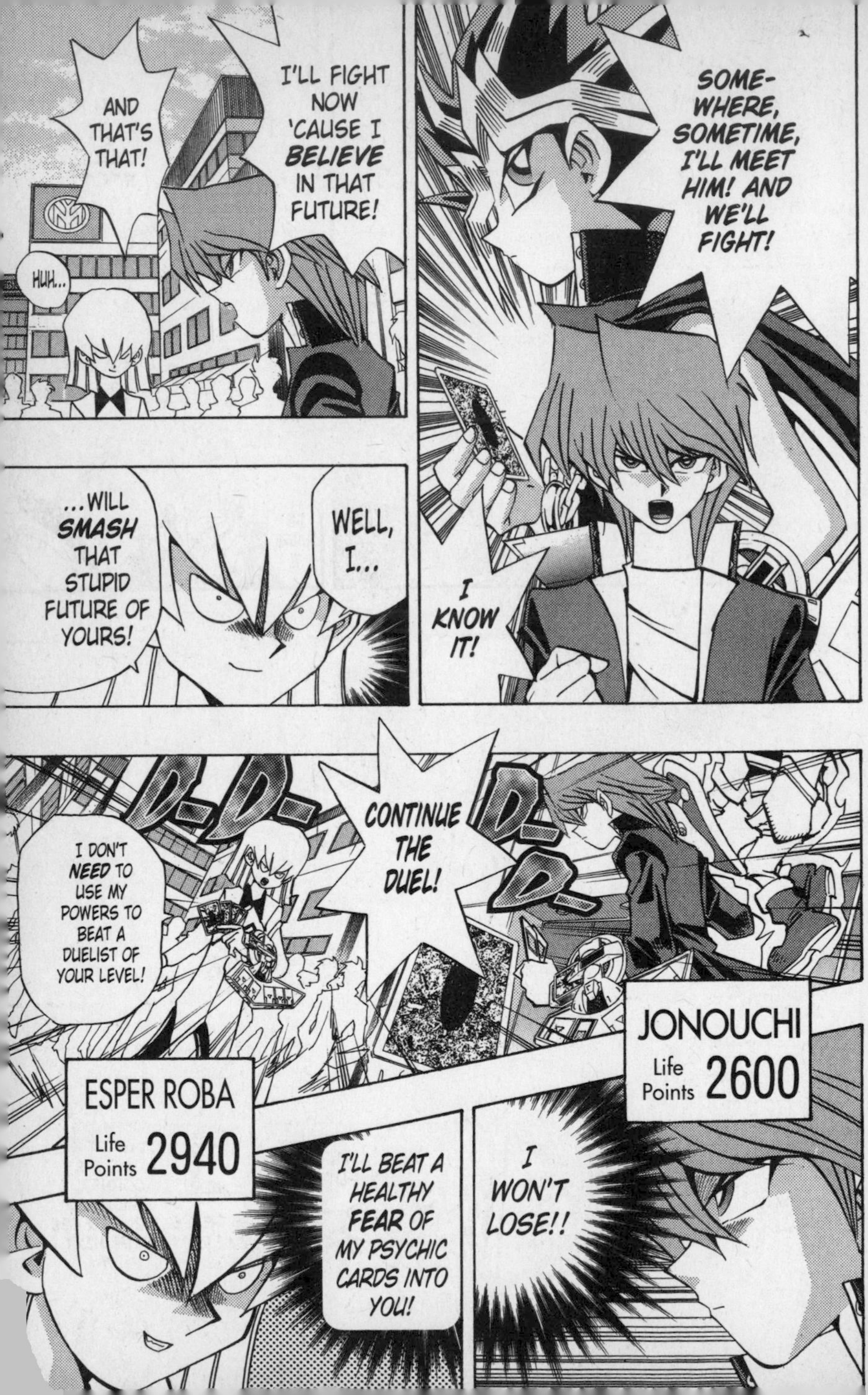
SOME-WHERE, SOMETIME, I'LL MEET HIM! AND WE'LL FIGHT!
I KNOW IT!
I'LL FIGHT NOW 'CAUSE I BELIEVE IN THAT FUTURE!
AND THAT'S THAT!
HUH...
WELL, I...
...WILL SMASH THAT STUPID FUTURE OF YOURS!
D-D-
D-D-
CONTINUE THE DUEL!
JONOUCHI Life Points 2600
I DON'T NEED TO USE MY POWERS TO BEAT A DUELIST OF YOUR LEVEL!
ESPER ROBA Life Points 2940
I WON'T LOSE!!
I'LL BEAT A HEALTHY FEAR OF MY PSYCHIC CARDS INTO YOU!

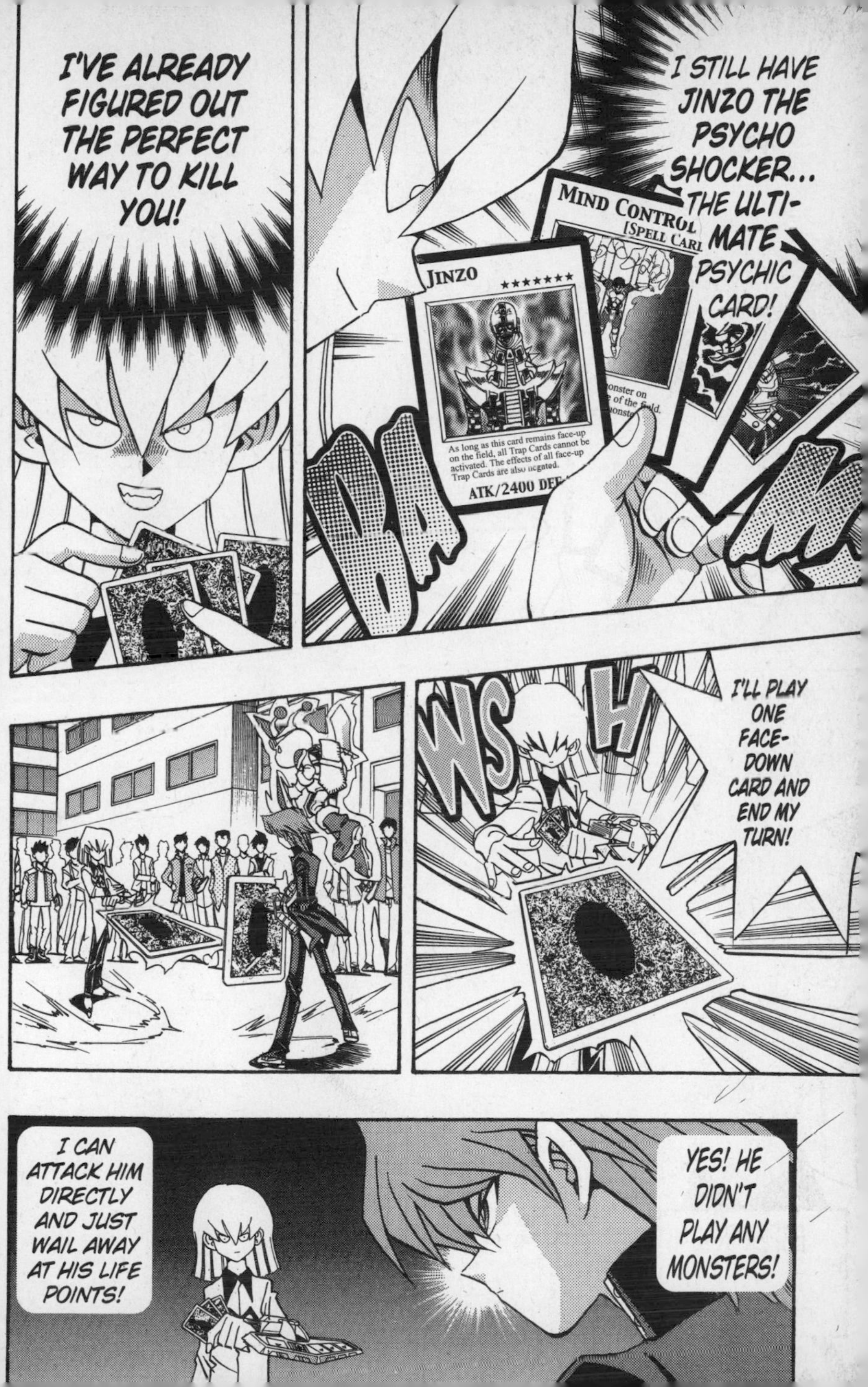
I STILL HAVE JINZO THE PSYCHO SHOCKER... THE ULTIMATE PSYCHIC CARD!
MIND CONTROL
[SPELL CARD]
JINZO
As long as this card remains face-up on the field, all Trap Cards cannot be activated. The effects of all face-up Trap Cards are also negated.
ATK/2400
I'VE ALREADY FIGURED OUT THE PERFECT WAY TO KILL YOU!
I'LL PLAY ONE FACE-DOWN CARD AND END MY TURN!
YES! HE DIDN'T PLAY ANY MONSTERS!
I CAN ATTACK HIM DIRECTLY AND JUST WAIL AWAY AT HIS LIFE POINTS!

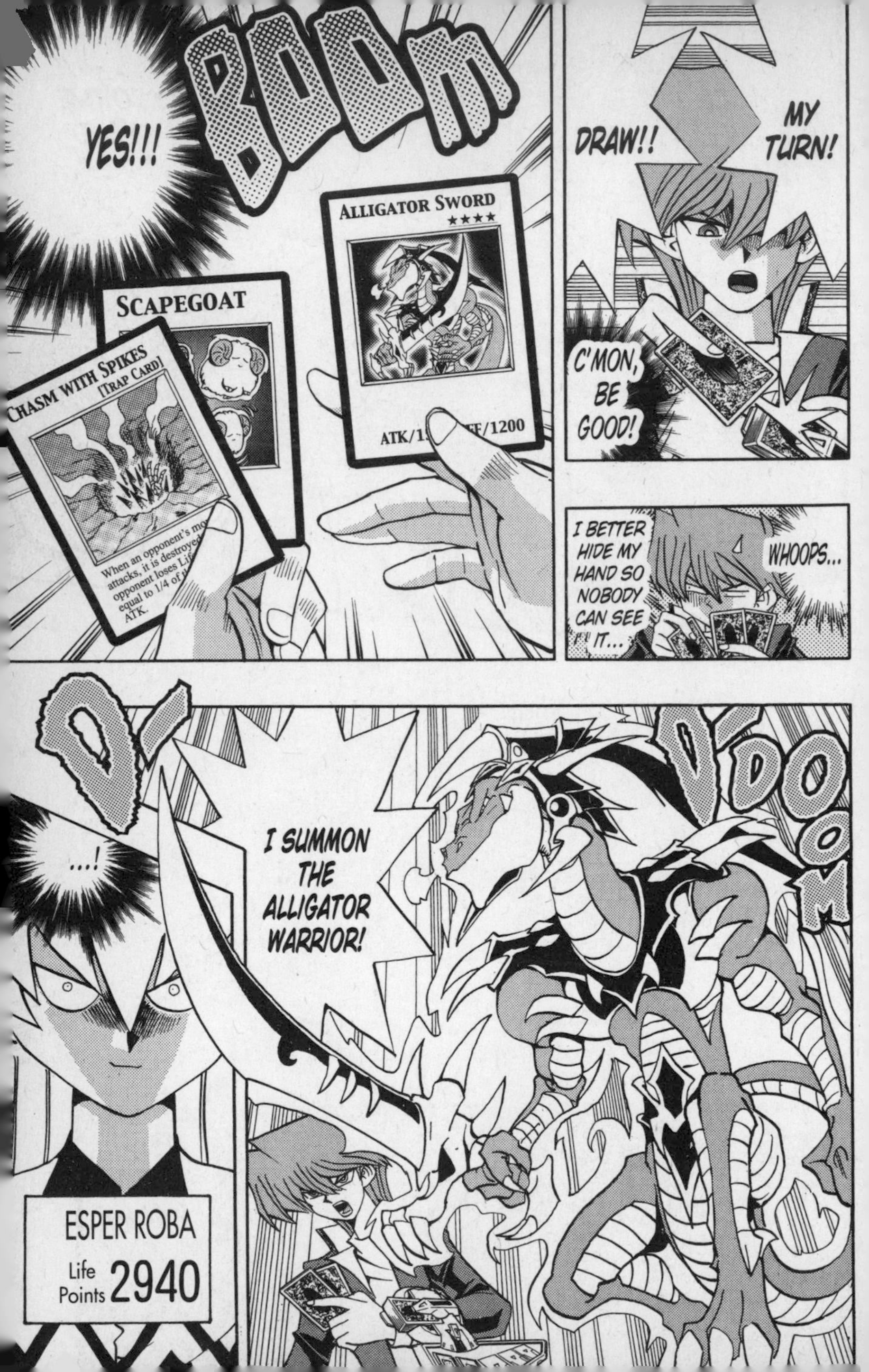
MY TURN!
DRAW!!
C'MON, BE GOOD!
WHOOPS...
I BETTER HIDE MY HAND SO NOBODY CAN SEE IT...
BOOM
YES!!!
ALLIGATOR SWORD
SCAPEGOAT
CHASM WITH SPIKES [TRAP CARD]
D-DOOOM
I SUMMON THE ALLIGATOR WARRIOR!
D-
...!
ESPER ROBA
Life Points 2940

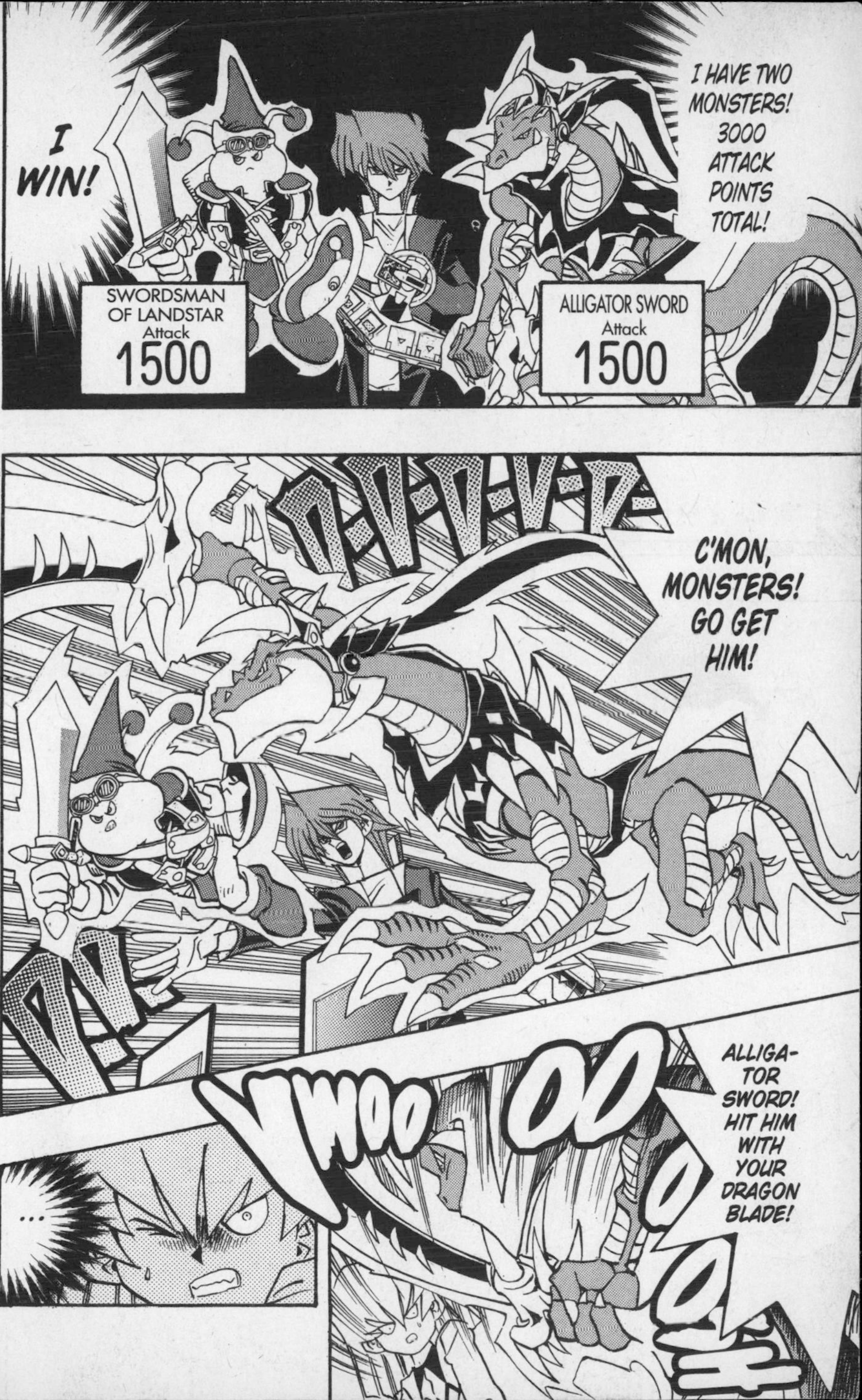
I HAVE TWO MONSTERS! 3000 ATTACK POINTS TOTAL!
I WIN!
ALLIGATOR SWORD
Attack
1500
SWORDSMAN OF LANDSTAR
Attack
1500
C'MON, MONSTERS! GO GET HIM!
ALLIGA-TOR SWORD! HIT HIM WITH YOUR DRAGON BLADE!
...

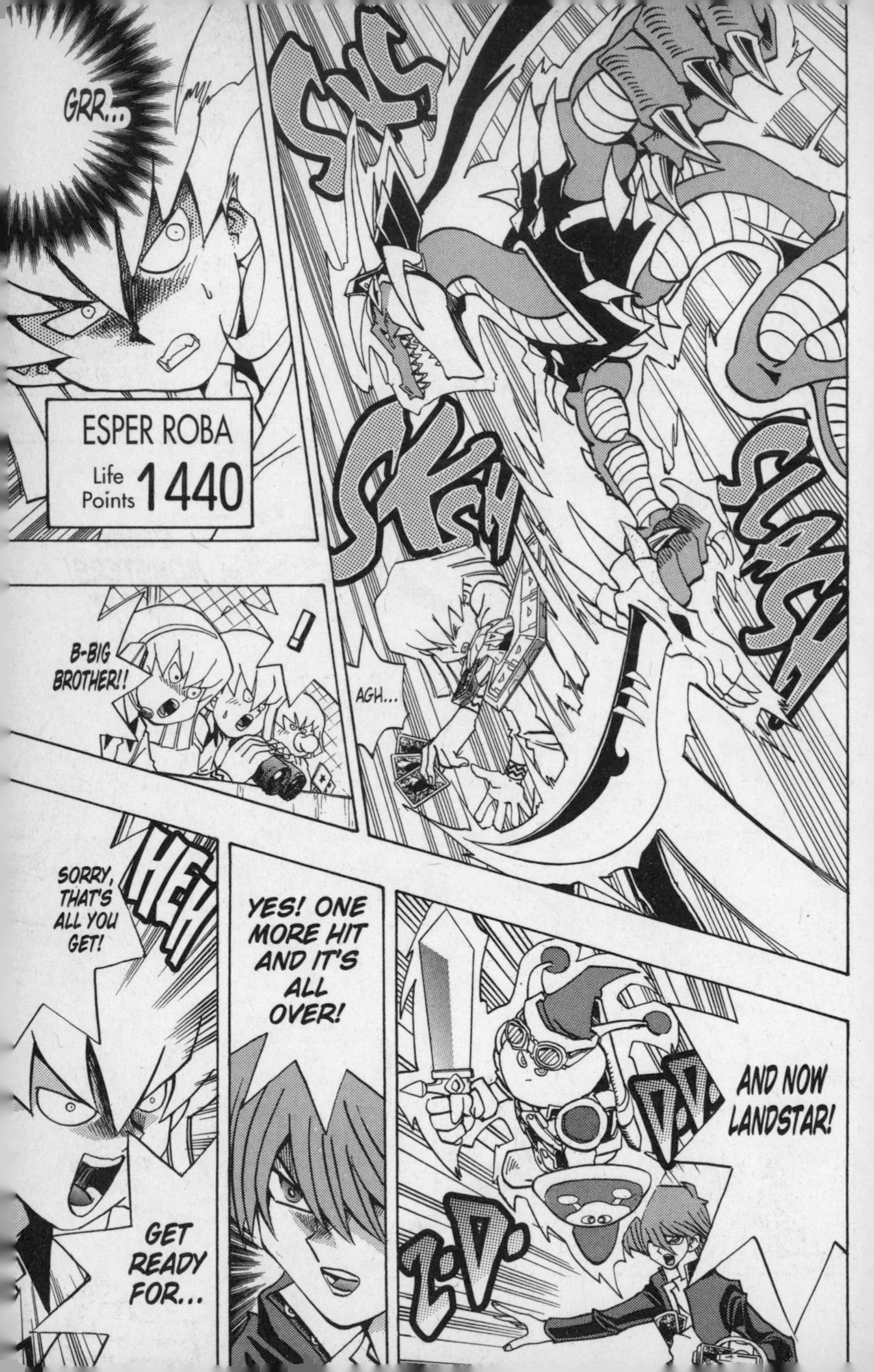

AGH...
GRR...
ESPER ROBA
Life Points 1440
!
B-BIG BROTHER!!
AND NOW LANDSTAR!
YES! ONE MORE HIT AND IT'S ALL OVER!
HEH
SORRY, THAT'S ALL YOU GET!
GET READY FOR...

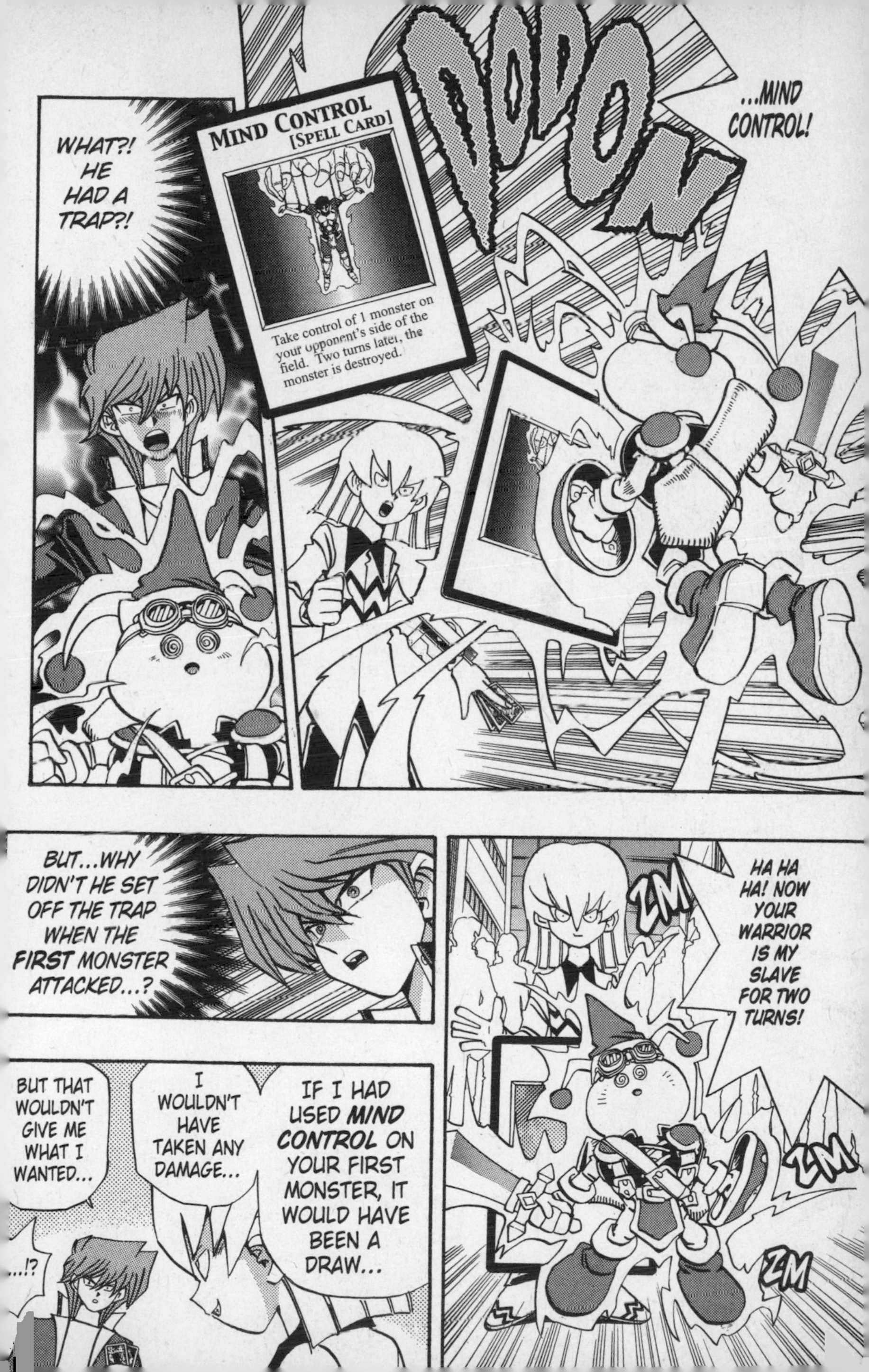
...MIND CONTROL!
DODON
MIND CONTROL [SPELL CARD]
Take control of 1 monster on your opponent's side of the field. Two turns later, the monster is destroyed.
WHAT?! HE HAD A TRAP?!
HA HA HA! NOW YOUR WARRIOR IS MY SLAVE FOR TWO TURNS!
ZM
ZM
ZM
BUT...WHY DIDN'T HE SET OFF THE TRAP WHEN THE FIRST MONSTER ATTACKED...?
IF I HAD USED MIND CONTROL ON YOUR FIRST MONSTER, IT WOULD HAVE BEEN A DRAW...
I WOULDN'T HAVE TAKEN ANY DAMAGE...
BUT THAT WOULDN'T GIVE ME WHAT I WANTED...
...!?

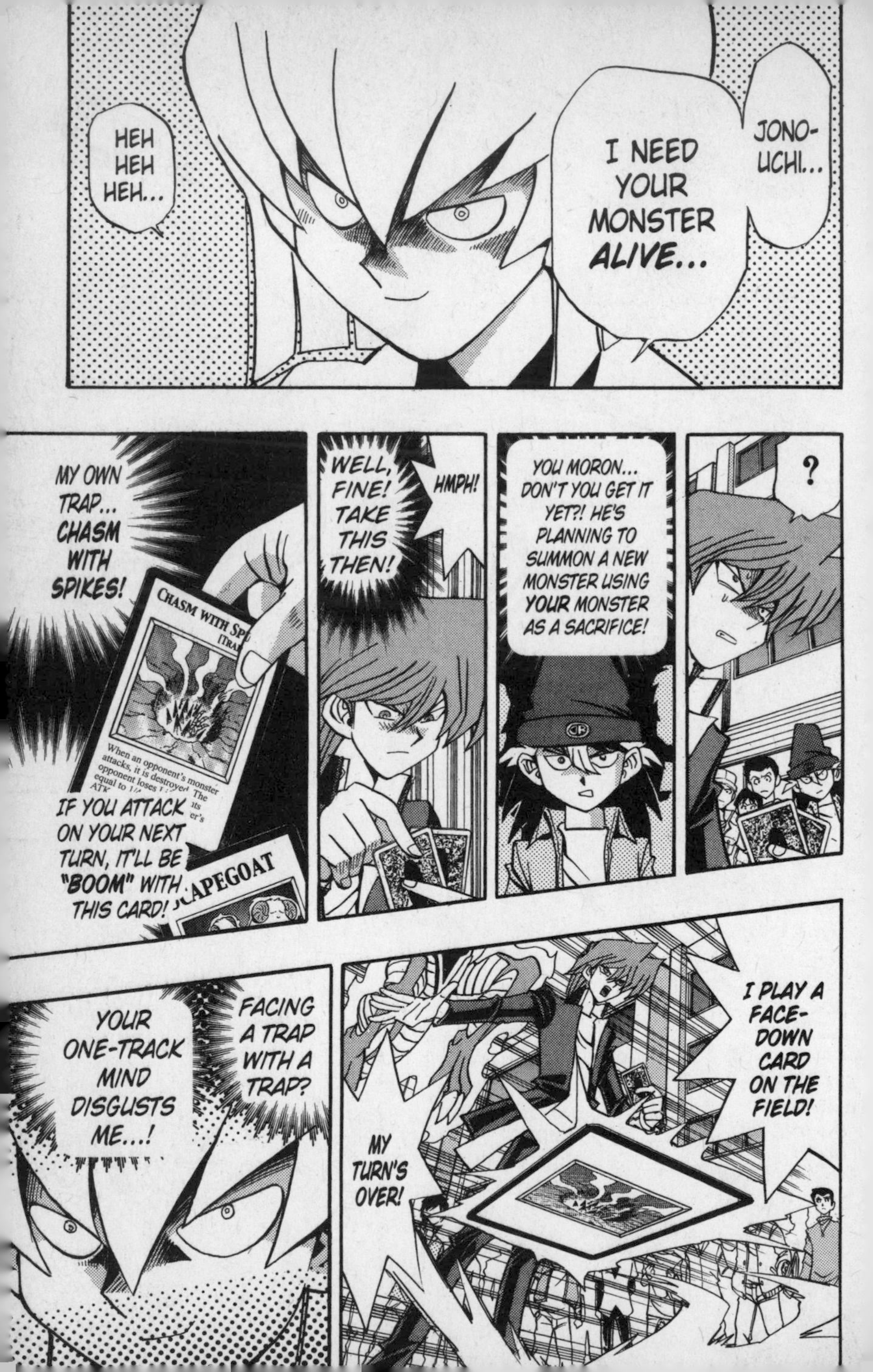
JONO-UCHI...
I NEED YOUR MONSTER ALIVE...
HEH HEH HEH...
?
YOU MORON... DON'T YOU GET IT YET?! HE'S PLANNING TO SUMMON A NEW MONSTER USING YOUR MONSTER AS A SACRIFICE!
HMPH!
WELL, FINE! TAKE THIS THEN!
MY OWN TRAP... CHASM WITH SPIKES!
IF YOU ATTACK ON YOUR NEXT TURN, IT'LL BE "BOOM" WITH THIS CARD!
I PLAY A FACE-DOWN CARD ON THE FIELD!
MY TURN'S OVER!
FACING A TRAP WITH A TRAP?
YOUR ONE-TRACK MIND DISGUSTS ME...!

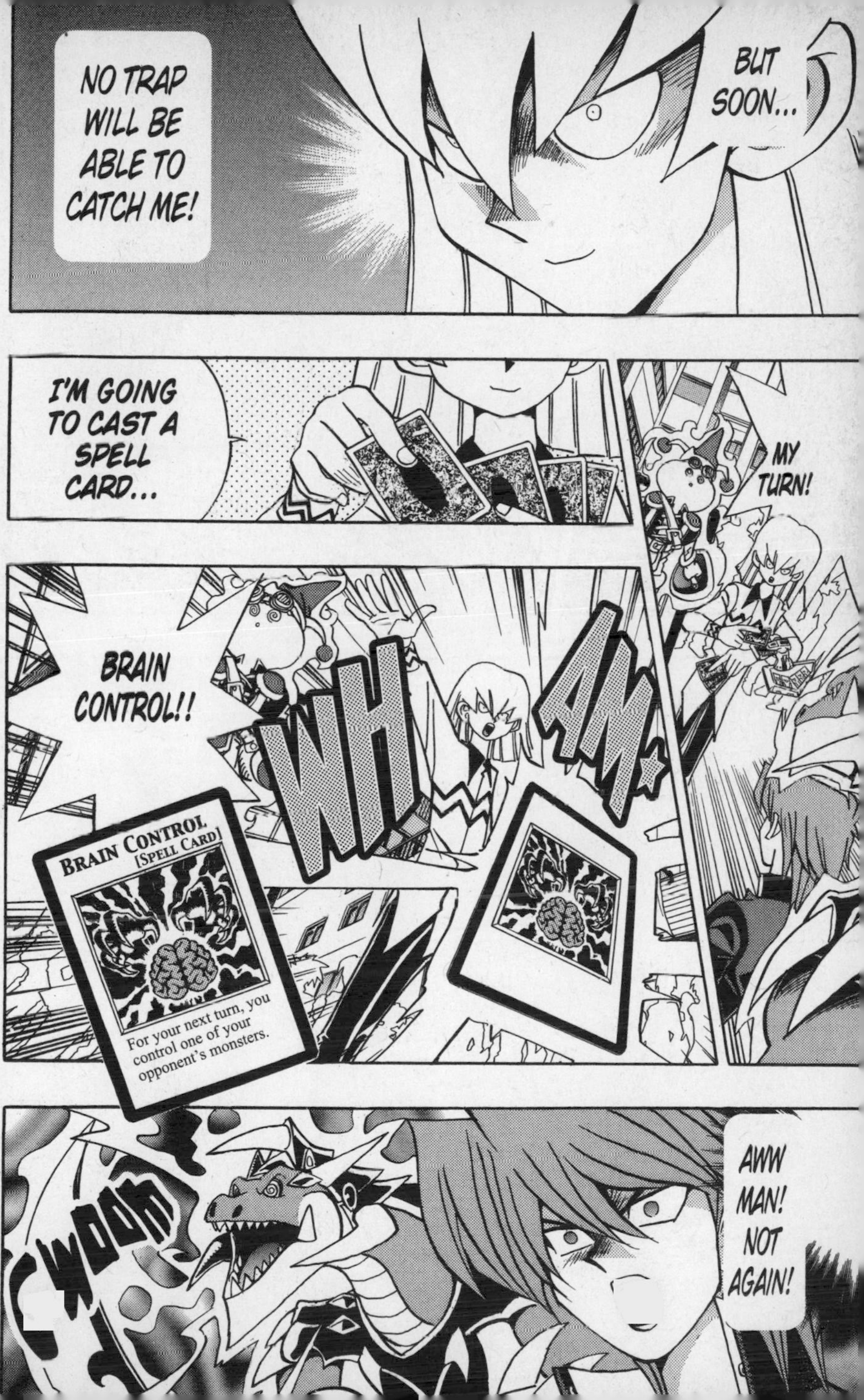
BUT SOON...
NO TRAP WILL BE ABLE TO CATCH ME!
MY TURN!
I'M GOING TO CAST A SPELL CARD...
BRAIN CONTROL!!
WHAM
BRAIN CONTROL
[SPELL CARD]
For your next turn, you control one of your opponent's monsters.
AWW MAN! NOT AGAIN!
WOOM

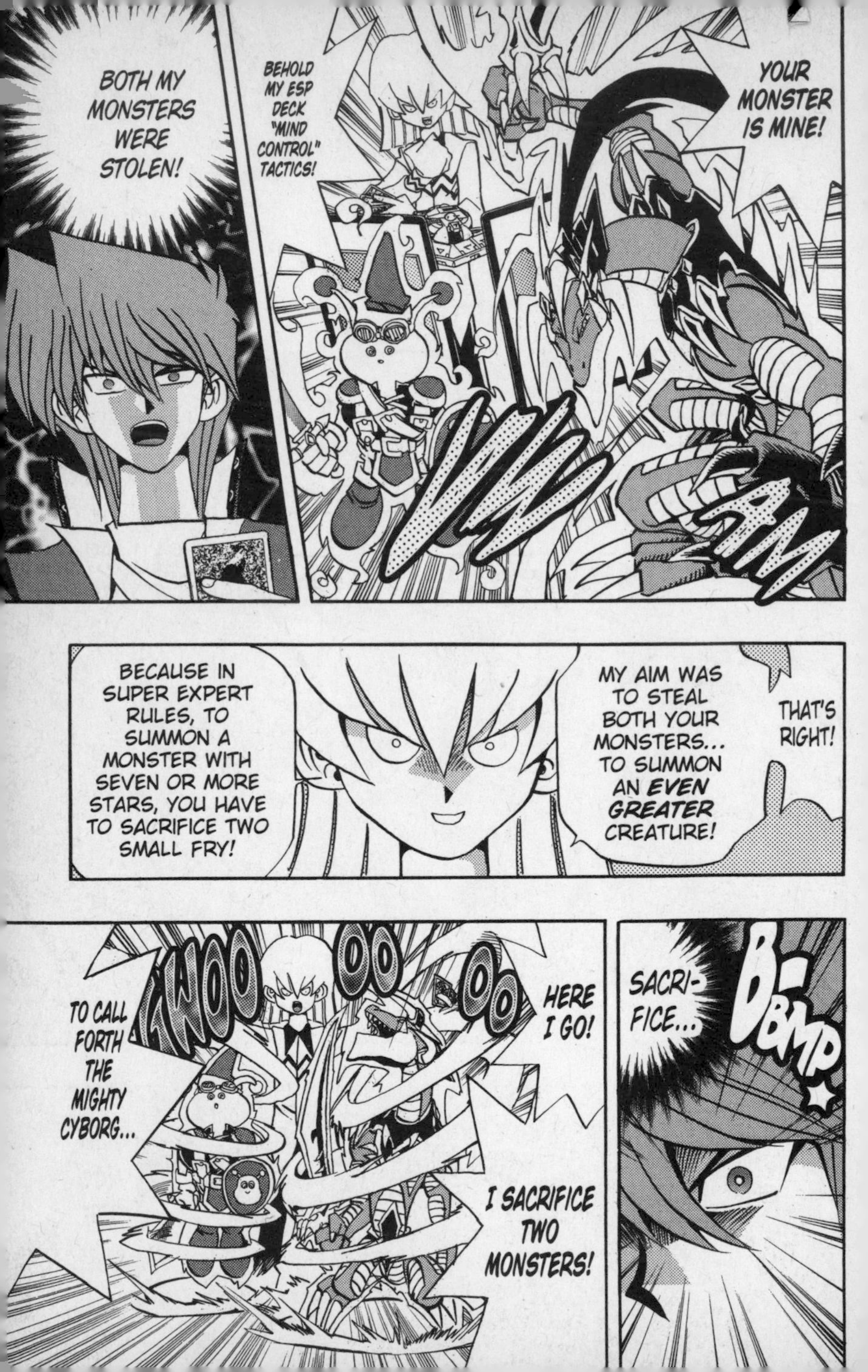
YOUR MONSTER IS MINE!
BEHOLD MY ESP DECK "MIND CONTROL" TACTICS!
VWM
AM
BOTH MY MONSTERS WERE STOLEN!
THAT'S RIGHT!
MY AIM WAS TO STEAL BOTH YOUR MONSTERS... TO SUMMON AN *EVEN GREATER* CREATURE!
BECAUSE IN SUPER EXPERT RULES, TO SUMMON A MONSTER WITH SEVEN OR MORE STARS, YOU HAVE TO SACRIFICE TWO SMALL FRY!
B-BMP
SACRI-FICE...
HERE I GO!
WOO OO OO
TO CALL FORTH THE MIGHTY CYBORG...
I SACRIFICE TWO MONSTERS!

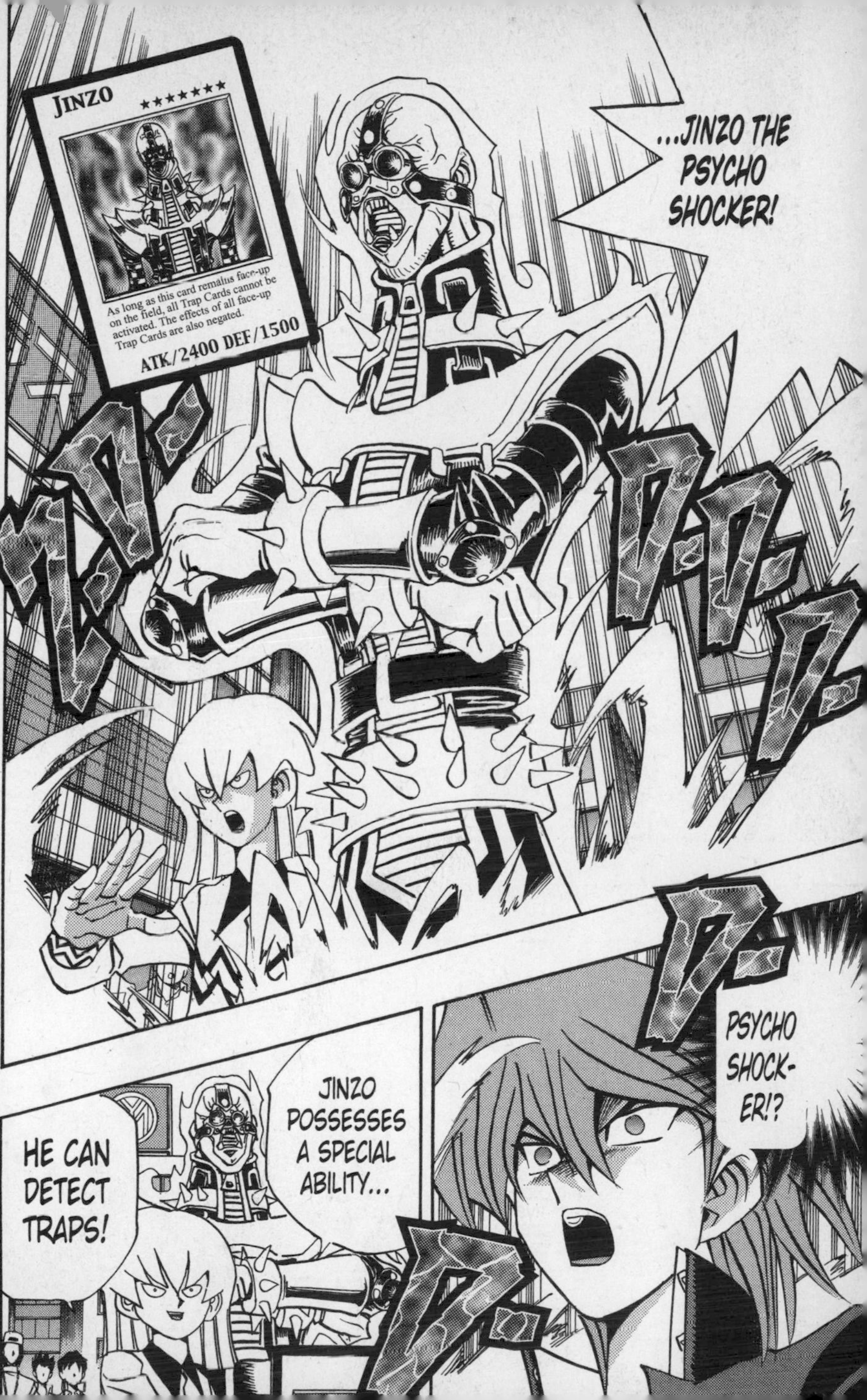
...JINZO THE PSYCHO SHOCKER!
JINZO ★★★★★★★
As long as this card remains face-up on the field, all Trap Cards cannot be activated. The effects of all face-up Trap Cards are also negated.
ATK/2400 DEF/1500
PSYCHO SHOCK-ER!?
JINZO POSSESSES A SPECIAL ABILITY...
HE CAN DETECT TRAPS!

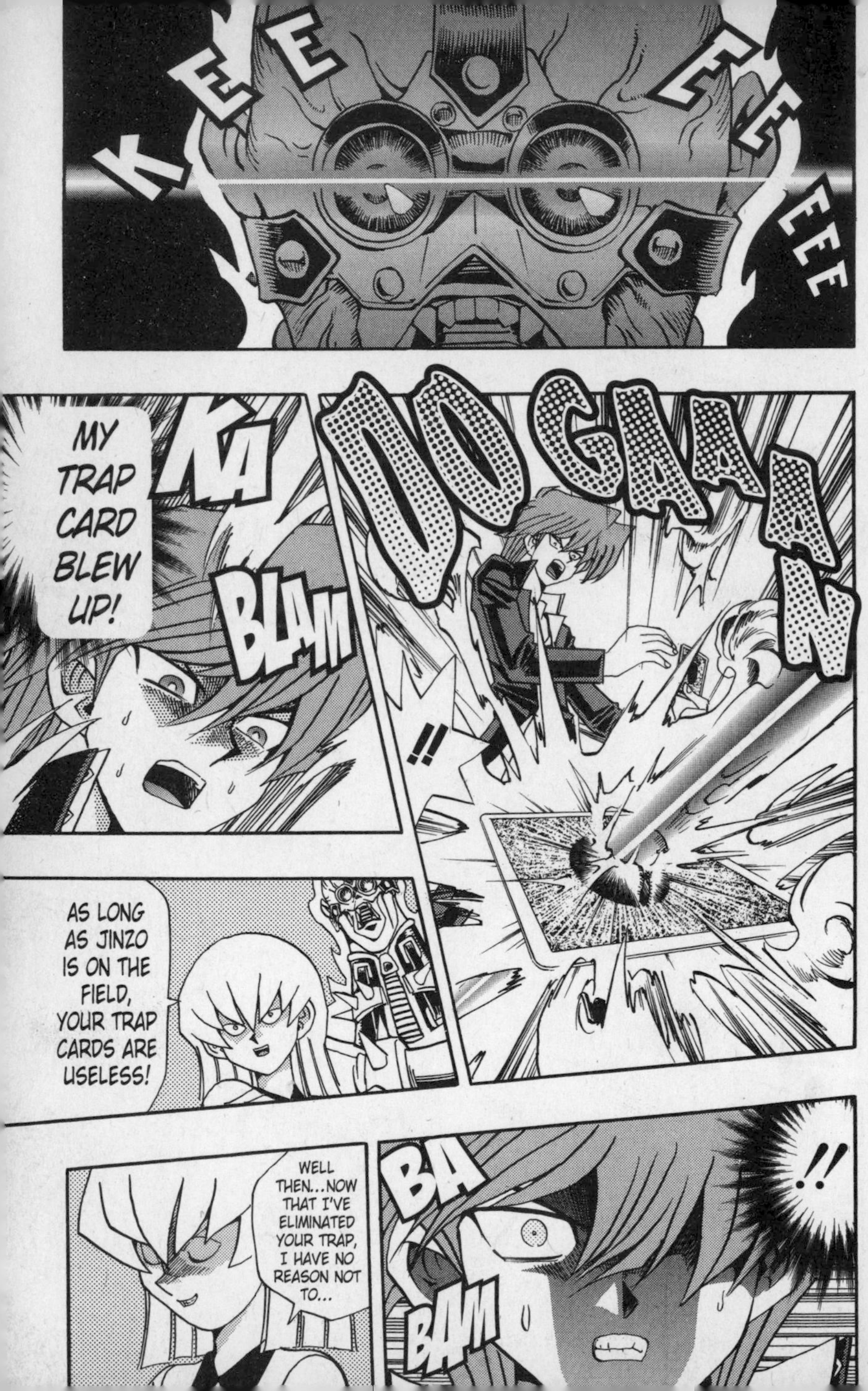
KEEEEEEE
DOGAAAN
!!
KA
MY TRAP CARD BLEW UP!
BLAM
AS LONG AS JINZO IS ON THE FIELD, YOUR TRAP CARDS ARE USELESS!
BA
!!
BAM
WELL THEN...NOW THAT I'VE ELIMINATED YOUR TRAP, I HAVE NO REASON NOT TO...

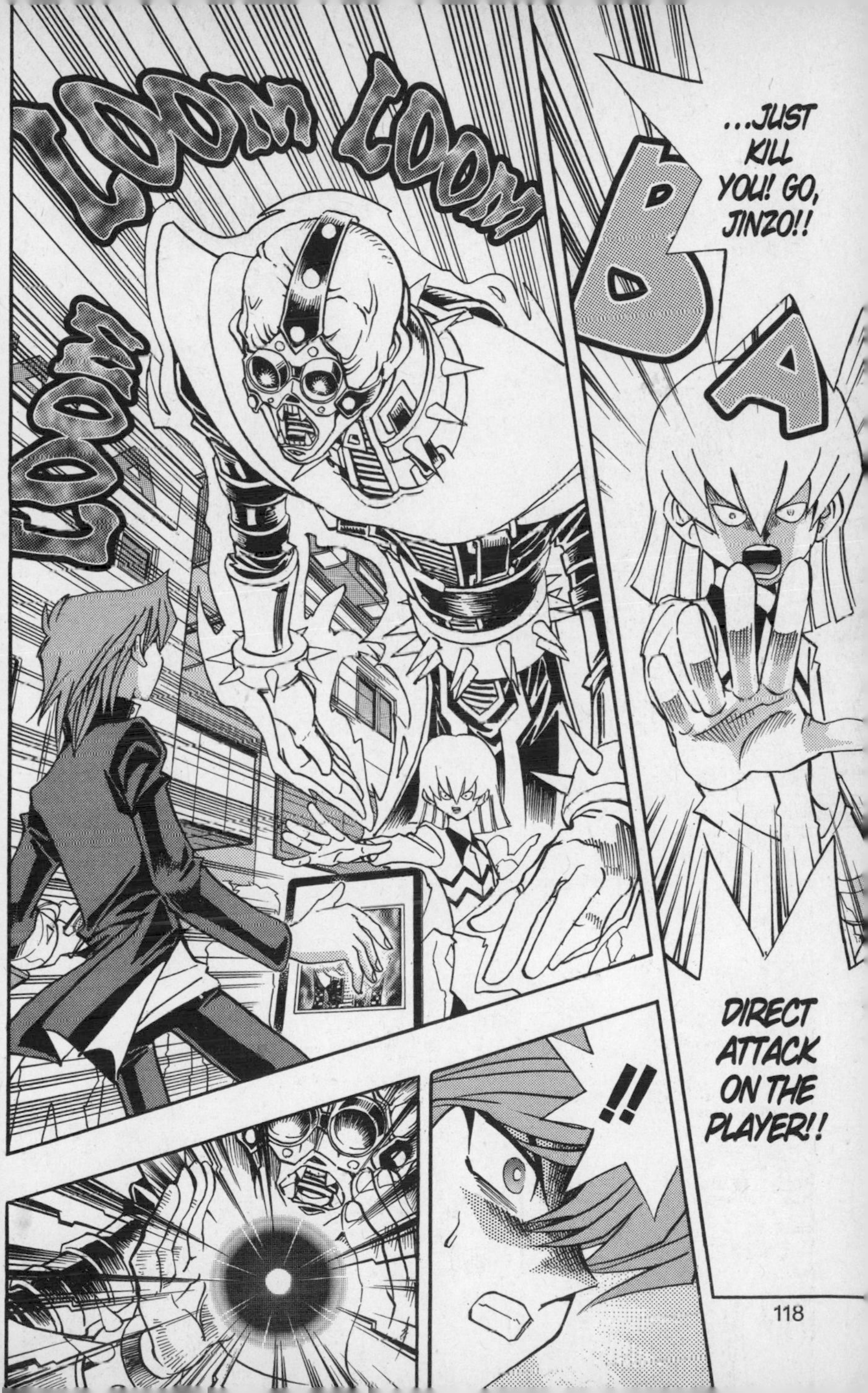

...JUST KILL YOU! GO, JINZO!!
BA
LOOM LOOM
LOOM
DIRECT ATTACK ON THE PLAYER!!
!!

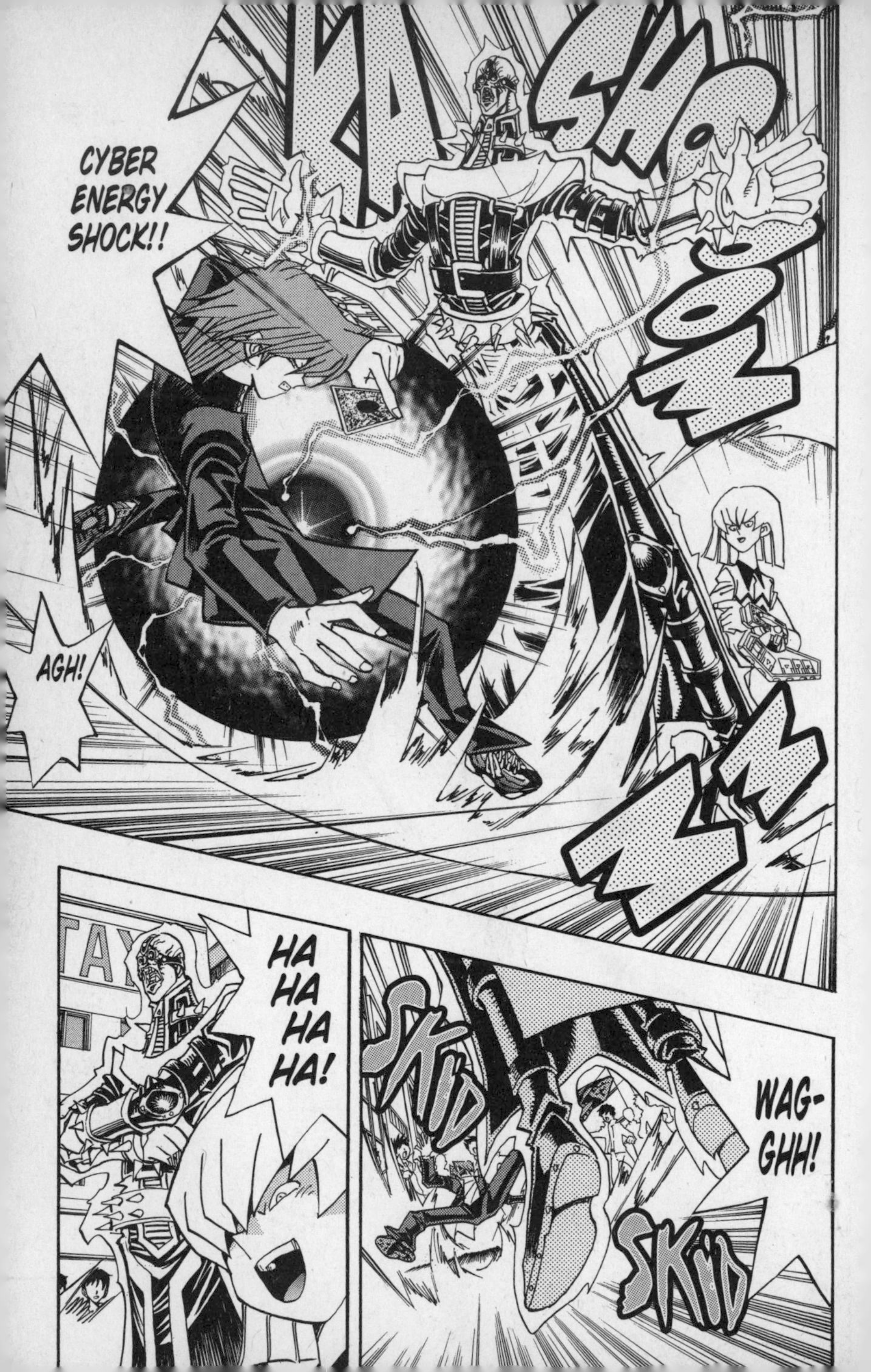
CYBER ENERGY SHOCK!!
AGH!
SKID
WAG-GHH!
SKID
HA HA HA HA!

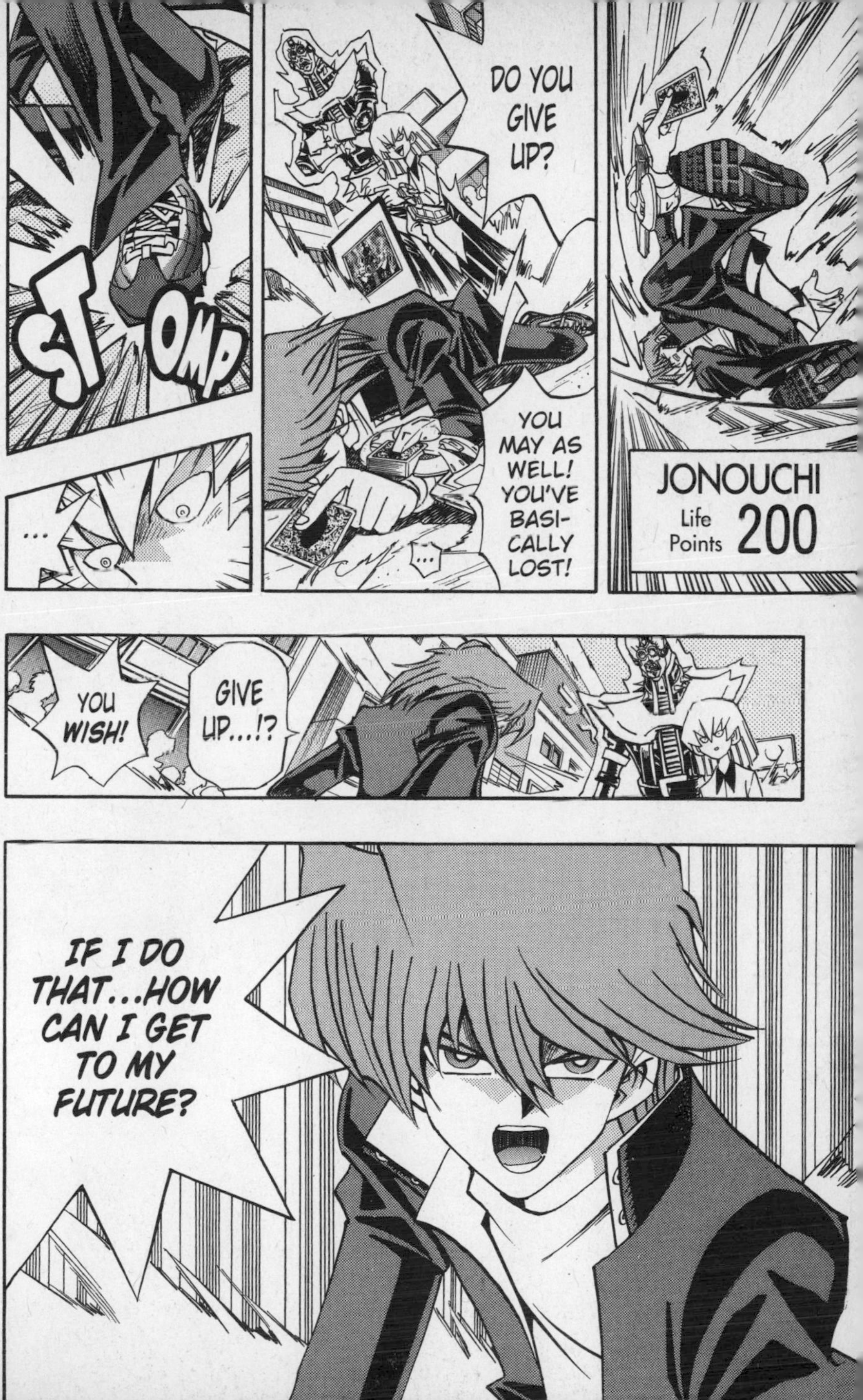
JONOUCHI Life Points 200
DO YOU GIVE UP?
YOU MAY AS WELL! YOU'VE BASI- CALLY LOST!
...
STOMP
...
GIVE UP...!?
YOU WISH!
IF I DO THAT...HOW CAN I GET TO MY FUTURE?

Duel 99: A Brave Gamble

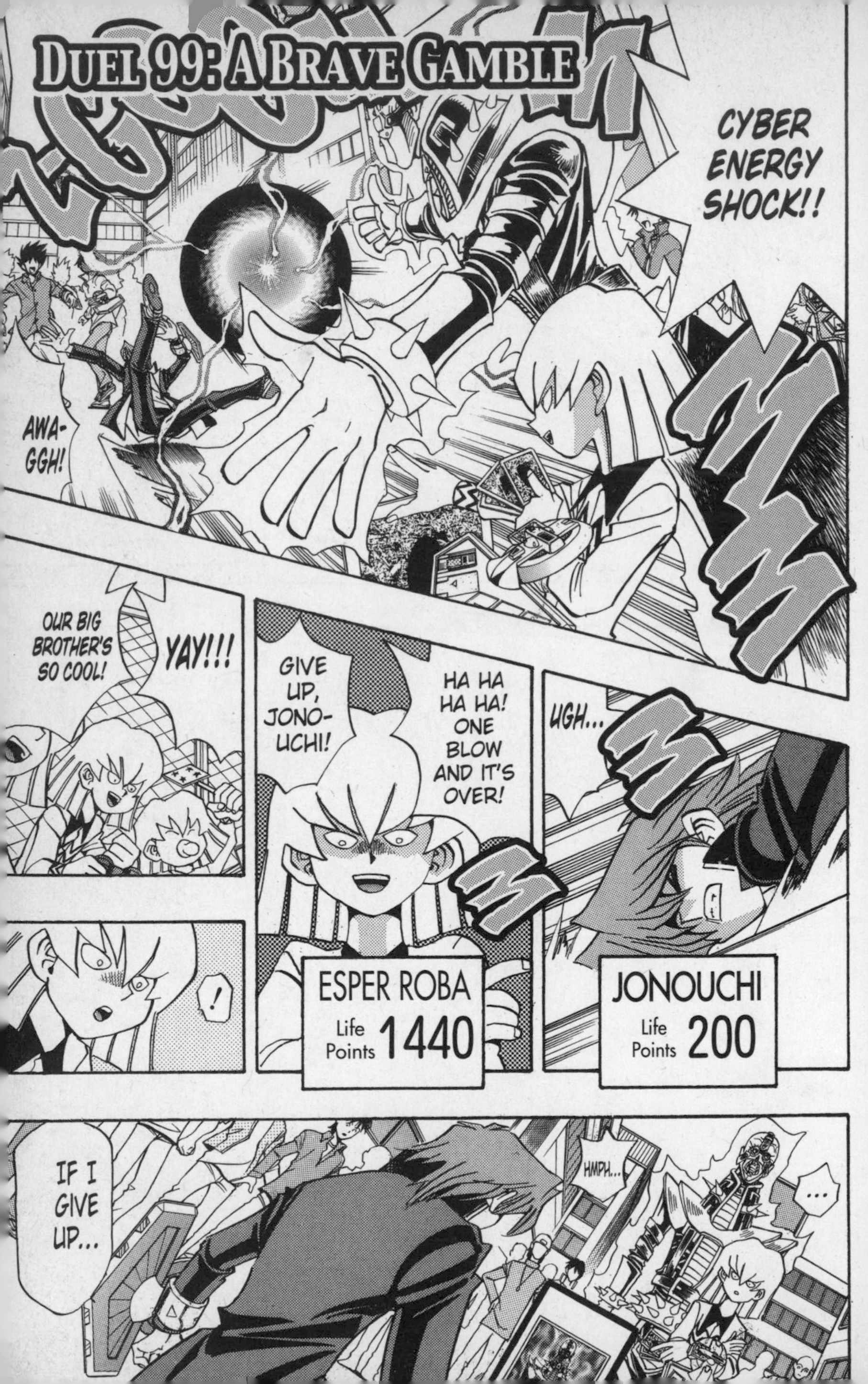
CYBER ENERGY SHOCK!!
AWA-GGH!
UGH...
JONOUCHI Life Points 200
HA HA HA HA! ONE BLOW AND IT'S OVER!
GIVE UP, JONOUCHI!
ESPER ROBA Life Points 1440
YAY!!!
OUR BIG BROTHER'S SO COOL!
!
...
HMPH...
IF I GIVE UP...

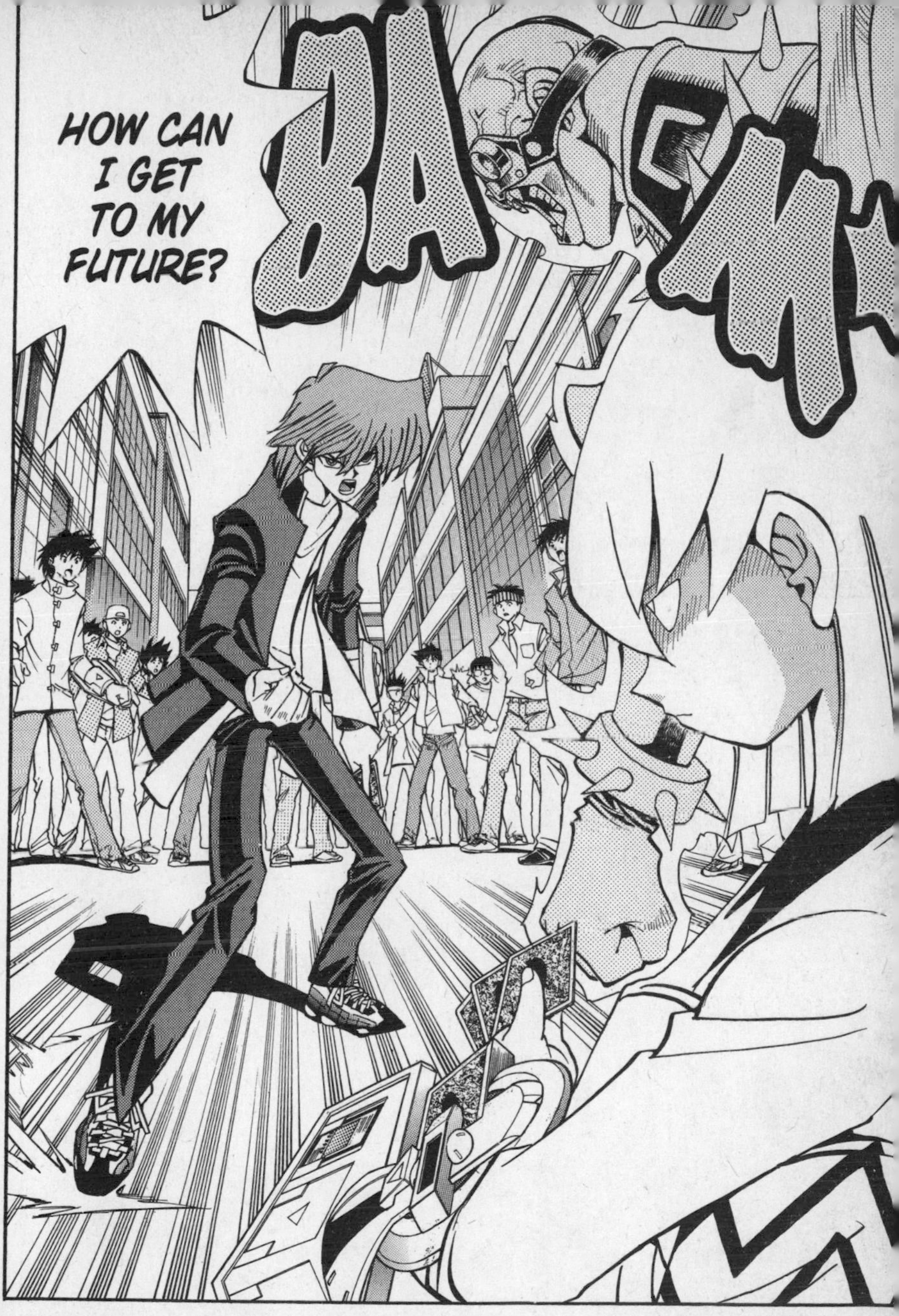
HOW CAN I GET TO MY FUTURE?
BA

Duel 99: A Brave Gamble

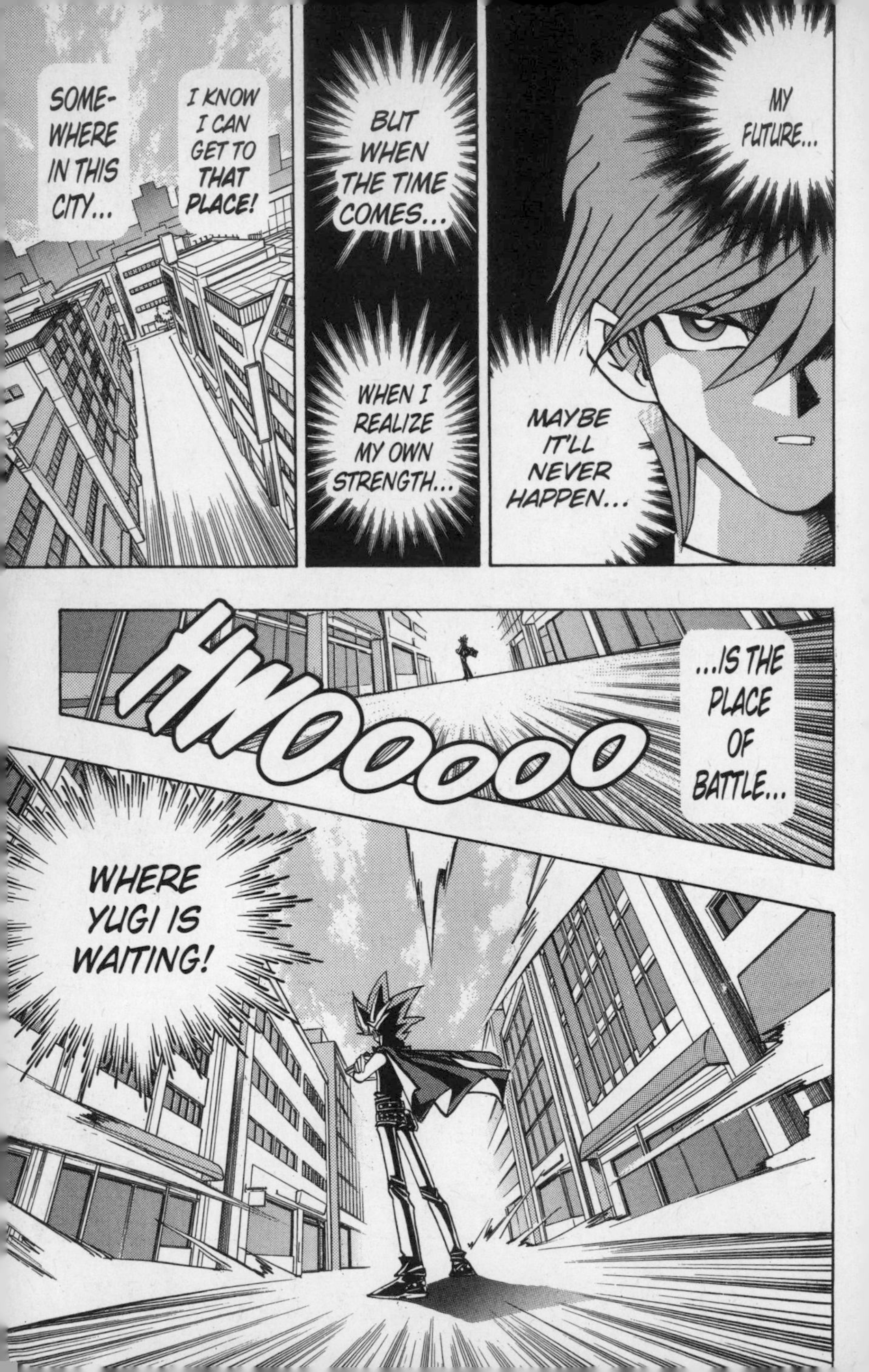
SOME-WHERE IN THIS CITY...
I KNOW I CAN GET TO THAT PLACE!
BUT WHEN THE TIME COMES...
WHEN I REALIZE MY OWN STRENGTH...
MY FUTURE...
MAYBE IT'LL NEVER HAPPEN...
HWOOOOOO
...IS THE PLACE OF BATTLE...
WHERE YUGI IS WAITING!

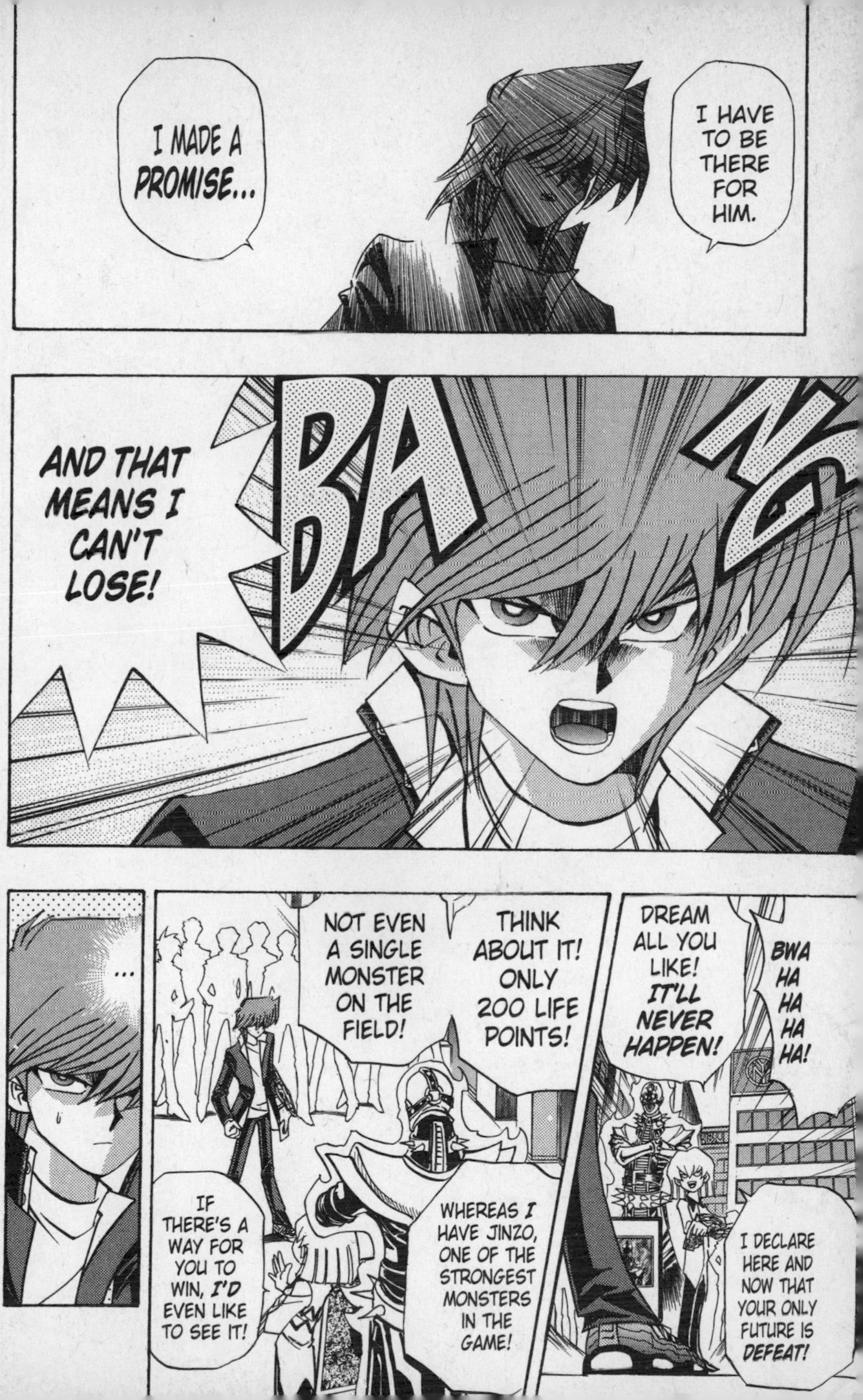
I HAVE TO BE THERE FOR HIM.
I MADE A PROMISE...
BAN
AND THAT MEANS I CAN'T LOSE!
BWA HA HA HA HA!
DREAM ALL YOU LIKE! IT'LL NEVER HAPPEN!
I DECLARE HERE AND NOW THAT YOUR ONLY FUTURE IS DEFEAT!
THINK ABOUT IT! ONLY 200 LIFE POINTS!
NOT EVEN A SINGLE MONSTER ON THE FIELD!
WHEREAS I HAVE JINZO, ONE OF THE STRONGEST MONSTERS IN THE GAME!
IF THERE'S A WAY FOR YOU TO WIN, I'D EVEN LIKE TO SEE IT!
...

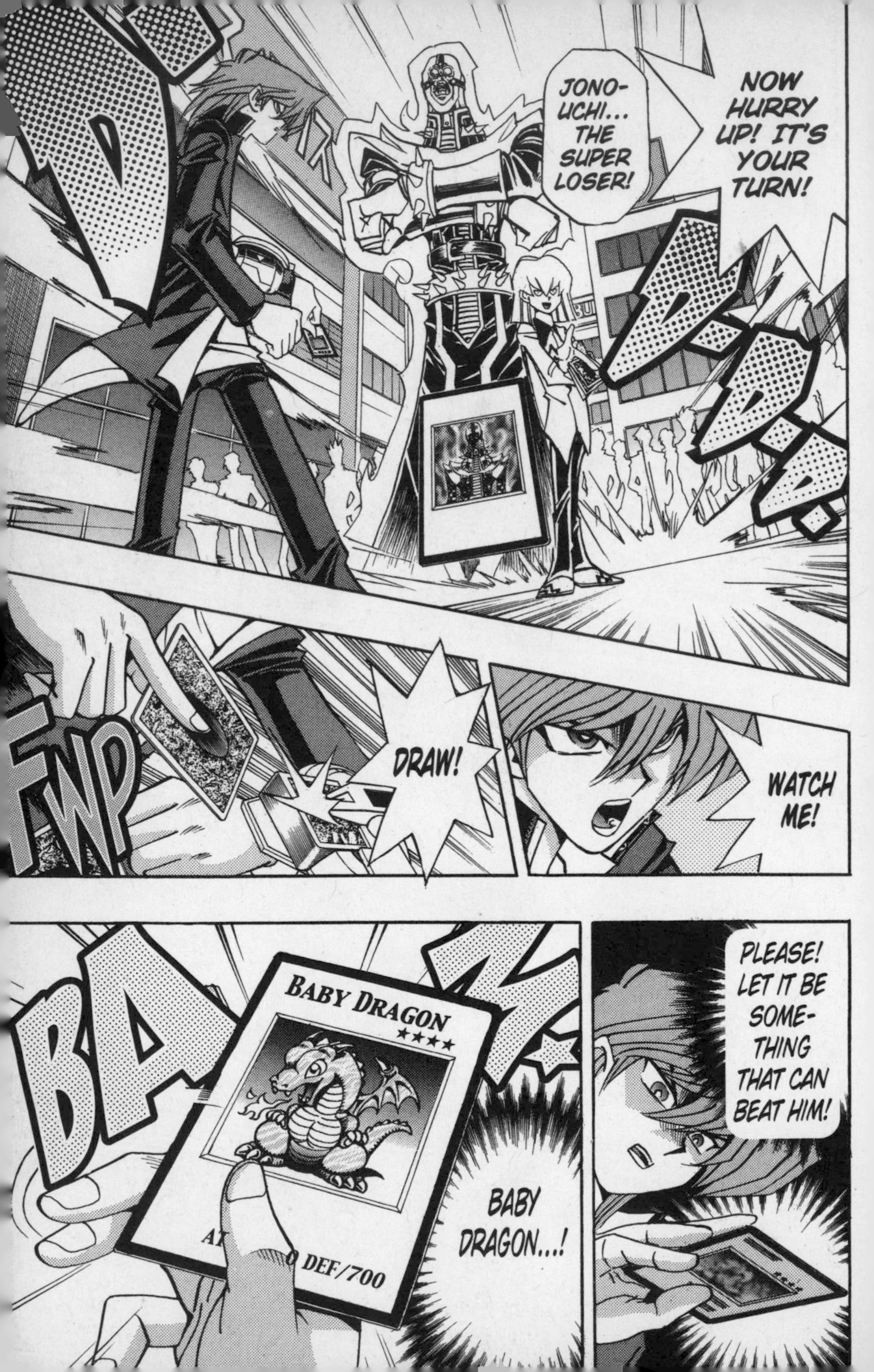
NOW HURRY UP! IT'S YOUR TURN!
JONO-UCHI... THE SUPER LOSER!
WATCH ME!
DRAW!
FWP
PLEASE! LET IT BE SOME-THING THAT CAN BEAT HIM!
BABY DRAGON...!
BABY DRAGON
DEF/700
BA

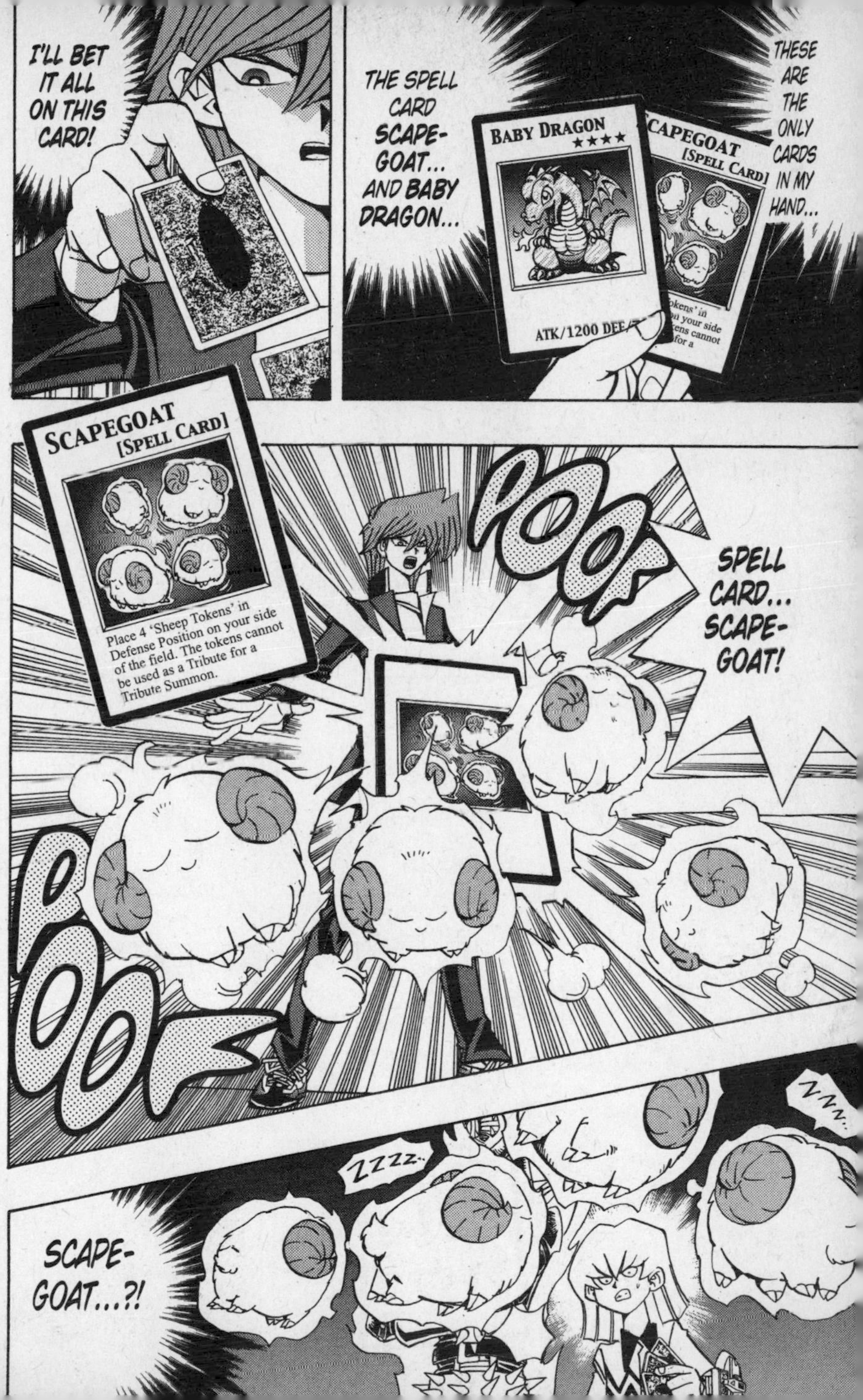
THESE ARE THE ONLY CARDS IN MY HAND...
BABY DRAGON ★★★★
ATK/1200
SCAPEGOAT [SPELL CARD]
THE SPELL CARD SCAPE-GOAT... AND BABY DRAGON...
I'LL BET IT ALL ON THIS CARD!
SPELL CARD... SCAPE-GOAT!
POOOF
SCAPEGOAT [SPELL CARD]
Place 4 'Sheep Tokens' in Defense Position on your side of the field. The tokens cannot be used as a Tribute for a Tribute Summon.
POOOF
ZZZZ..
ZZZ..
SCAPE-GOAT...?!

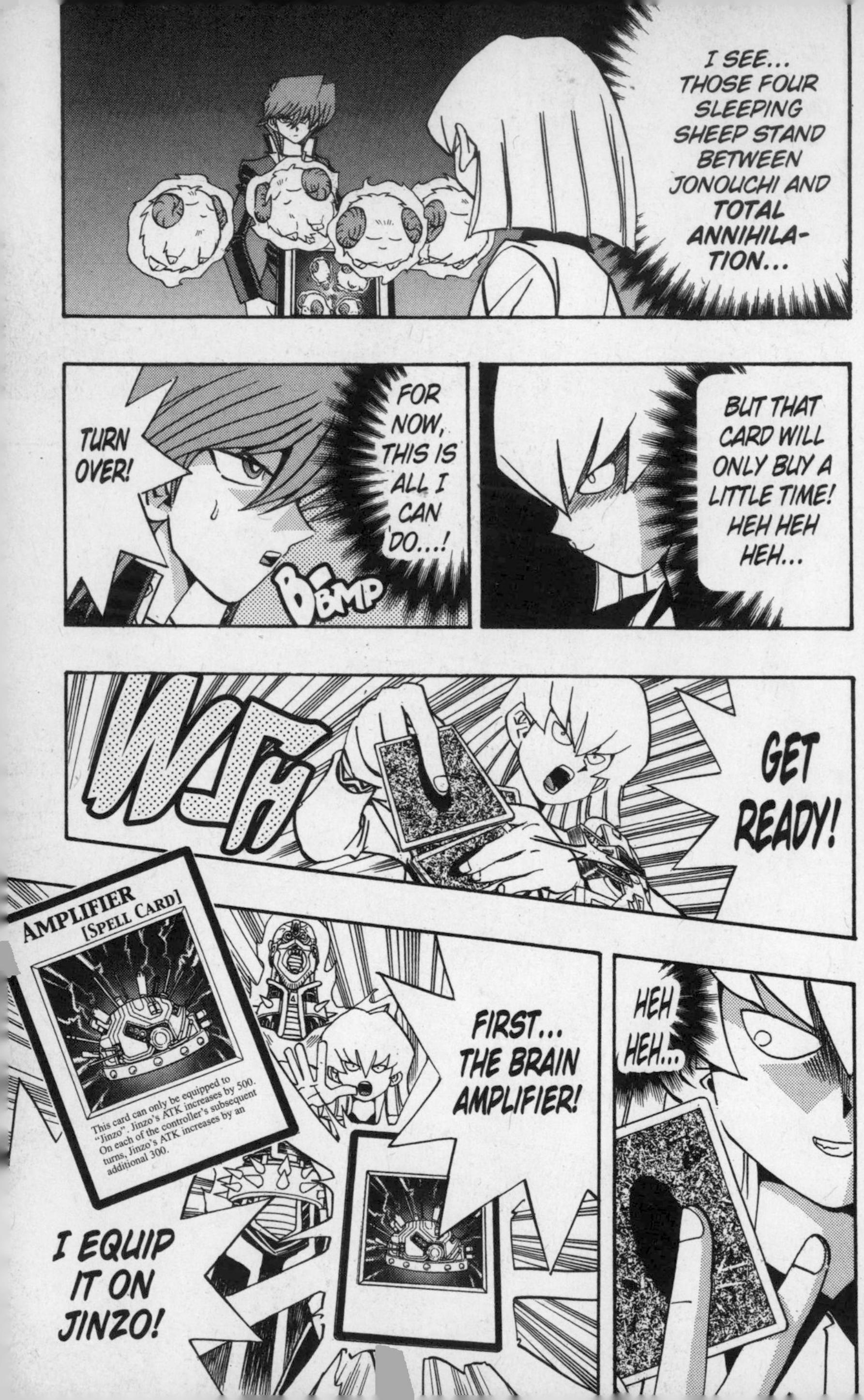
I SEE... THOSE FOUR SLEEPING SHEEP STAND BETWEEN JONOUCHI AND TOTAL ANNIHILATION...
BUT THAT CARD WILL ONLY BUY A LITTLE TIME! HEH HEH HEH...
FOR NOW, THIS IS ALL I CAN DO...!
TURN OVER!
BBMP
GET READY!
WSH
HEH HEH...
FIRST... THE BRAIN AMPLIFIER!
AMPLIFIER [SPELL CARD]
This card can only be equipped to "Jinzo". Jinzo's ATK increases by 500. On each of the controller's subsequent turns, Jinzo's ATK increases by an additional 300.
I EQUIP IT ON JINZO!

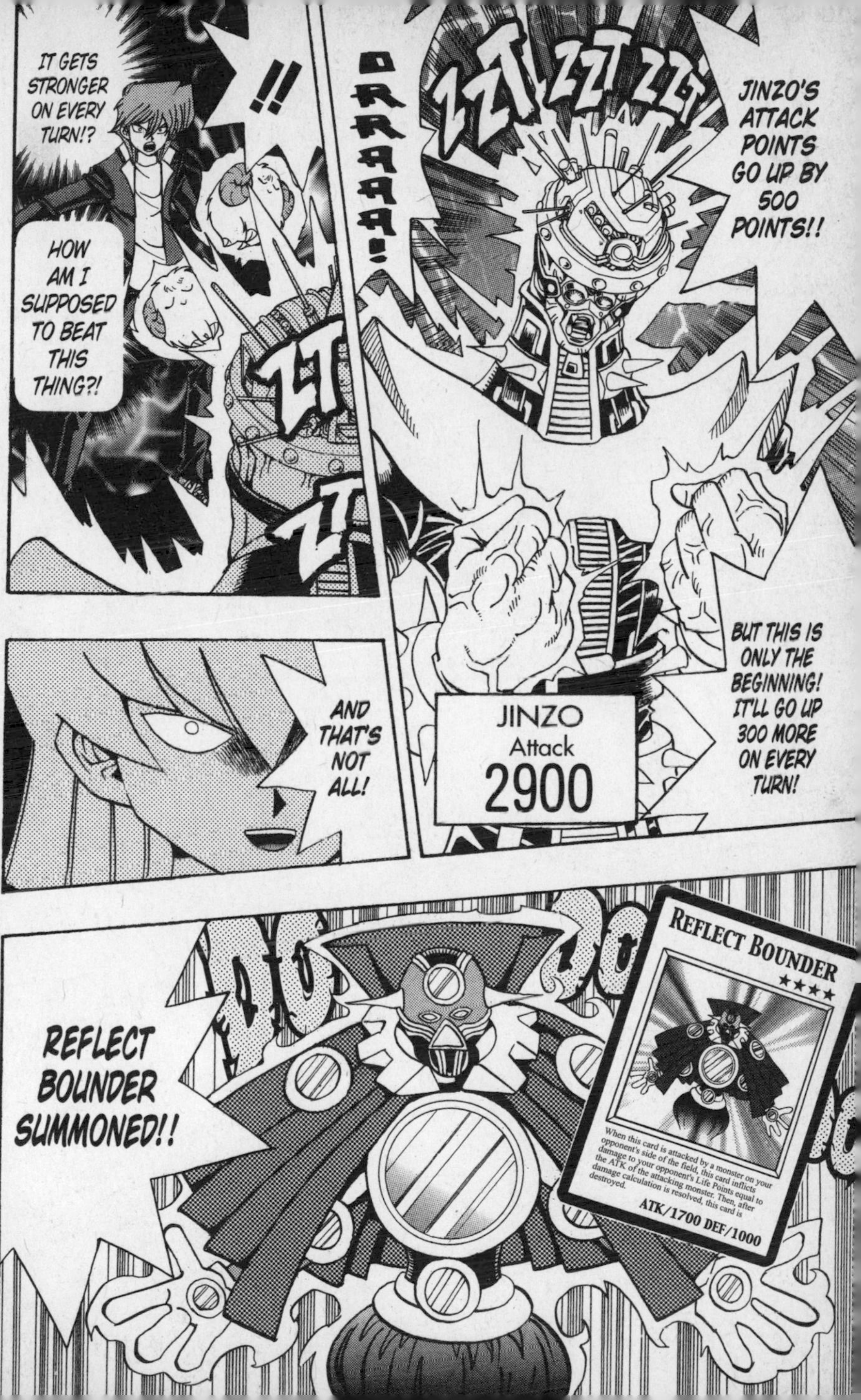

ZZT ZZT ZZT
JINZO'S ATTACK POINTS GO UP BY 500 POINTS!!
DRRAAAA!!
BUT THIS IS ONLY THE BEGINNING! IT'LL GO UP 300 MORE ON EVERY TURN!
JINZO Attack 2900
!!
IT GETS STRONGER ON EVERY TURN!?
HOW AM I SUPPOSED TO BEAT THIS THING?!
ZZT
ZZT
AND THAT'S NOT ALL!
REFLECT BOUNDER
★★★★
When this card is attacked by a monster on your opponent's side of the field, this card inflicts damage to your opponent's Life Points equal to the ATK of the attacking monster. Then, after damage calculation is resolved, this card is destroyed.
ATK/1700 DEF/1000
REFLECT BOUNDER SUMMONED!!

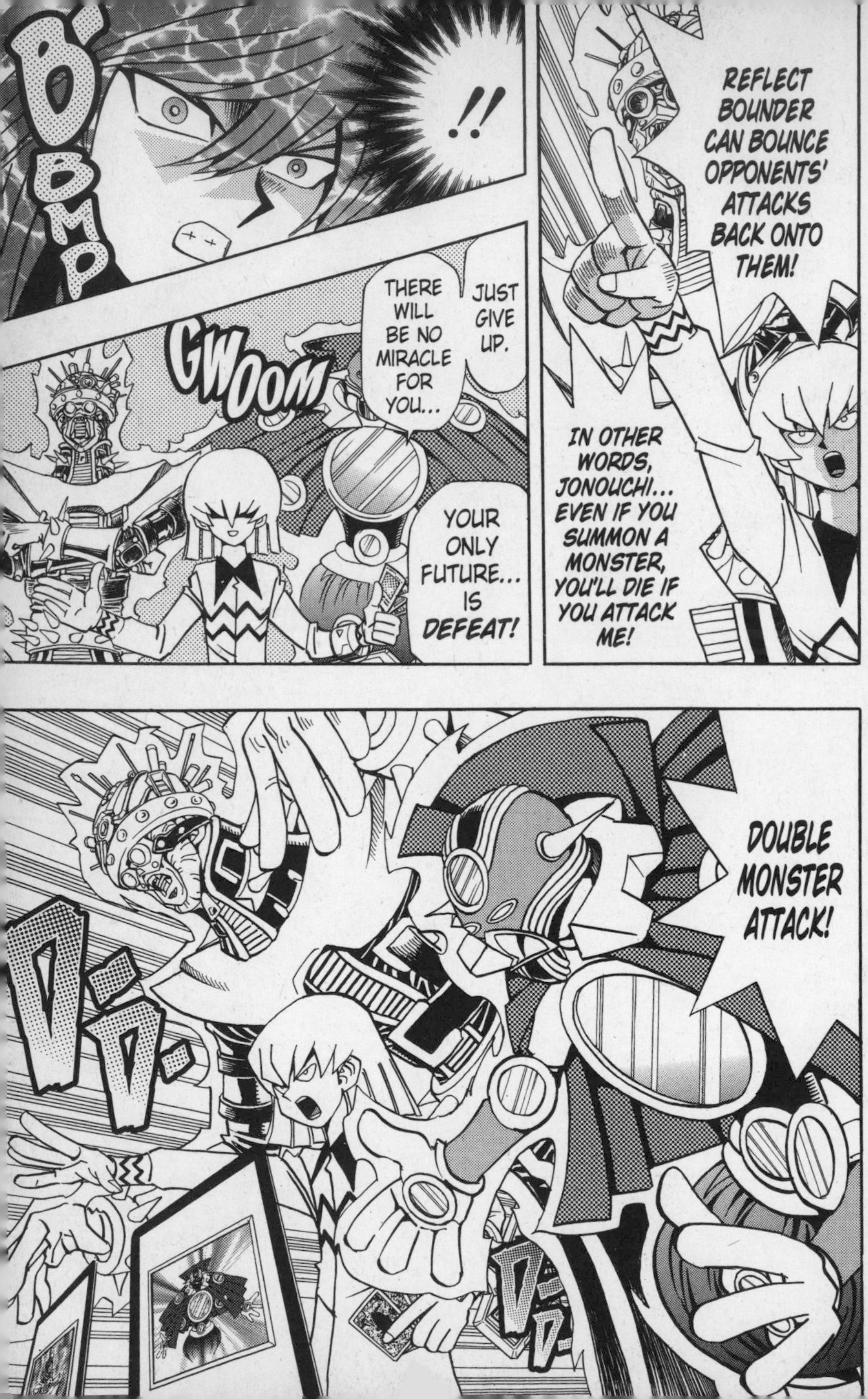
REFLECT BOUNDER CAN BOUNCE OPPONENTS' ATTACKS BACK ONTO THEM!
IN OTHER WORDS, JONOUCHI... EVEN IF YOU SUMMON A MONSTER, YOU'LL DIE IF YOU ATTACK ME!
!!
GWOOM
JUST GIVE UP.
THERE WILL BE NO MIRACLE FOR YOU...
YOUR ONLY FUTURE... IS DEFEAT!
DOUBLE MONSTER ATTACK!

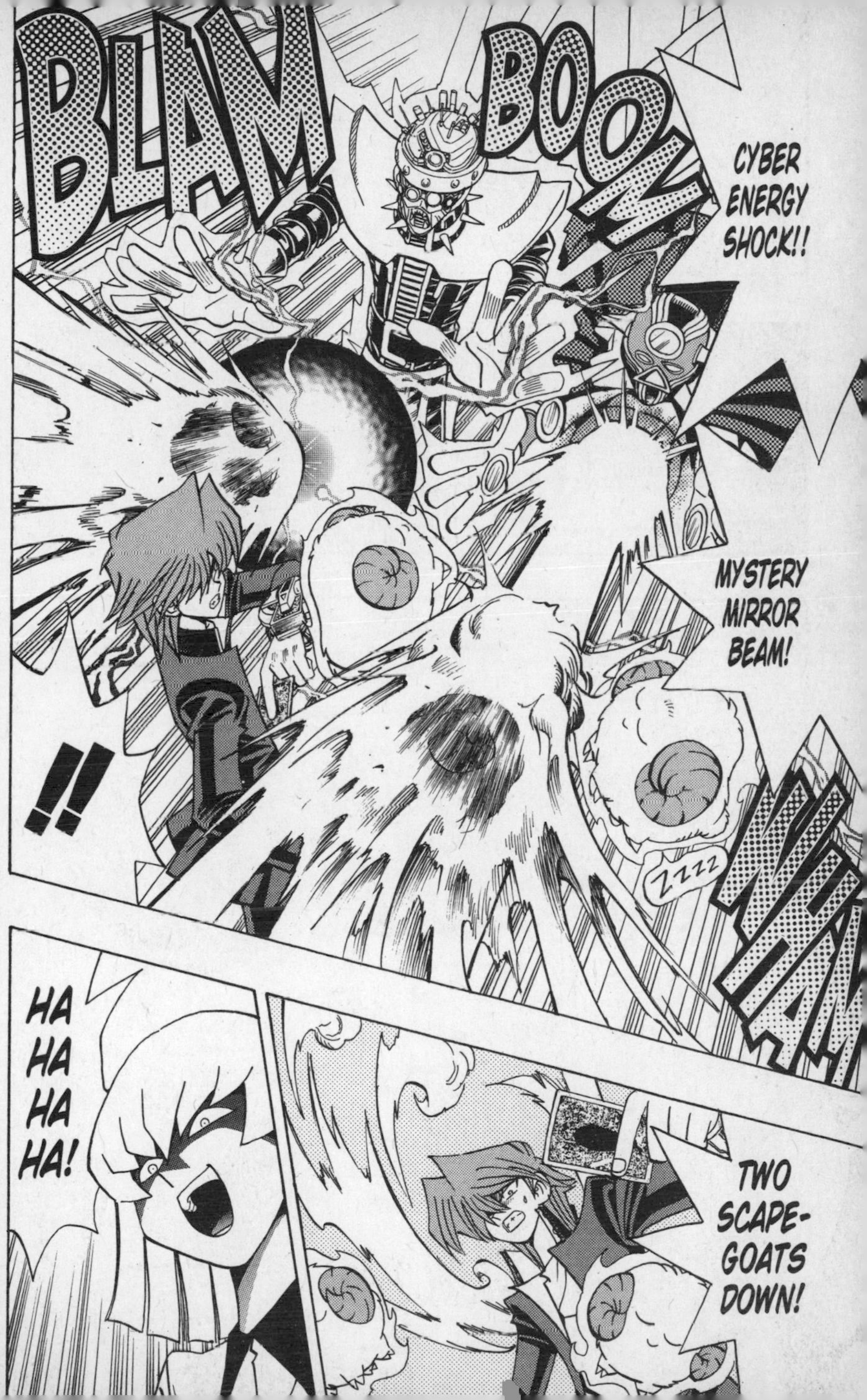
BOOM
CYBER ENERGY SHOCK!!
BLAM
MYSTERY MIRROR BEAM!
!!
ZZZZ
TWO SCAPE-GOATS DOWN!
HA HA HA HA!

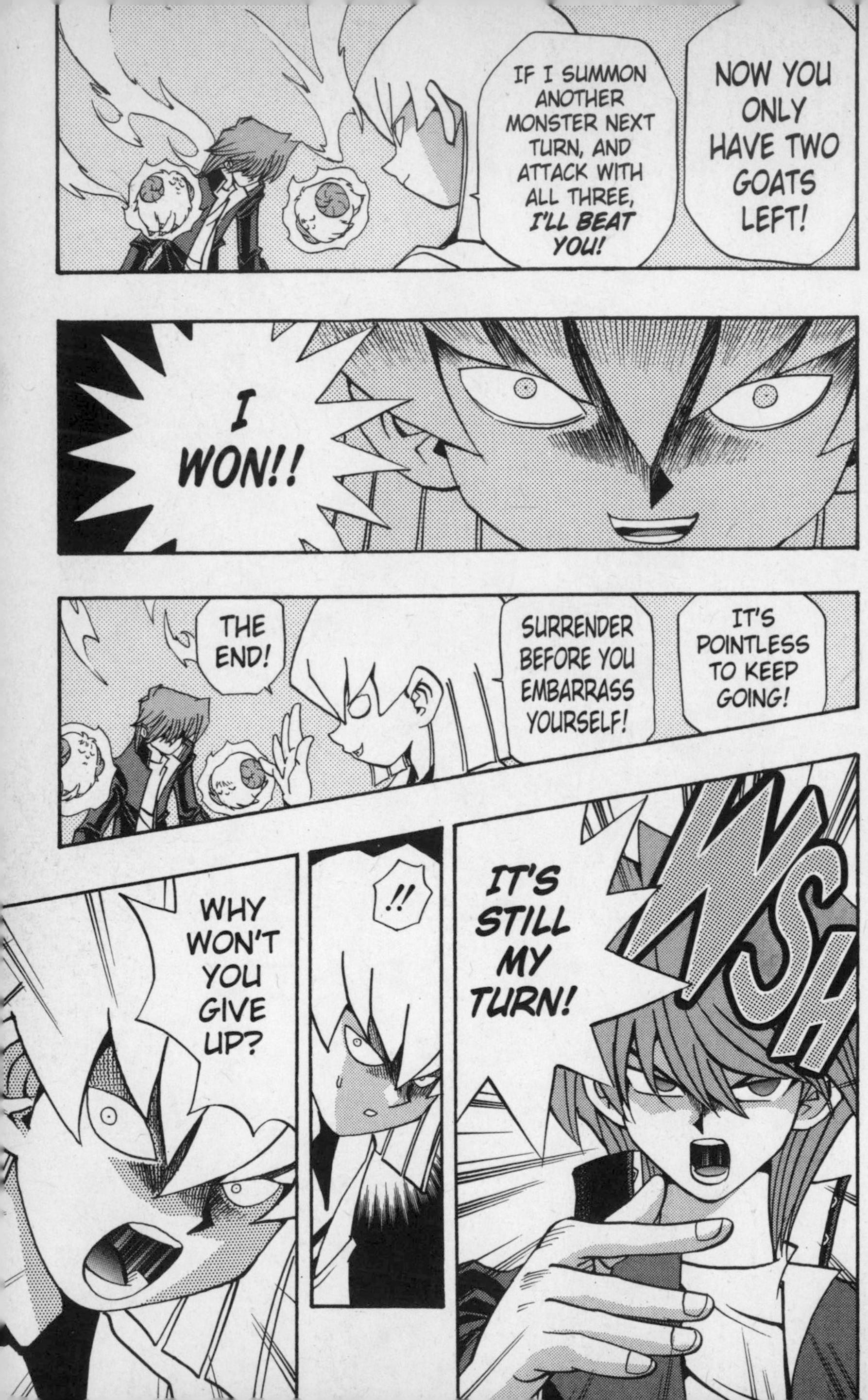
NOW YOU ONLY HAVE TWO GOATS LEFT!
IF I SUMMON ANOTHER MONSTER NEXT TURN, AND ATTACK WITH ALL THREE, *I'LL BEAT YOU!*
I WON!!
IT'S POINTLESS TO KEEP GOING!
SURRENDER BEFORE YOU EMBARRASS YOURSELF!
THE END!
WSH
IT'S STILL MY TURN!
!!
WHY WON'T YOU GIVE UP?

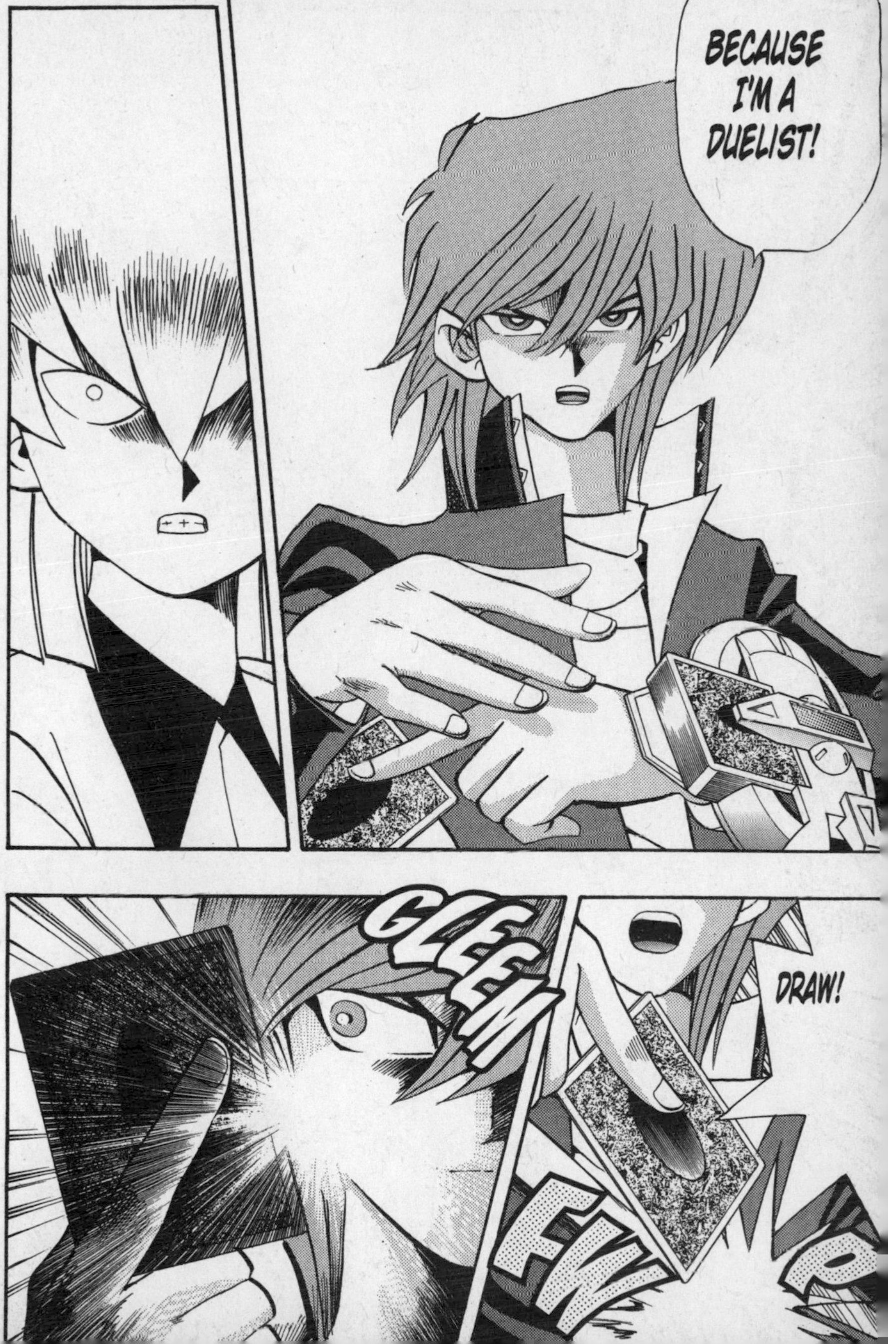
BECAUSE I'M A DUELIST!
DRAW!
GLEEM

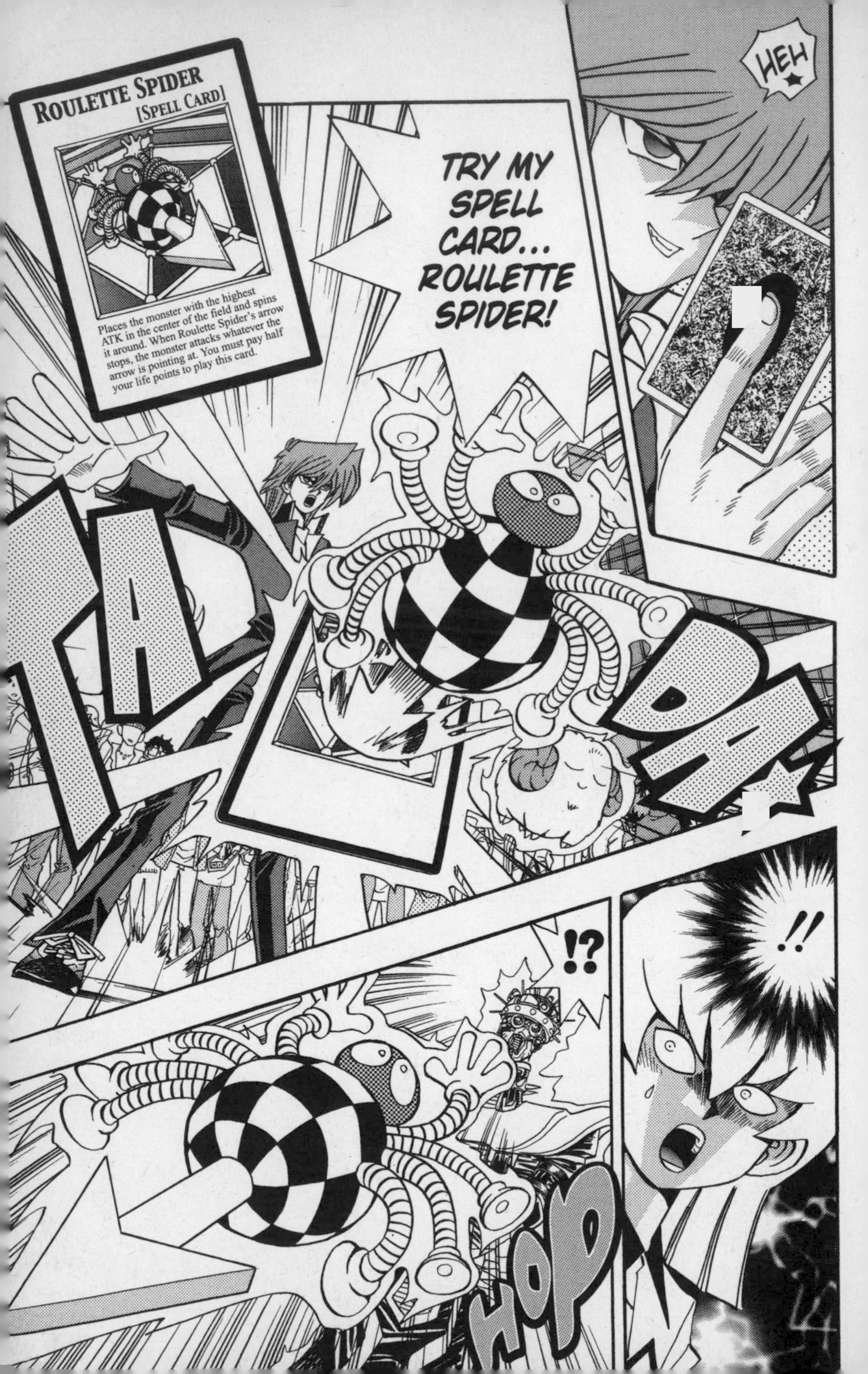
HEH★
TRY MY SPELL CARD... ROULETTE SPIDER!
ROULETTE SPIDER
[SPELL CARD]
Places the monster with the highest ATK in the center of the field and spins it around. When Roulette Spider's arrow stops, the monster attacks whatever the arrow is pointing at. You must pay half your life points to play this card.
TA DA★
!!
!?
HOP

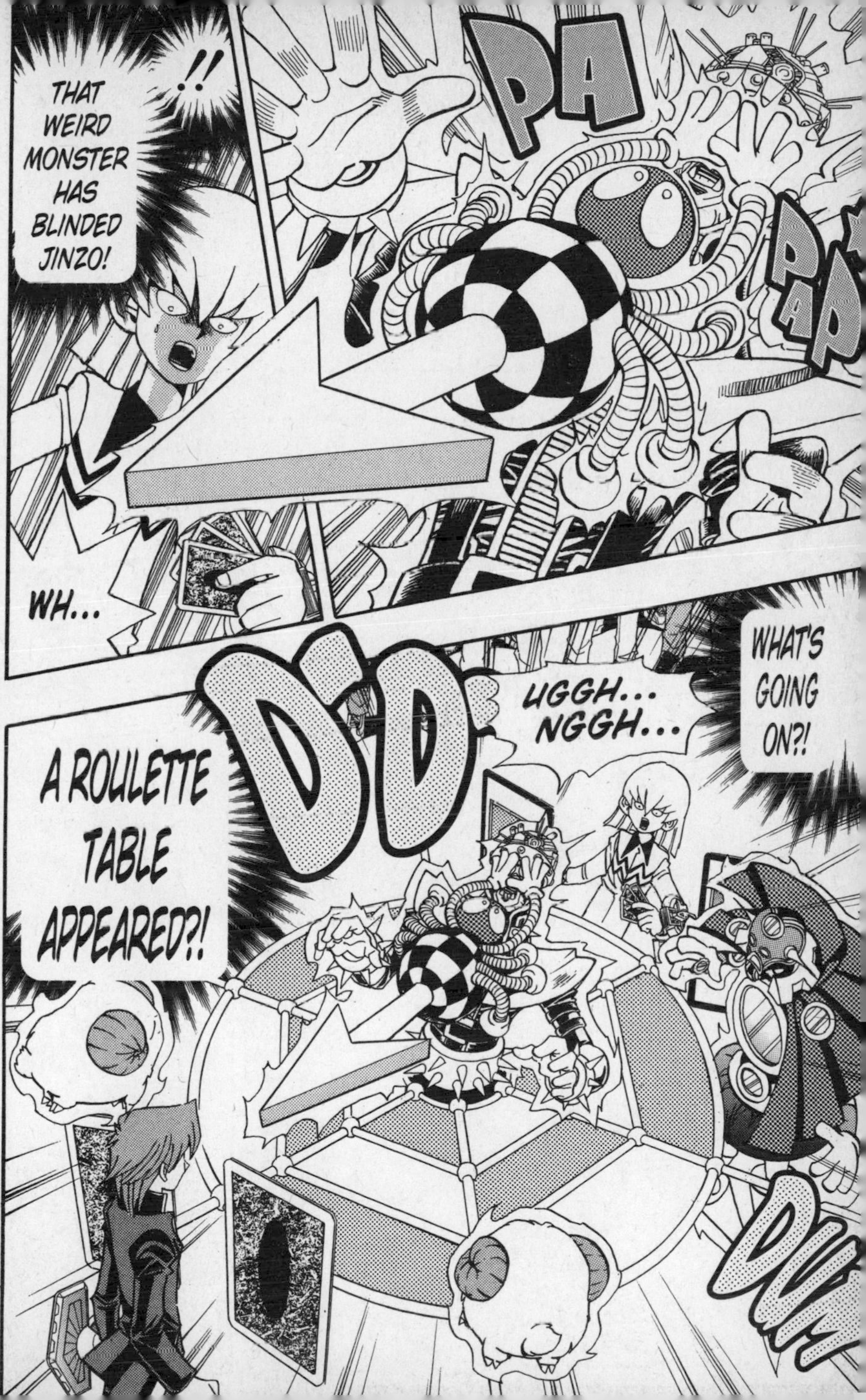

PA
PAPA
!!
THAT WEIRD MONSTER HAS BLINDED JINZO!
WH...
WHAT'S GOING ON?!
UGGH... NGGH...
DO
A ROULETTE TABLE APPEARED?!
DUN

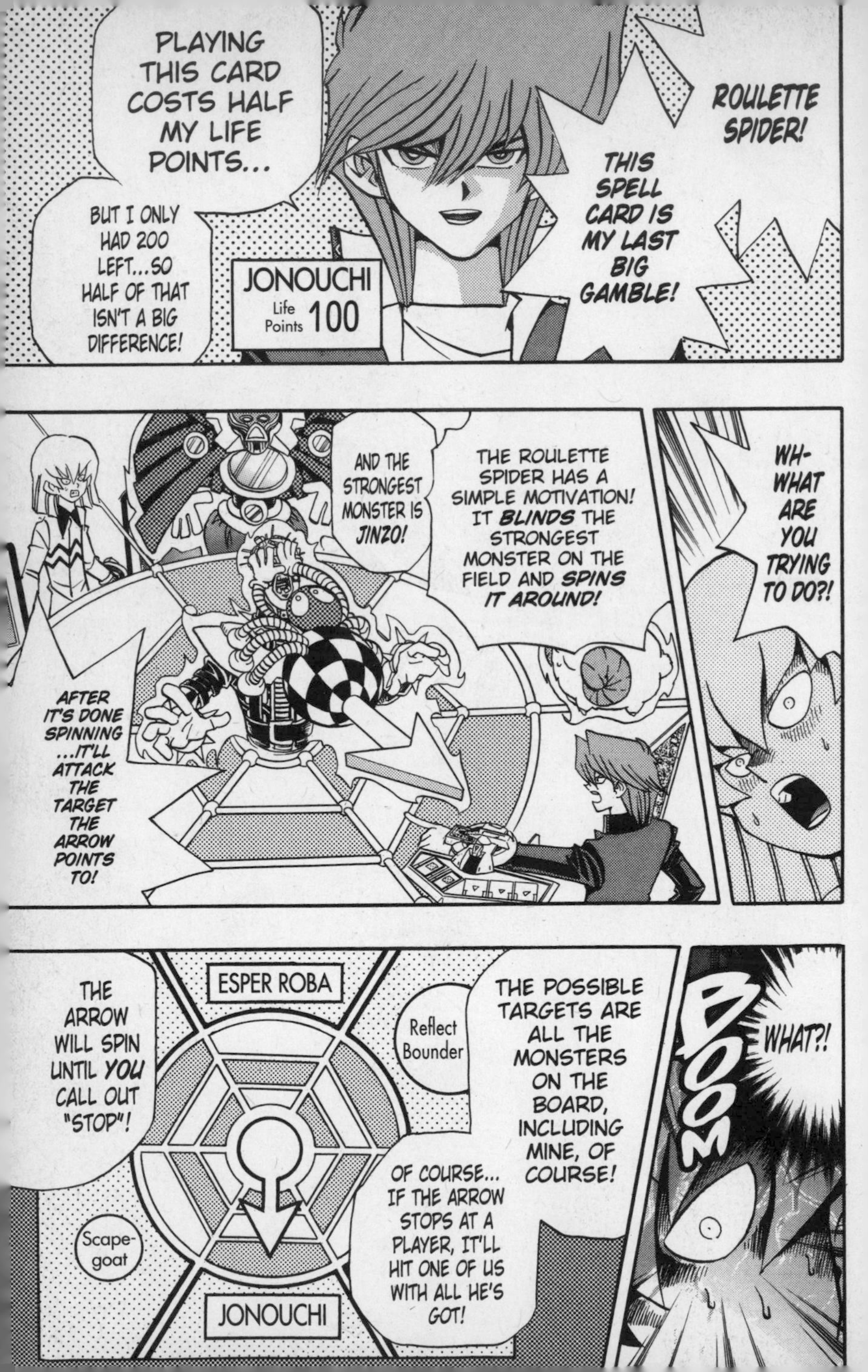
ROULETTE SPIDER!
THIS SPELL CARD IS MY LAST BIG GAMBLE!
PLAYING THIS CARD COSTS HALF MY LIFE POINTS...
JONOUCHI Life Points 100
BUT I ONLY HAD 200 LEFT...SO HALF OF THAT ISN'T A BIG DIFFERENCE!
WH-WHAT ARE YOU TRYING TO DO?!
THE ROULETTE SPIDER HAS A SIMPLE MOTIVATION! IT *BLINDS* THE STRONGEST MONSTER ON THE FIELD AND *SPINS IT AROUND!*
AND THE STRONGEST MONSTER IS *JINZO!*
AFTER IT'S DONE SPINNING ...IT'LL ATTACK THE TARGET THE ARROW POINTS TO!
BOOM
WHAT?!
THE POSSIBLE TARGETS ARE ALL THE MONSTERS ON THE BOARD, INCLUDING MINE, OF COURSE!
Reflect Bounder
ESPER ROBA
THE ARROW WILL SPIN UNTIL *YOU* CALL OUT "STOP"!
OF COURSE... IF THE ARROW STOPS AT A PLAYER, IT'LL HIT ONE OF US WITH ALL HE'S GOT!
Scape-goat
JONOUCHI

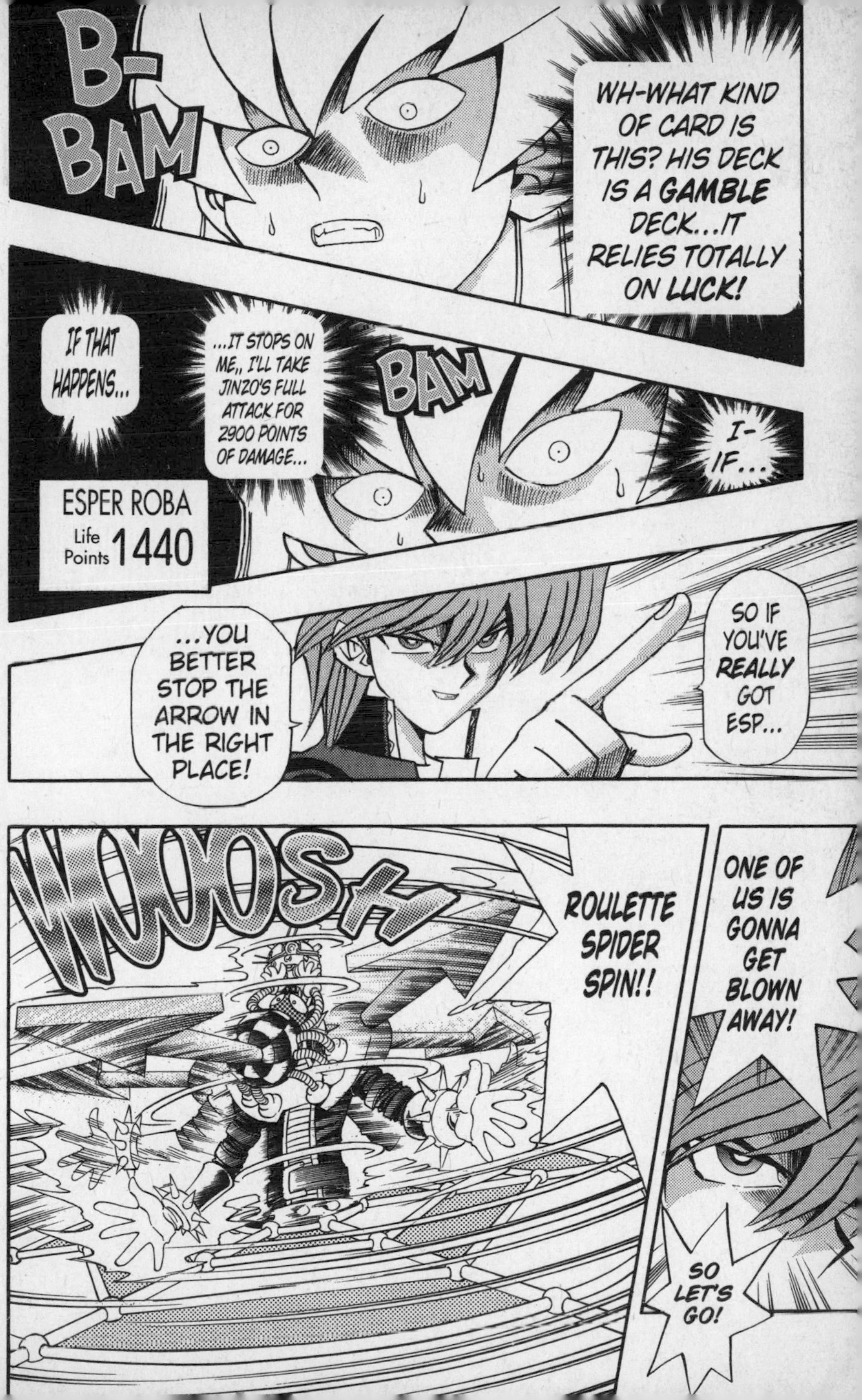
WH-WHAT KIND OF CARD IS THIS? HIS DECK IS A **GAMBLE** DECK...IT RELIES TOTALLY ON **LUCK!**
B-BAM
I- IF...
BAM
...IT STOPS ON ME,, I'LL TAKE JINZO'S FULL ATTACK FOR 2900 POINTS OF DAMAGE...
IF THAT HAPPENS...
ESPER ROBA Life Points 1440
SO IF YOU'VE **REALLY** GOT ESP...
...YOU BETTER STOP THE ARROW IN THE RIGHT PLACE!
ONE OF US IS GONNA GET BLOWN AWAY!
SO LET'S GO!
ROULETTE SPIDER SPIN!!
WHOOSH

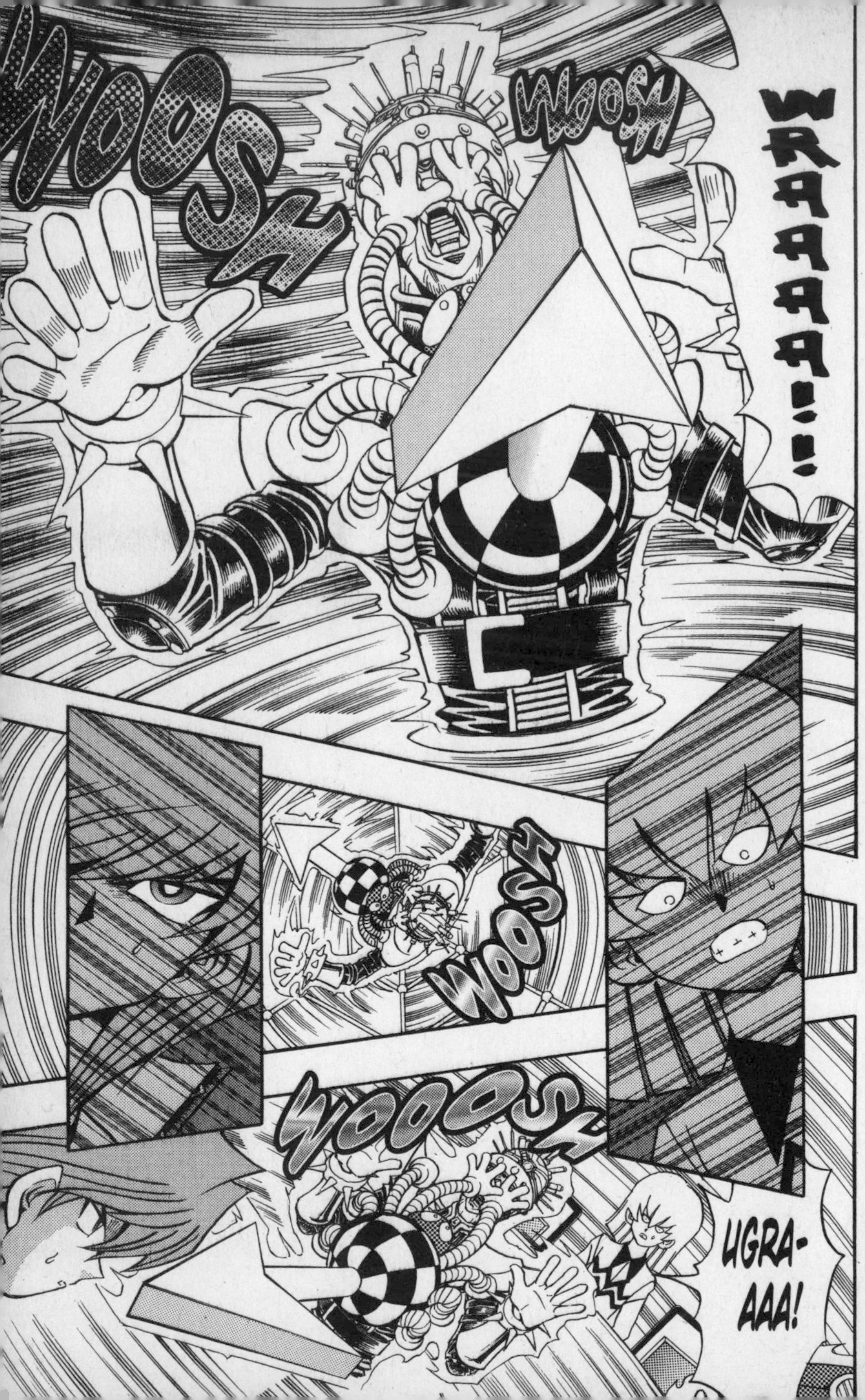
WRAAAA!!
WOOSH
WOOSH
WOOOSH
UGRA-
AAA!
WOOOSH

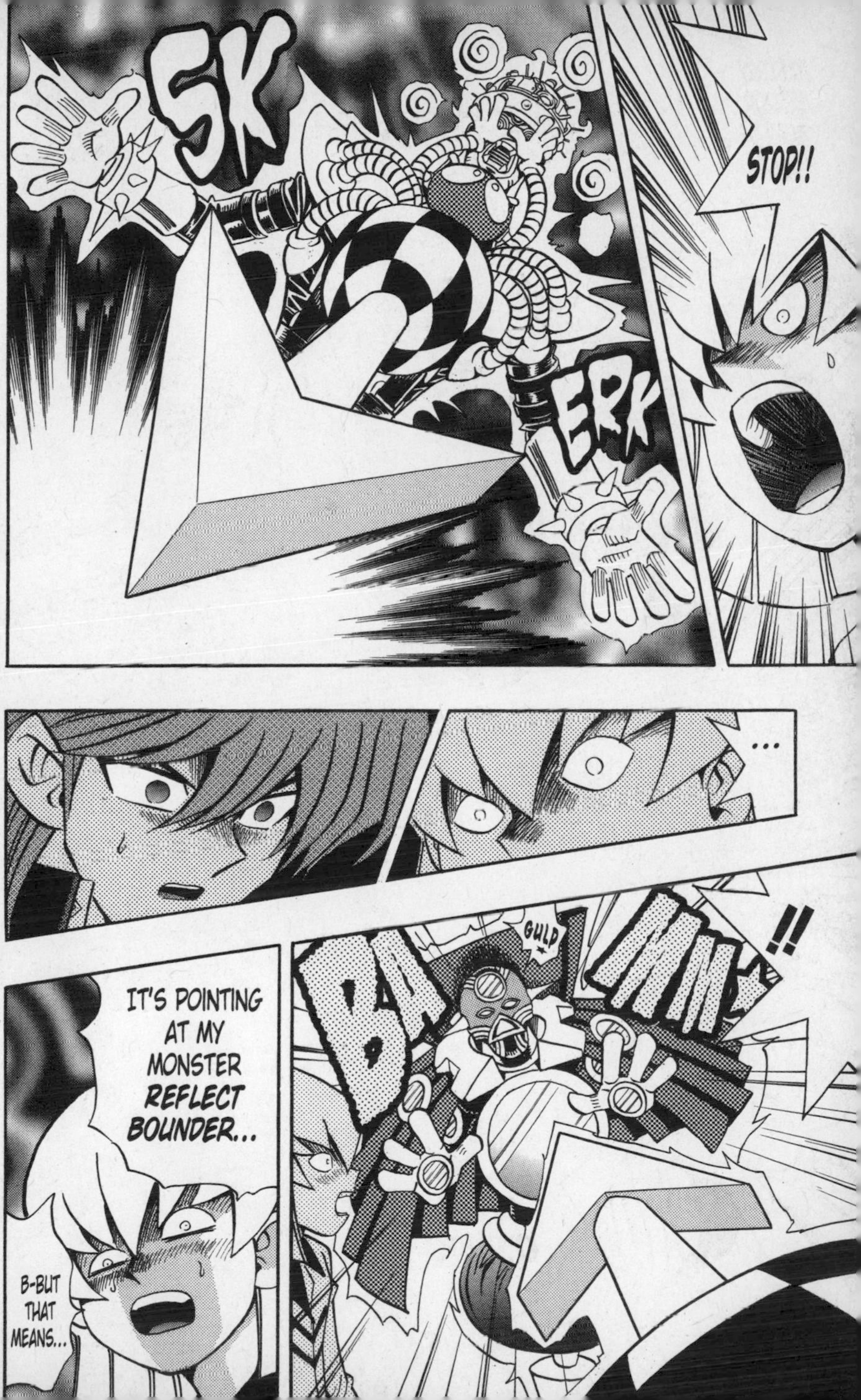
STOP!!
SK
ERK
...
GULP
BAMMM!!
IT'S POINTING AT MY MONSTER *REFLECT BOUNDER*...
B-BUT THAT MEANS...

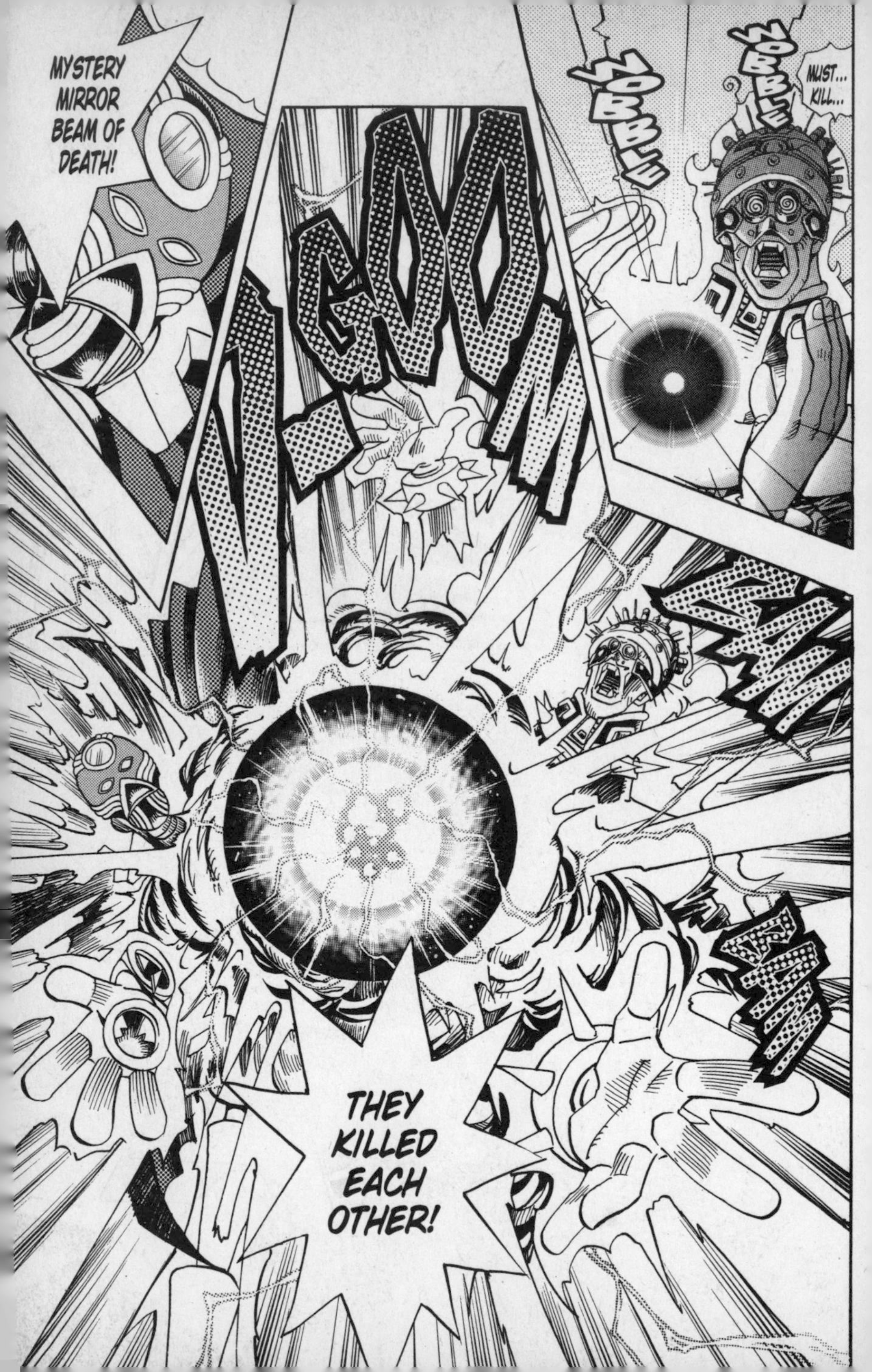
WOBBLE
WOBBLE
MUST... KILL...
MYSTERY MIRROR BEAM OF DEATH!
THEY KILLED EACH OTHER!

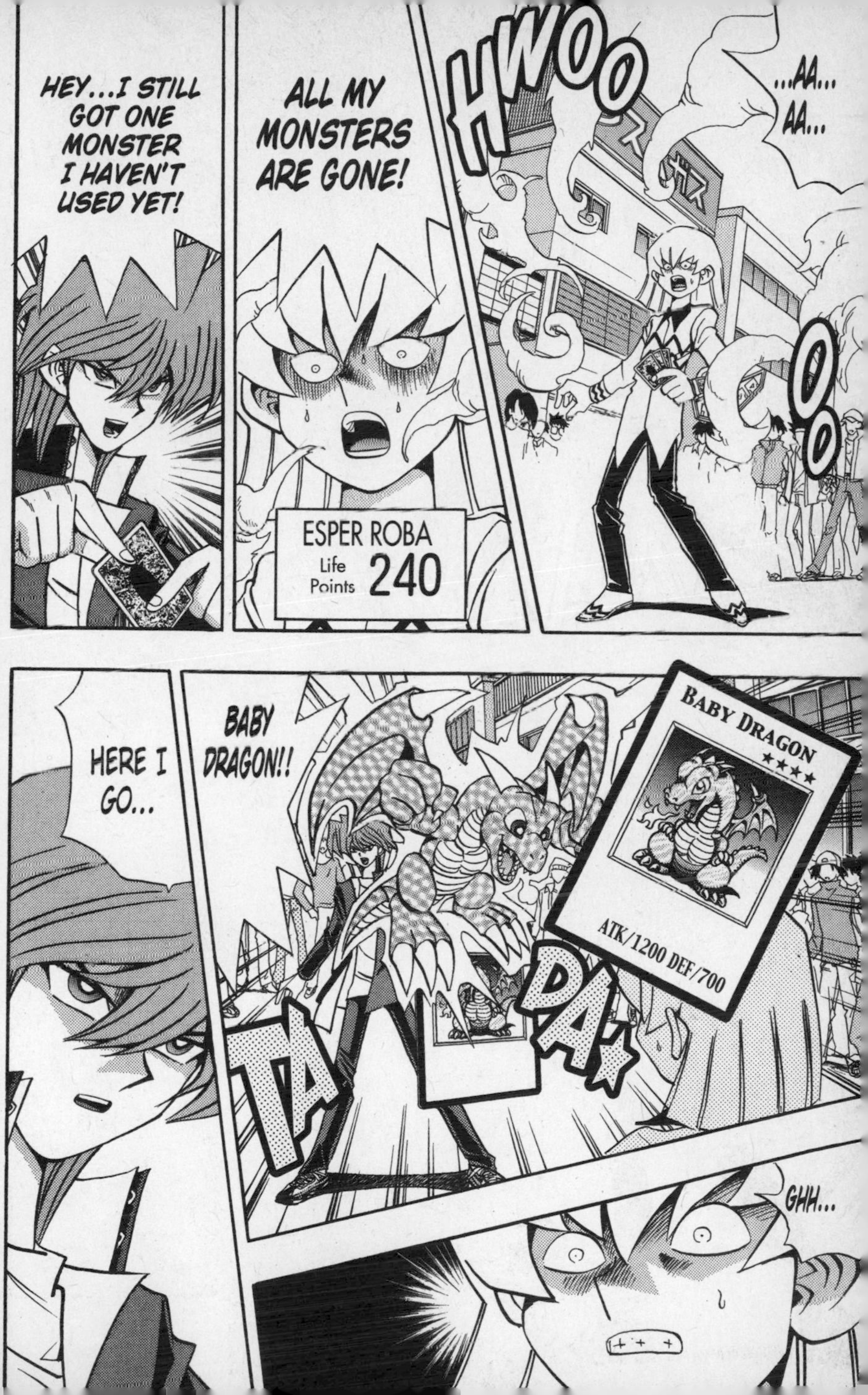

...AA... AA...
HWOOOO
ALL MY MONSTERS ARE GONE!
ESPER ROBA
Life Points 240
HEY...I STILL GOT ONE MONSTER I HAVEN'T USED YET!
BABY DRAGON!!
BABY DRAGON
★★★★
ATK/1200 DEF/700
TA DA★
GHH...
HERE I GO...

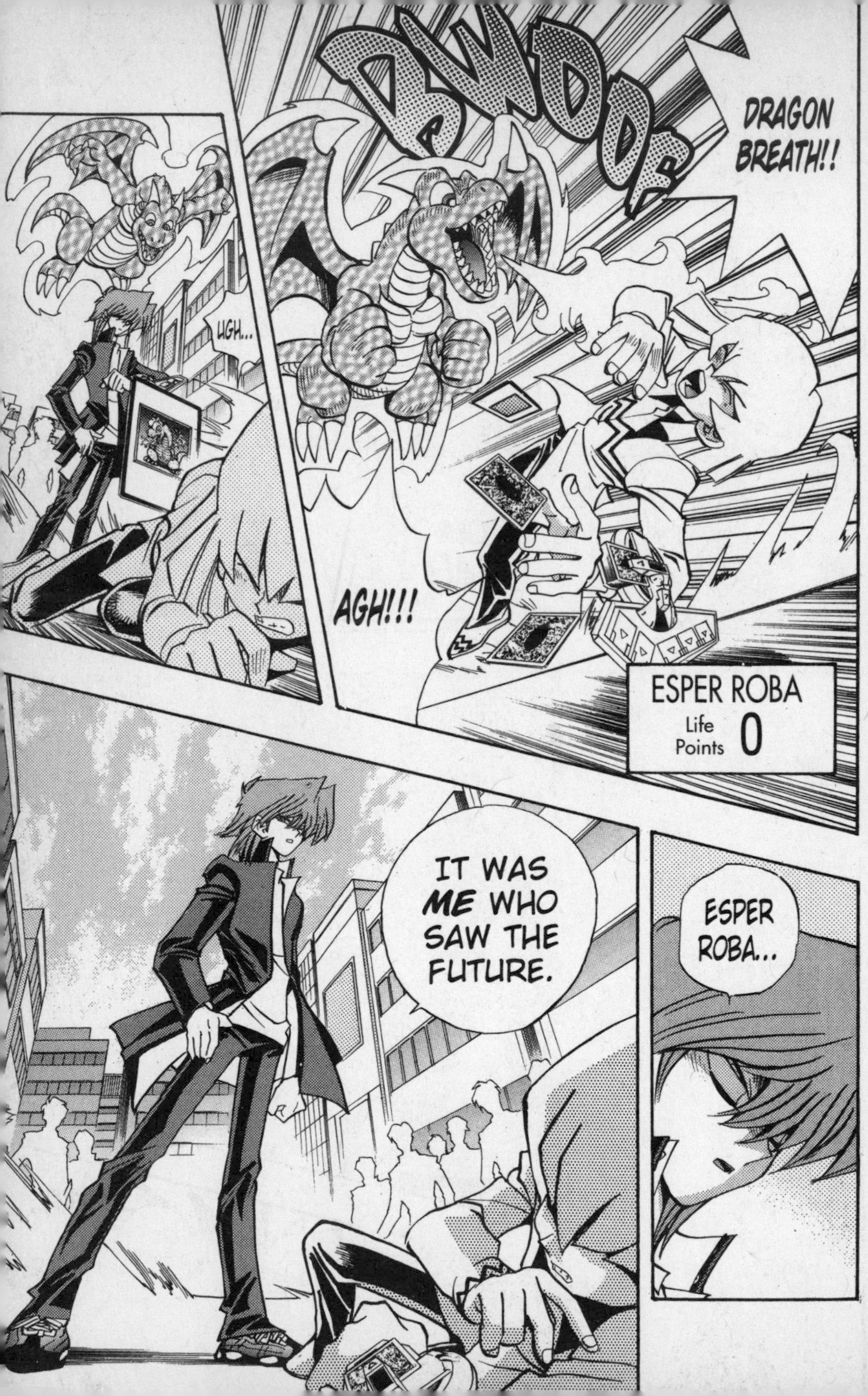
DRAGON BREATH!!
AGH!!!
ESPER ROBA Life Points 0
UGH...
ESPER ROBA...
IT WAS ME WHO SAW THE FUTURE.

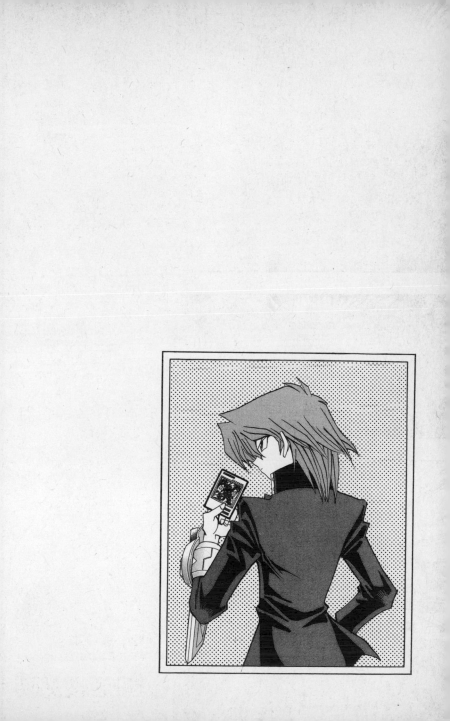

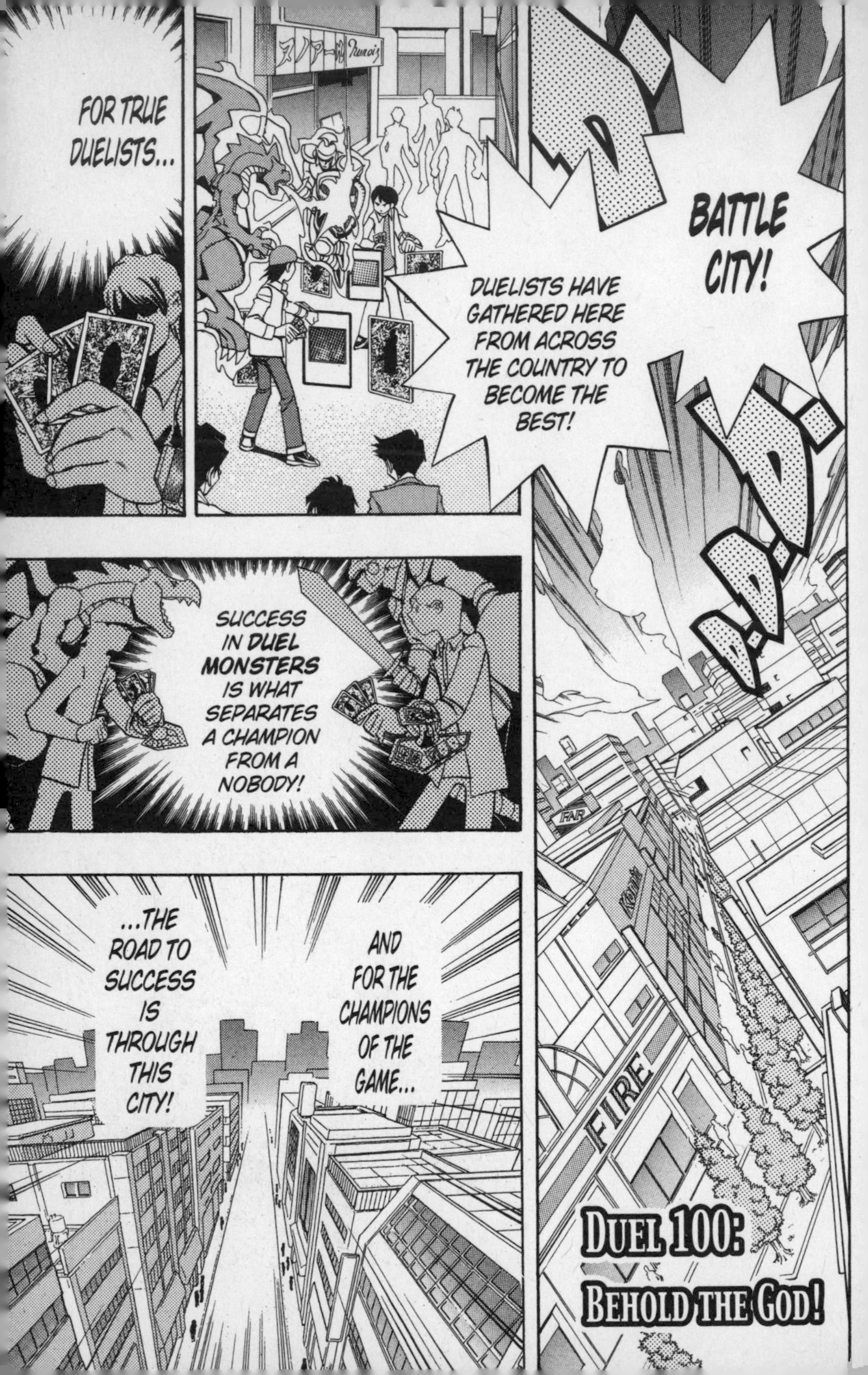

BATTLE CITY!
DUELISTS HAVE GATHERED HERE FROM ACROSS THE COUNTRY TO BECOME THE BEST!
FIRE
DUEL 100: BEHOLD THE GOD!
FOR TRUE DUELISTS...
SUCCESS IN DUEL MONSTERS IS WHAT SEPARATES A CHAMPION FROM A NOBODY!
AND FOR THE CHAMPIONS OF THE GAME...
...THE ROAD TO SUCCESS IS THROUGH THIS CITY!

Duel 100: Behold the God!

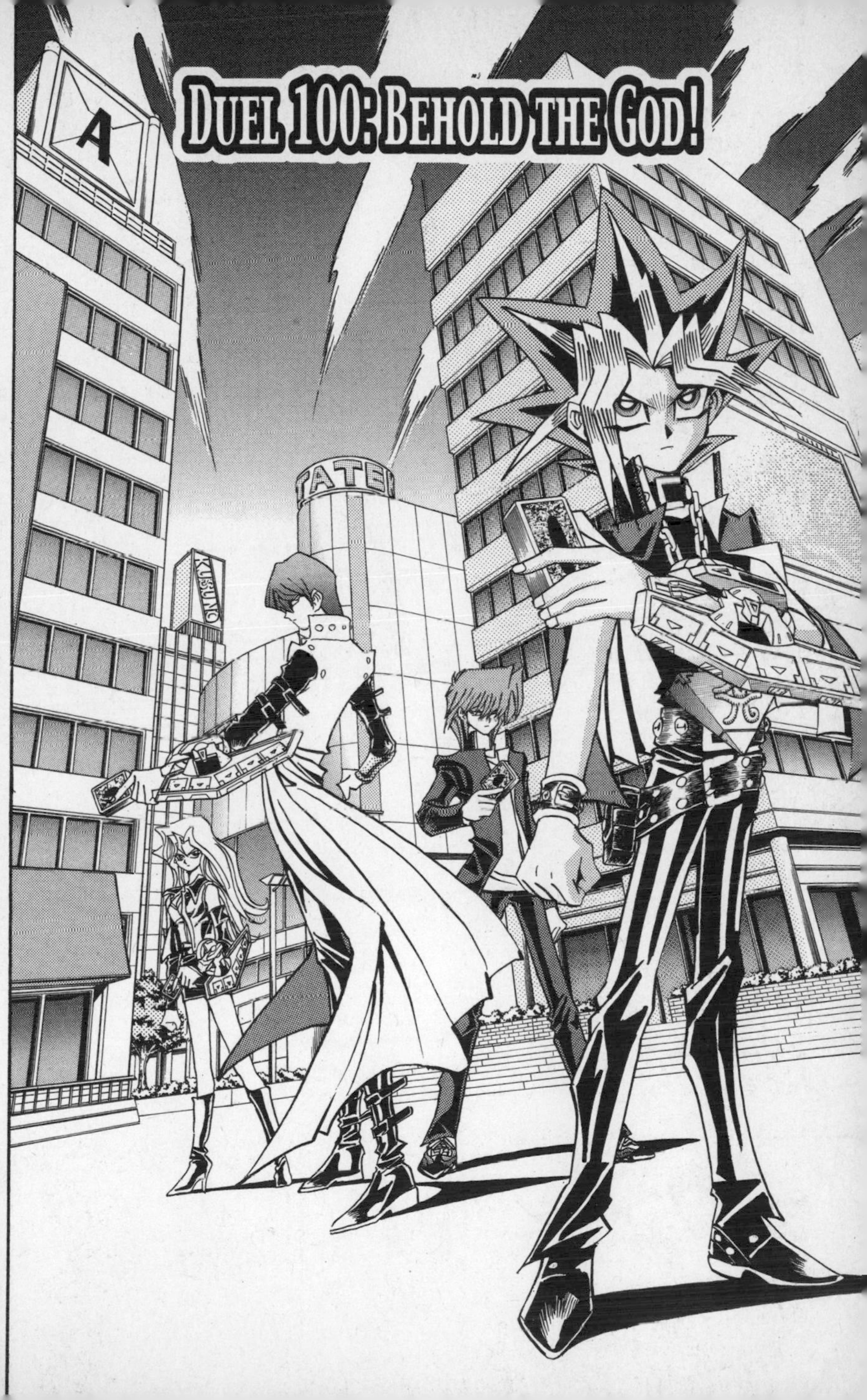

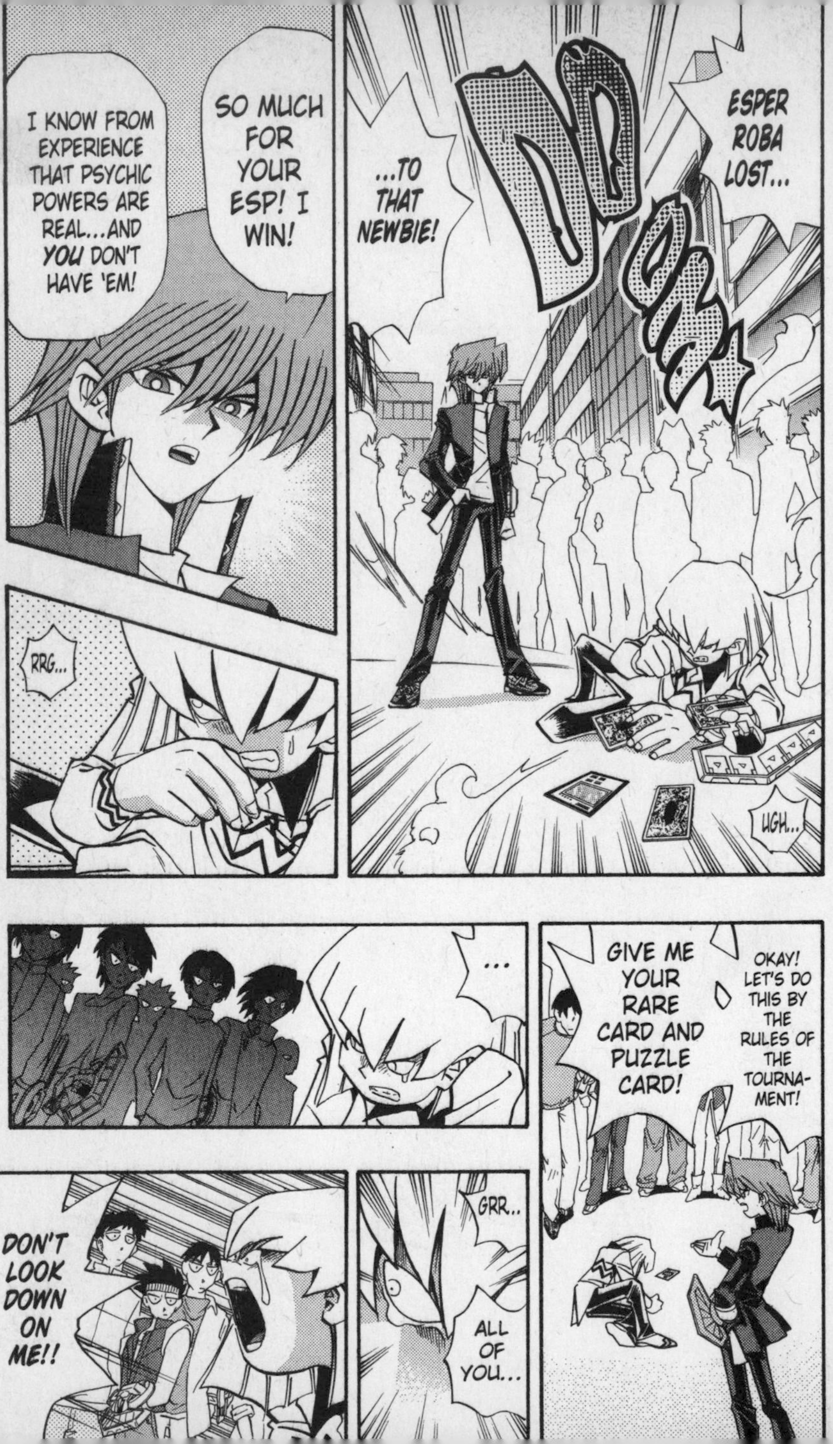
ESPER ROBA LOST...
...TO THAT NEWBIE!
UGH...
SO MUCH FOR YOUR ESP! I WIN!
I KNOW FROM EXPERIENCE THAT PSYCHIC POWERS ARE REAL...AND *YOU* DON'T HAVE 'EM!
RRG...
OKAY! LET'S DO THIS BY THE RULES OF THE TOURNA-MENT!
GIVE ME YOUR RARE CARD AND PUZZLE CARD!
...
GRR...
ALL OF YOU...
DON'T LOOK DOWN ON ME!!

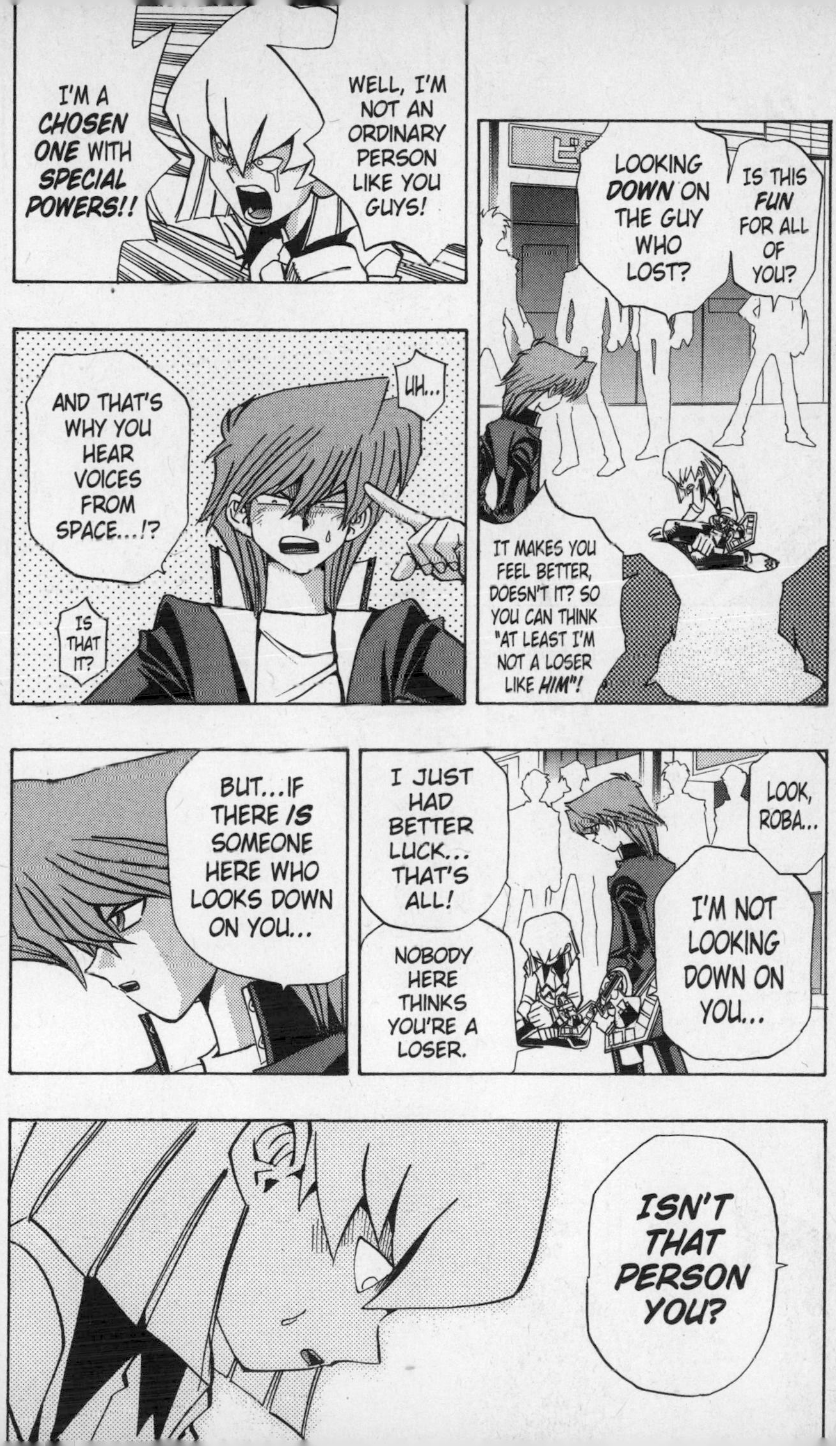
IS THIS FUN FOR ALL OF YOU?
LOOKING DOWN ON THE GUY WHO LOST?
IT MAKES YOU FEEL BETTER, DOESN'T IT? SO YOU CAN THINK "AT LEAST I'M NOT A LOSER LIKE HIM"!
WELL, I'M NOT AN ORDINARY PERSON LIKE YOU GUYS!
I'M A CHOSEN ONE WITH SPECIAL POWERS!!
UH...
AND THAT'S WHY YOU HEAR VOICES FROM SPACE...!?
IS THAT IT?
LOOK, ROBA...
I'M NOT LOOKING DOWN ON YOU...
I JUST HAD BETTER LUCK... THAT'S ALL!
NOBODY HERE THINKS YOU'RE A LOSER.
BUT...IF THERE IS SOMEONE HERE WHO LOOKS DOWN ON YOU...
ISN'T THAT PERSON YOU?

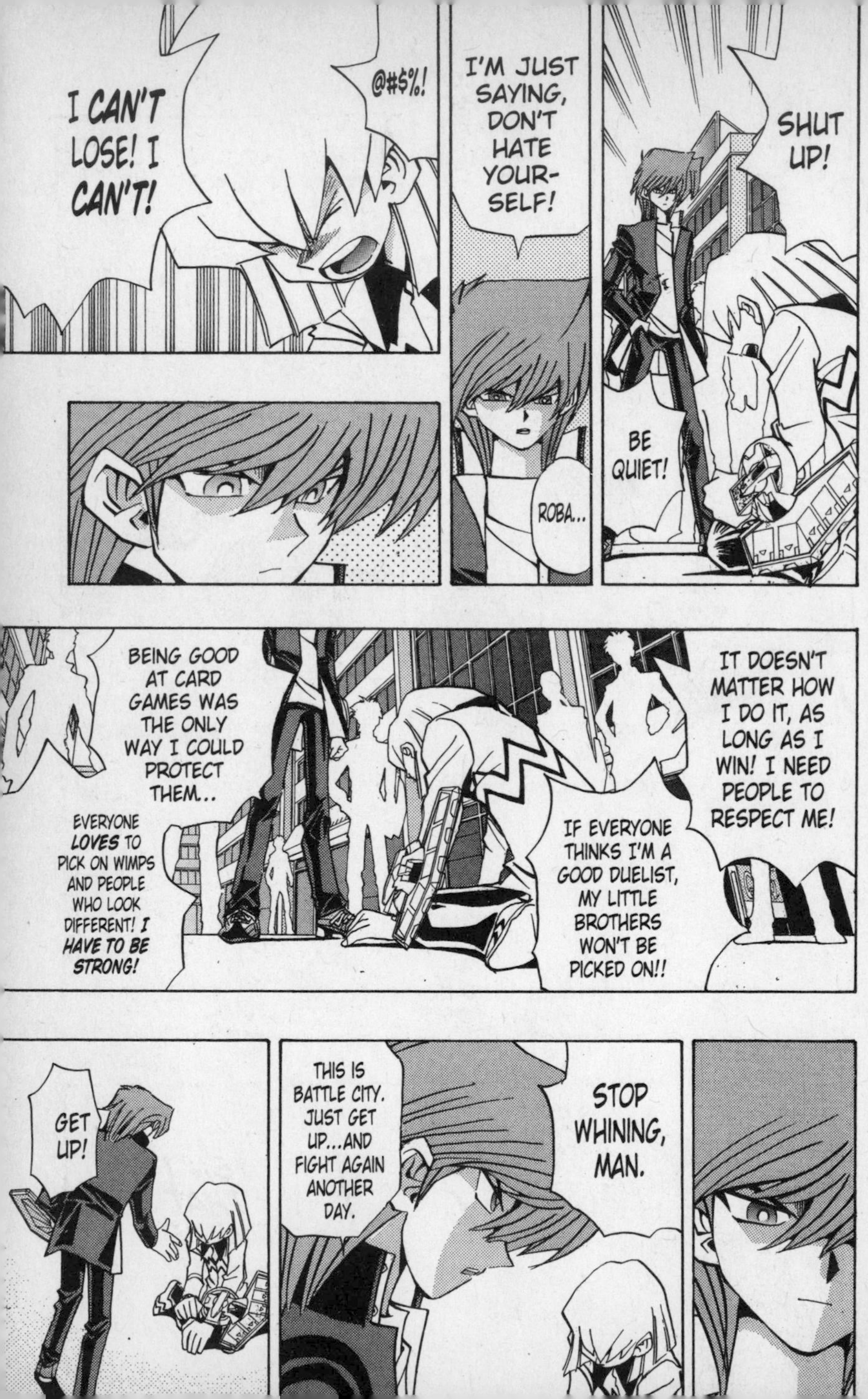

SHUT UP!
BE QUIET!
I'M JUST SAYING, DON'T HATE YOURSELF!
ROBA...
@#$%!
I CAN'T LOSE! I CAN'T!
IT DOESN'T MATTER HOW I DO IT, AS LONG AS I WIN! I NEED PEOPLE TO RESPECT ME!
IF EVERYONE THINKS I'M A GOOD DUELIST, MY LITTLE BROTHERS WON'T BE PICKED ON!!
BEING GOOD AT CARD GAMES WAS THE ONLY WAY I COULD PROTECT THEM...
EVERYONE LOVES TO PICK ON WIMPS AND PEOPLE WHO LOOK DIFFERENT! I HAVE TO BE STRONG!
STOP WHINING, MAN.
THIS IS BATTLE CITY. JUST GET UP...AND FIGHT AGAIN ANOTHER DAY.
GET UP!

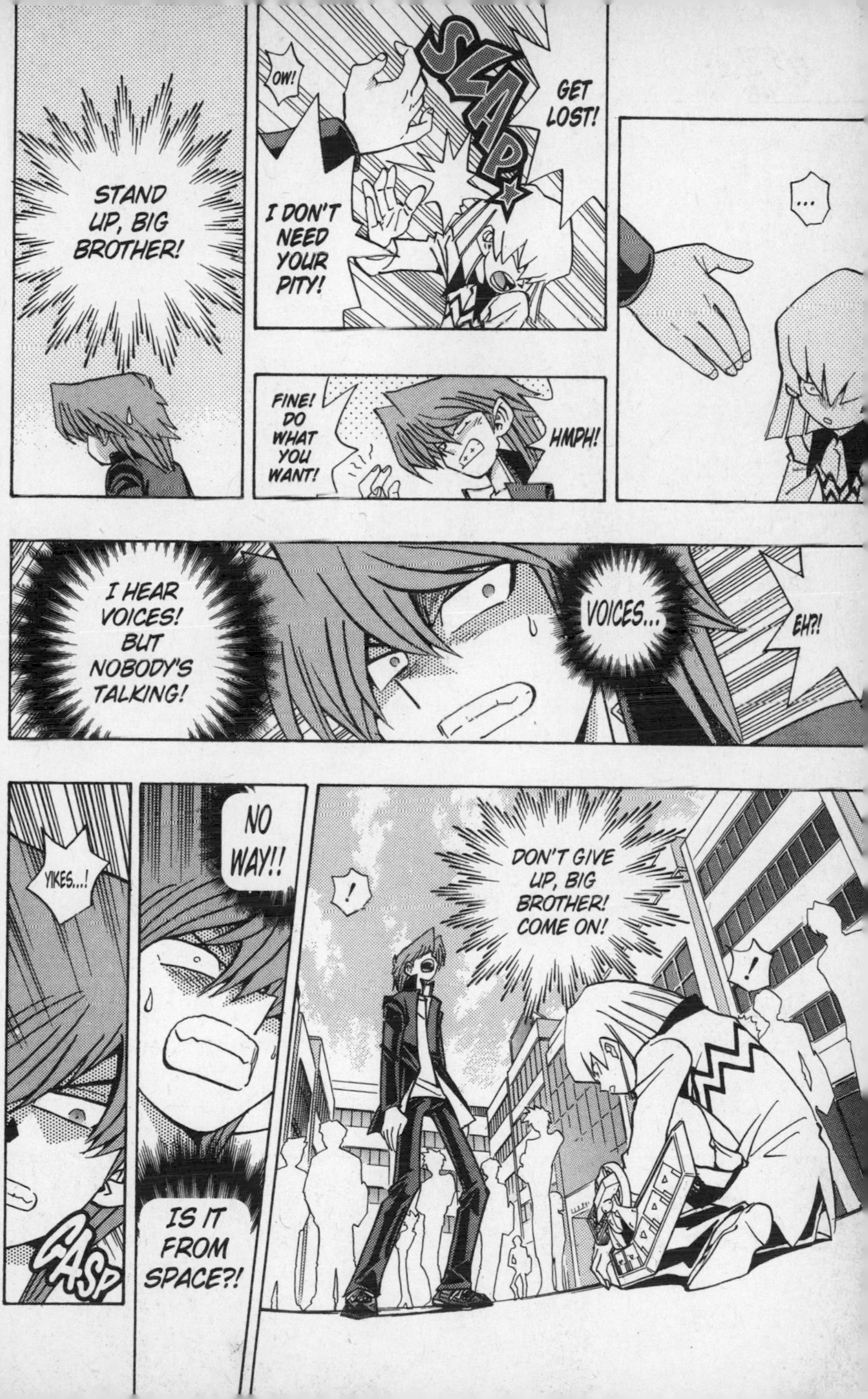
...
GET LOST!
SLAP
OW!
I DON'T NEED YOUR PITY!
HMPH!
FINE! DO WHAT YOU WANT!
STAND UP, BIG BROTHER!
EH?!
VOICES...
I HEAR VOICES! BUT NOBODY'S TALKING!
DON'T GIVE UP, BIG BROTHER! COME ON!
!
!
NO WAY!!
IS IT FROM SPACE?!
YIKES...!
GASP

READ THIS WAY

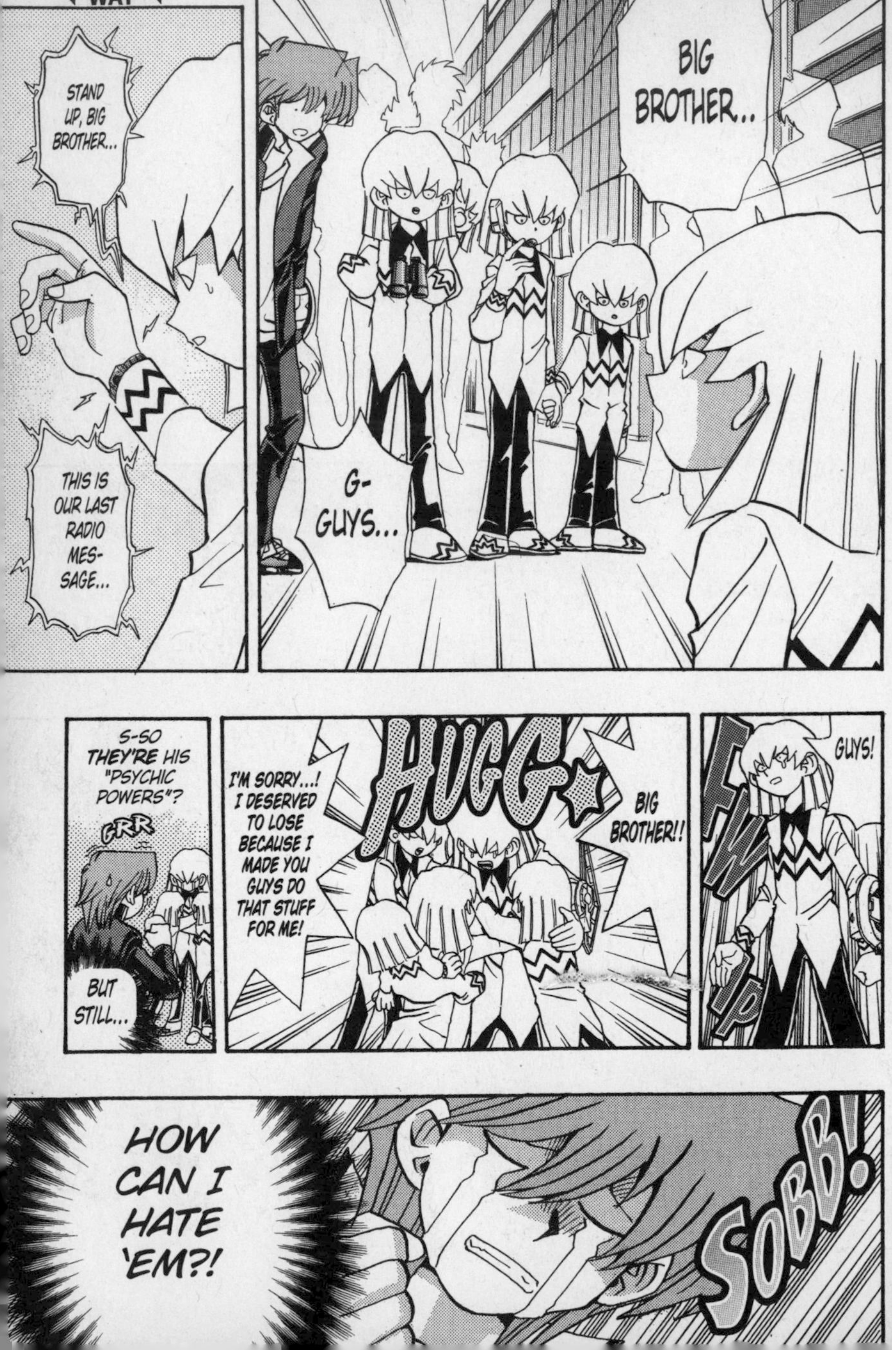
BIG BROTHER...
G-GUYS...
STAND UP, BIG BROTHER...
THIS IS OUR LAST RADIO MESSAGE...
GUYS!
FWIP
BIG BROTHER!!
HUGG
I'M SORRY...! I DESERVED TO LOSE BECAUSE I MADE YOU GUYS DO THAT STUFF FOR ME!
S-SO THEY'RE HIS "PSYCHIC POWERS"?
GRR
BUT STILL...
SOBB!
HOW CAN I HATE 'EM?!

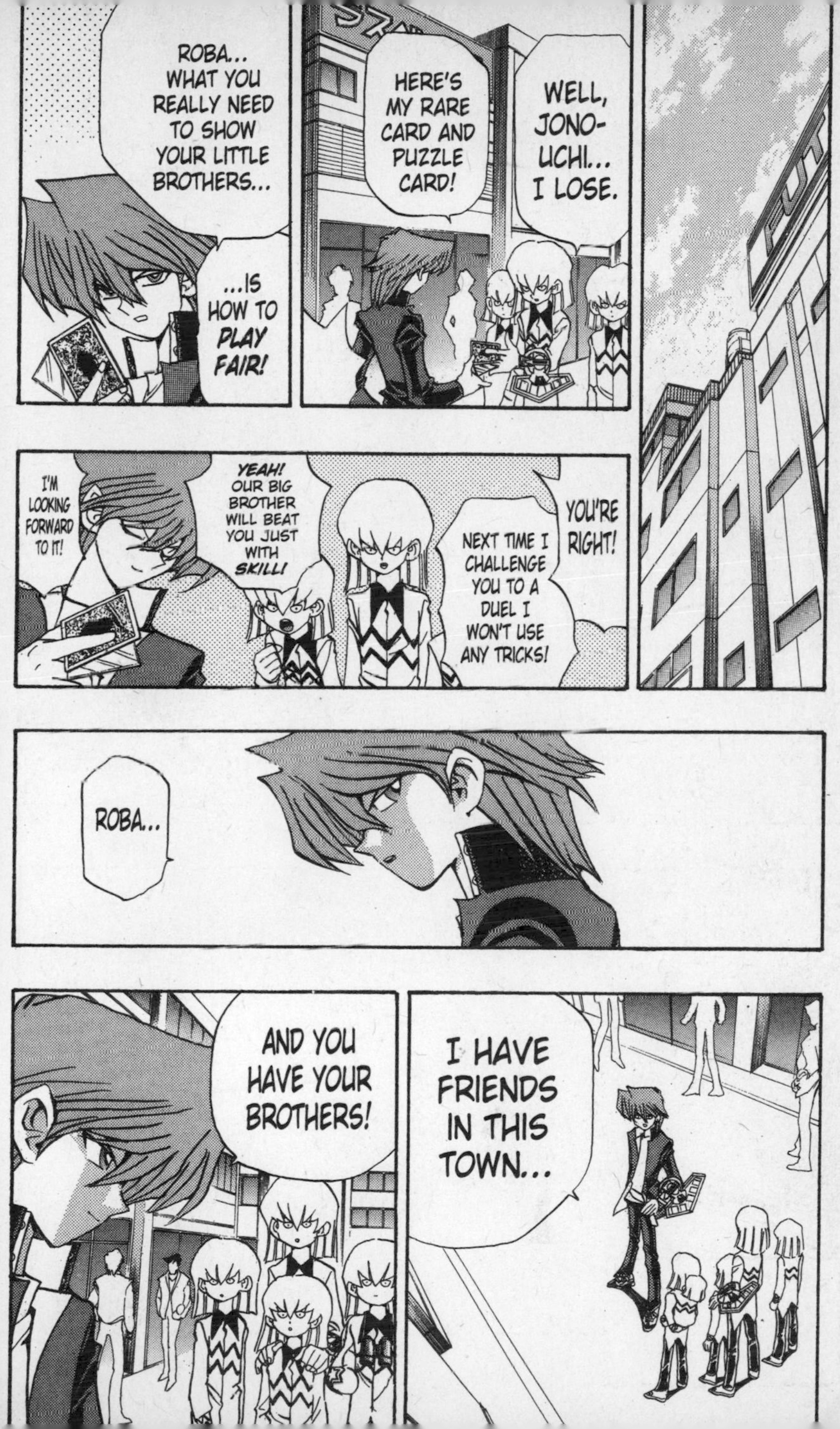
WELL, JONO-UCHI... I LOSE.
HERE'S MY RARE CARD AND PUZZLE CARD!
ROBA... WHAT YOU REALLY NEED TO SHOW YOUR LITTLE BROTHERS...
...IS HOW TO PLAY FAIR!
YOU'RE RIGHT!
NEXT TIME I CHALLENGE YOU TO A DUEL I WON'T USE ANY TRICKS!
YEAH! OUR BIG BROTHER WILL BEAT YOU JUST WITH SKILL!
I'M LOOKING FORWARD TO IT!
ROBA...
I HAVE FRIENDS IN THIS TOWN...
AND YOU HAVE YOUR BROTHERS!

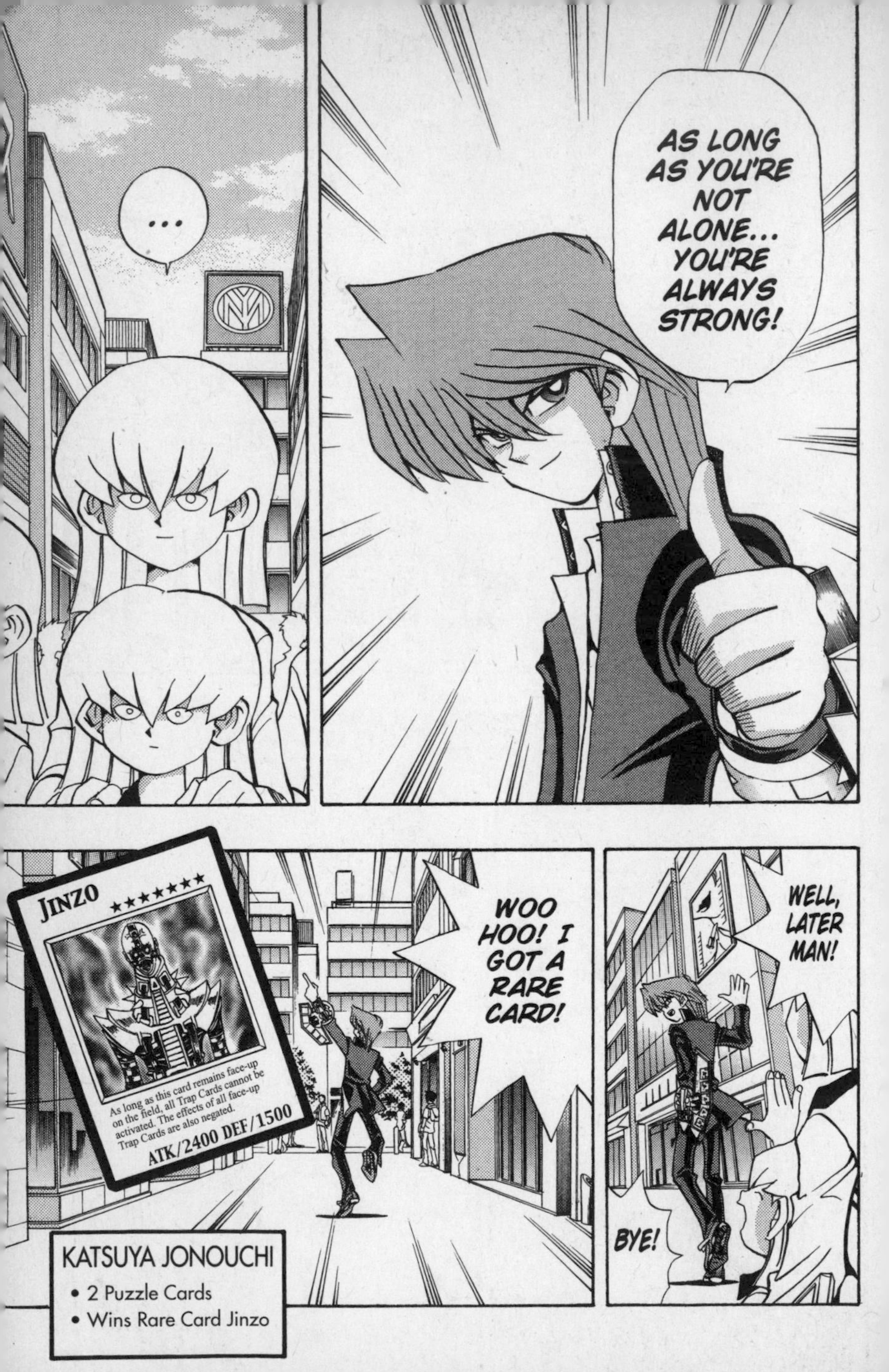
AS LONG AS YOU'RE NOT ALONE... YOU'RE ALWAYS STRONG!
...
WELL, LATER MAN!
BYE!
WOO HOO! I GOT A RARE CARD!
JINZO
As long as this card remains face-up on the field, all Trap Cards cannot be activated. The effects of all face-up Trap Cards are also negated.
ATK/2400 DEF/1500
KATSUYA JONOUCHI
• 2 Puzzle Cards
• Wins Rare Card Jinzo

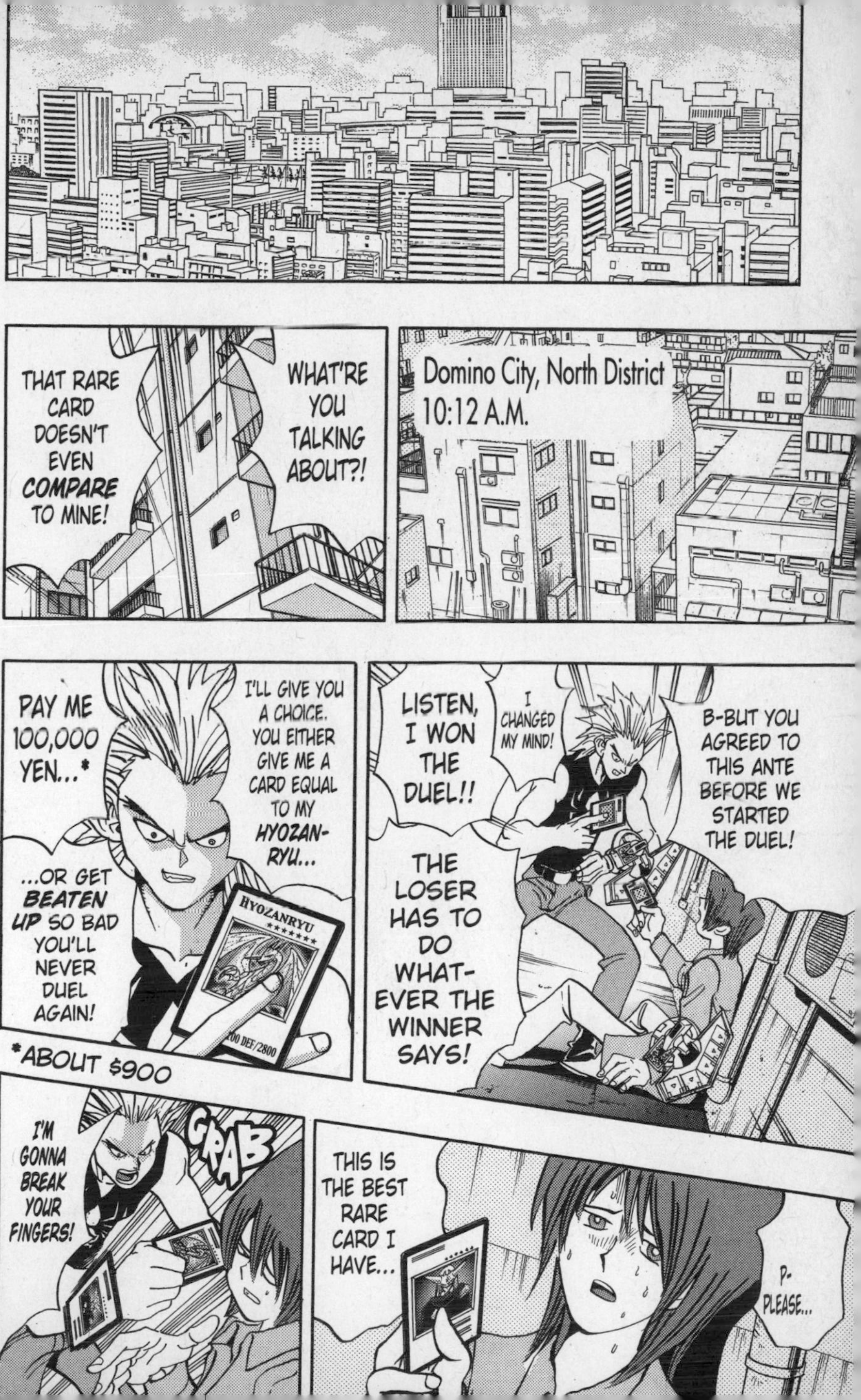
Domino City, North District
10:12 A.M.
WHAT'RE YOU TALKING ABOUT?!
THAT RARE CARD DOESN'T EVEN COMPARE TO MINE!
B-BUT YOU AGREED TO THIS ANTE BEFORE WE STARTED THE DUEL!
I CHANGED MY MIND!
LISTEN, I WON THE DUEL!!
THE LOSER HAS TO DO WHATEVER THE WINNER SAYS!
I'LL GIVE YOU A CHOICE. YOU EITHER GIVE ME A CARD EQUAL TO MY HYOZANRYU...
PAY ME 100,000 YEN...*
...OR GET BEATEN UP SO BAD YOU'LL NEVER DUEL AGAIN!
HYOZANRYU
DEF/2800
*ABOUT $900
P-PLEASE...
THIS IS THE BEST RARE CARD I HAVE...
GRAB
I'M GONNA BREAK YOUR FINGERS!

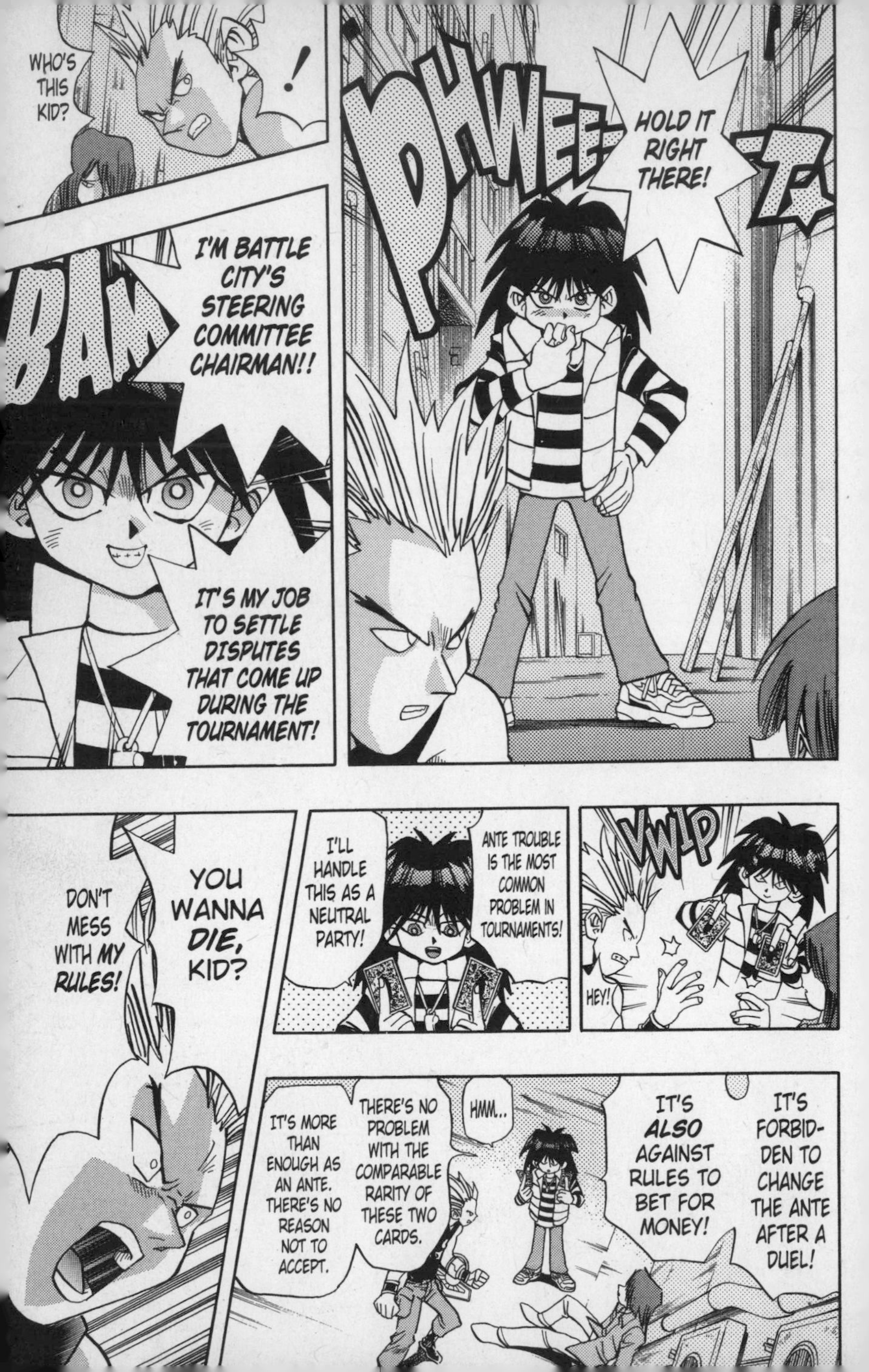
DHWEE-Z!
HOLD IT RIGHT THERE!
WHO'S THIS KID?
!
BAM
I'M BATTLE CITY'S STEERING COMMITTEE CHAIRMAN!!
IT'S MY JOB TO SETTLE DISPUTES THAT COME UP DURING THE TOURNAMENT!
VWIP
HEY!
ANTE TROUBLE IS THE MOST COMMON PROBLEM IN TOURNAMENTS!
I'LL HANDLE THIS AS A NEUTRAL PARTY!
IT'S FORBIDDEN TO CHANGE THE ANTE AFTER A DUEL!
IT'S ALSO AGAINST RULES TO BET FOR MONEY!
HMM...
THERE'S NO PROBLEM WITH THE COMPARABLE RARITY OF THESE TWO CARDS.
IT'S MORE THAN ENOUGH AS AN ANTE. THERE'S NO REASON NOT TO ACCEPT.
YOU WANNA DIE, KID?
DON'T MESS WITH MY RULES!

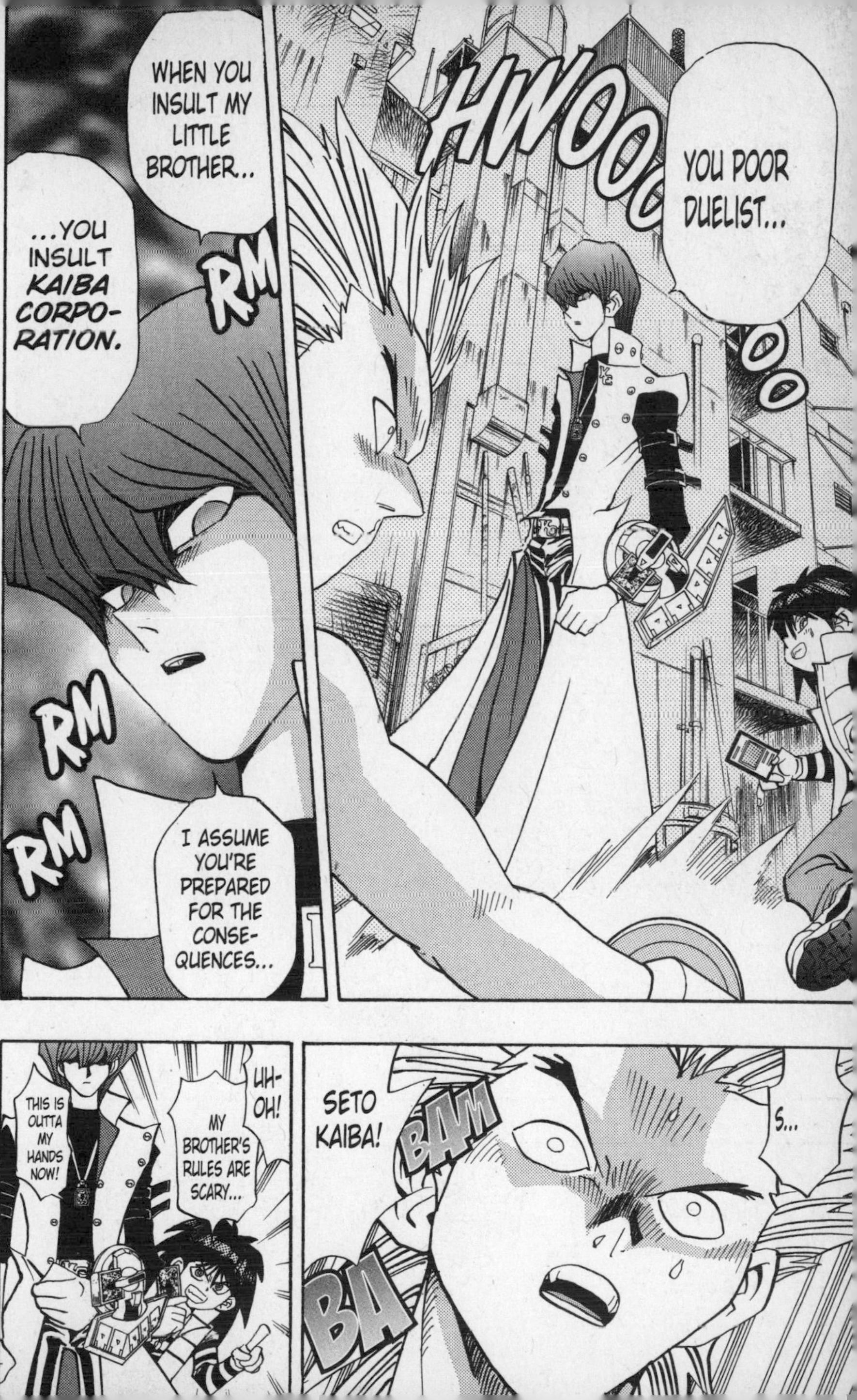
HWOOOOOOO
YOU POOR DUELIST...
WHEN YOU INSULT MY LITTLE BROTHER...
...YOU INSULT KAIBA CORPORATION.
RM
RM
RM
I ASSUME YOU'RE PREPARED FOR THE CONSEQUENCES...
S...
BAM
SETO KAIBA!
BA
UH-OH!
MY BROTHER'S RULES ARE SCARY...
THIS IS OUTTA MY HANDS NOW!

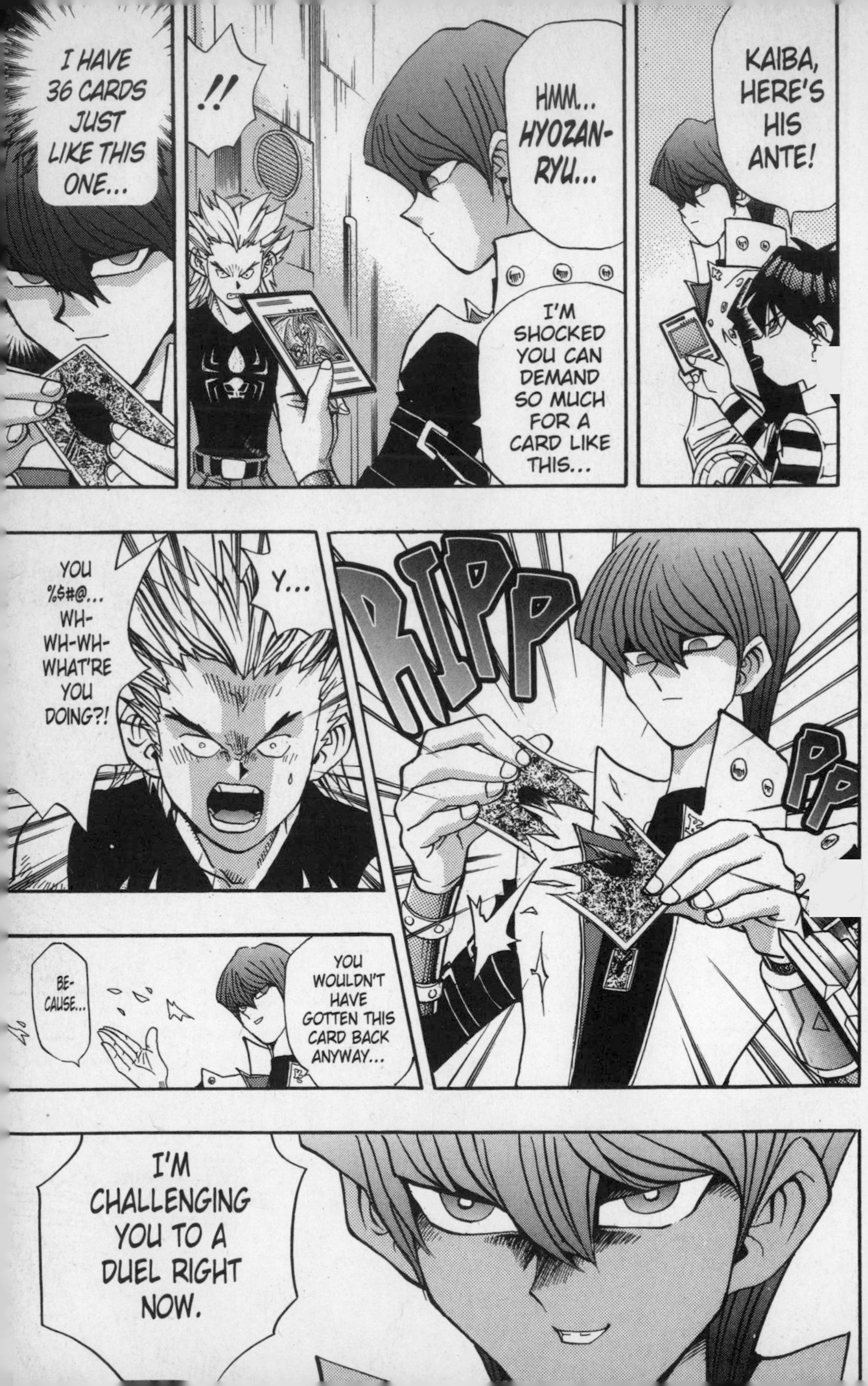
KAIBA, HERE'S HIS ANTE!
HMM... HYOZAN-RYU...
I'M SHOCKED YOU CAN DEMAND SO MUCH FOR A CARD LIKE THIS...
!!
I HAVE 36 CARDS JUST LIKE THIS ONE...
RIPP
PP
Y...
YOU %$#@... WH-WH-WH-WHAT'RE YOU DOING?!
YOU WOULDN'T HAVE GOTTEN THIS CARD BACK ANYWAY...
BE-CAUSE...
I'M CHALLENGING YOU TO A DUEL RIGHT NOW.

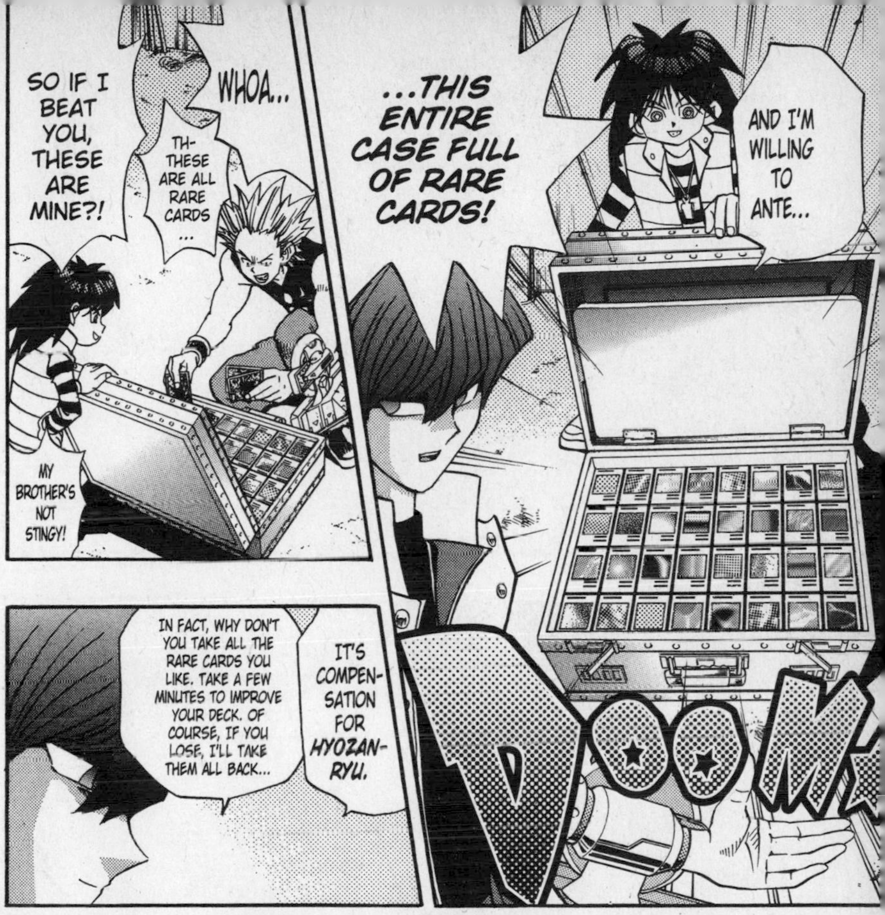
AND I'M WILLING TO ANTE...
...THIS ENTIRE CASE FULL OF RARE CARDS!
DOOM
WHOA...
TH-THESE ARE ALL RARE CARDS...
SO IF I BEAT YOU, THESE ARE MINE?!
MY BROTHER'S NOT STINGY!
IT'S COMPENSATION FOR HYOZAN-RYU.
IN FACT, WHY DON'T YOU TAKE ALL THE RARE CARDS YOU LIKE. TAKE A FEW MINUTES TO IMPROVE YOUR DECK. OF COURSE, IF YOU LOSE, I'LL TAKE THEM ALL BACK...

*ABOUT $450,000,000

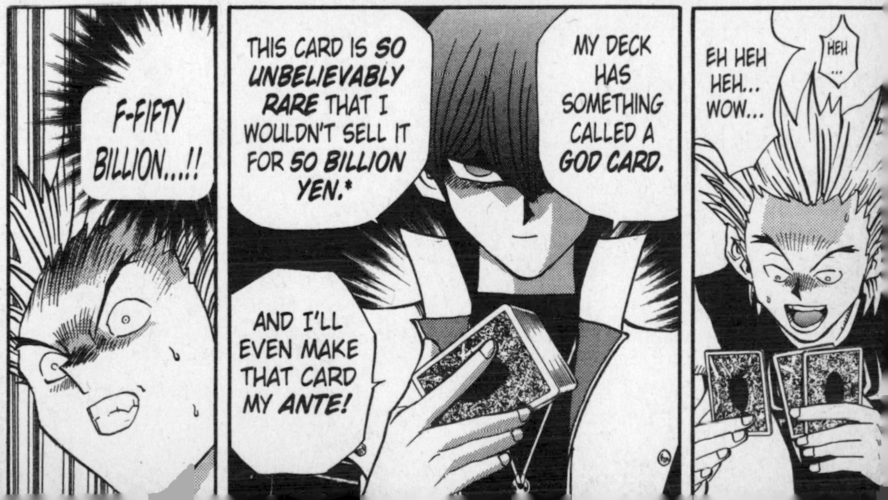
HEH...
EH HEH HEH... WOW...
MY DECK HAS SOMETHING CALLED A GOD CARD.
THIS CARD IS SO UNBELIEVABLY RARE THAT I WOULDN'T SELL IT FOR 50 BILLION YEN.*
AND I'LL EVEN MAKE THAT CARD MY ANTE!
F-FIFTY BILLION...!!

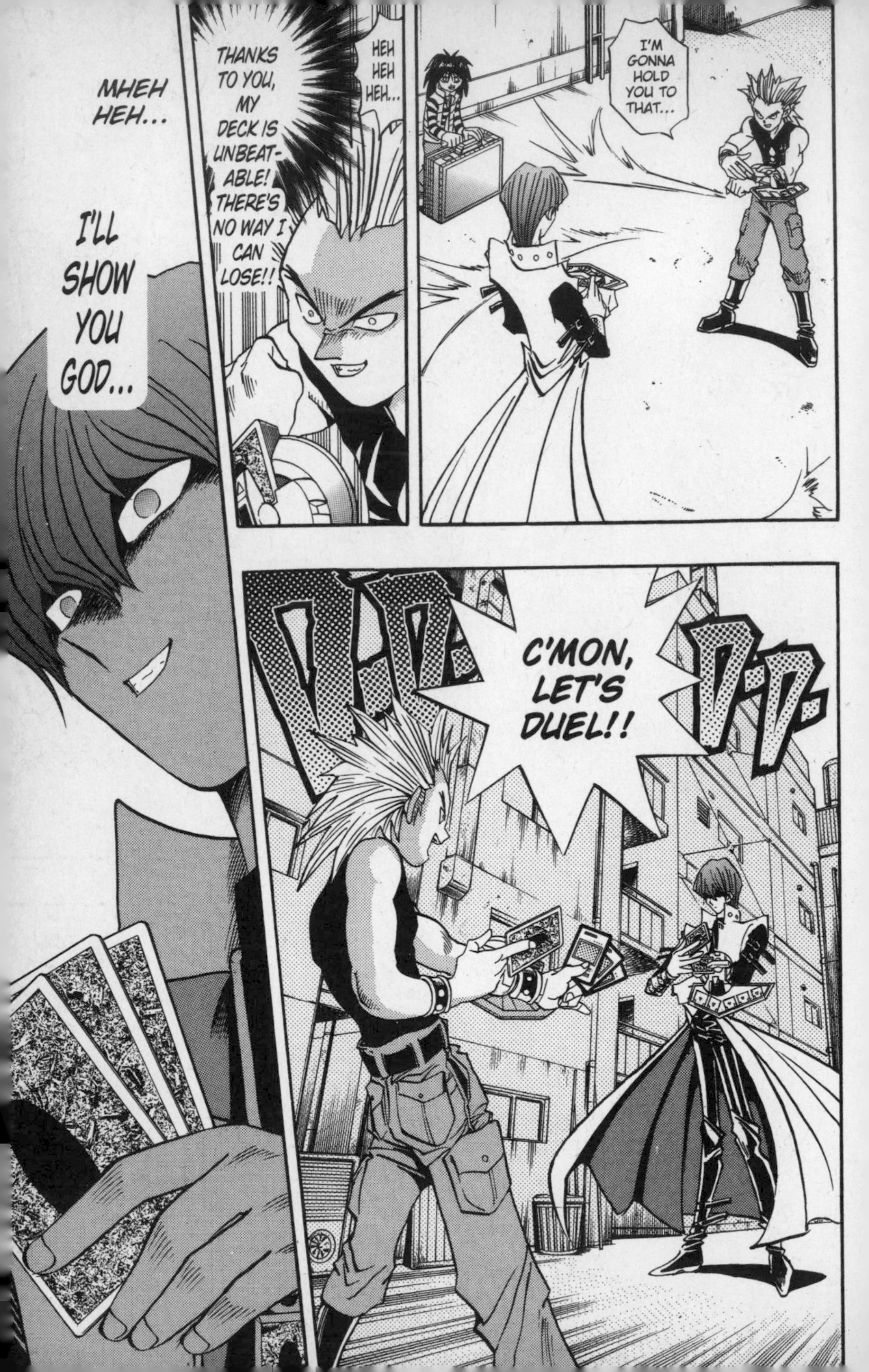
I'M GONNA HOLD YOU TO THAT...
HEH HEH HEH...
THANKS TO YOU, MY DECK IS UNBEATABLE! THERE'S NO WAY I CAN LOSE!!
C'MON, LET'S DUEL!!
MHEH HEH...
I'LL SHOW YOU GOD...

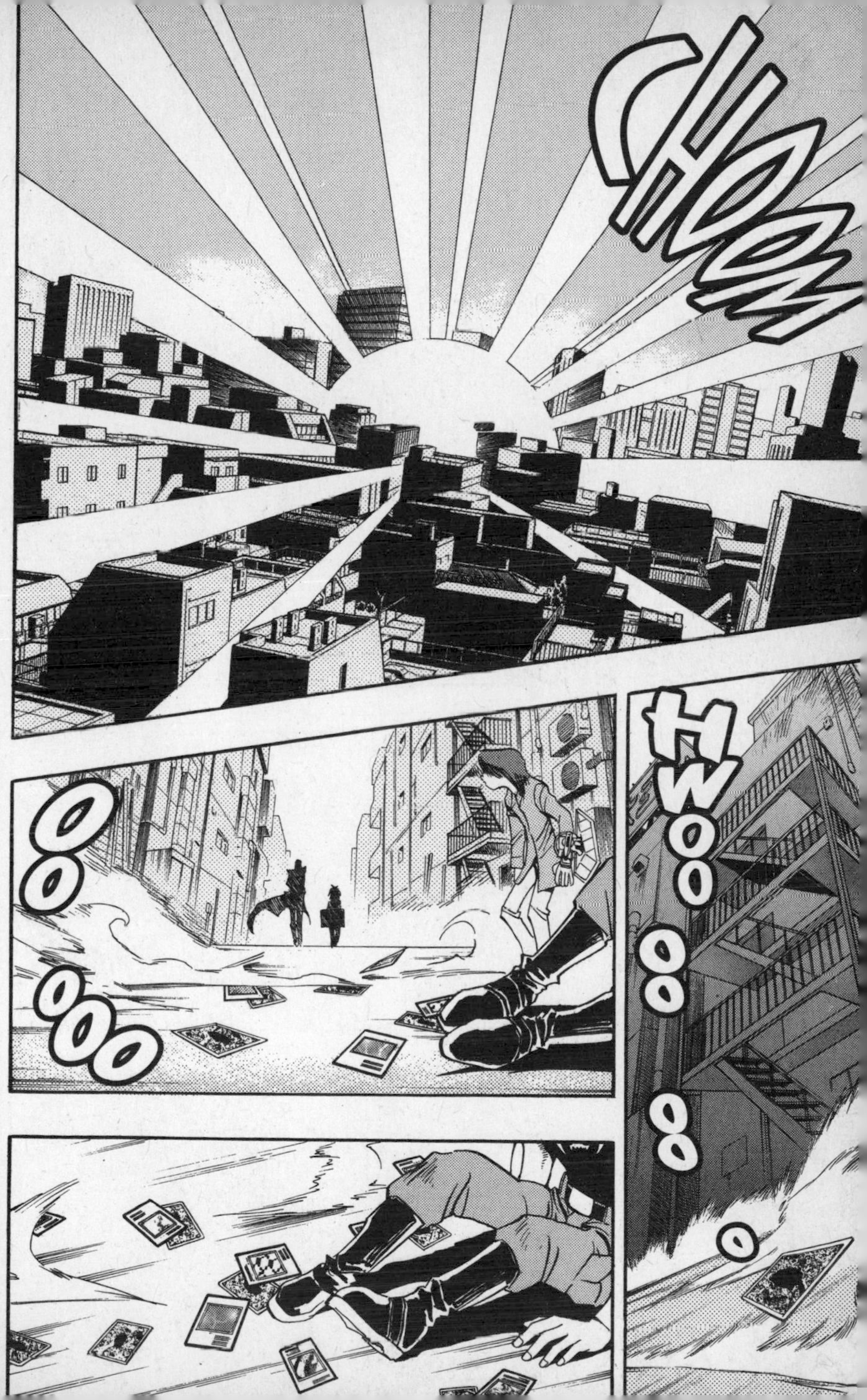
CHOOM
HWOOOOOO
OOOOOO

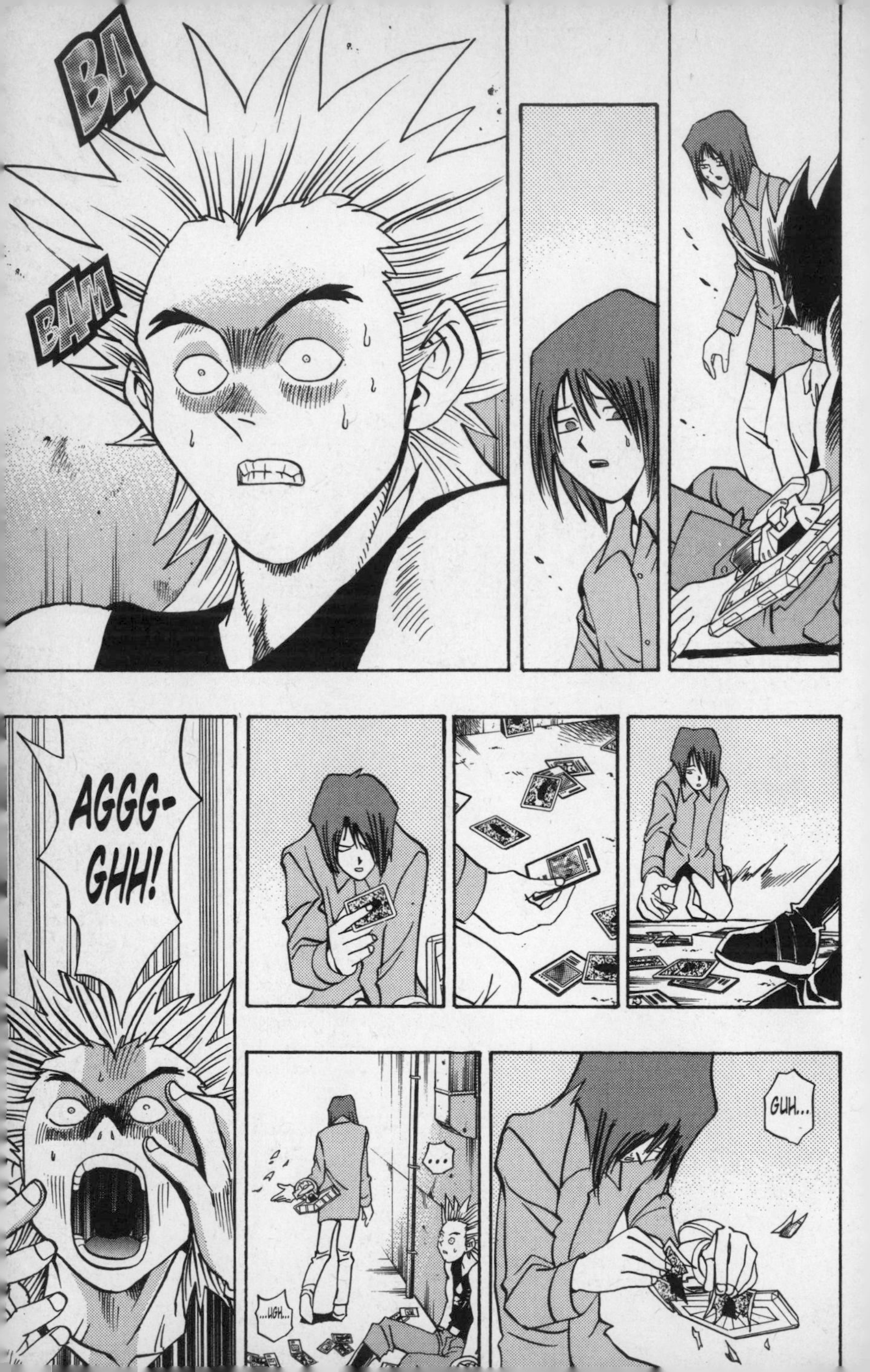
BA
BAM
GUH...
...
...UGH...
AGGG-GHH!

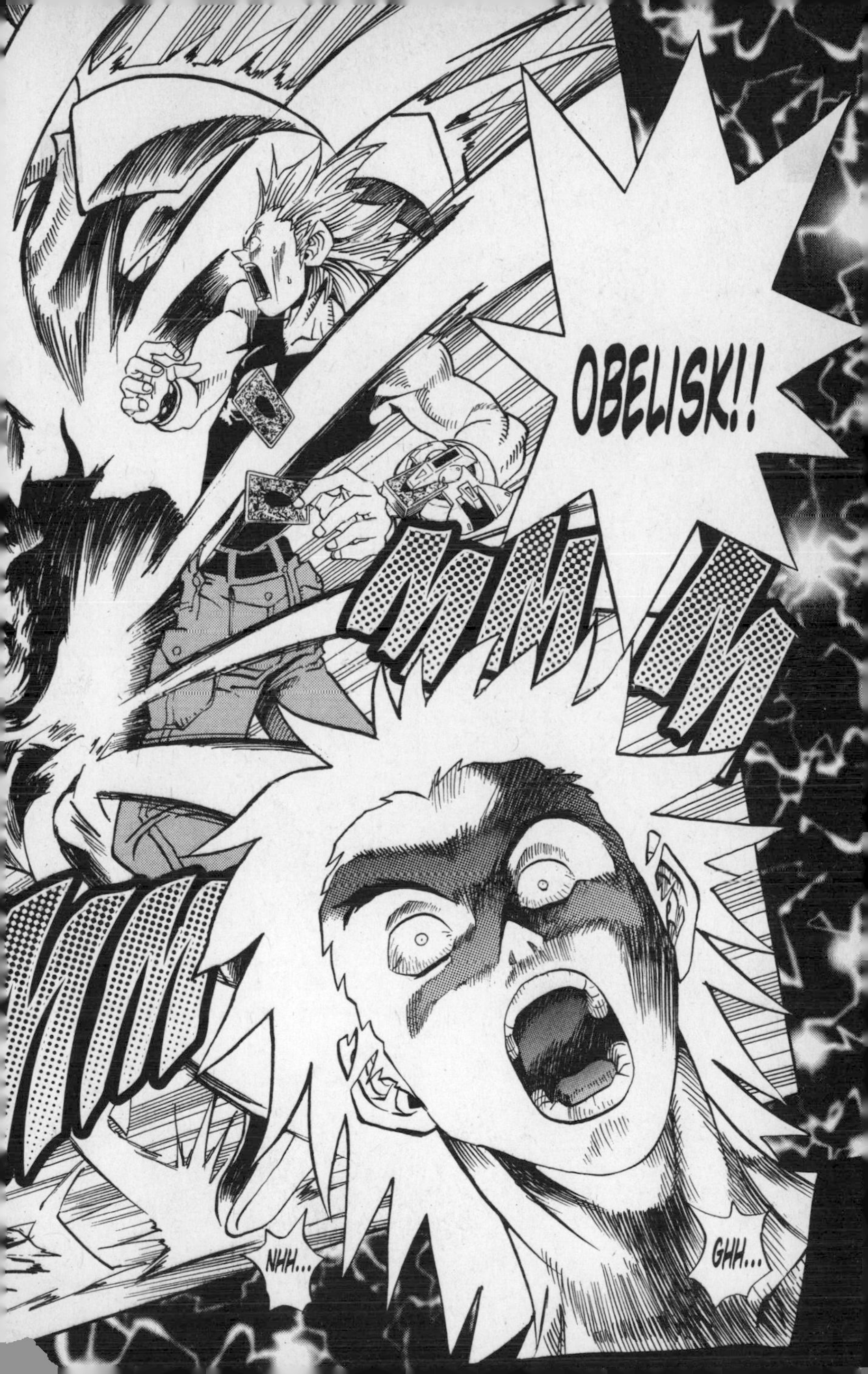
OBELISK!!
MMMM
MMM
GHH...
NHH...

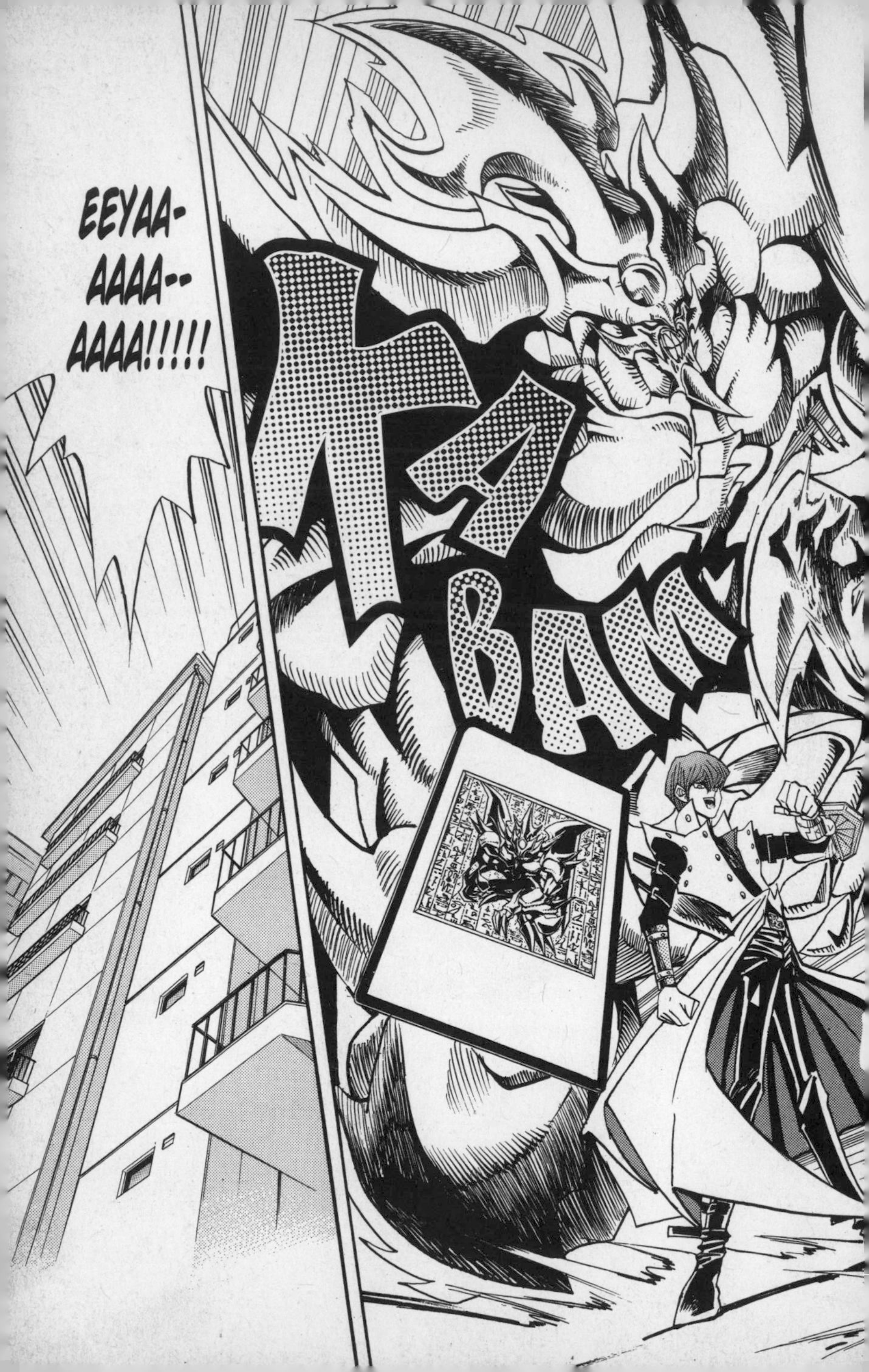
TA BAM
EEYAA-
AAAA--
AAAA!!!!!

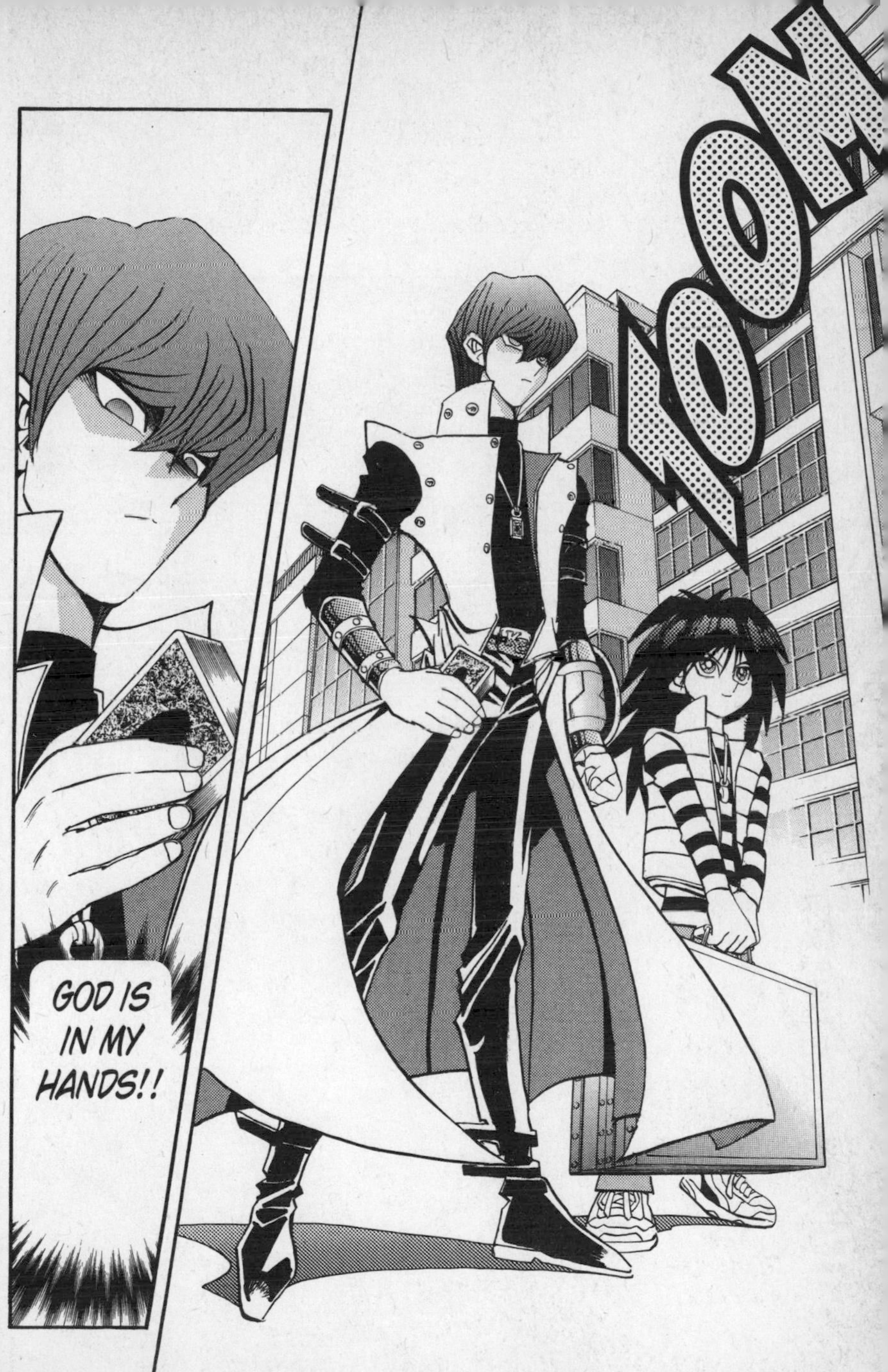
ZOOM
GOD IS IN MY HANDS!!

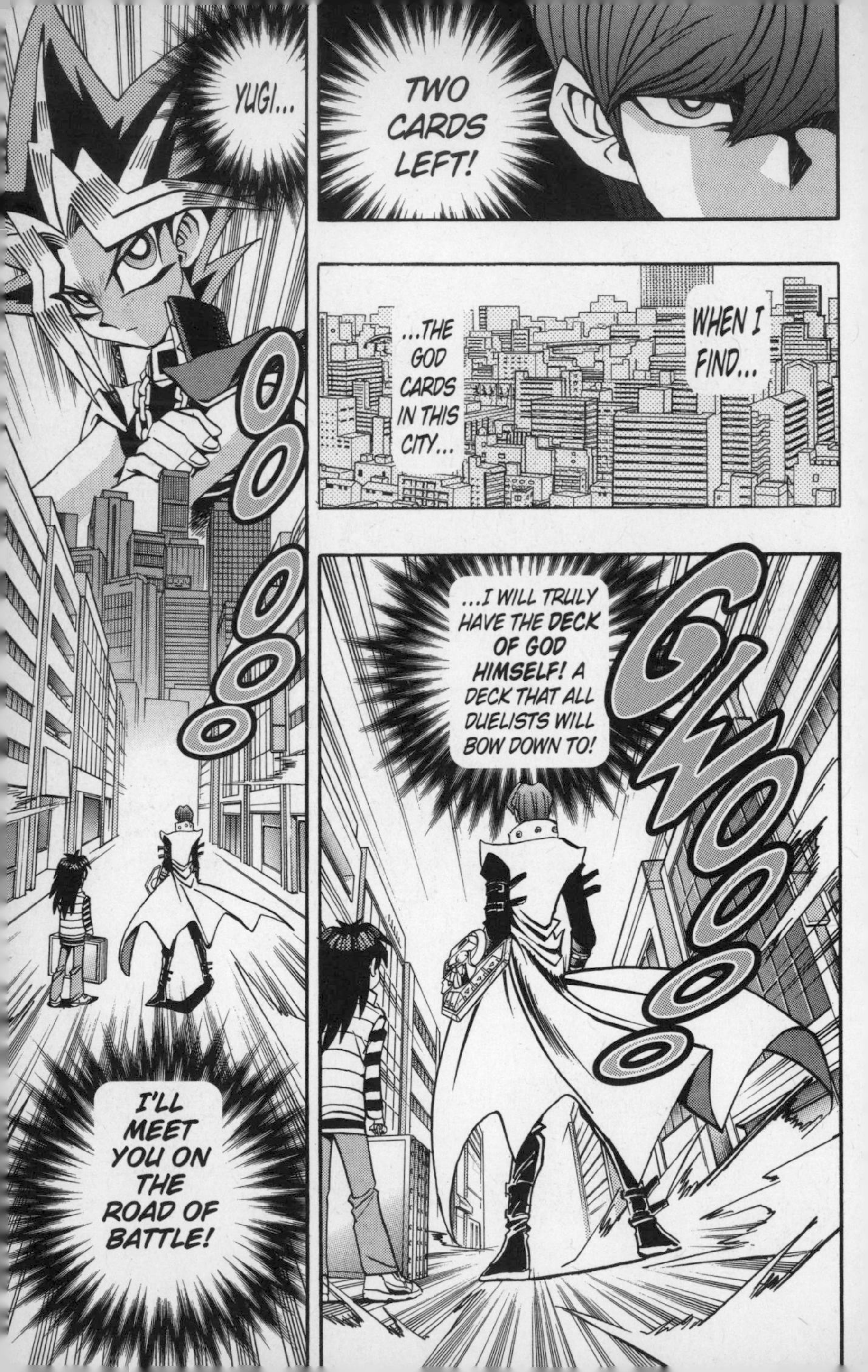
TWO CARDS LEFT!
WHEN I FIND...
...THE GOD CARDS IN THIS CITY...
...I WILL TRULY HAVE THE DECK OF GOD HIMSELF! A DECK THAT ALL DUELISTS WILL BOW DOWN TO!
GWOOOOO
YUGI...
OOOOOOOO
I'LL MEET YOU ON THE ROAD OF BATTLE!

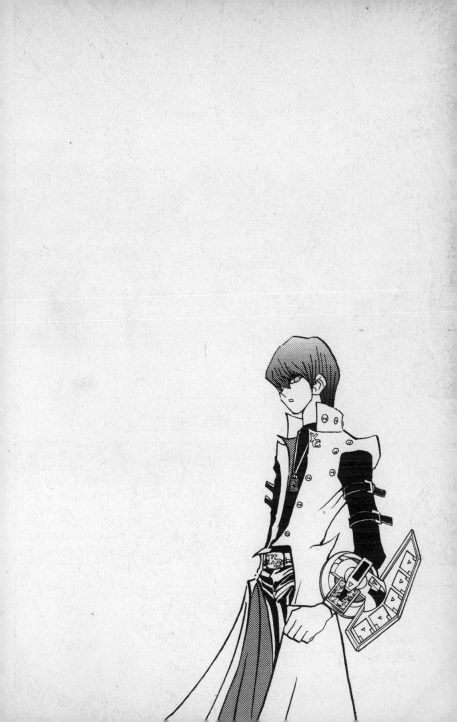

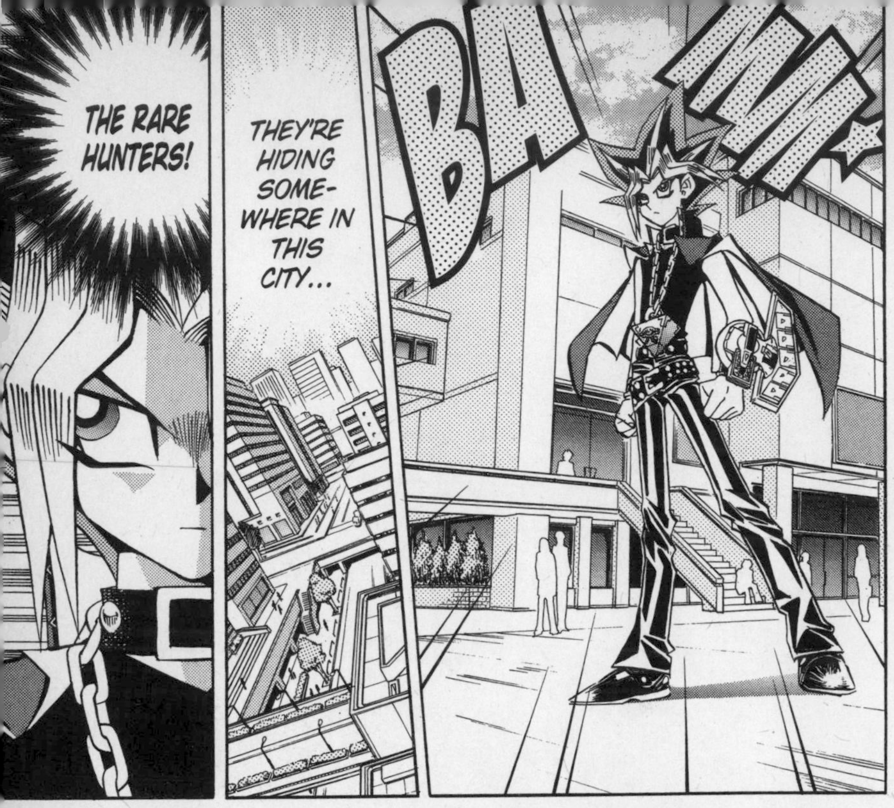
BAM
THEY'RE HIDING SOMEWHERE IN THIS CITY...
THE RARE HUNTERS!

DUEL 101: MARIK STRIKES!

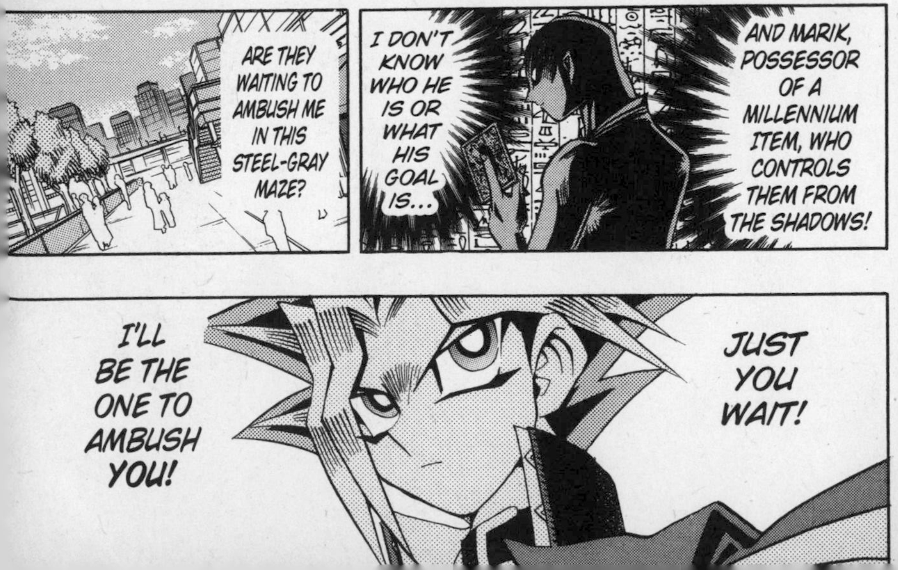
AND MARIK, POSSESSOR OF A MILLENNIUM ITEM, WHO CONTROLS THEM FROM THE SHADOWS!
I DON'T KNOW WHO HE IS OR WHAT HIS GOAL IS...
ARE THEY WAITING TO AMBUSH ME IN THIS STEEL-GRAY MAZE?
JUST YOU WAIT!
I'LL BE THE ONE TO AMBUSH YOU!

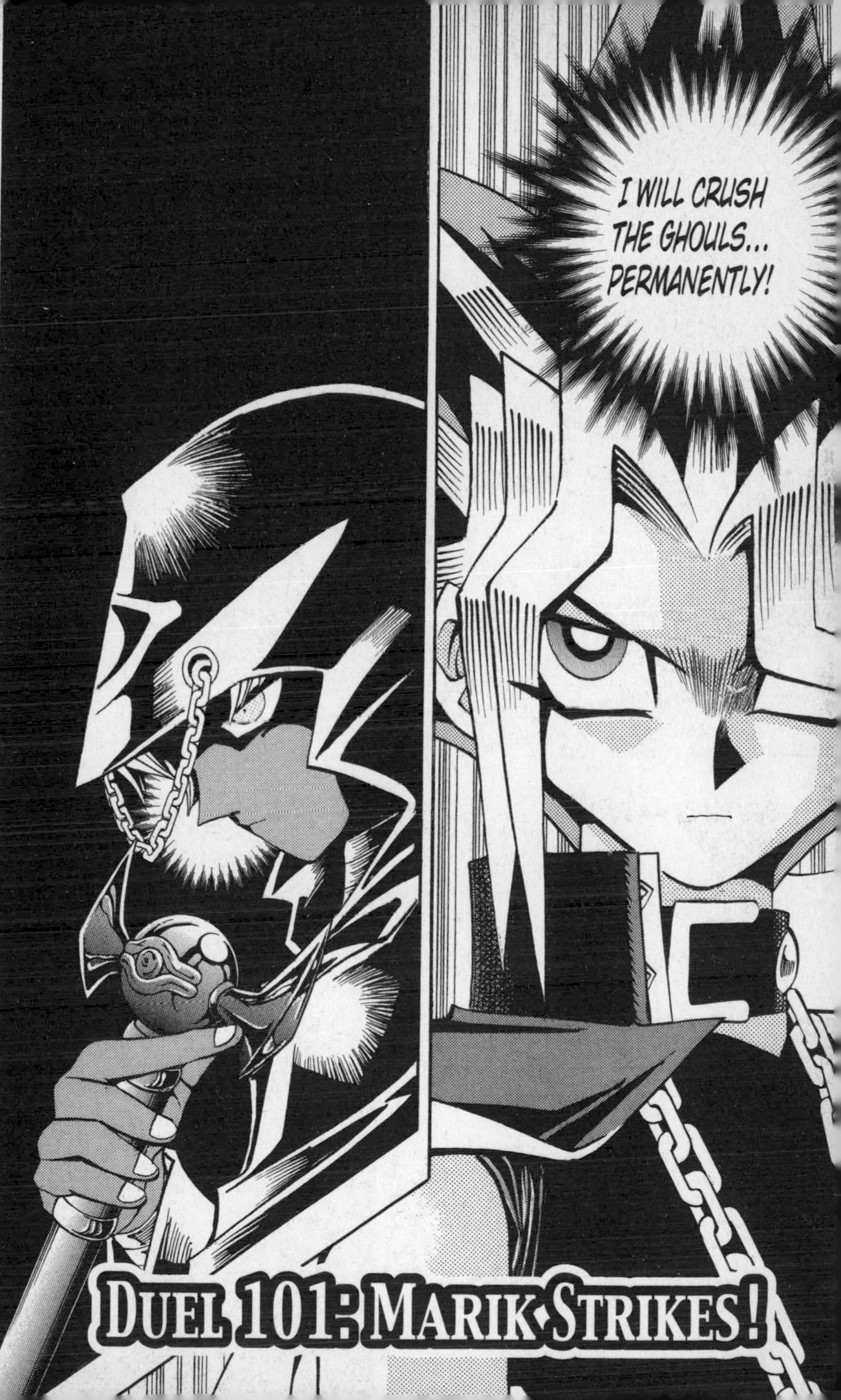
I WILL CRUSH THE GHOULS... PERMANENTLY!

DUEL 101: MARIK STRIKES!

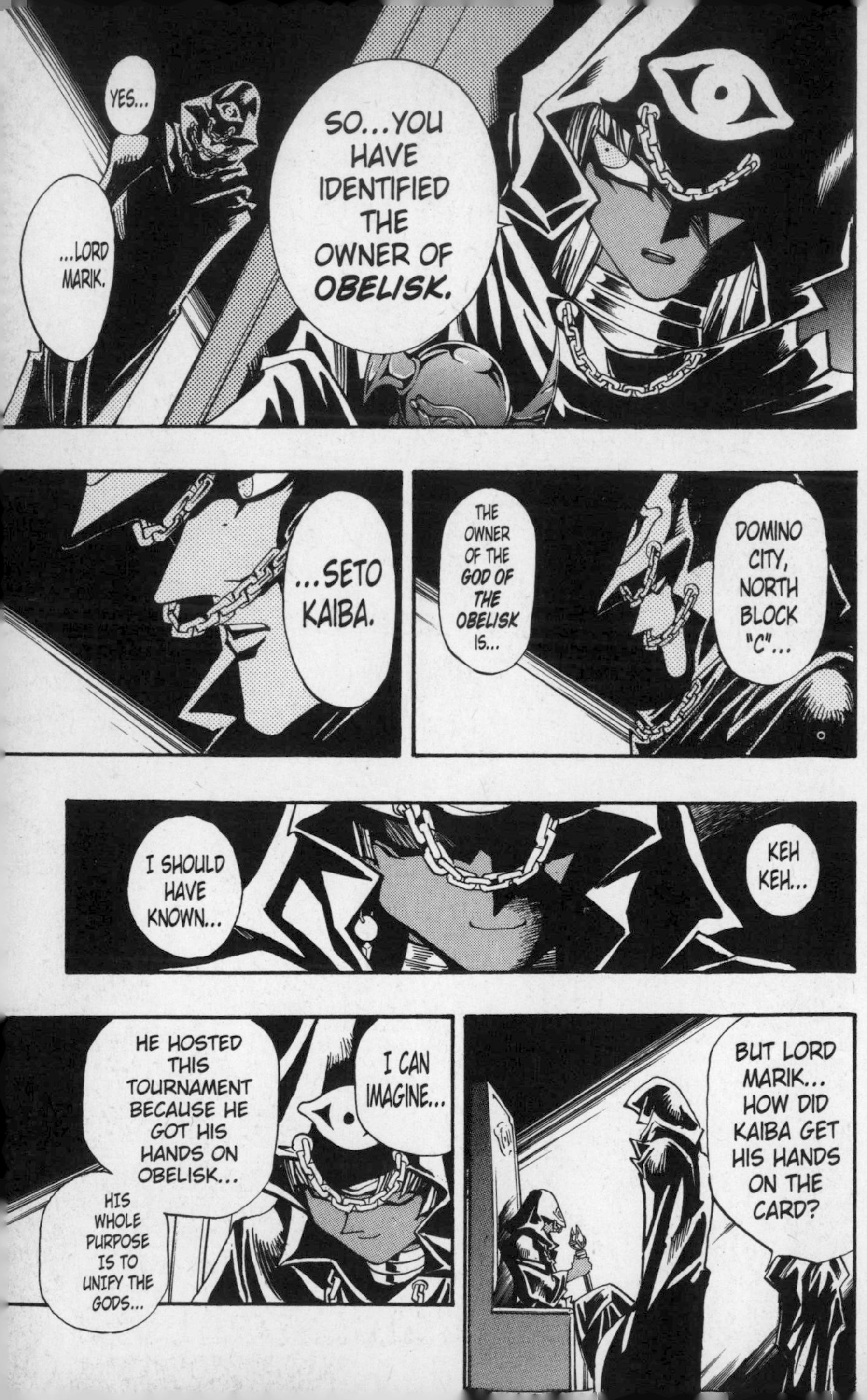
SO...YOU HAVE IDENTIFIED THE OWNER OF OBELISK.
YES...
...LORD MARIK.
DOMINO CITY, NORTH BLOCK "C"...
THE OWNER OF THE GOD OF THE OBELISK IS...
...SETO KAIBA.
KEH KEH...
I SHOULD HAVE KNOWN...
BUT LORD MARIK... HOW DID KAIBA GET HIS HANDS ON THE CARD?
I CAN IMAGINE...
HE HOSTED THIS TOURNAMENT BECAUSE HE GOT HIS HANDS ON OBELISK...
HIS WHOLE PURPOSE IS TO UNIFY THE GODS...

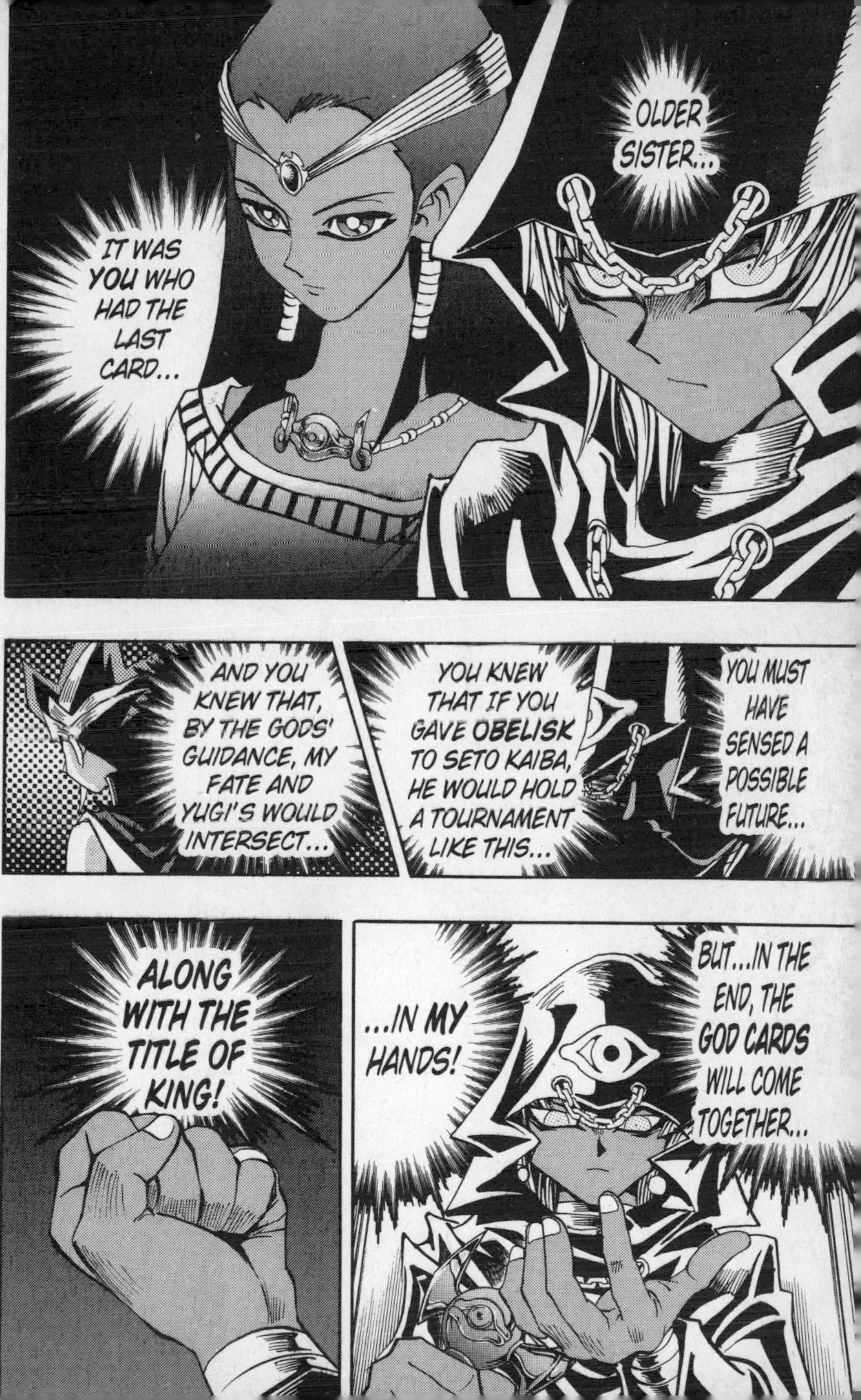
OLDER SISTER...
IT WAS YOU WHO HAD THE LAST CARD...
YOU MUST HAVE SENSED A POSSIBLE FUTURE...
YOU KNEW THAT IF YOU GAVE OBELISK TO SETO KAIBA, HE WOULD HOLD A TOURNAMENT LIKE THIS...
AND YOU KNEW THAT, BY THE GODS' GUIDANCE, MY FATE AND YUGI'S WOULD INTERSECT...
BUT...IN THE END, THE GOD CARDS WILL COME TOGETHER...
...IN MY HANDS!
ALONG WITH THE TITLE OF KING!

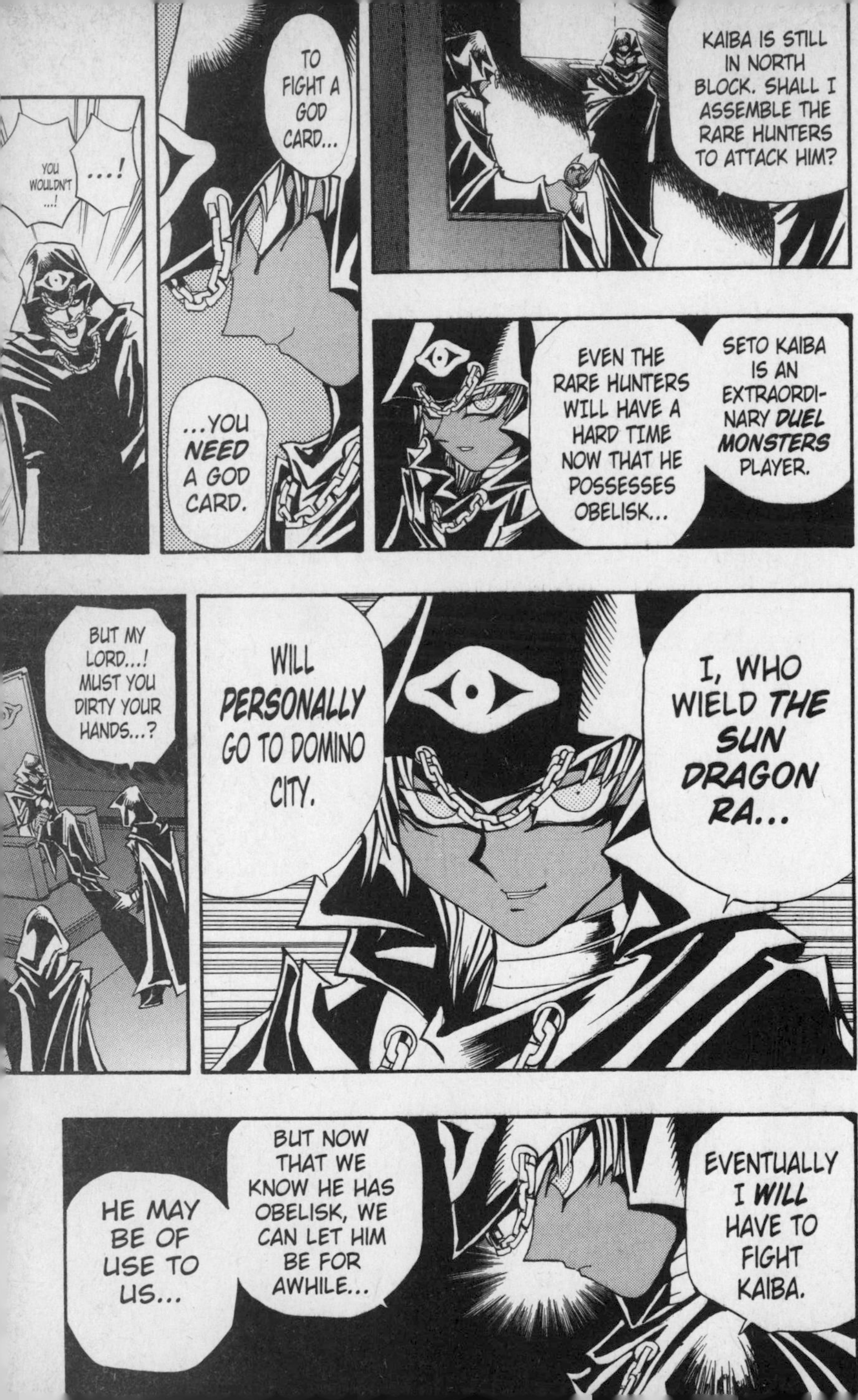
KAIBA IS STILL IN NORTH BLOCK. SHALL I ASSEMBLE THE RARE HUNTERS TO ATTACK HIM?
SETO KAIBA IS AN EXTRAORDINARY DUEL MONSTERS PLAYER.
EVEN THE RARE HUNTERS WILL HAVE A HARD TIME NOW THAT HE POSSESSES OBELISK...
TO FIGHT A GOD CARD...
...YOU NEED A GOD CARD.
...!
YOU WOULDN'T ...!
I, WHO WIELD THE SUN DRAGON RA...
WILL PERSONALLY GO TO DOMINO CITY.
BUT MY LORD...! MUST YOU DIRTY YOUR HANDS...?
EVENTUALLY I WILL HAVE TO FIGHT KAIBA.
BUT NOW THAT WE KNOW HE HAS OBELISK, WE CAN LET HIM BE FOR AWHILE...
HE MAY BE OF USE TO US...

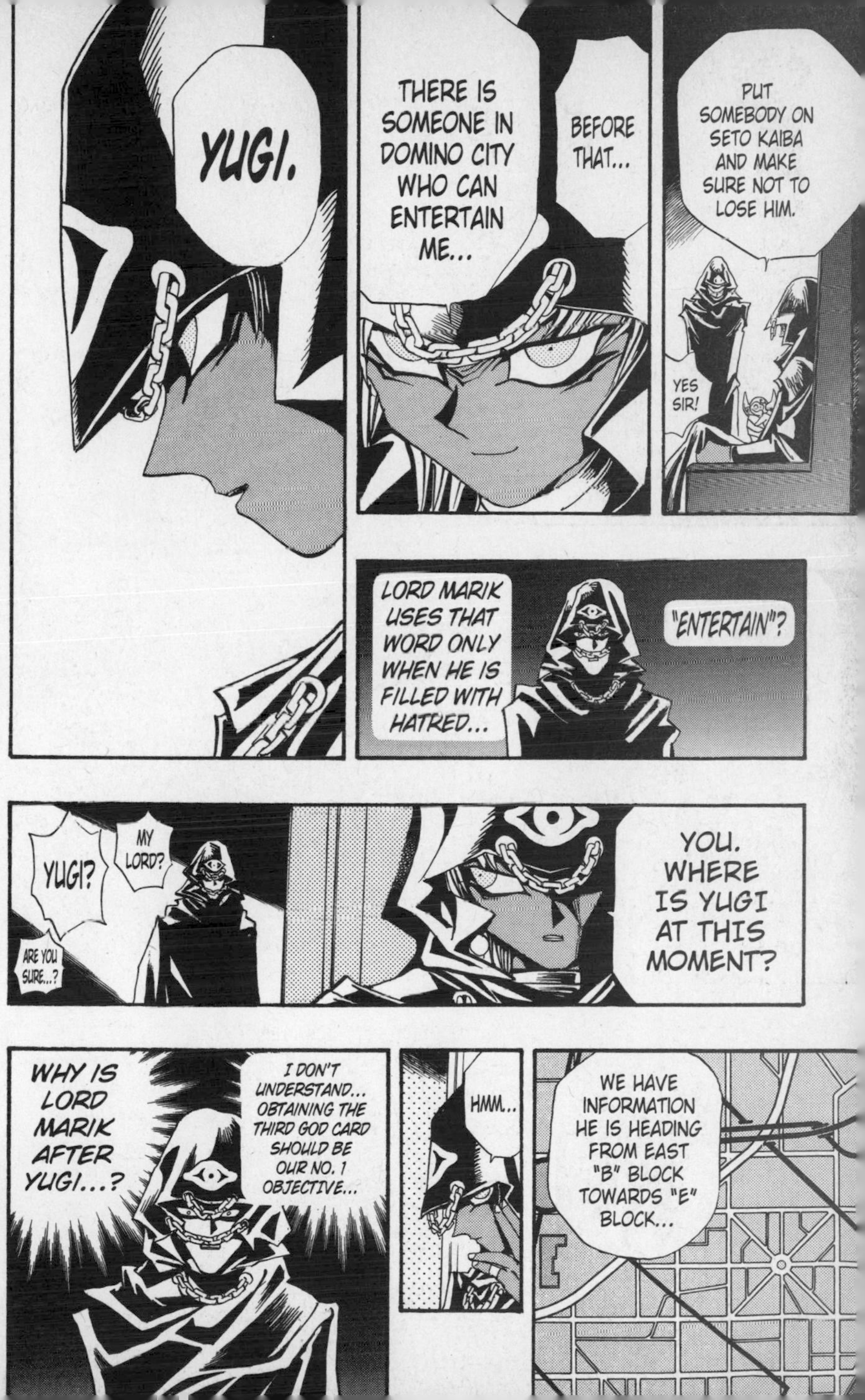
PUT SOMEBODY ON SETO KAIBA AND MAKE SURE NOT TO LOSE HIM.
YES SIR!
BEFORE THAT...
THERE IS SOMEONE IN DOMINO CITY WHO CAN ENTERTAIN ME...
"ENTERTAIN"?
LORD MARIK USES THAT WORD ONLY WHEN HE IS FILLED WITH HATRED...
YUGI.
YOU. WHERE IS YUGI AT THIS MOMENT?
MY LORD?
YUGI?
ARE YOU SURE...?
WE HAVE INFORMATION HE IS HEADING FROM EAST "B" BLOCK TOWARDS "E" BLOCK...
HMM...
I DON'T UNDERSTAND... OBTAINING THE THIRD GOD CARD SHOULD BE OUR NO. 1 OBJECTIVE...
WHY IS LORD MARIK AFTER YUGI...?

READ THIS WAY

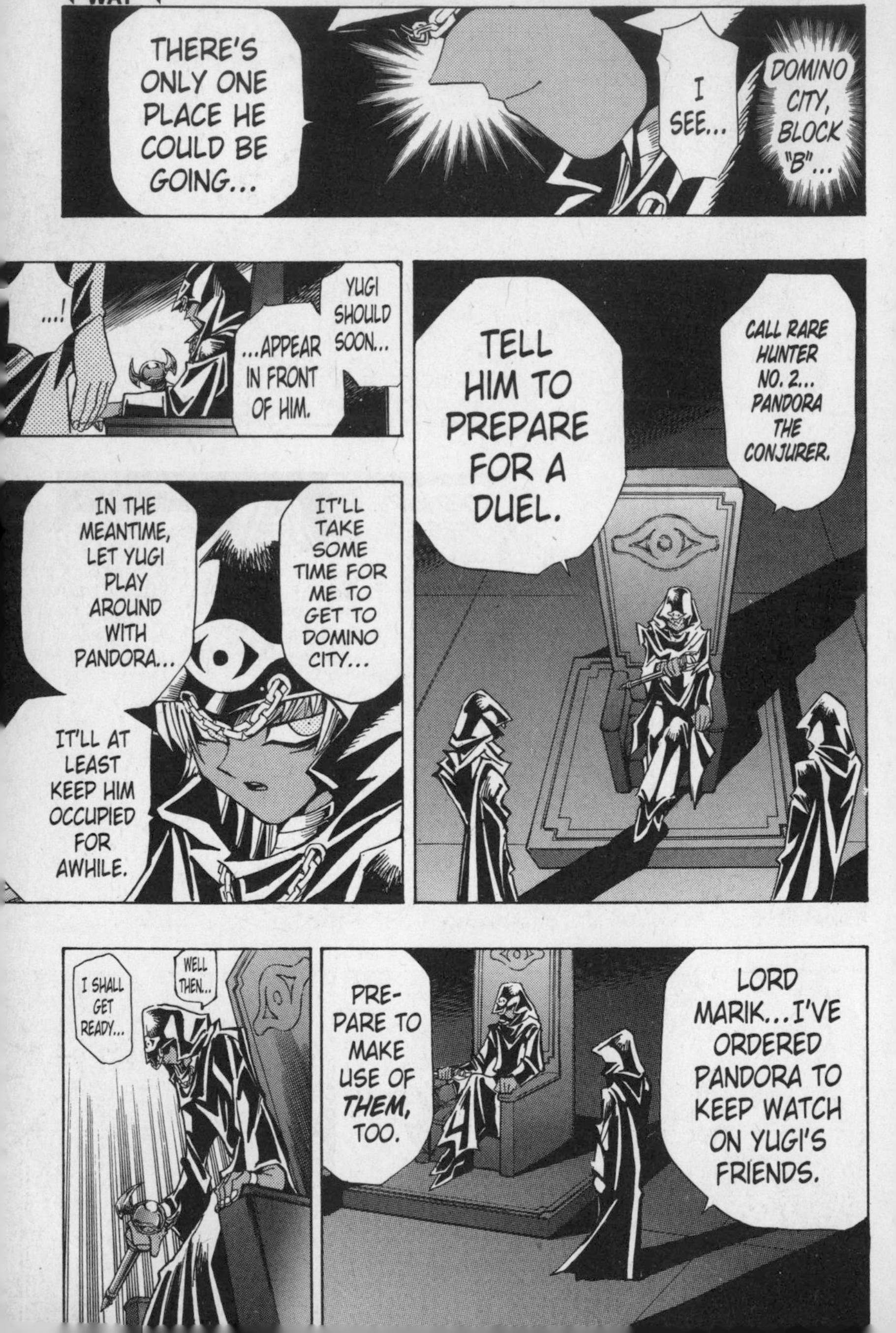
DOMINO CITY, BLOCK "B"...
I SEE...
THERE'S ONLY ONE PLACE HE COULD BE GOING...
CALL RARE HUNTER NO. 2... PANDORA THE CONJURER.
TELL HIM TO PREPARE FOR A DUEL.
YUGI SHOULD SOON...
...APPEAR IN FRONT OF HIM.
...!
IT'LL TAKE SOME TIME FOR ME TO GET TO DOMINO CITY...
IN THE MEANTIME, LET YUGI PLAY AROUND WITH PANDORA...
IT'LL AT LEAST KEEP HIM OCCUPIED FOR AWHILE.
LORD MARIK...I'VE ORDERED PANDORA TO KEEP WATCH ON YUGI'S FRIENDS.
PRE-PARE TO MAKE USE OF THEM, TOO.
WELL THEN...
I SHALL GET READY...

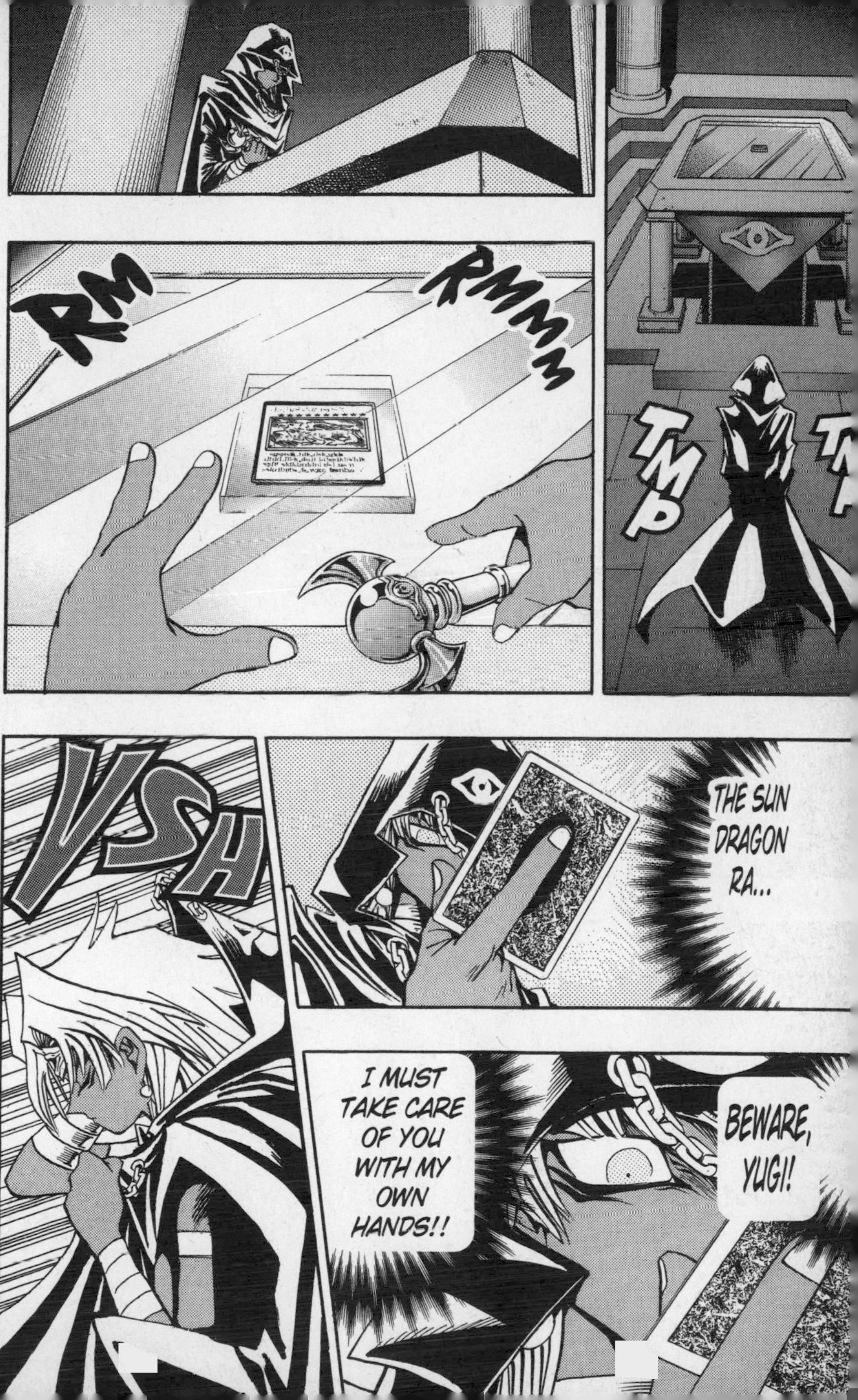
TMP
TMP
RM
RMMM
THE SUN DRAGON RA...
BEWARE, YUGI!
I MUST TAKE CARE OF YOU WITH MY OWN HANDS!!
VSH

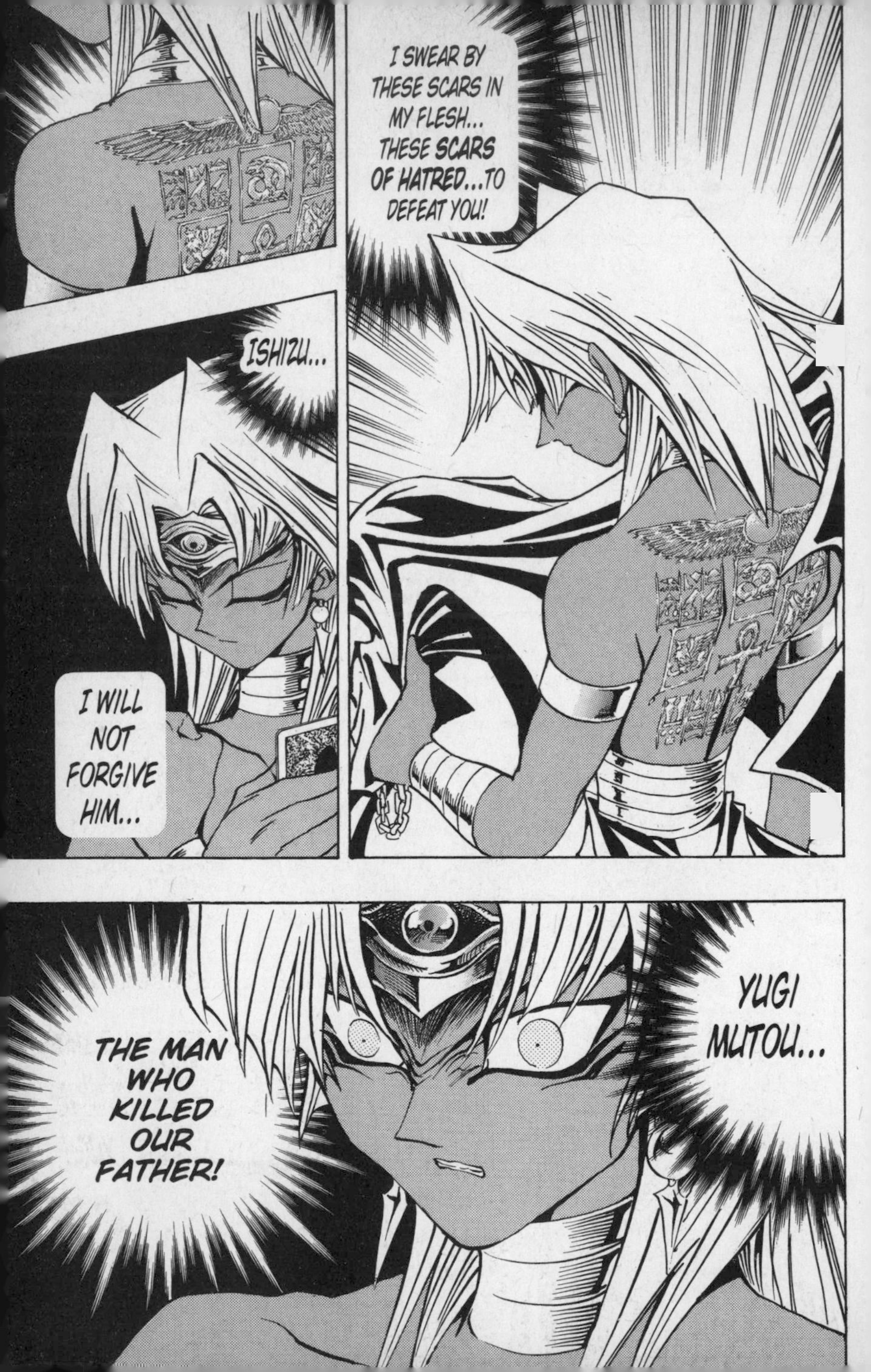
I SWEAR BY THESE SCARS IN MY FLESH... THESE SCARS OF HATRED...TO DEFEAT YOU!
ISHIZU...
I WILL NOT FORGIVE HIM...
YUGI MUTOU...
THE MAN WHO KILLED OUR FATHER!

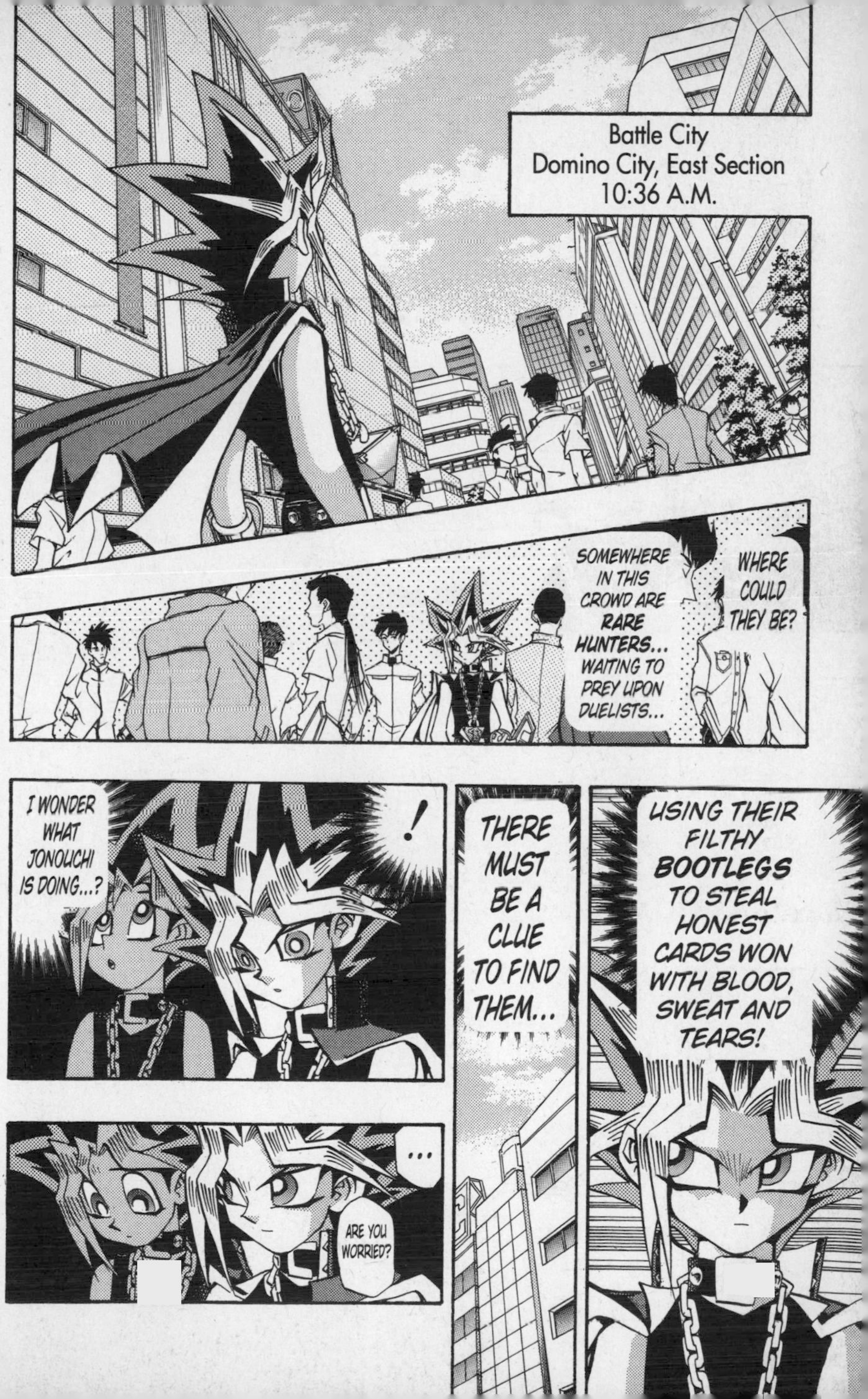
Battle City
Domino City, East Section
10:36 A.M.
WHERE COULD THEY BE?
SOMEWHERE IN THIS CROWD ARE RARE HUNTERS... WAITING TO PREY UPON DUELISTS...
USING THEIR FILTHY BOOTLEGS TO STEAL HONEST CARDS WON WITH BLOOD, SWEAT AND TEARS!
THERE MUST BE A CLUE TO FIND THEM...
!
I WONDER WHAT JONOUCHI IS DOING...?
...
ARE YOU WORRIED?

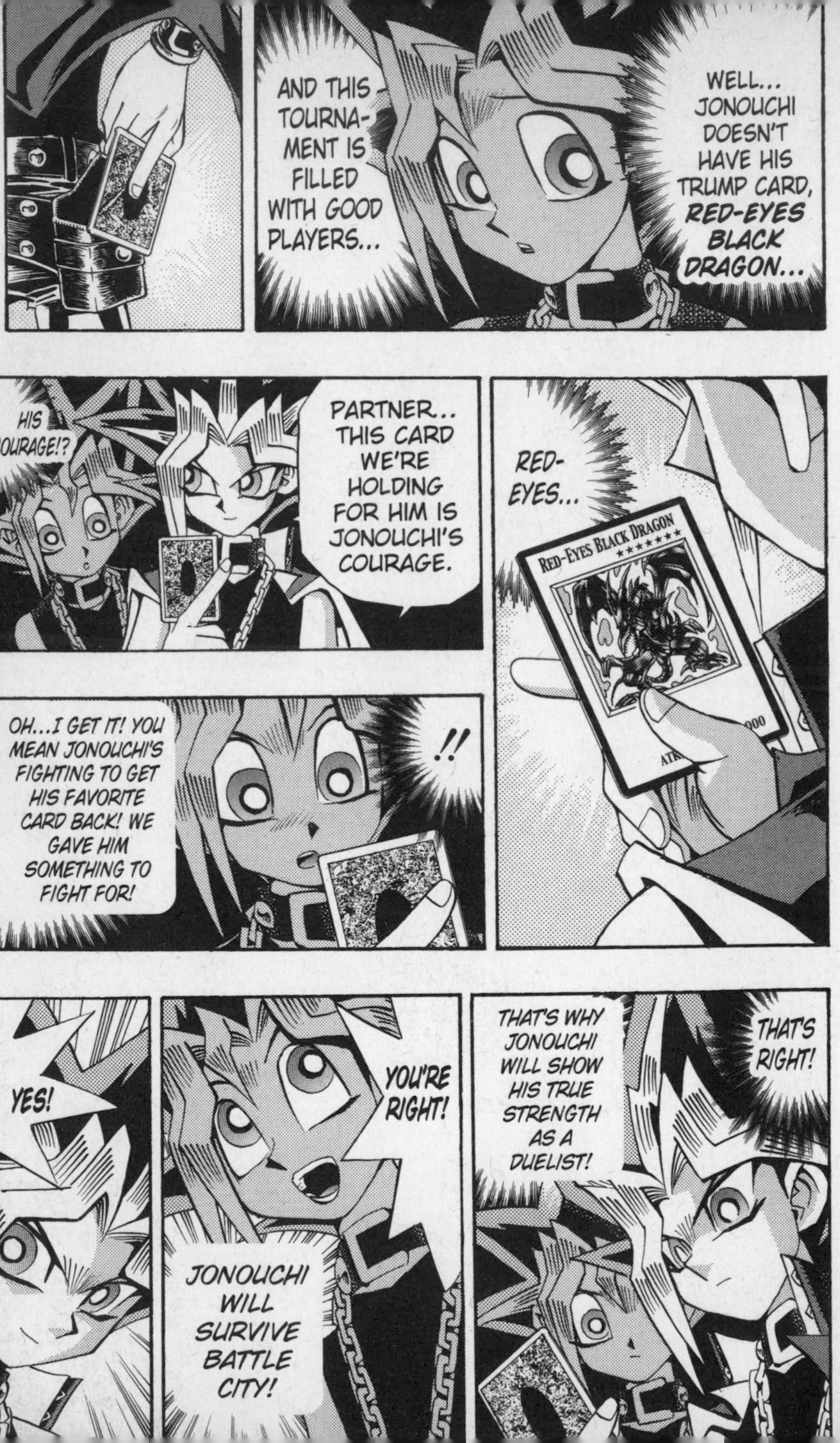
WELL... JONOUCHI DOESN'T HAVE HIS TRUMP CARD, RED-EYES BLACK DRAGON...
AND THIS TOURNA-MENT IS FILLED WITH GOOD PLAYERS...
RED-EYES...
RED-EYES BLACK DRAGON
PARTNER... THIS CARD WE'RE HOLDING FOR HIM IS JONOUCHI'S COURAGE.
HIS COURAGE!?
!!
OH...I GET IT! YOU MEAN JONOUCHI'S FIGHTING TO GET HIS FAVORITE CARD BACK! WE GAVE HIM SOMETHING TO FIGHT FOR!
THAT'S RIGHT!
THAT'S WHY JONOUCHI WILL SHOW HIS TRUE STRENGTH AS A DUELIST!
YOU'RE RIGHT!
JONOUCHI WILL SURVIVE BATTLE CITY!
YES!

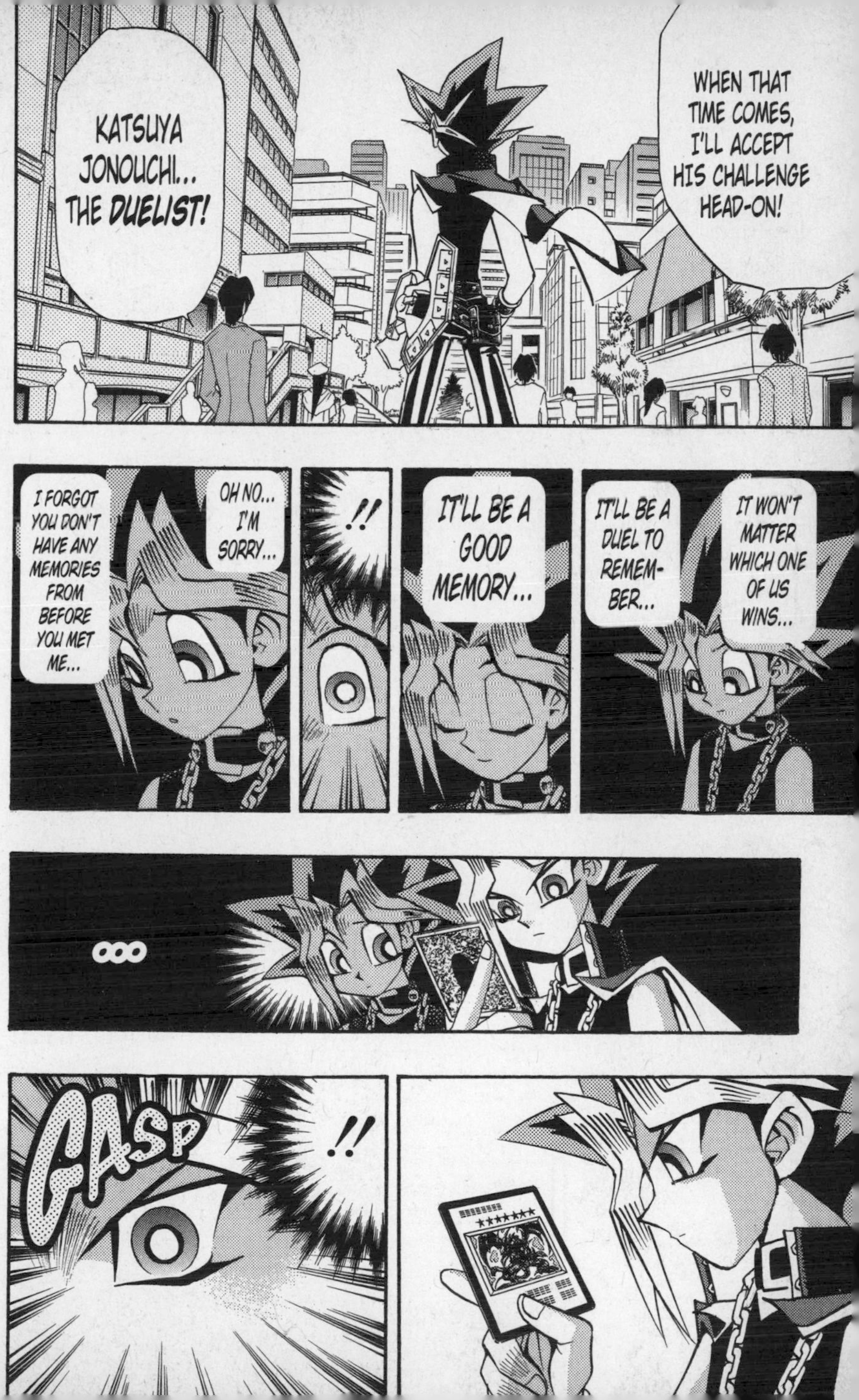
WHEN THAT TIME COMES, I'LL ACCEPT HIS CHALLENGE HEAD-ON!
KATSUYA JONOUCHI... THE *DUELIST*!
IT WON'T MATTER WHICH ONE OF US WINS...
IT'LL BE A DUEL TO REMEMBER...
IT'LL BE A GOOD MEMORY...
!!
OH NO... I'M SORRY...
I FORGOT YOU DON'T HAVE ANY MEMORIES FROM BEFORE YOU MET ME...
...
!!
GASP

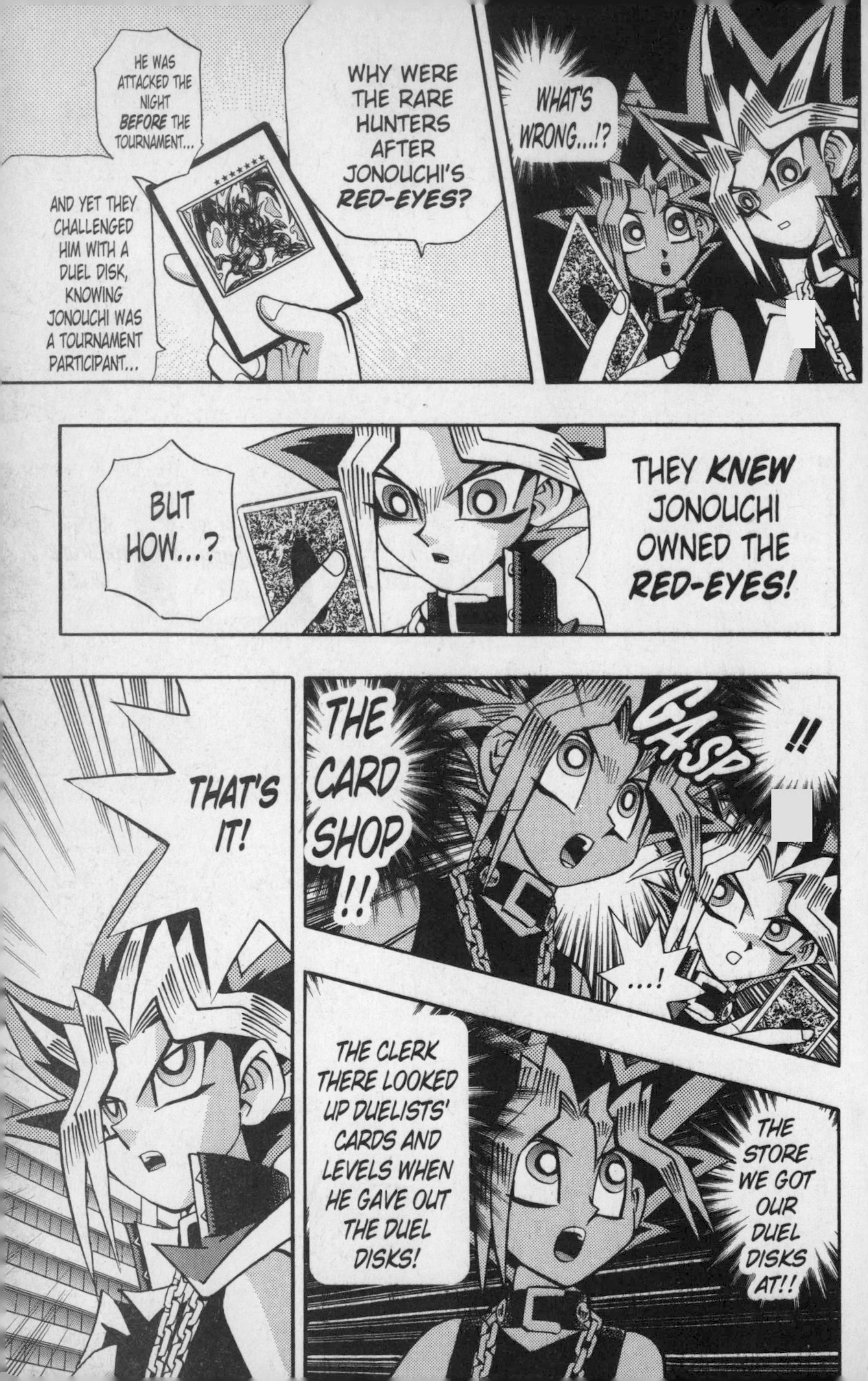
WHAT'S WRONG...!?
WHY WERE THE RARE HUNTERS AFTER JONOUCHI'S *RED-EYES?*
HE WAS ATTACKED THE NIGHT *BEFORE* THE TOURNAMENT...
AND YET THEY CHALLENGED HIM WITH A DUEL DISK, KNOWING JONOUCHI WAS A TOURNAMENT PARTICIPANT...
THEY *KNEW* JONOUCHI OWNED THE *RED-EYES!*
BUT HOW...?
GASP!!
THE CARD SHOP!!
...!
THE STORE WE GOT OUR DUEL DISKS AT!!
THE CLERK THERE LOOKED UP DUELISTS' CARDS AND LEVELS WHEN HE GAVE OUT THE DUEL DISKS!
THAT'S IT!

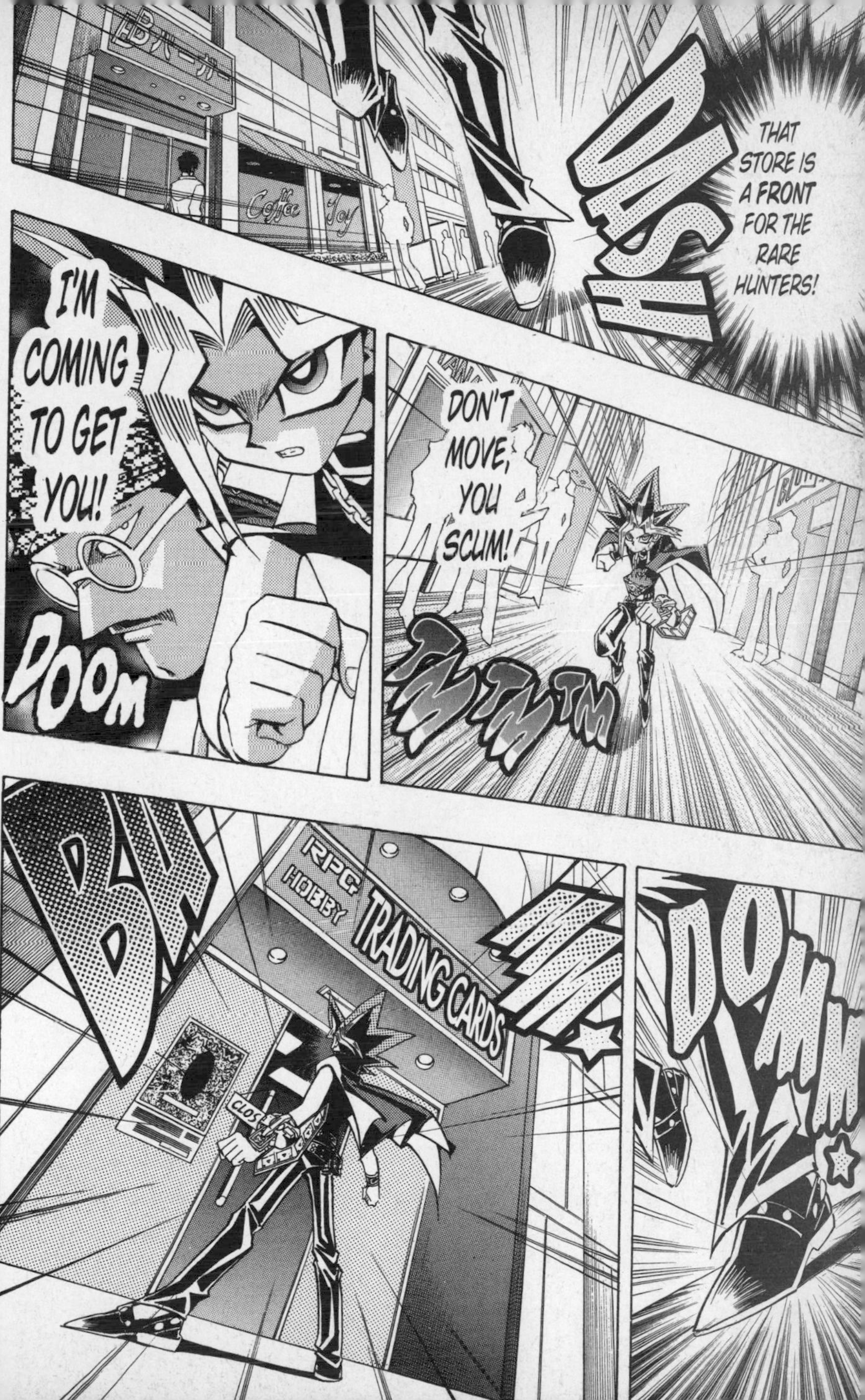
THAT STORE IS A FRONT FOR THE RARE HUNTERS!
DASH
Coffee Joy
DON'T MOVE, YOU SCUM!
TM TM TM
I'M COMING TO GET YOU!
DOOM
RPG
HOBBY
TRADING CARDS
CLOS

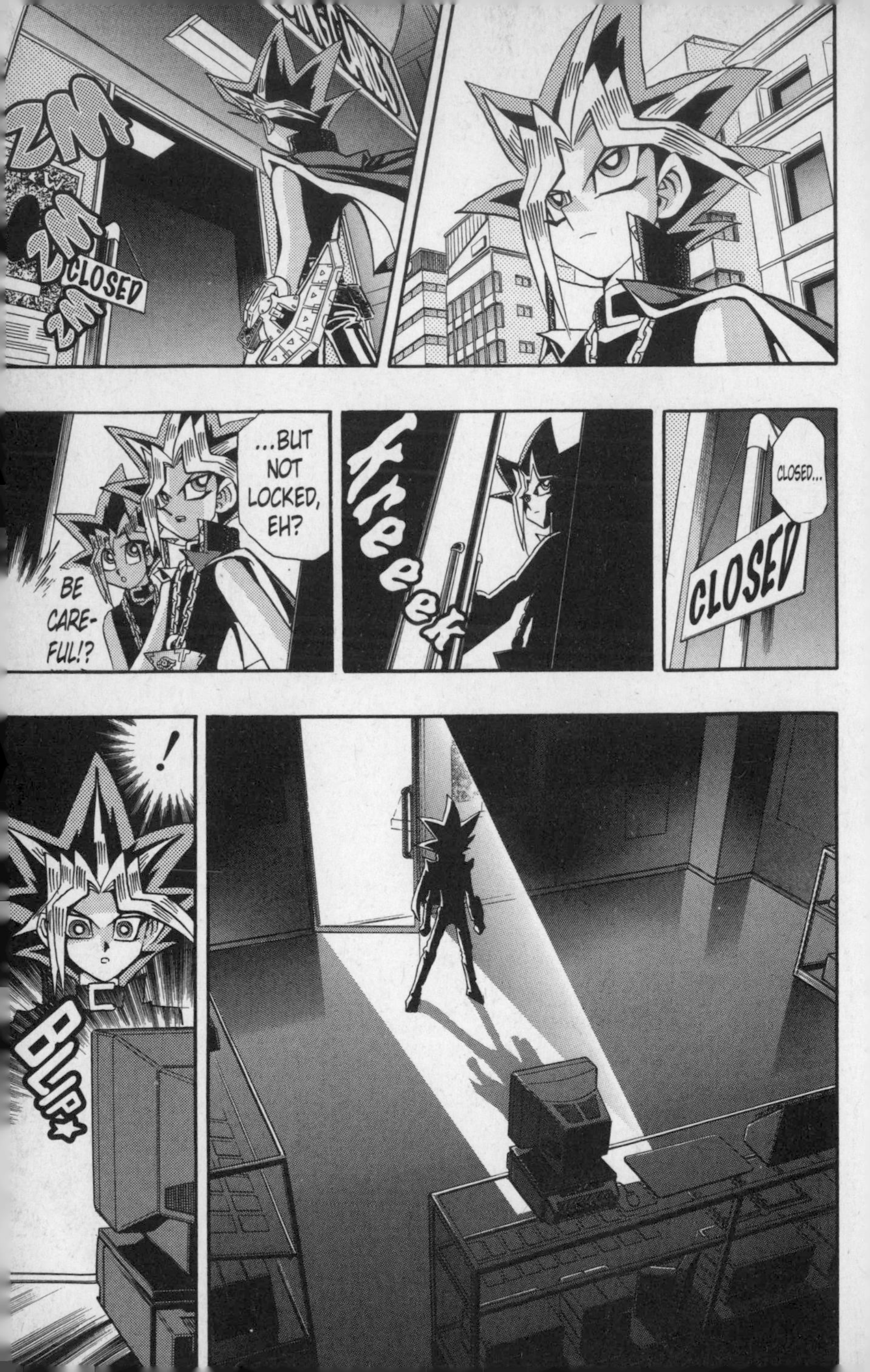
ZM
ZM
ZM
CLOSED
CLOSED...
CLOSED
kreeek
...BUT NOT LOCKED, EH?
BE CARE-FUL!?
!
BLIP

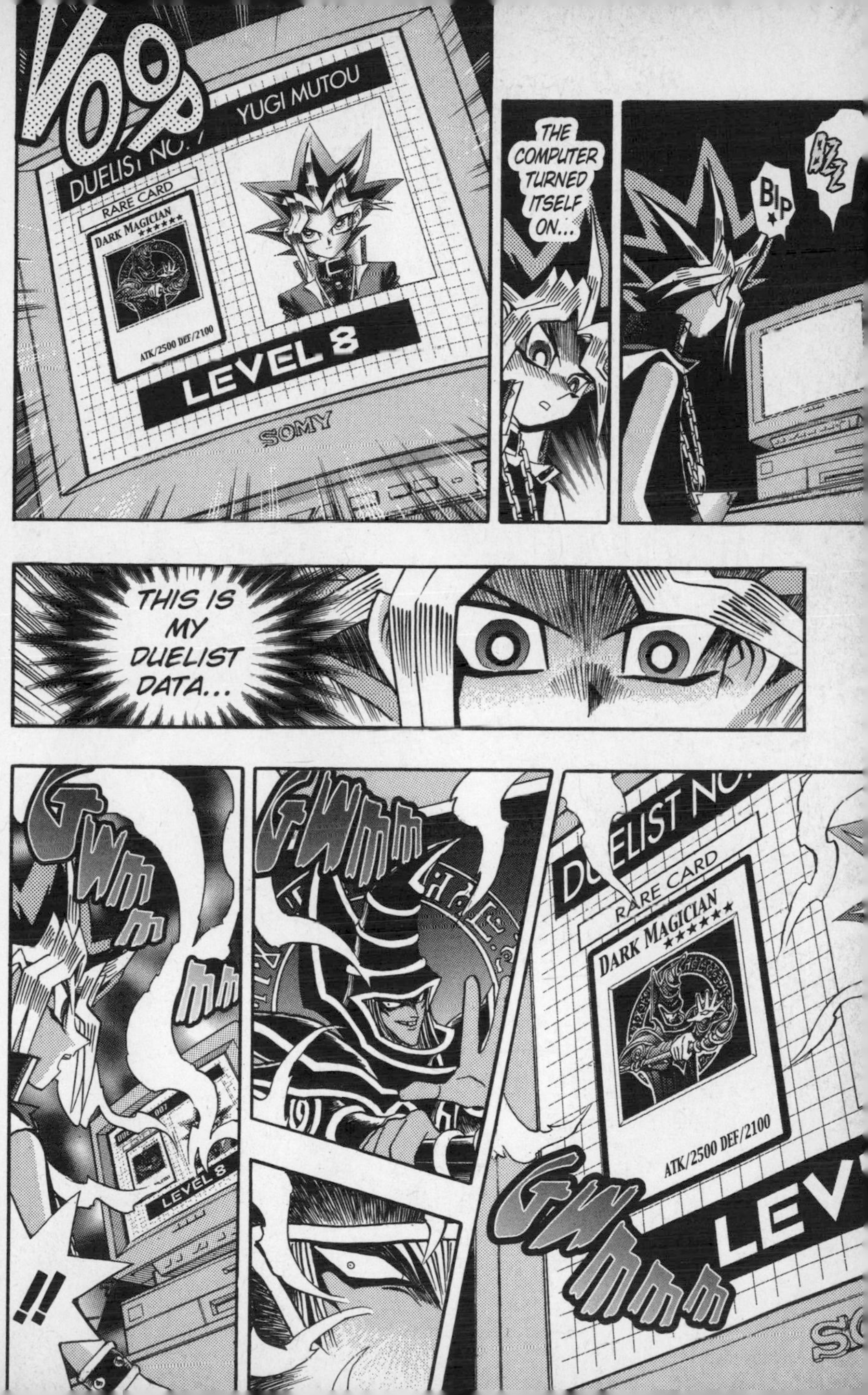
BIP
BZZ
THE COMPUTER TURNED ITSELF ON...
VOOP
DUELIST NO.
YUGI MUTOU
RARE CARD
DARK MAGICIAN
ATK/2500 DEF/2100
LEVEL 8
SOMY
THIS IS MY DUELIST DATA...
DUELIST NO.
RARE CARD
DARK MAGICIAN
ATK/2500 DEF/2100
LEV
GWMMM
GWMMMM
GWMMM
LEVEL 8
!!

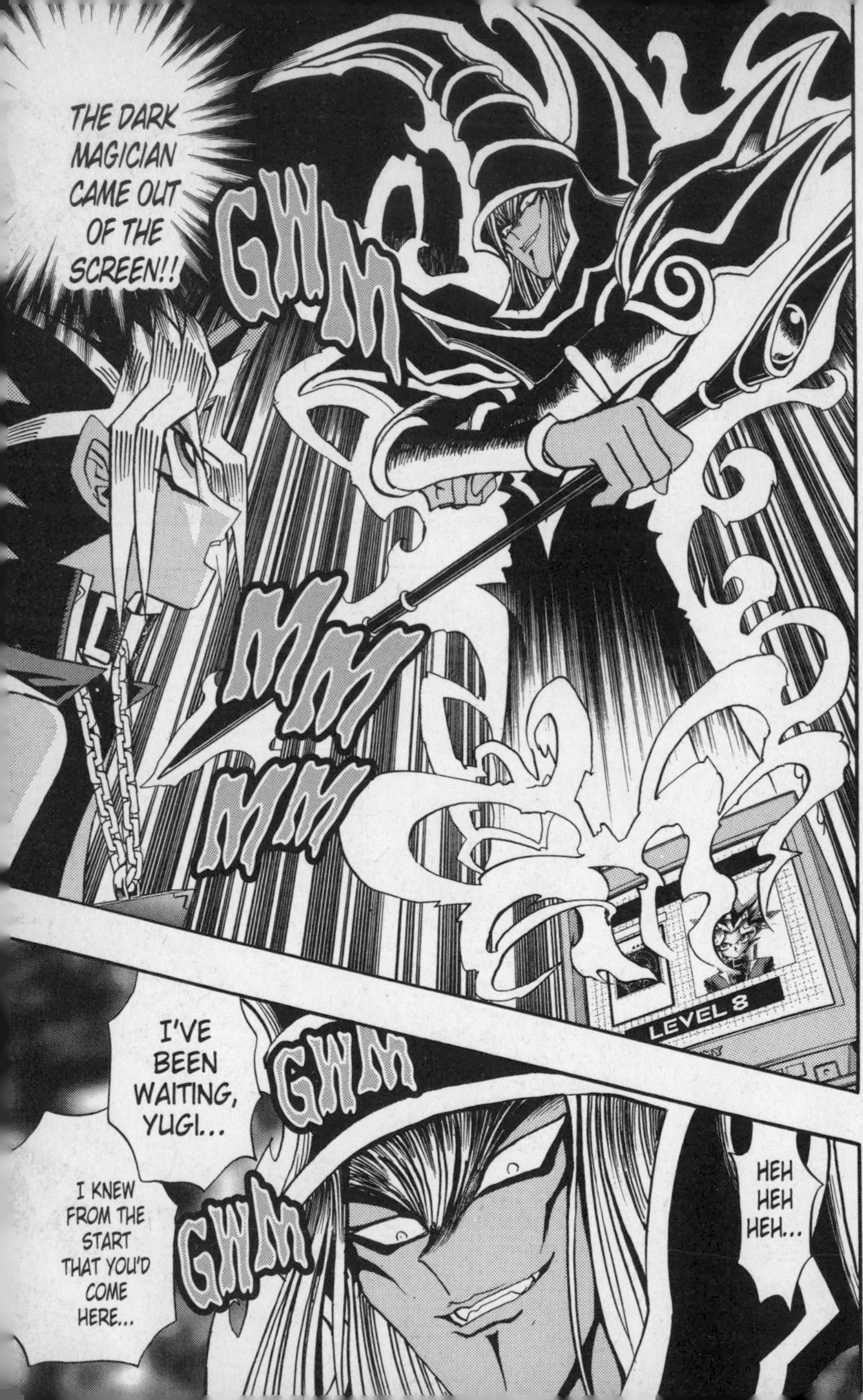
THE DARK MAGICIAN CAME OUT OF THE SCREEN!!
GHM
MMM
MM
LEVEL 8
GHM
I'VE BEEN WAITING, YUGI...
HEH HEH HEH...
I KNEW FROM THE START THAT YOU'D COME HERE...
GHM

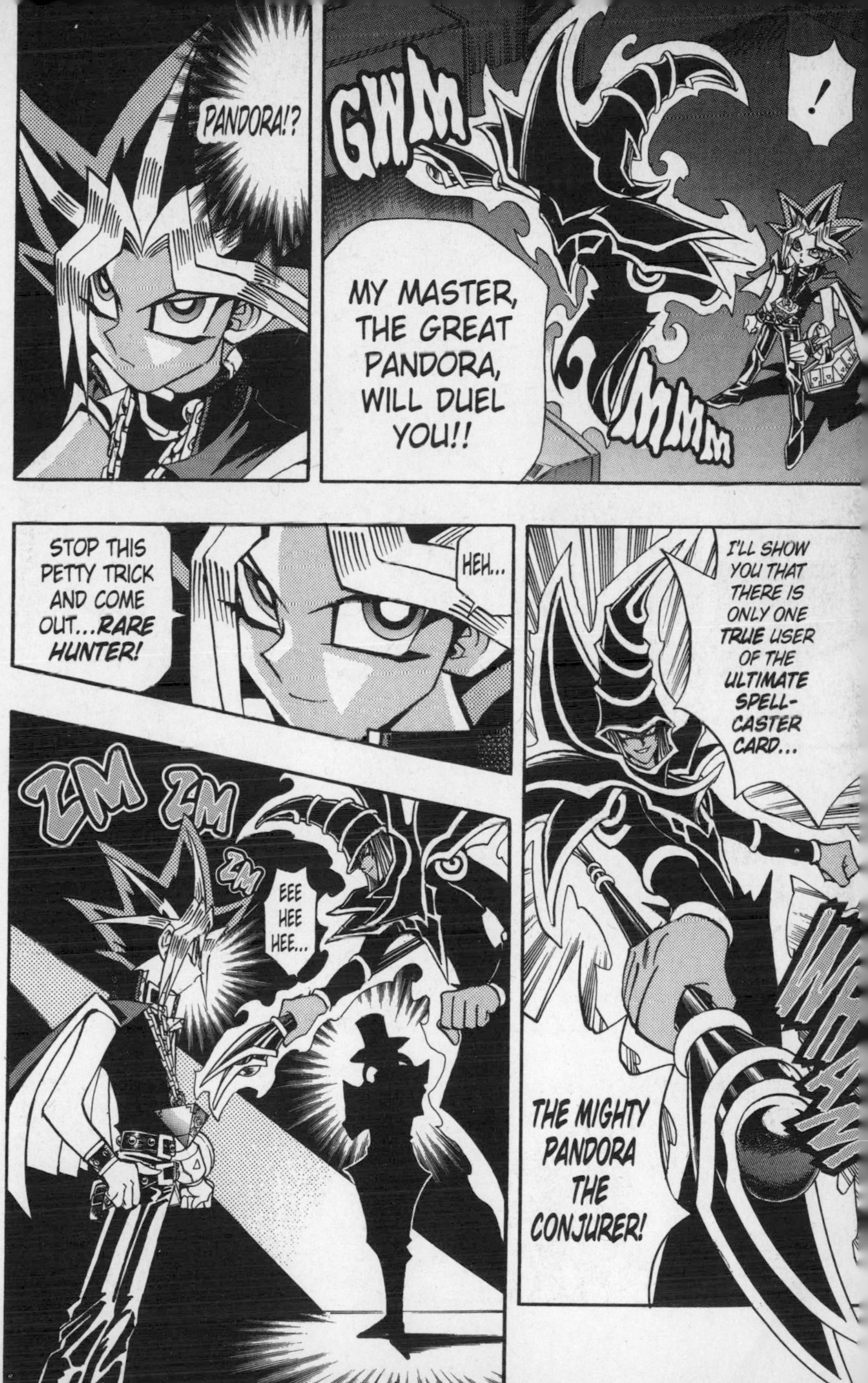
!
GWM
MY MASTER, THE GREAT PANDORA, WILL DUEL YOU!!
MMMM
PANDORA!?
I'LL SHOW YOU THAT THERE IS ONLY ONE TRUE USER OF THE ULTIMATE SPELL-CASTER CARD...
THE MIGHTY PANDORA THE CONJURER!
HEH...
STOP THIS PETTY TRICK AND COME OUT...RARE HUNTER!
ZM ZM
ZM
EEE HEE HEE...

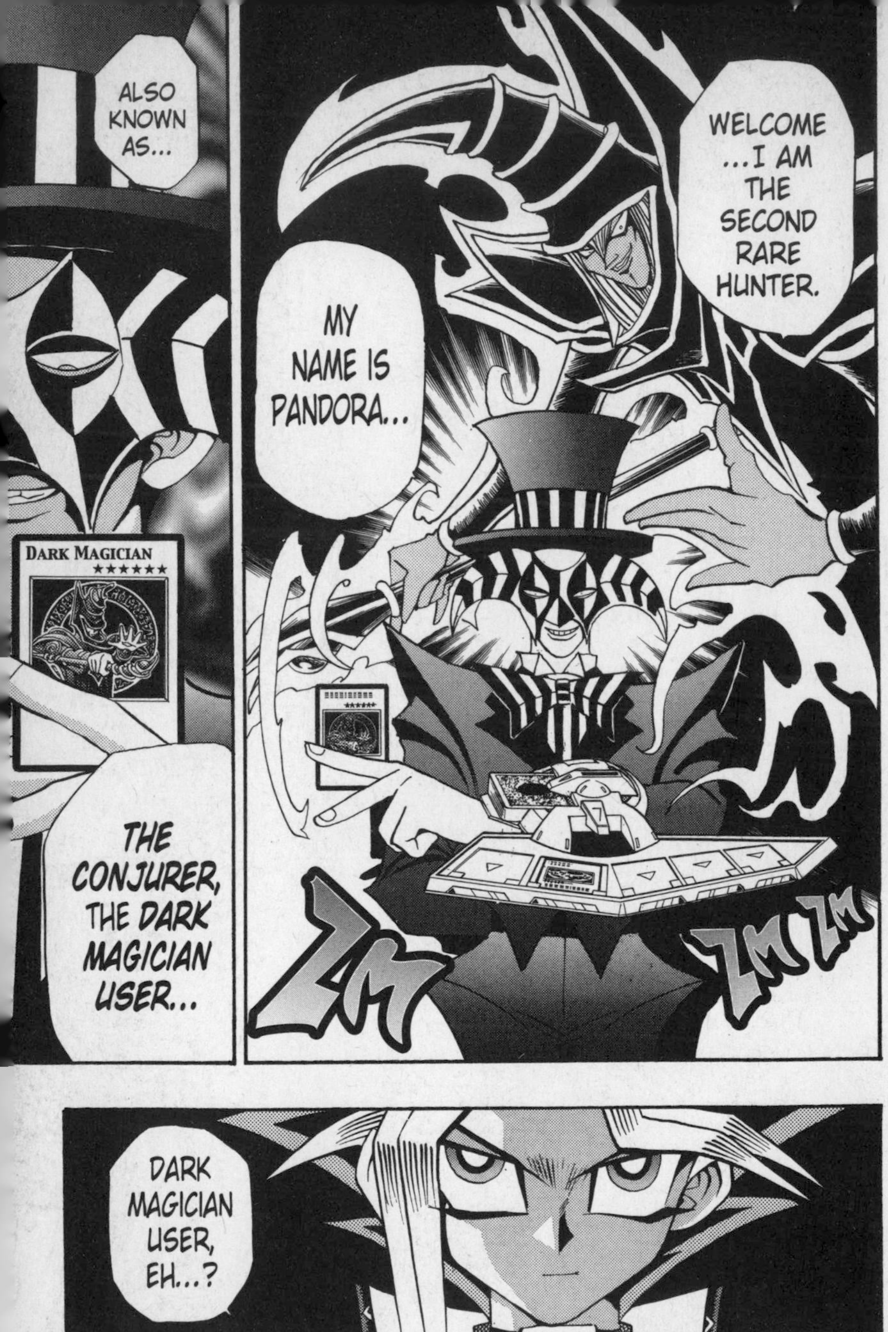
WELCOME ...I AM THE SECOND RARE HUNTER.
MY NAME IS PANDORA...
ZM ZM
ZM
ALSO KNOWN AS...
DARK MAGICIAN
THE CONJURER, THE DARK MAGICIAN USER...
DARK MAGICIAN USER, EH...?

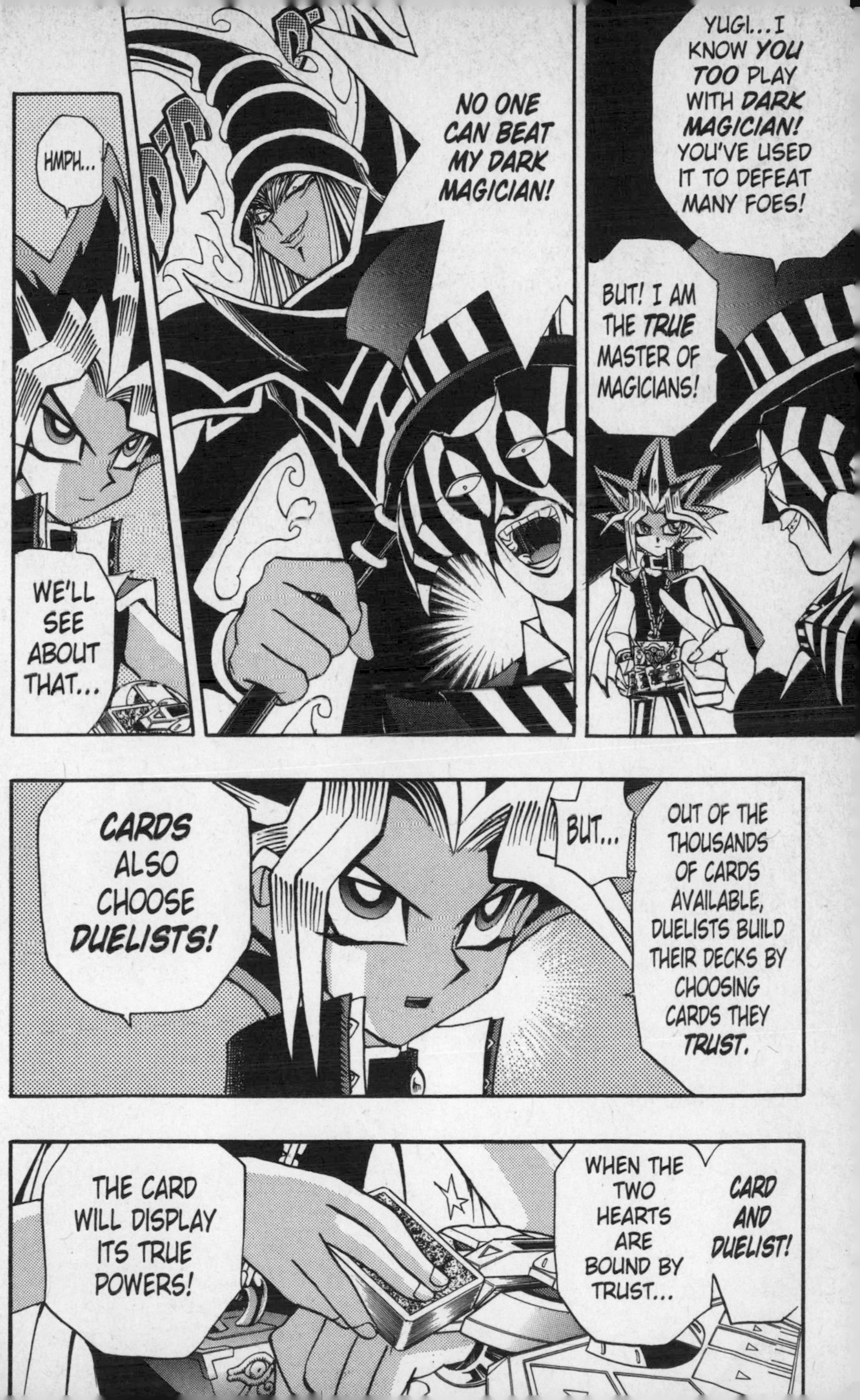
YUGI...I KNOW YOU TOO PLAY WITH DARK MAGICIAN! YOU'VE USED IT TO DEFEAT MANY FOES!
BUT! I AM THE TRUE MASTER OF MAGICIANS!
NO ONE CAN BEAT MY DARK MAGICIAN!
HMPH...
WE'LL SEE ABOUT THAT...
OUT OF THE THOUSANDS OF CARDS AVAILABLE, DUELISTS BUILD THEIR DECKS BY CHOOSING CARDS THEY TRUST.
BUT...
CARDS ALSO CHOOSE DUELISTS!
CARD AND DUELIST!
WHEN THE TWO HEARTS ARE BOUND BY TRUST...
THE CARD WILL DISPLAY ITS TRUE POWERS!

Graceful Charity
[SPELL CARD]
Draw 3 cards from your Deck, then discard any 2 cards from your hand.
©1996 KAZUKI TAKAHASHI

[MACHINE / EFFECT]
Points directly this turn.
ATK/ 800 DEF/2200
©1996 KAZUKI TAKAHASHI

Hyozanryu
[DRAGON]
A dragon created from a massive diamond that sparkles with blinding light.
ATK/2100 DEF/2800
©1996 KAZUKI TAKAHASHI

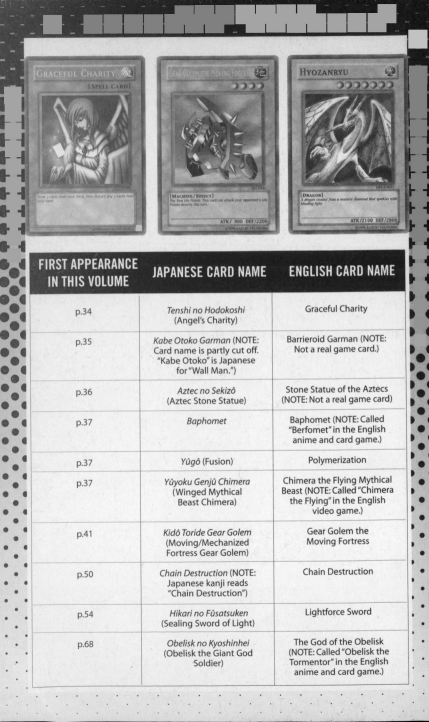

FIRST APPEARANCE IN THIS VOLUME	JAPANESE CARD NAME	ENGLISH CARD NAME
p.34	*Tenshi no Hodokoshi* (Angel's Charity)	Graceful Charity
p.35	*Kabe Otoko Garman* (NOTE: Card name is partly cut off. "Kabe Otoko" is Japanese for "Wall Man.")	Barrieroid Garman (NOTE: Not a real game card.)
p.36	*Aztec no Sekizô* (Aztec Stone Statue)	Stone Statue of the Aztecs (NOTE: Not a real game card)
p.37	*Baphomet*	Baphomet (NOTE: Called "Berfomet" in the English anime and card game.)
p.37	*Yûgô* (Fusion)	Polymerization
p.37	*Yûyoku Genjû Chimera* (Winged Mythical Beast Chimera)	Chimera the Flying Mythical Beast (NOTE: Called "Chimera the Flying" in the English video game.)
p.41	*Kidô Toride Gear Golem* (Moving/Mechanized Fortress Gear Golem)	Gear Golem the Moving Fortress
p.50	*Chain Destruction* (NOTE: Japanese kanji reads "Chain Destruction")	Chain Destruction
p.54	*Hikari no Fûsatsuken* (Sealing Sword of Light)	Lightforce Sword
p.68	*Obelisk no Kyoshinhei* (Obelisk the Giant God Soldier)	The God of the Obelisk (NOTE: Called "Obelisk the Tormentor" in the English anime and card game.)

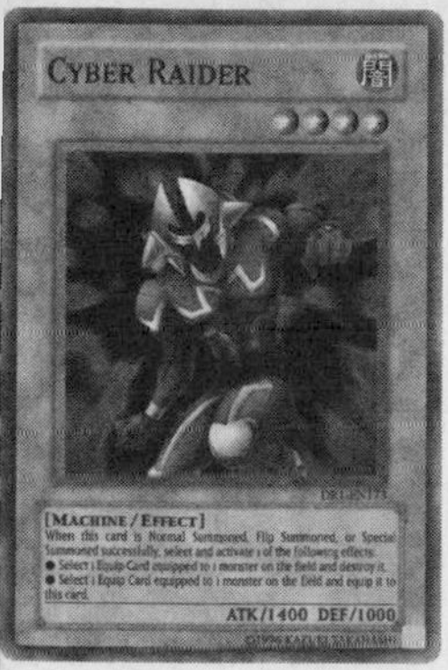
CYBER RAIDER
[MACHINE / EFFECT]
ATK/1400 DEF/1000

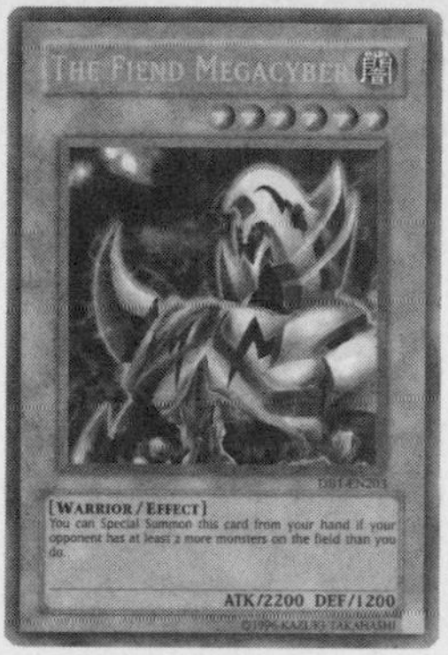
THE FIEND MEGACYBER
[WARRIOR / EFFECT]
ATK/2200 DEF/1200

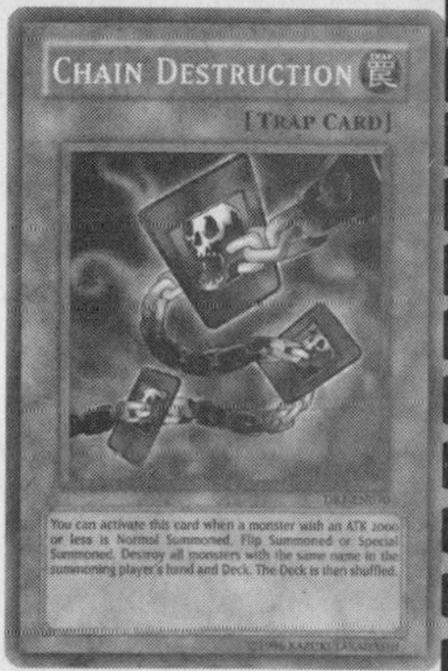
CHAIN DESTRUCTION
[TRAP CARD]

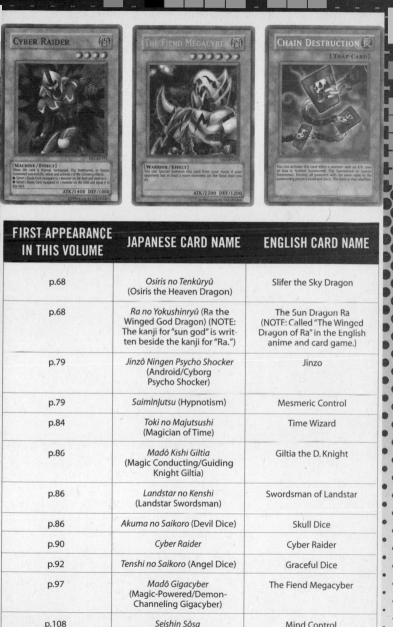

FIRST APPEARANCE IN THIS VOLUME	JAPANESE CARD NAME	ENGLISH CARD NAME
p.68	*Osiris no Tenkûryû* (Osiris the Heaven Dragon)	Slifer the Sky Dragon
p.68	*Ra no Yokushinryû* (Ra the Winged God Dragon) (NOTE: The kanji for "sun god" is written beside the kanji for "Ra.")	The Sun Dragon Ra (NOTE: Called "The Winged Dragon of Ra" in the English anime and card game.)
p.79	*Jinzô Ningen Psycho Shocker* (Android/Cyborg Psycho Shocker)	Jinzo
p.79	*SaiminJutsu* (Hypnotism)	Mesmeric Control
p.84	*Toki no Majutsushi* (Magician of Time)	Time Wizard
p.86	*Madô Kishi Giltia* (Magic Conducting/Guiding Knight Giltia)	Giltia the D. Knight
p.86	*Landstar no Kenshi* (Landstar Swordsman)	Swordsman of Landstar
p.86	*Akuma no Saikoro* (Devil Dice)	Skull Dice
p.90	*Cyber Raider*	Cyber Raider
p.92	*Tenshi no Saikoro* (Angel Dice)	Graceful Dice
p.97	*Madô Gigacyber* (Magic-Powered/Demon-Channeling Gigacyber)	The Fiend Megacyber
p.108	*Seishin Sôsa* (Mind Manipulation)	Mind Control

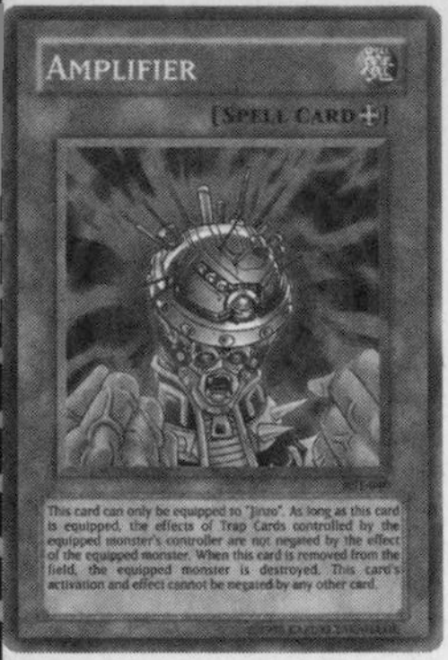
AMPLIFIER
[SPELL CARD]

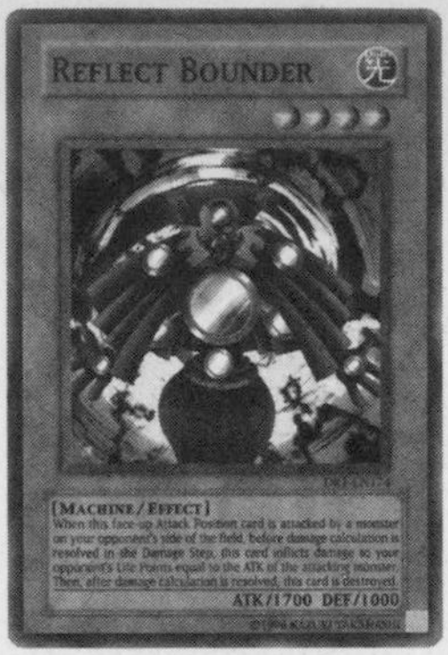
REFLECT BOUNDER
[MACHINE / EFFECT]
ATK/1700 DEF/1000

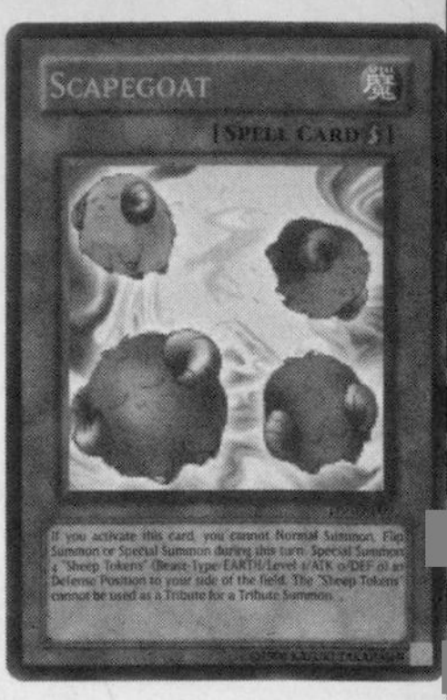
SCAPEGOAT
[SPELL CARD]

FIRST APPEARANCE IN THIS VOLUME	JAPANESE CARD NAME	ENGLISH CARD NAME
p.108	*Sennô Brain Control* (Brainwashing/Brain Control)	Brain Control
p.109	*Wyvern no Senshi* (Wyvern Warrior)	Alligator Sword (NOTE: Not a real game card.)
p.109	*Scape Goat*	Scapegoat
p.109	*Otoshiana* (Pitfall)	Chasm with Spikes
p.127	*Dennôzôfukuki* (Electric Brain Amplificatrion Machine)	Amplifier
p.125	*Baby Dragon*	Baby Dragon
p.128	*Reflect Bounder*	Reflect Bounder
p.133	*Roulette Spider*	Roulette Spider (NOTE: Not a real game card.)
p.152	*Diamond Dragon*	Hyozanryu (NOTE: "Hyozanryu" is Japanese for "Iceberg Dragon")
p.180	*Black Magician*	Dark Magician

IN THE NEXT VOLUME...

Yugi fights Pandora the Conjurer! Who is the greatest master of magicians? Can Yugi duel *while chained to the path of a roaring buzzsaw?* Meanwhile, Insector Haga returns, challenging Jonouchi with an army of vicious bugs! But that's not all... Jonouchi's own deck has been infected with Haga's parasitic insects! Is this the end?

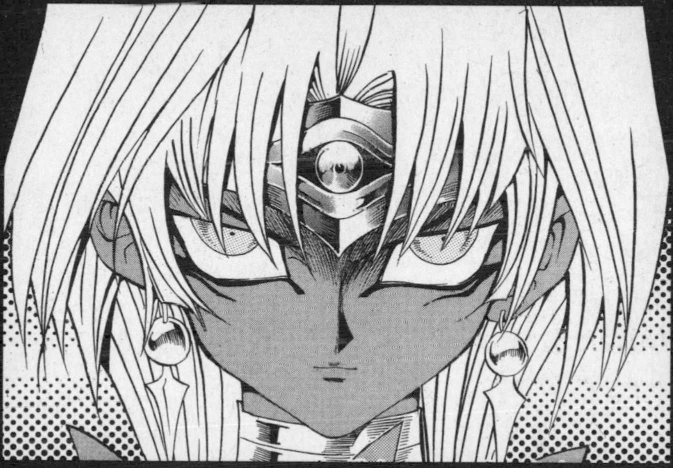

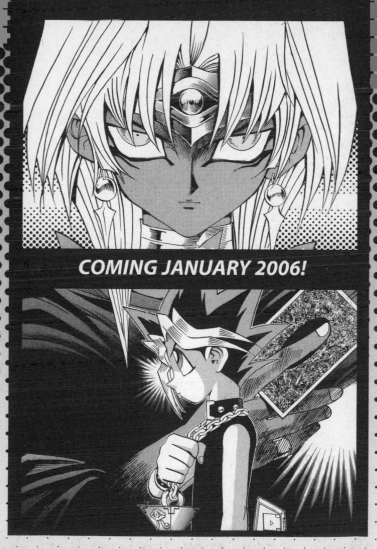

COMING JANUARY 2006!

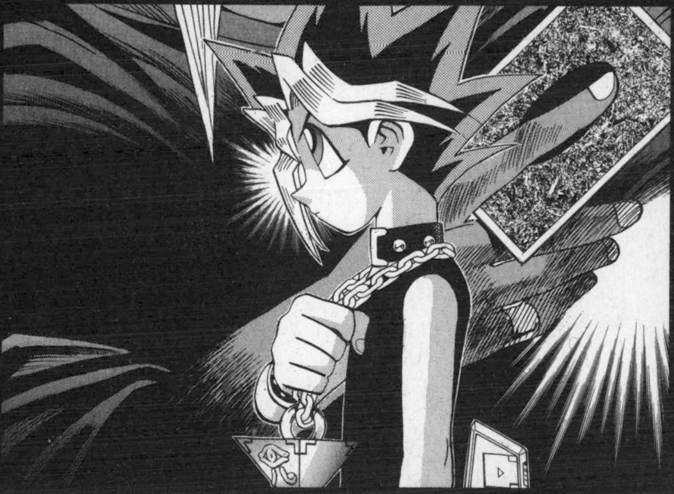

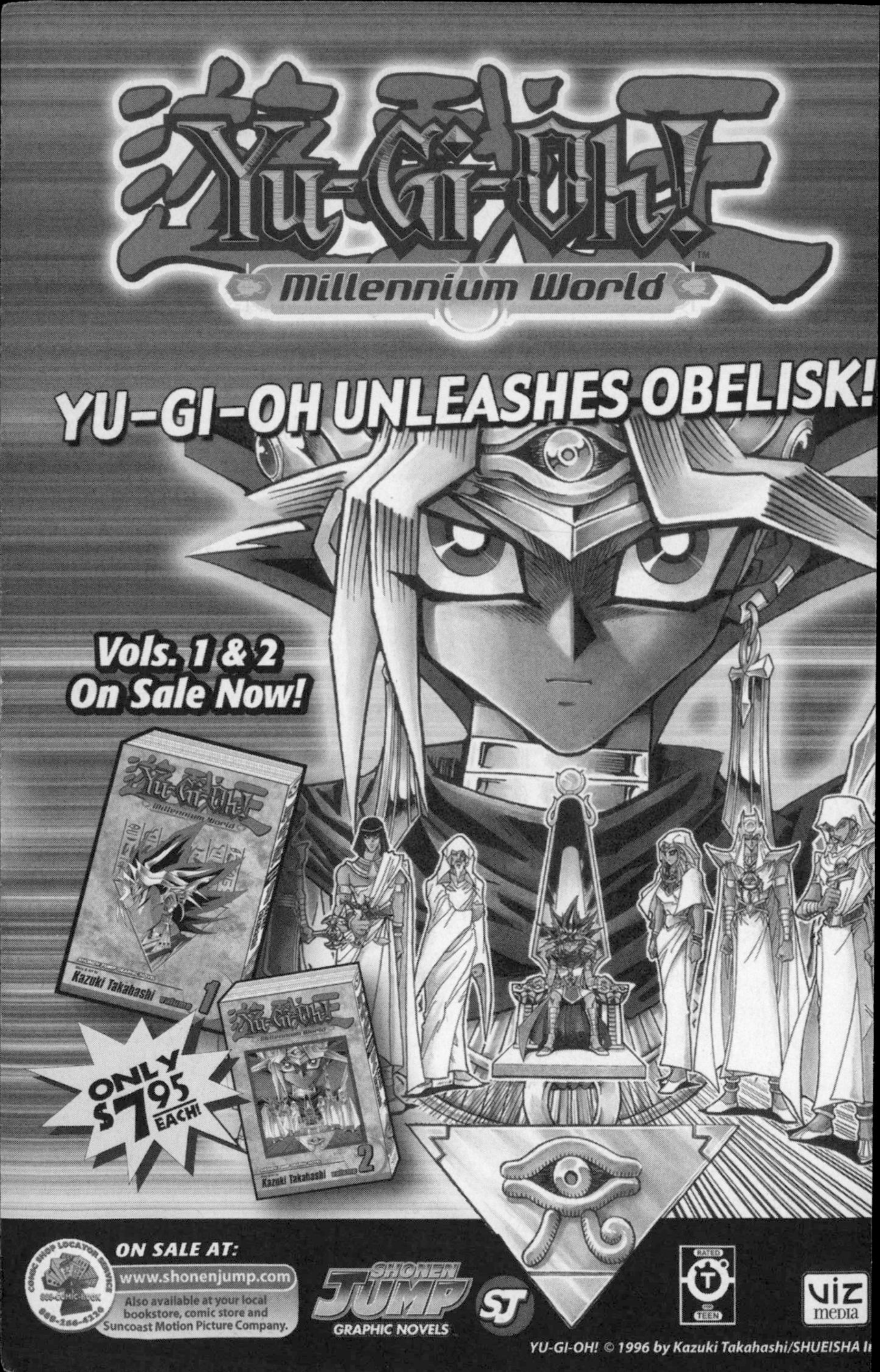
YU-GI-OH! Millennium World
YU-GI-OH UNLEASHES OBELISK!
Vols. 1 & 2 On Sale Now!
Kazuki Takahashi volume 1
Kazuki Takahashi volume 2
ONLY $7.95 EACH!
ON SALE AT:
www.shonenjump.com
Also available at your local bookstore, comic store and Suncoast Motion Picture Company.
SHONEN JUMP GRAPHIC NOVELS
SJ
RATED T TEEN
VIZ media
YU-GI-OH! © 1996 by Kazuki Takahashi/SHUEISHA I

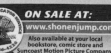

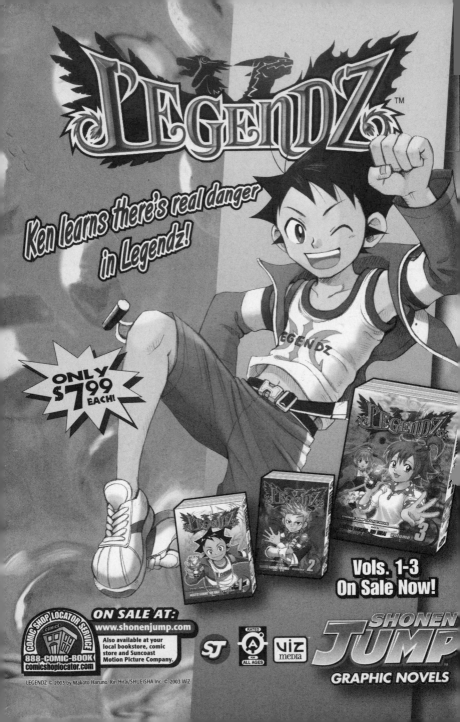

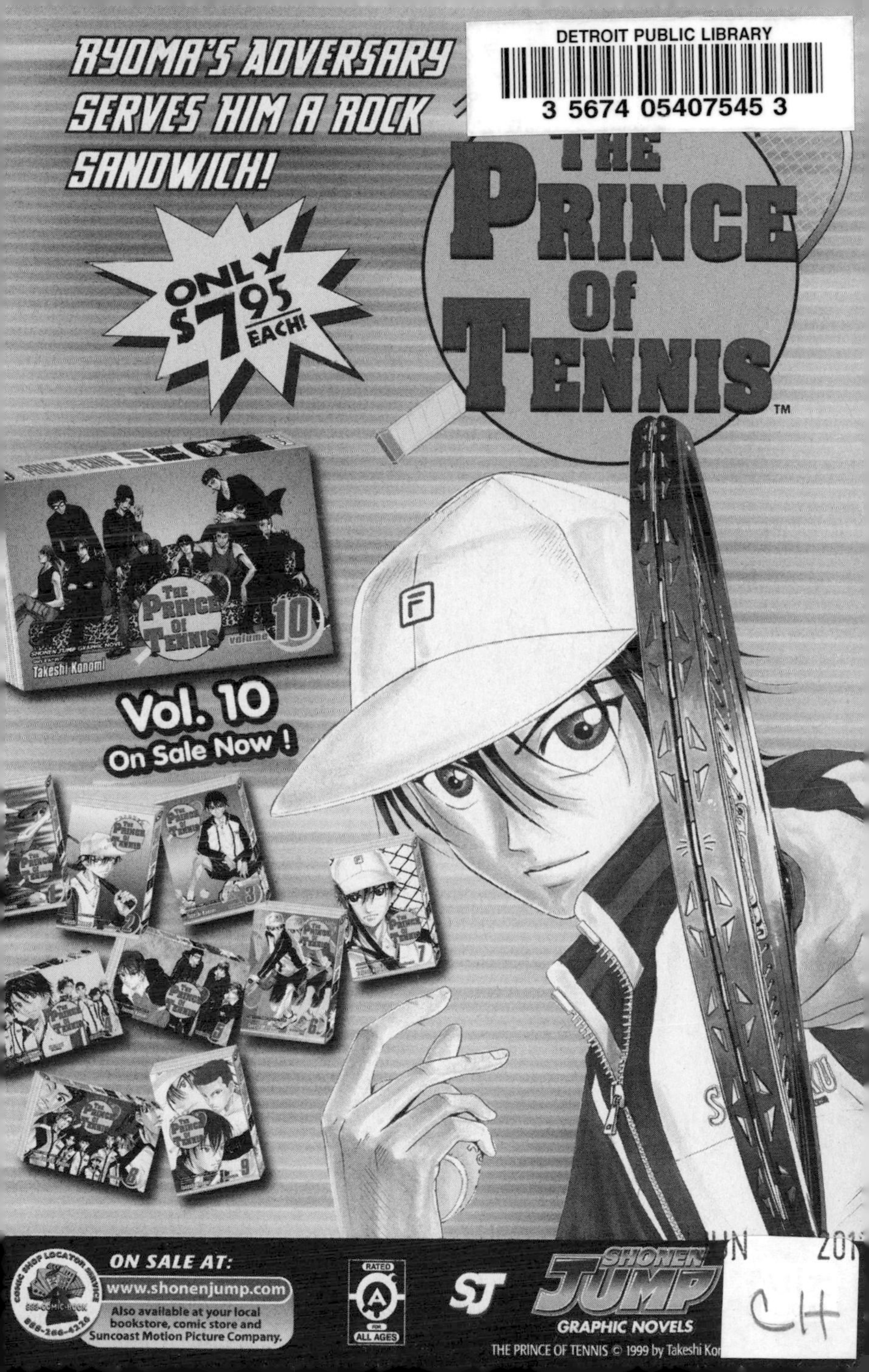
RYOMA'S ADVERSARY SERVES HIM A ROCK SANDWICH!
ONLY $7.95 EACH!
THE PRINCE OF TENNIS™
Vol. 10
On Sale Now !
ON SALE AT:
www.shonenjump.com
Also available at your local bookstore, comic store and Suncoast Motion Picture Company.
RATED A FOR ALL AGES
SJ
SHONEN JUMP
GRAPHIC NOVELS

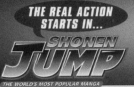

Check us out on the web!

www.shonenjump.com

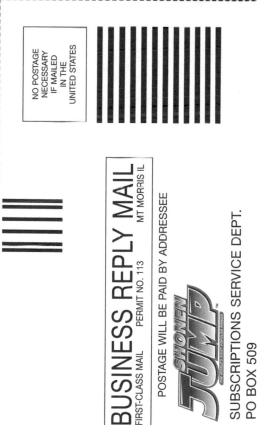

SHONEN JUMP
THE WORLD'S MOST POPULAR MANGA

COMPLETE OUR SURVEY AND LET US KNOW WHAT YOU THINK!

☐ Please do NOT send me information about VIZ Media and SHONEN JUMP products, news and events, special offers, or other information.

☐ Please do NOT send me information from VIZ Media's trusted business partners.

Name: _____

Address: _____

City: _____ State: _____ Zip: _____

E-mail: _____

☐ Male ☐ Female   Date of Birth (mm/dd/yyyy): ___/___/___   (Under 13? Parental consent required.)

1 Do you purchase SHONEN JUMP Magazine?

☐ Yes   ☐ No

If **YES**, do you subscribe?
☐ Yes   ☐ No

If **NO**, how often do you purchase SHONEN JUMP Magazine?
☐ 1-3 issues a year   ☐ 4-6 issues a year   ☐ more than 7 issues a year

2 Which SHONEN JUMP Manga did you purchase this time? (please check only one)

☐ Beet the Vandel Buster   ☐ Bleach   ☐ Bobobo-bo Bo-bobo
☐ Death Note   ☐ Dragon Ball   ☐ Dragon Ball Z
☐ Dr. Slump   ☐ Eyeshield 21   ☐ Hikaru no Go
☐ Hunter x Hunter   ☐ I"s   ☐ JoJo's Bizarre Adventure
☐ Knights of the Zodiac   ☐ Legendz   ☐ Naruto
☐ One Piece   ☐ Rurouni Kenshin   ☐ Shaman King
☐ The Prince of Tennis   ☐ Ultimate Muscle   ☐ Whistle!
☐ Yu-Gi-Oh!   ☐ Yu-Gi-Oh!: Duelist   ☐ Yu-Gi-Oh!: Millennium World
☐ YuYu Hakusho   ☐ Other _____

Will you purchase subsequent volumes?
☐ Yes   ☐ No

3 How did you learn about this title? (check all that apply)

☐ Favorite title   ☐ Advertisement   ☐ Article
☐ Gift   ☐ Read excerpt in SHONEN JUMP Magazine
☐ Recommendation   ☐ Special offer   ☐ Through TV animation
☐ Website   ☐ Other _____

4 Of the titles that are serialized in SHONEN JUMP paperback manga volumes?

☐ Yes ☐ No

If **YES**, which ones have you purchased? (check all that apply)

☐ Hikaru no Go ☐ Naruto ☐ One Piece ☐ Shaman King
☐ Yu-Gi-Oh!: Millennium World ☐ YuYu Hakusho

If **YES**, what were your reasons for purchasing? (please pick up to 3)

☐ A favorite title ☐ A favorite creator/artist ☐ I want to read it in one go
☐ I want to read it over and over again ☐ There are extras that aren't in the magazine
☐ The quality of printing is better than the magazine ☐ Recommendation
☐ Special offer ☐ Other

If **NO**, why did/would you not purchase it?

☐ I'm happy just reading it in the magazine ☐ It's not worth buying the manga volume
☐ All the manga pages are in black and white, unlike the magazine
☐ There are other manga volumes that I prefer ☐ There are too many to collect for each title
☐ It's too small ☐ Other ____________

5 Of the titles NOT serialized in the magazine, which ones have you purchased?
(check all that apply)

☐ Beet the Vandel Buster ☐ Bleach ☐ Bobobo-bo Bo-bobo ☐ Death Note
☐ Dragon Ball ☐ Dragon Ball Z ☐ Dr. Slump ☐ Eyeshield 21
☐ Hunter x Hunter ☐ I"s ☐ JoJo's Bizarre Adventure ☐ Knights of the Zodiac
☐ Legendz ☐ The Prince of Tennis ☐ Rurouni Kenshin ☐ Ultimate Muscle
☐ Whistle! ☐ Yu-Gi-Oh! ☐ Yu-Gi-Oh!: Duelist ☐ None
☐ Other ____________

If you did purchase any of the above, what were your reasons for purchasing?

☐ A favorite title ☐ A favorite creator/artist
☐ Read a preview in SHONEN JUMP Magazine and wanted to read the rest of the story
☐ Recommendation ☐ Other

Will you purchase subsequent volumes?

☐ Yes ☐ No

6 What race/ethnicity do you consider yourself? (please check one)

☐ Asian/Pacific Islander ☐ Black/African American ☐ Hispanic/Latino
☐ Native American/Alaskan Native ☐ White/Caucasian ☐ Other

THANK YOU! Please send the completed form to: VIZ Media Survey
42 Catharine St.
Poughkeepsie, NY 12601

VIZ media™

All information provided will be used for internal purposes only. We promise not to sell or otherwise divulge your information.